Understanding the Knowledgeable Organization

Nurturing Knowledge Competence

Endorsements for Understanding the Knowledgeable Organization

'This book combines excellent insight with practical application. It is suitable both for the reader who seeks intellectual stimulation and the practitioner who strives to bring change to his/her own organization.'

Philip Ramsell
Group Knowledge Manager, Abbey National

'This remarkable book brings order to a very complex topic. I found that it brought into focus many things I intuitively knew and the structure made it accessible at many different levels. Uniquely, it is both a practical handbook and an academic treatise.'

Professor Richard Potter
Chief Knowledge Officer, QinetiQ

'An excellent book reviewing for the first time (I think) Knowledge Management as a series of competencies within the organizational context. Each chapter contains a great breadth of references including the most recent thinking on the subject. Well researched and very articulate. An excellent source book for the knowledge professional.'

Deborah Lawley
Group Knowledge Manager, Orange Group

'*Understanding the Knowledgeable Organization* is a must-have for practitioners. It provides conceptual and practical guidelines for professionals dealing with the dynamics of knowledge management. Managing tensions and paradoxes in management is never easy but is made possible when the thinking in this book is applied.'

Bob de Wit
Professor of Strategy at the Strategy Academy, The Netherlands
(Co-author of the bestselling books Strategy *and* Strategy Synthesis*)*

'In *Understanding the Knowledgeable Organization*, McKenzie and van Winkelen have brought to the surface some of the fundamental characteristics of knowledge and its application in business that make it so difficult to manage.

'By identifying and exploring the tensions associated with each area of competence, the authors provide a fresh and insightful perspective into knowledge management. This book will prove to be very useful to any CKO creating or reviewing their KM strategy for two reasons. First, at a high level, it provides an approach to validating such a strategy; and second, at the detailed level, it includes a great many pointers and suggestions for interventions that will help ensure any KM strategy is effective, sustainable and aligned with business needs.'

Alex Goodall
Knowledge Management Consulting Services and Solutions, Unisys

'Through a comprehensive review of the many diverse aspects of knowledge management and a synthesis of models and theories the authors provide a clear and logical framework that offers new and important insights for the forward-thinking manager. The approach through dialectic provides an excellent roadmap for the many strategic and operational decisions that need to be taken in building and managing tomorrow's knowledge-based organization.'

Dr Edward Truch
Director, Knowledge Management Research Institute, Henley Management College, UK
and Visiting Professor at the Warsaw Academy of Management

Understanding the Knowledgeable Organization

Nurturing Knowledge Competence

Jane McKenzie
Christine van Winkelen

THOMSON

Australia • Canada • Mexico • Singapore • Spain • United Kingdom • United States

THOMSON

™

Understanding the Knowledgeable Organization

Copyright © Jane McKenzie and Christine van Winkelen 2004

The Thomson logo is a registered trademark used herein under licence.

For more information, contact Thomson Learning, High Holborn House, 50–51 Bedford Row, London, WC1R 4LR or visit us on the World Wide Web at: http://www.thomsonlearning.co.uk

British Library Cataloguing-in-Publication Data
A catalogue record for this book is available from the British Library

ISBN 1-86152-895-7

First edition 2004

Typeset by Photoprint, Torquay, Devon

Printed by TJ International, Padstow, Cornwall

To all of the many people who helped make
this book possible, and in particular
Simon van Winkelen for his unstinting
advice, support and thoughtful
contributions

Contents

List of figures

List of tables

Foreword

The mindful organization

The industrial economy based on managing material things seems to be drawing to a close. We often hear this change referred to as the shift to the knowledge economy, but what does this mean? In practice, the shift from the material to the intangible, in effect, a dematerialization of business, places more and more emphasis on the tacit dimensions of managerial activity. This book seeks to understand how managers can handle that dematerialization. In concert with Boisot (1998) the authors agree that one vital element of the understanding is that: 'Tacit knowledge provides greater potential for long-term business value . . .' A key to performance in this emerging knowledge economy is the development of organizational tools that continuously nourish and nurture tacit knowledge.

The importance of paying attention to tacit knowledge is evident when we start to consider the global speed of data and information diffusion, as well as packaged and codified insights, in other words, knowledge. As an example, in the medical science field the growth rate of the production of new written material is now said to be around 100 per cent per year. But gaining value from this new material requires expertise developed from years of experience – the tacit dimension of knowledge. To survive the deluge of information and explicit knowledge and apply it constructively to business problems challenges human minds and brains to focus on a healthy balance between what we know and what we need to know. As the authors of this book conclude, organizations must balance constantly between the comfortable stability of the present and the need for future renewal.

Looking backwards does not help organizations to find this balance. The present tools of economics and the theory of the firm focus heavily on organizing to harvest revenues from what was invested in previous years, they don't help us to understand the needs of the future. Efficiency and keeping costs and budgets in balance are another common focus. These offer a kind of linear analysis of how to increase revenues and wealth in an extrapolated business context that can be forecasted because of assumed stability. These assumptions seem more and more to be out of alignment with the continuously evolving world around us.

We learn from the famous MIT researcher Jay Forrester that there is some pattern in the world economy. Global economics has life cycles, which are manifest in phases of attention paid to nurturing renewal and development, not only for products, but also for business sectors, regions and nations. Forrester called these patterns 'world dynamics'. For example, if we track the pattern of the European economy since 1945, we see cycles of rapid renewal between roughly 1945–1970, followed by periods characterized more by maintenance than innovation. The driver behind these so-called world dynamics is whether people pay attention to existence and survival or to nurturing and renewal. As humans we have internal systems that monitor the speed of renewal in our bodies. How can our societies and organizations monitor their renewal rate, and assess whether it is right for their environment? Biological research suggests that the human body renews itself at a rate of about 2 kg of new cells per day! This is just renewal, not growth. What is the equivalent for organizations?

Although leaders in our organizations and political leaders are all using the language of growth, this can only occur when the deeper dimension of renewal is nourished and strong. According to Richard Normann, the symbolizing activity in the mind is the core of renewal. If we further penetrate this dimension of renewal we might see that at its heart lies the power of thought. This is how the human brain functions. The key question is how to build knowledgeable organizations where there is this power of renewal. What form should new organizational manifestos take in order to remain synchronized with the complex context? Is our organizational approach mindful enough?

Societal development is moving beyond the simple production of goods towards generating a living from thoughts. Critical to the intelligence of modern societies are the dual capabilities of knowledge navigation and questioning. Professor Stevan Dedijer has coined the term 'quizzics' to describe this science of intelligence. A quizzics approach encourages managers to shift their sights beyond the social construct of an organization to its wider context. To move from vertical perspectives on wealth creation to lateral or longitudinal perspectives (see www.corporatelongitude.com) represents a shift from present to future, from known to unknown, from management to renewal, from assets to flows, from harvesting to cultivation and nurturing. This might result in a shift towards building the knowledgeable firm, as well as intelligence of societies. I challenge you to take charge of the future and become a prime mover!

This book offers us six inter- as well as intra-related components for nurturing the knowledgeable firm in this new societal and market context. It gives us a very helpful holistic view of the complex interactions between two mental perspectives: one focused on internal efficiency and current value from knowledge, and one focused on external adaptation and future value creation. Overall it provides an integrated model for value creation through building competence in dealing with these issues. It is highly recommended as a guide to practical knowledge interventions that will generate strategic leadership through shaping a knowledgeable enterprise.

When there is no vision people will perish

Book of Proverbs

Leif Edvinsson, 2003

Introduction

Enabling everyone to gain from the intellect, imagination, potential and enthusiasm of those working in and with our organizations is the aim of effective knowledge management. So far it has proved a hard goal to achieve. Most of the time, in today's pressured business environment, the majority of us struggle to make the best decisions we can with incomplete information and limited time. The issue at stake is how do we improve the situation we find ourselves in so that we can make better choices, more timely and informed decisions and come up with more new ideas? If this were easy, it would have happened yesterday (if not years ago). There are good reasons why our organizations are still working towards the ideal of managing internal and external knowledge resources effectively. This book is written to help speed up the journey by increasing understanding of why knowledge management is difficult and identifying ways to overcome the obstacles.

What do we mean by 'The Knowledgeable Organization'? More than anything, we mean an organization in which there is:

1 Recognition that knowledge resources are crucial to business success.

2 A strong focus on accessing and leveraging both internal and external knowledge resources for business value.

3 An appreciation of how the tensions implicit in knowledge-related choices can make it hard to achieve the expected outcomes without recognizing and resolving conflicting interests.

4 An understanding of how to pursue an integrated approach to managing knowledge, seeing the choices and activities as part of an interconnected pattern that needs to be dynamically adjusted as the competitive environment changes.

The pressures acting on our organizations pull us in many different directions. For example, we are pressured to deliver results to satisfy the stock market today and to invest for the long term to insure our future. Often, the pressures of these conflicting forces, combined with differences in the strategic objectives of our organizations, make designing a suitable 'recipe' to manage knowledge a complex challenge. If we add in the fact that any recipe will need constant adjustment to respond to ever-changing business priorities and competitor activity, we have an even thornier problem. Finally, the very characteristics of knowledge itself create their own tensions: for example, existing knowledge can get in the way of new knowledge being accepted, making the co-ordination of knowledge-based activities that much more difficult. We begin to appreciate why knowledge competence can be hard to achieve.

Giving people better access to available knowledge and helping them use it gives our organizations an unrivalled opportunity to improve performance. The potential is huge. Access to the right knowledge at the right time can sharpen both operational and strategic decisions, whether made by individuals or groups, as well as enhance the value-generating potential of our relationships with colleagues and external partners. The Knowledgeable Organization is a place where such opportunities are being actively pursued in a way that pays attention to the conflicting interests in all knowledge-based decisions and dynamically adjusts the balance between opposing alternatives to select a more effective route to competitive advantage.

Failure to take account of the conflicting pressures that pull against intended outcomes and failure to accept that it is necessary to make dynamic adjustments to strategies are two of the main reasons why many knowledge management initiatives have not delivered the anticipated value. This view forms the foundation of our approach in this book. We have identified six areas of competence that enable our organizations to leverage their knowledge resources and operate effectively within the knowledge economy. These are:

Competence Area 1: Competing
Competence Area 2: Deciding
Competence Area 3: Learning
Competence Area 4: Connecting
Competence Area 5: Relating
Competence Area 6: Monitoring

Each chapter explores one area of competence and is based on understanding how to achieve a particular objective by designing an appropriate balance of the activities and processes through which knowledge resources are deployed and linked together. We use the term 'appropriate balance' because each area of competence involves a tension between two apparently conflicting interests or alternatives, which tend to pull organizational attention in opposite directions. We suggest attaining competence means that both sides of the tension are beneficially active within the organization and the issues this generates have been resolved in a way most suited to the context. The first three areas of competence focus our attention on internal issues. The second three focus on our organization's position in the wider external environment. Within each chapter, we have adopted a similar pattern of discussion that helps us explore the tension related to that area of competence and reach a balanced conclusion on how to overcome it. This is represented graphically in Figure I.1.

We start by reviewing what is needed to build that area of knowledge competence. This process identifies the root source of each conflicting pull. For each pull we consider the main approaches that can be pursued to manage it well, then explore the sources of tension that occur when we try to optimize both

Figure I.1 Developing each area of competence by resolving the tensions between approaches that maintain stability and drive change

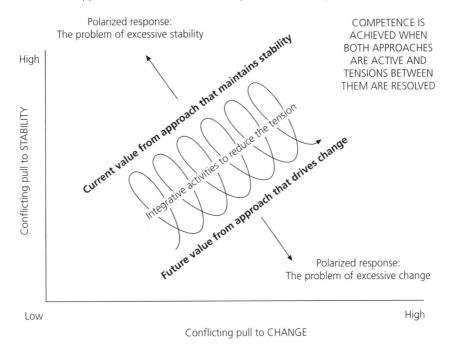

pulls at the same time. Generally, one aspect of the tension pulls towards stability and the delivery of current value from knowledge; the second largely supports change and the creation of future potential value from knowledge. Understanding why paying attention to both creates tension is the first step to handling it. However, we also offer suggestions for additional activities that can to some extent resolve or reduce the tensions. The aim is to adopt an approach that can allow both conflicting pulls to work as complementary forces instead of counter-productive arguments, by recognizing the benefits of each.

In times of uncertainty, we all have a tendency to cling to what we know best: we try to do more of the same to overcome a problem. Unfortunately, paying too much attention to the extremes of either approach produces a polarized response, which is generally detrimental for the organization. Too much stability when outside conditions are changing can quickly leave our organizations uncompetitive. Too much change and our organizations become unstable and difficult to co-ordinate efficiently. The art of providing both stability and change brings the competence to adapt and thrive in a rapidly changing world.

One of our main arguments is that these six areas of competence are highly interrelated, mutually reinforcing and part of an holistic system. In our final chapter, we see how all six areas of competence fit together into an integrated picture of a Knowledgeable Organization. Although we have to present a sequential story through the chapters of the book, the important message is to recognize that the areas of competence are mutually interdependent. To make this easier, in addition to the final integrative chapter, we draw attention to the inter-relationships throughout the book by using signposts.

Signpost *A signpost points to a related competence area.* It either shows a related topic in a later chapter or summarizes key points that we have already covered.

Knowledge, knowledge management and the knowledge economy

Before we move on to summarize the ideas behind each of the six areas of competence, we need to adopt some definitions. As we will see later, particularly in *Competence Area 3: Learning*, language is the means by which we construct and communicate knowledge. However, the way words are interpreted often differs between sender and receiver. To avoid misunderstanding, we would like to start developing a shared language for our communications by defining what we mean by knowledge, knowledge management and the knowledge economy.

People have been classifying types of knowledge since the days of the early philosophers. Some of the most frequently encountered classifications are:

- Explicit and tacit (Polanyi, 1958).
- Know how, know what, know why, know when, know who (Wikstrom and Norman, 1994).
- Embedded, embodied, encultured, embrained and encoded (Blackler, 1995).

Simple categorizations help us think about our ability to strategically influence knowledge flows and how value can be realized from each type of knowledge resource. Take the most often used distinction, explicit and tacit knowledge. Explicit knowledge is knowledge that has been codified into words and so is easily transferable in essence, if not in value (for example, providing a salesperson with an overview of the buying patterns of a customer organization and the characteristics of decision-makers in that company). Explicit knowledge produces greater value when widely applied, but it also leaks to others because it is easy to transfer. In contrast, tacit knowledge is knowledge that cannot easily be put into words. It takes time and considerable investment to develop (for example, the experience of a salesperson in recognizing sales opportunities and overcoming difficulties that arise through the negotiations). Ultimately, tacit knowledge promises greater potential for long-term business value because it tends to be more widely applicable to different circumstances, creates greater differentiation and is easier to protect; however, that potential is much harder to realize (Boisot, 1998).

Although we can categorize knowledge in different ways, it is another matter again to say what knowledge actually is. In *Competence Area 3: Learning* we will be looking in detail at learning, as both the process and the outcome of knowledge development. To do this, we must explore two of the main perspectives on what knowledge is. We will argue that knowledge is less an abstract entity that we can search for and more a highly context-specific interpretation that individuals and social groups give to their observations of the world around them.

For the rest of the book, we have adopted a definition of knowledge consistent with this view and one that we feel addresses the practical realities of our organizations. It recognizes the fact that when we do anything, we use two types of knowledge: we draw on knowledge about what the right course of action is and we apply knowledge about how to pursue that course of action. Both of these are included in the following definition of knowledge (Sveiby, 2002):

Justified true belief – 'know what' or 'know that' which provides the raw material for deciding what to do and includes facts , assumptions and values,
and

The capacity to act – 'know how' derived from resources such as procedures, rules, practical experiences, mental and physical abilities. This is the knowledge base that we draw on to show us how to take action.

This definition reinforces the inevitable difficulties in 'managing' something as subjective and contextualized as knowledge. It has even been questioned whether it is actually possible to manage knowledge (Stacey, 2002). However, again in the practical realities of our organizations, we have to try to make a difference to the value that knowledge can deliver by focusing time and resources on specific knowledge-based initiatives. We therefore accept the definition: 'knowledge management means using the ideas and experience of employees, customers and suppliers to improve the organization's performance.' (Skapinker, 2002)

In recent years, many organizations have adopted a wide range of knowledge-related practices. For example:

- Human resource management-based practices to encourage knowledge flows directly between people (such as incentives for knowledge sharing, networking initiatives and community building).
- Information and communications technology projects to facilitate explicit knowledge flows (such as designing portals, intranets and group decision support systems).
- Marketing activities that build relationships to encourage knowledge flows into our organizations (such as creating customer relationship management systems).
- Financial re-evaluations (such as intellectual capital measurement) that provide feedback on the effectiveness of knowledge flows.

We will be looking at how these and many others can all fit together into a coherent strategic approach. We place particular emphasis on the fact that the unusual characteristics of knowledge as an organizational resource demand that internally-driven developments be closely linked to and shaped by external activity in the knowledge economy. This is yet another tension that needs to be understood.

Much has been written about the knowledge economy. It has been made to sound like some new phenomenon that challenges all we know about business. In fact, knowledge has been the driver behind economic and cultural development since Stone Age man first started specializing in particular activities within communities (Grant, 2002). However, until recently, we did not pay as much attention to knowledge as to other resources, such as raw materials or labour, and therefore we did not take the time to nurture it as an economic value driver. The Organization for Economic Co-operation and Development highlighted the role of knowledge in modern national economic development:

> OECD economies are increasingly based on knowledge and information. Knowledge is now recognized as the driver of productivity and growth, leading to a new focus on the role of information technology and learning in economic performance. The term 'knowledge economy' stems from this fuller recognition of the place of knowledge and technology in modern OECD economies.
>
> *OECD, 1996*

We need a way to determine which knowledge interventions are strategic. In other words, which ones help our organizations to adapt appropriately to the ebb and flow of the external knowledge activity of competitors, collaborators, customers, suppliers and others operating in our industry space. The six areas of competence provide the understanding and the tool kit to make these strategic choices.

Six areas of competence needed by the Knowledgeable Organization

First Competence Area: Competing

Twenty years of rationalization, re-engineering, total quality management and activity-based costing have helped us to make our organizations highly efficient. The drive to improvements in efficiency and productivity has focused on encouraging a disciplined approach to adopting best practices and sharing knowledge to continuously improve. Yet all of the issues arising from the knowledge economy (rapidly changing and increasing customer expectations, global competition, changing relationships with suppliers, partners and employees) require sustained flexibility and creativity. Our organizations are pulled to optimize efficiency to 'stay in the game' and generate the returns required by investors today. Yet we also need to create the fluid and creative environment that is essential for innovation.

Building competence in competing through knowledge involves two conflicting pulls:

- paying attention to creating new knowledge *and*
- paying attention to exploiting existing knowledge.

Existing knowledge can get in the way of new knowledge so we also have to be able to 'unlearn'. Encouraging both the exploitation of current knowledge and the creation of new knowledge requires careful people management practices and the conversion of individual expertise into practices and procedures that everyone can adopt. We need to use excellent examples of current practice to inspire even higher levels of innovation.

Second Competence Area: Deciding

Knowledge underpins effective decision-making in that we need to know both what to do and how to do it. For decisions to be appropriate and relevant, our organizations need access to sufficiently varied sources of knowledge to make sense of the rapid changes in the competitive environment. Yet decision-making often has to be distributed so that knowledge is applied as closely as possible to the point of need. This makes it difficult to align actions. To achieve competence in the area of deciding, we have to ensure that collectively we are attentive to and aware of the needs and diverse capabilities of our colleagues, so that together we can use the best knowledge available to make consistent decisions.

Building competence in using knowledge to make better decisions involves two conflicting pulls:

- paying attention to accessing and integrating diverse information and knowledge *and*
- paying attention to aligning decisions.

Encouraging a diverse range of perspectives can undermine alignment if politics and power are allowed to get in the way. We need to create a culture in our organizations in which there is not a gap between knowing what the right thing to do is and actually doing it, and in which employees are able to and expect to make decisions when and where they are needed.

Third Competence Area: Learning

This area of competence explores how to enable individuals and social groups to learn more efficiently and effectively. We need to understand the processes involved in learning, and in particular the role language plays. We can help individuals in our organizations to learn by providing opportunities to gain experience through work and through interactions with colleagues. Meaningful experience, social interactions and reflection are all important elements of the process. We can also use language carefully in our organizations, such as through dialogue and stories, to support collective learning. Building trust and effective relationships to create a shared understanding between people who rarely if ever meet are now recognized as essential elements of effective knowledge management.

Developing competence in knowledge sharing and knowledge creation through more effective learning processes involves two conflicting pulls:

- paying attention to individual learning *and*
- paying attention to organizational learning.

Although language is the way we build and transfer knowledge, it can also cause knowledge to 'stick' with individuals, or within particular groups, if specialist language is not shared with others. Connecting communities of practice across our organization allows knowledge to flow to where it will add most value.

Fourth Competence Area: Connecting

Here we move away from an internal perspective on knowledge-based operations. We start to look at how to actively channel knowledge flows in both directions across organizational boundaries, so as to influence our own options and shape the competitive environment we find ourselves in. To avoid being caught out by competitors, we must make sure our existing knowledge base does not act as a blind spot, preventing us from seeing important changes in our environment or lucrative opportunities we could pursue. Yet connections should be two way. We can also shape the environment for others and ourselves if we control the outward flow of knowledge from our organizations. We need to know when to share our knowledge for advantage, either by driving the adoption of common standards, or by teaming up with partners offering complementary products or services. We also need to know when to protect our knowledge so that we can get the most value from it.

Building competence in connecting with the outside world to use knowledge for internal and external influence involves two conflicting pulls:

- paying attention to 'outside-in' knowledge flows *and*
- paying attention to 'inside-out' knowledge flows.

To avoid wasting energy trying to integrate too much knowledge from outside or losing value by releasing too much from the inside, we need to manage the rate at which knowledge flows in both directions. We can adjust the permeability of the boundaries of our organizations to knowledge flows by adjusting the nature of our relationships within a knowledge-sharing network.

Fifth Competence Area: Relating

Having recognized that our organizations need to operate within a network, this area of competence is about designing and working in many different forms of knowledge-sharing relationships, whilst still maintaining a coherent organizational identity. The structure and configuration of the connections in our network, the quality of relationships and the level of shared understanding between the different parties all influence the way knowledge flows and the type of knowledge that is accessible. This in turn affects our organization's competitive position in the knowledge economy. We need to maintain appropriate forms of relationships with customers, suppliers and other organizations (including competitors) in order to respond intelligently to business conditions. Close ties are needed for meaningful knowledge, particularly tacit knowledge, to be exchanged. We can help relationships to become progressively closer by investing more time and effort to build up trust, but there are only so many close relationships we can manage effectively. Loose associations offer the benefit of flexible access to diverse knowledge sources. Although such relationships are primarily conduits for explicit knowledge, they take less time and commitment to maintain and make an essential contribution to the responsiveness of our organization. We have to understand what is the most appropriate configuration of relationships in our network, given the business conditions that we find ourselves in and our strategic goals.

Building competence in forming and sustaining a viable network of knowledge-sharing relationships involves two conflicting pulls:

- paying attention to close ties *and*
- paying attention to loose associations.

To reduce the risks from too many close ties limiting the ideas that we have to draw on, and of too many loose associations causing fragmentation and little valuable knowledge transfer, we need to dynamically manage the mix in a number of ways, such as allocating responsibility for the relationships within our own organizations, continuously re-evaluating the knowledge potential from each of these, and then adapting our management style to each type of collaborative activity.

Sixth Competence Area: Monitoring

Many organizations now find themselves in a position where a high proportion of stock market valuation does not lie in bricks and mortar, in raw materials or inventory. Instead it lies in analysts' perceptions of the value of intangibles, such as the potential to be innovative, the value of brands, relationships with customers and partners, and the skills and judgement of employees and leaders to make good decisions. Intellectual capital cannot be built overnight, or even over the next two quarters (although they can be destroyed on that timescale by poor decisions).

Managing intellectual capital and communicating its current and potential value requires competence in measuring and assessing the return on knowledge investments. A comprehensive Knowledgeability Monitor should provide insights into whether value is currently being delivered from the ways in which we are co-ordinating the stocks of knowledge accessible to our organizations. It should also provide us with the means of foreseeing future trends in our external environment, and our own capacity to shape these trends and change in response to them.

Competence in monitoring the returns and potential of knowledge resources involves two conflicting pulls:

- paying attention to generating insights into the current performance of intellectual capital *and*
- paying attention to generating foresight as to our capability to adapt to change.

There is a risk if we place too great an emphasis on current performance and stability in our organizations. We can end up refining our current way of doing things to such an extent that it becomes a source of inertia, discouraging more radical change when it becomes necessary. Similarly, if we place too great an emphasis on being able to change, we can dissolve into chaos and fail to achieve sufficient value from the knowledge we create. We need to include ways of monitoring the strength of the stabilizing mechanisms and the drivers for change to adapt the balance as the turbulence of the external environment changes.

Box: example

We have recognized that some readers may be interested in more background detail about some of the topics we cover. We have captured this material in Boxes like this and tried to make them optional reading. In principle, each chapter can be understood without them if the reader chooses.

Integrating six areas of competence into an holistic view of managing knowledge for value

Recognizing that there is a lot to handle in each of the six areas of competence, we feel it is important for the reader to have an overview of the whole book in one place. In the final chapter we assemble the pieces of the 'jigsaw puzzle' and connect the six areas of competence into a picture of the key issues in managing knowledge. We summarize the recommendations for handling each of the tensions and use the graphical illustration format of Figure I.1 to describe the dangers of a polarized response and the benefits of a balanced approach. We start to see why the tensions in Competing, Deciding and Learning are complementary internal priorities designed to address the unusual characteristics of knowledge and the requirements of managing knowledge effectively. It also becomes evident why Connecting, Relating and Monitoring are complementary strategic activities necessary for handling the external dynamics of the knowledge economy. Finally, we consider how it may be possible to view the six competence areas as a pattern of interaction between two complex mental perspectives, one focused on managing internal priorities and the other on the broader perspective of an organization's role in the external knowledge economy.

References

Blackler, F. (1995) 'Knowledge, knowledge work and organizations: An overview and interpretation', *Organization Studies* 16(6): 1021–46.

Boisot, M. H. (1998) *Knowledge Assets: Securing Competitive Advantage in the Knowledge Economy*. Oxford: Oxford University Press.

Grant, R. M. (2002) 'The knowledge based view of the firm', in *The Strategic Management of Intellectual Capital and Organizational Knowledge* (ed. C. W. Choo and N. Bontis). Oxford: Oxford University Press.

OECD (1996) 'The knowledge based economy in 1996. Science technology and industry outlook'. Paris: Organization for Economic Co-operation and Development.

Polanyi, M. (1958) *Personal Knowledge: Towards a Post-Critical Philosophy*. Chicago: University of Chicago Press.

Skapinker, M. (2002) 'The Change Agenda'. London: CIPD.

Stacey, R. (2002) 'The impossibility of managing knowledge', www.theRSA.org.uk (accessed December 2002).

Sveiby, K.-E. (2002) 'Creating knowledge focused strategies – good and bad practices', Second Annual Conference of the Henley Knowledge Management Forum, Henley Management College, UK.

Wikstrom, S. and Norman, R. (1994) *Knowledge and Value: A New Perspective on Corporate Transformation*: London: Routledge.

1 First Competence Area
Competing

Business Challenges

- How does the way knowledge is harnessed make an organization more successful?

- How is new knowledge created?

- Which knowledge should we focus our attention on?

- How can existing knowledge create more value?

- What makes it hard to shift the knowledge emphasis of an organization?

- Which people management practices make a difference?

Introduction

In this chapter we set out to understand how our organizations can mobilize knowledge for competitive success. Many companies have effective knowledge management practices that *either* improve innovation *or* increase efficiency. Here we look at how to harness knowledge resources to do *both*, so that our organizations can thrive now and in the future.

To compete in a global market, we have to continuously differentiate our products or services. In the face of increasingly sophisticated customer demands, it takes sustained innovation to keep products and services at the forefront of choice. Investments in innovations can be an adaptive response to environmental changes or a deliberate choice to actively influence the competitive conditions for others. Either way, innovation is key to our ability to survive whilst simultaneously preparing the ground for future success. Sustained innovation requires the ability to continuously develop and refine new knowledge.

We will look at how our organizations can create the right conditions to encourage new knowledge development, including ways to assess the value of knowledge so that efforts can be focused and potential converted into real returns.

Competing successfully also needs efficient operations to deliver robust products and services that meet or exceed customer expectations today. An organization delivers value by exploiting knowledge efficiently to satisfy customer needs, either within the boundaries of the firm or by providing mechanisms to put outside knowledge to work. We will look at how knowledge management initiatives can improve operational effectiveness by capturing and distributing knowledge and good practices in a structured way.

Yet orchestrating the right conditions for both new knowledge creation *and* efficient use of existing knowledge within a single organization poses two different challenges. The faculties needed to develop new knowledge include enough specialization to get beyond what is commonly known about a subject, and sufficient flexibility (effectively 'slack' in the system) to give people time to think laterally and experiment. These requirements appear to be in stark contrast to the structure and discipline needed to integrate the knowledge resources distributed around an organization, continuously improve products and ensure the spread of best practices. Simultaneously optimizing knowledge creation and knowledge exploitation can also be difficult because the accumulated effort invested in refining the existing knowledge base can become a deterrent to change. To accept new ways of doing things, we have to be willing to give up or 'unlearn' knowledge that is no longer valuable.

Despite the tension between knowledge creation and knowledge exploitation, we will look at how it is possible to institutionalize them both into our organizations. It takes a combination of several complementary mechanisms to both deliver value from current knowledge today *and* nurture the potential value of new knowledge for the future.

How can knowledge be a source of competitive advantage?

Our starting point is to think of knowledge as a resource for an organization to draw upon. In general, resources and capabilities are now recognized as the concern of strategists. If you are interested in the way that thinking about strategy has developed in recent years to reach this view, then more detail is provided in Box 1.1.

An organization possesses unique bundles of resources generated by past investments and the historical decisions of its owners and managers. These include: tangible resources, such as buildings, manufacturing and testing equipment; financial resources; and raw materials and other inventory. They also include intangible resources like reputation (including ownership of brands) and proprietary technology that is protected through patents. These cannot be 'seen and touched' in the same way. Other intangible resources that can make a

Box 1.1

An historical perspective on strategy development

To appreciate how knowledge has come to be recognized as a source of competitive advantage, we need to start by taking a look at what competitive advantage means. An organization gains competitive advantage when it is following a different value-creating strategy to other organizations in the same market space, and when others cannot copy the way the benefits are achieved (Barney, 1991). Business strategists seek to explain what drives and sustains superior performance in a market space so that they can use this understanding to devise alternative courses of action for their organizations.

Strategists have not always viewed competitive advantage in this way, but the evolutionary path of their thinking sheds light on why knowledge is now seen as a significant source of advantage. Confidence in rational and largely linear analytical approaches to strategy making was undermined by the largely unforeseen oil shocks of 1974 and 1979, when strategists started to look for other approaches (Whittington, 1993). They quickly recognized that bounded rationality (that is, human error and inadequacy) makes complete analysis of the environment and options impossible. In fact, Mintzberg (1994) questioned the entire strategic planning process which searched for 'one best way' to devise and implement strategies to enhance competitiveness. Further evidence showed that organizations with the same apparent industry position, size and so on, actually performed differently in the marketplace. Internal factors relating to how the business was structured and managed accounted for six times more of the variation in performance (measured by return on capital) than did the long-term attractiveness of the industry itself (Rumelt, 1991).

Recognizing that neither information nor the ability to understand it is ever complete, a gradual approach to strategy known as logical incrementalism (Quinn, 1980) was proposed in which an underlying logic, or strategic intent, is used to inform step-by-step decision-making, allowing for opportunism and flexibility along the way. The Resource Based approach to strategy was also developed to explain how sustainable superior performance was the product of internal resources that take time and learning to evolve (Grant, 1991). The resources and capabilities that are likely to make a difference are those which ▶

competitive difference include: knowledge of customers, suppliers and partners; knowledge embedded in products, systems and processes; and knowledge of people acting on behalf of the organization.

How we put these resources to work affects the success of our organizations. Once we recognize that organization-specific resources matter, questions of how they can be acquired and developed become more important.

are long-lasting, not so transparent as to be obvious to competitors, not easily transferred between firms and not easily imitated through replication. So, strategists became concerned with constructing and consolidating distinctive internal capabilities over the long term. It was now clear that business performance could be maximized by paying attention to effective practices, by exploiting imperfect markets for resources to build distinctive capabilities, and by cultivating flexibility for incremental adaptation as more information becomes available about the environment and the choices available.

Behavioural Decision Theory added to these ideas by taking into account that we often make less than ideal choices in the face of uncertainty and complexity (Amit and Schoemaker, 1993). In making investment decisions about the resources and capabilities underpinning the firm's competitive advantage, we have to:

- anticipate possible futures
- foresee competitive interactions with each projected future
- overcome organizational inertia and internal dispute in order to realign the firm's strategic assets to the desired new configuration.

Inevitably we approach this mix of uncertainty, complexity and conflict with considerable bias, illusion and sub-optimality. This re-enforces the validity of the Resource Based approach by highlighting the barriers that prevent an organization's resources and capabilities being transferred to or copied by a competitor. Yet it also emphasizes the risks inherent in selecting what resources will make a difference.

Signpost

See *Competence Area 2: Deciding* to find out how our view of the world, our experience and our relationships with others affect the decisions we make.

The task for managers and leaders is to optimize the investments made in developing capabilities, given the resources available. Organizational learning is a 'higher-order' capability that improves the strategic flexibility of an organization to build leverage and maintain other capabilities.

The debate has now gone beyond just recognizing the importance of knowledge in strategic choice and competitive advantage. Turning knowledge into value is now regarded as the reason for firms' existence. A knowledge-based theory of the firm draws attention to its role in a number of different areas, many of which we explore in this and later chapters of this book. These include:

- co-ordinating activities
- innovative capability

- effective decision-making
- determining the boundaries of the organization
- the design of organizational structures
- management roles and responsibilities.

From this perspective, organizations exist primarily to integrate knowledge from many sources into goods and services. The purpose of management is to establish the co-ordination necessary to achieve this (Grant, 1996). In these terms, organizations become a series of 'enduring alliances between independent knowledge-creating entities, be they individuals, teams or other organizations' (Spender, 1996). Under such circumstances it becomes important to understand how knowledge transfers between these 'knowledge-creating entities' form the basis for creating value in an organization.

Knowledge flows create value

We can look at an organization as a series of knowledge transfers and conversions (Sveiby, 2001; Toffler, 1990). Knowledge transfers are different to transfers of tangible resources in that knowledge grows when it is used. In contrast, other resources tend to depreciate with use. When one person transfers knowledge to another, both now have access to that knowledge. In practice, the process the giver uses to access their knowledge may result in him/her seeing the subject from a new perspective, as well as allowing the receiver to combine the new knowledge with that gained from previous experience to generate a completely new insight.

 See *Competence Area 3: Learning* to find out more about the practicalities of knowledge transfer and knowledge development.

We have emphasized the differences in approach needed to manage tangible resources and knowledge resources in Figure 1.1. Tangible resources require strategies to manage convergence, that is, their increasing scarcity as they are used up. Knowledge resources need strategies to manage divergence, that is, the potential for them to multiply as they are put to use.

Simultaneously integrating both capabilities into an organization can create operating tensions, because different behaviours are needed to manage each effectively. For example,

- Managing convergence requires attention to detail, precision, risk control and focused and targeted action to get the most from distinctive resources that are scarce, valuable and durable (Barney, 1991). Quality and value are produced through objective decisions that produce tangible and directly measurable results.

- Managing divergence requires acceptance of ambiguity, risk reduction and flexibility. Quality and value are subjective interpretations of potential and there are non-linear consequences of the choices that are made.

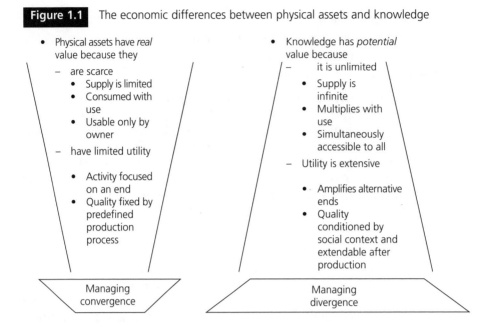

Figure 1.1 The economic differences between physical assets and knowledge

- Physical assets have *real* value because they
  - are scarce
    - Supply is limited
    - Consumed with use
    - Usable only by owner
  - have limited utility

    - Activity focused on an end
    - Quality fixed by predefined production process

  Managing convergence

- Knowledge has *potential* value because
  - it is unlimited
    - Supply is infinite
    - Multiplies with use
    - Simultaneously accessible to all
  - Utility is extensive

    - Amplifies alternative ends
    - Quality conditioned by social context and extendable after production

  Managing divergence

We can make sense of knowledge transfers and conversions within our organizations by grouping the divergent properties of knowledge resources into three categories or 'families' (Sveiby, 2001):

External structure: relationships with customers and suppliers (including reputation, brand names and trademarks).

Internal structure: the business processes, ways of organizing, culture, systems and people in those functions such as finance, IT and HR that support the operation of the organization.

Individual competence: the competence of all the people who have direct contact with customers, or who directly produce the goods and services offered to customers.

Knowledge transfers and conversions within each family and between families, together with the ability to integrate all of the flows, provide potential opportunities for our organizations to deliver value from knowledge resources.

 Signpost In *Competence Area 6: Monitoring* we look at how to measure and monitor the value of knowledge resources within an organization.

Our final step in thinking about knowledge as a source of competitive advantage is to add in the dimension of sustainability over time. Although knowledge appreciates rather than depreciates with use, it can still become redundant if other knowledge supersedes it or competitors catch up. So managers need to focus on how to turn existing knowledge resources into value to compete effectively today *and* look to the future by exploring the potential business opportunities offered by new ideas and knowledge.

Regenerative knowledge processes sustain value and difference over time

Recognizing and managing the tension between exploiting existing knowledge resources and exploring the future potential of new knowledge has been described as a 'primary factor in system survival and prosperity' (March, 1991) and has been the subject of considerable discussion (see, for example, Brown and Duguid, 2001b; Crossan and Holland, 2002). The two complementary ideas can be summed up in one word: 'regeneration'. At a strategic level, successful regeneration involves both reinforcing the existing purpose and identity of an organization and evolving them, taking into account both external and internal influences.

 See *Competence Area 2: Deciding* to see how the sense of identity of the members of an organization impacts what they pay attention to and the decisions they make.

Evolving the purpose and identity of our organizations takes time, flexibility, courage and the opportunity to stimulate new connections between ideas, thereby creating knowledge outside the scope of existing practices. Often we have to invest effort without a clear appreciation of where the most valuable opportunities lie. Yet, exploring the potential of new ideas feeds innovation, and we need to innovate to adapt in response to external changes and to favourably shape the competitive environment for the future.

 See *Competence Area 4: Connecting* to learn more about how adjusting the permeability of the boundaries of an organization affects regeneration by changing the flow of knowledge in and out of operations.

As Michael Dell, the CEO of Dell Computers, has said: 'innovation is about taking risks'. Taking risks is particularly important to prevent complacency when the company is doing well. Managers at Dell are actively encouraged to experiment and the company tries to ensure that people are not afraid of the possibility of failure (Dell, 2002).

In contrast, using knowledge resources to produce products and services (effectively exploiting the value of current expertise) offers more certain returns and reinforces an organization's purpose and identity. However, it requires different skills. Efficiently integrating and applying the diverse knowledge resources accessible to an organization (including through networks of relationships that reach across the firm's boundaries) takes careful, detailed effort to refine, standardize and seamlessly link knowledge activities. The organizational capability to integrate and refine knowledge resources accumulates knowledge incrementally through a process of learning by doing. The mobile phone manufacturer Nokia attributes its success in part to concerted and consistent efforts to make sure that all areas of the organization communicate with each other and with suppliers (Skapinker, 2002). It takes great care to ensure there are streamlined routes for anyone who knows anything about their products (designers, specialists who look at how consumers use phones, manufacturing managers and component suppliers) to share their knowledge constantly.

Figure 1.2 summarizes some of the ways people have described these two aspects of regeneration. Organizations are often biased towards either knowledge creation or knowledge exploitation in the way people are managed, the way systems and procedures are structured, or the focus of investment in information and communication technology.

Unfortunately, the luxury of choosing to focus on one side or the other of the balance is rapidly disappearing. Increasing pressure to adapt continuously to environmental upheaval means that 'there will no longer be a simple choice or static balance between exploration and exploitation, or spontaneity and structure, but a constant and pervasive need to dynamically balance and coordinate the two throughout the organization' (Brown and Duguid, 2001b).

In practice, all living systems exist because they have both capabilities. All organisms have evolved to make best use of the resources they have and adapt in order to survive in the face of danger. In so doing, they create the evolutionary learning that drives the need for further adaptation for other species. Box 1.2 includes more information about what we can learn about knowledge processes in organizations from this self-reinforcing cycle in living organisms.

Figure 1.2 Balancing orientations towards generating value from knowledge

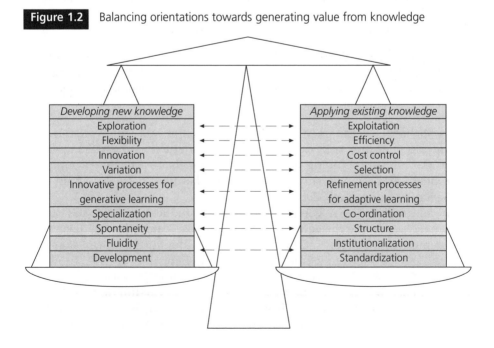

Developing new knowledge	Applying existing knowledge
Exploration	Exploitation
Flexibility	Efficiency
Innovation	Cost control
Variation	Selection
Innovative processes for generative learning	Refinement processes for adaptive learning
Specialization	Co-ordination
Spontaneity	Structure
Fluidity	Institutionalization
Development	Standardization

Box 1.2

Sensing and remembering

Living organisms can be distinguished from non-living systems by one fundamental feature: each contains within its own boundary the mechanisms and processes that enable it to produce and reproduce itself. Each constantly creates and recreates its own identity because it has an internal model of itself and its world (for example, genetically we stay the same person even though all the cells in our body die regularly and are replaced). Higher life- forms can translate the input from their senses into new knowledge as they interact with their environment. This enables them to rise above pre-programmed instinct and create a further internal structure (memory in the form of brain function or competent muscle action) that is used to recall and organize their existing experiences and knowledge (Maula, 2000). Over time, this combination of genetic code, sensing and remembering creates identity.

Every living system is conservative in that it distinguishes itself by setting a boundary between itself and the outside world. Regardless of intelligence, it also acts to preserve its identity through that boundary. Yet at the same time, the ever-changing signals coming in from the environment provoke change and an urge to improve relative to others which it perceives as similar. We can look at this in terms of the balance between survival in the face of immediate threats and the process of evolutionary learning and adaptation.

We can focus on human systems at three different levels: groups of cells (these make up the organs in our body); groups of organs (these form individual people); and social groups (for example teams, communities and organizations). Teams, communities and organizations are all coherent living systems, albeit socially rather than biologically connected. We can look for insights into how they compete and adapt by making comparisons with the processes observed in other complex ecologies. Most importantly, we find that at each level in any ecology the best operational properties of a group emerge from the interactions between the elements in the group and the interactions across the boundaries between the groups that come together as a larger entity. Groups share resources for mutual benefit. Internally, resource ▶

Now we will focus on what we can do practically in our organizations to build the capacity to create new knowledge and also to exploit and refine existing knowledge. We will look at how to pay attention to each in turn, before examining those areas where tensions arise from the different practices each requires.

flows are guided by 'tags' – small, codified markers that facilitate and channel random flows to appropriate places. Keywords are a simple example of tags for information. They help us make useful connections between groups of knowledge. Values are another example of tags that guide the use of resources.

Signpost See *Competence Area 3*: *Learning* for a more in-depth look at individuals and organizations as living systems and what this means for how they learn.

Two important knowledge flows maintain the 'life' of organizations as social collectives:

- Knowledge flowing from the environment provides the raw material for 'groups' and 'cells' (that is, individuals) to operate, learn and adapt.
- Knowledge flowing around the system gives access to memories about what to do and how to do it. This assures the immediate survival of the organization.

These flows are interconnected and their integration is the basis for continuous regeneration of an organization. Successful knowledge-based organizations implement and connect these knowledge flows.

An organization's ability to sustain its identity as it learns and evolves depends to a large extent on the permeability of its boundary and the practices it puts in place to 'feed' the creation and accumulation of new knowledge, without tearing itself apart. Absorptive capacity at the boundary is of particular importance. We can improve the capability of our organizations to regenerate by proactively paying attention to boundary practices.

Signpost See *Competence Area 4: Connecting* to find out more about the permeability of organizational boundaries and how to develop absorptive capacity.

Paying attention to creating new knowledge: knowledge exploration

New knowledge allows our organizations to differentiate themselves from competitors by creating unique characteristics within a range of products and services, or by reshaping the competitive structure of an industry. In this section we will look at what our organizations can do to create knowledge and examine how to assess its potential value so that investment decisions can be managed.

We will also look at the conditions that support the knowledge creation process, including the people management practices that need to be adopted.

Identify what knowledge is required

The first thing to decide is what new knowledge do we need? Zack (2002) suggests that mapping the knowledge resources of an organization from a strategic perspective helps show where to focus effort. Is there a gap between what an organization must do to compete and what it can currently do, or a gap between the knowledge resources it has access to and those of the main competitors? The purpose and strategic objectives of an organization allow us to categorize knowledge resources into those that are needed to stay in the game (core); those that enable it to be competitively viable (advanced); and those that will allow it to significantly differentiate itself (innovative).

When there is less knowledge than is needed to execute the strategy (an internal knowledge gap), or less advanced or innovative knowledge than competitors in the industry (an external knowledge gap), then an organization needs to be a knowledge explorer and either create the knowledge resources internally or acquire them through networks or markets.

Zack suggests that it is helpful to differentiate between the knowledge strategy and the knowledge management strategy of an organization. The knowledge strategy is about understanding what knowledge is needed to achieve the strategic objectives of the organization, and why. The knowledge management strategy guides and defines the processes and infrastructure for managing knowledge, focusing action on strategic knowledge gaps or surpluses.

This is certainly a helpful approach and mapping knowledge gaps should be undertaken seriously and systematically. However, it is worth remembering that this will never provide a complete picture. As we saw earlier in Box 1.1, a planned approach to strategy has distinct limitations because information about, for example, the knowledge base of competitors will always be incomplete. New knowledge often creates the most value when it leads to the development of products and services that no-one has yet seen a need for.

So, as well as mapping knowledge gaps, we also need to think about how we can access radically new ideas from the network of knowledge resources available to the organization; ideas that bear no resemblance to current planning, yet have the potential to change the shape of the competitive landscape. Generally, this sort of knowledge arises at the boundary of two distinct knowledge domains. The most obvious example is the convergence of IT and telecommunications expertise, which has resulted in a mass of new products and services. A similar combination process is happening in the pharmaceutical industry as chemical drugs are replaced by treatments produced from live fermentation, botanical extracts or genetically engineered organisms.

It is important to understand what conditions will enable new knowledge to emerge and be recognized as valuable. How can we overcome the inertia of existing ways of doing things so that change can be seen as acceptable? To answer these questions, we need to start by understanding more about how knowledge is created and then move on to look at how the potential value of new knowledge can be recognized.

Understand how knowledge is created

Nonaka (1991) has proposed a 'dynamic theory of organizational knowledge creation', with the central theme that organizational knowledge is created through a continuous interplay between the tacit and explicit knowledge of individuals. While individuals develop new knowledge, organizations play a critical role in articulating and amplifying it. Nonaka describes four modes of knowledge conversion that create a spiral of knowledge creation as experienced by individuals. We can explain these modes using Figure 1.3.

1 Tacit to tacit: where connections are made between tacit experiences and past knowledge (points 1 and 7 on the diagram).
2 Tacit to explicit: conversion occurs as a result of dialogue (points 2, 3 and 8 on the diagram).
3 Explicit to explicit: when different aspects of knowledge are combined (points 4 and 5 on the diagram).
4 Explicit to tacit: internalization of new knowledge through experimentation and practice (points 6 and 9 on the diagram).

Clearly there are obstacles that can derail this process at various points. Tacit knowledge is made explicit though language and people interpret language differently. Explicit knowledge is carried by technological systems that can distort the communication process. The timing of an idea will affect its acceptance and the background context will affect how willing and able people are to consider and take up the idea. The idea will change as it goes round the spiral and people interpret and re-interpret it, so what comes out may not be what was envisaged at the outset. Emotions, cultural filters and political power bases will all affect the negotiation process (Blackler, 1995).

Organizational knowledge creation, as distinct from individual knowledge creation, occurs when the flow is 'managed' through all four modes of knowledge creation, so that the spiral extends onwards, unbroken. Nonaka (1991; 1994) describes various triggers that an organization can use to induce shifts between different modes of knowledge conversion and cause a progression around the spiral.

Socialization (tacit to tacit). This usually starts with building of a 'team' or 'field' of interaction that encourages people to make connections between experiences, ideas and different perspectives. People need to trust one another to be able to participate in this process.

Externalization (tacit to explicit). This is the result of successive rounds of meaningful 'dialogue'. The sophisticated use of metaphors and analogies are useful to help team members articulate deeply-held perspectives and reveal hidden tacit knowledge. Gradually, a shared mental model crystallizes into some explicit insights and concepts.

Figure 1.3 The knowledge creation spiral

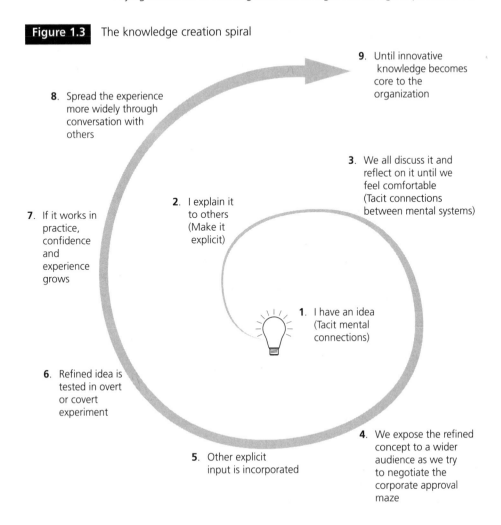

9. Until innovative knowledge becomes core to the organization

8. Spread the experience more widely through conversation with others

3. We all discuss it and reflect on it until we feel comfortable (Tacit connections between mental systems)

2. I explain it to others (Make it explicit)

7. If it works in practice, confidence and experience grows

1. I have an idea (Tacit mental connections)

6. Refined idea is tested in overt or covert experiment

4. We expose the refined concept to a wider audience as we try to negotiate the corporate approval maze

5. Other explicit input is incorporated

Combination (explicit to explicit). These concepts are combined with existing data and external knowledge through co-ordination with other sections of the organization and by accessing existing sources of knowledge. The concepts are justified against the accepted business criteria for assessing ideas and the expectations of the organization.

Internalization (explicit to tacit). Through an iterative process of trial and error, concepts are made concrete and experimented with until they emerge in a viable form. The experience of experimenting helps people internalize new understanding through a process of 'learning by doing', in which the justified concept is transformed into something tangible, possibly a new product prototype.

This tangible output is not the end of the process. It leads to a new, expanded cycle of further knowledge creation, as the knowledge that has been generated feeds across an organization and impacts decisions made elsewhere. A customer's reaction to the new product concept may prompt further development work, or lead other customers to re-evaluate their own options. This 'cross-levelling' of knowledge depends on other parts of the organization having sufficient autonomy and interest to take on the knowledge developed elsewhere.

What does this mean in practice? Hewlett Packard used Work Innovation Networks to strengthen its innovation capability. A Work Innovation Network could be created by any of Hewlett Packard's businesses and was a means of focusing effort on developing a creative approach to a current problem (Stewart, 1997). A business announced itself as the host for a series of presentations, conferences and seminars on a topic it was currently striving to understand. An invitation was broadcast to the rest of the company and, if the 'market' responded, then the subject area took on a life of its own with on-going meetings and a community of practice evolving from the initial interest. This provides an example of the first two phases of Nonaka's knowledge creation spiral in action:

Socialization – the formation of the Work Innovation Network around a particular topic was a meaningful field of interaction. This often later turned into a community of practice to diffuse the knowledge more widely.

Externalization – seminars and conferences were the mechanism for rounds of meaningful dialogue.

The final phases of *Combination* and *Internalization* relied on developing proposals for applications of the concepts, getting formal approval to invest in these, and then 'learning by doing' in beta testing the products in the new field that emerged. If the knowledge that was created enhanced the company's ability to deliver superior performance and was in line with its intended strategy, then the investment required to utilize the new knowledge effectively in the organization would also be likely to be made.

Nonaka (1994) went on to describe 'enabling conditions' within an organization for an effective organizational knowledge creation process; effectively these are preconditions for progression through the spiral.

Organizational intention – identified in the strategic vision. This shapes each phase of knowledge conversion by determining what people pay attention to. It also influences the ways in which concepts are justified, affects the resources that are made available to support experimentation, and contributes to what knowledge is actively cross-fertilized across an organization.

Autonomy – the extent of trust in employees to act independently. This provides the freedom for people to think in different ways and for different businesses within a large corporation to take on knowledge developed elsewhere.

Fluctuation and creative chaos – disruption can create a feeling of urgency. Challenging goals can help people change their thinking in fundamental ways. Regular internal job rotations and structural changes also encourage knowledge flows around the organization.

Redundancy – the intentional overlapping of information, management systems and fields of activity in the organization. The same information presented from different perspectives helps people understand each other. It also helps the process of justifying concepts and securing cooperation to experiment with possible solutions. This is similar to the idea of 'organizational slack'.

Requisite variety – the inclusion of enough diversity in the organization to challenge complacency. Diversity encourages new ways of looking at issues and may also provide the basis for justifying concepts as they are developed.

 See *Competence Area 2: Deciding* to see why the diversity within an organization underpins its capacity to innovate.

3M is renowned for its entrepreneurial culture and ability to transfer knowledge through its organization (Graham and Pizzo, 1996). For many years it set business goals to achieve 30 per cent of its annual revenues from products less than four years old, and 10 per cent from products less than a year old. Examples of the knowledge management approaches 3M employed to support creativity in product design are:

- The idea that products belonged to divisions, but technology belonged to the company. This meant that technology was commonly used across divisional boundaries.
- A computerized database was developed to give employees instant access to all the company's technology experts.
- Formally organized networks were used to keep scientists in constant contact and encourage cross-unit technology transfer. Activities included annual meetings and technology fairs.
- The technical development department offered training courses, many of which were taught by 3M personnel.

Most of the 'enabling conditions' for an effective organizational knowledge creation process are evident in 3M's practices:

Organizational intention – 3M's business goals have placed a clear emphasis on innovation.

Autonomy – employees spend an agreed percentage of their work time pursuing personal research interests.

Fluctuation and creative chaos – employees have been encouraged to develop their product ideas in small, dynamic teams. More than 4000 profit centres have emerged from such teams.

Redundancy – slack has been built into project planning and employment practices to allow time for new ideas to be explored.

Requisite variety – cross-unit technology transfer has been actively encouraged so technology is shared to form new combinations.

There are many examples of how these mechanisms have resulted in the creation of unanticipated products. For example, Post-It Notes arose when a 3M chemist, who also sang in a church choir, connected the discovery of a new glue that didn't stick permanently with the need to be able to mark places in hymn books more effectively than with pieces of loose paper that could fall out.

In addition to these five enablers that support the effective progression of the knowledge spiral, it has been recognized that different forms of relationships between people are needed at each stage. These relationships are encouraged through the particular nature of the 'spaces' in which people interact. The Japanese term *'Ba'* has been used to describe these (Nonaka and Konno, 1998).

Signpost See *Competence Area 3: Learning* to find out more about improving the ability of the organization to learn through designing different kinds of *Ba* spaces.

Assess the potential value of new knowledge

We saw earlier that generating and communicating a knowledge strategy is one way to help us decide where to invest in knowledge resources. This provides a baseline of what an organization needs to know about in order to achieve its pre-defined objectives. We need other ways to discern how less obviously valuable new ideas fit with organizational intent and purpose. To find other ways to evaluate the potential value of radically new knowledge, we can build upon ideas from the field of organizational strategy.

Generally we cannot know how successful the outputs of a strategy-making process will be until we have tested them in practice. However, even though we cannot guarantee success, we can increase the chances by a process of 'disciplined imagination' (Weick, 1989). Imagination comes from deliberately introducing diversity into the ways of formulating the problem and generating alternatives. Discipline comes from identifying the rules used to evaluate and select alternatives. In knowledge terms, we have seen how the knowledge creating cycle and enabling conditions can feed and support a diversity of ideas. Knowledge creation becomes disciplined when the process for evaluating the worth of the concepts that are developed is applied consistently as a means to justify investment in the most valuable ideas.

The two principles below must work in harmony for knowledge creation to generate value:

1 Create the conditions for new knowledge to be generated and innovation to thrive.
2 Evaluate the new knowledge consistently against the value drivers of the organization.

The challenge is to be clear about how to evaluate the concepts developed through the knowledge creation process against the value drivers of the organization. The *combination* phase of the knowledge spiral suggests using outsiders, market data, comparative data, customer feedback and the organization's stated strategies and objectives to justify and build arguments for or against the concept. Figure 1.4 shows a framework for the evaluation process based on the

| Figure 1.4 | A framework for assessing the value of new knowledge (adapted from Earl and Hopwood, 1980) |

Value of new knowledge

	Relatively certain	Relatively uncertain
Relatively certain	**Formal planning** Use formal planning methods to define knowledge gaps and ways to access the knowledge. Measure progress using standard financial and risk management review processes.	**Bargaining** Negotiate with internal decision-makers and external network partners to agree on the value that will be achieved from the new knowledge.
Relatively uncertain	**Judgement** Use peer review processes, rules of thumb (heuristics) developed from experience and accepted practices in the industry to define and manage the process of developing the new knowledge.	**Intuition** Allow time to explore the issues and build in processes that encourage reflection. Use trusted advisers as sounding boards.

Outcome of developing new knowledge

extent of certainty about the value of the concepts that have been developed, and of the outcome of further knowledge development activities.

When there is relative certainty about the need for knowledge to be developed and the value it will bring to the organization (for example, to close a gap which has been identified through mapping the knowledge resources of the organization), as well as relative certainty about what that new knowledge will look like and what will be involved in creating it, then the knowledge development process can be integrated into the *formal planning and review processes* of the organization. Decisions can be made to develop the knowledge by investing in research and development, developing partnerships with other organizations or acquiring another firm. As this progresses, standard mechanisms for evaluating investment and risk can be used.

If there is less certainty within the organization about the value to be achieved from investing in further development of the concept, although there is a reasonably clear understanding of what the outcome would be if it were to be undertaken, then *bargaining* between various stakeholders can draw out more understanding of the risks and the potential. Negotiation between various influential decision-makers inside and outside the business builds consensus on the potential value of the new knowledge. The outcome may be deciding to develop the concept outside of the core business of the organization, thinking about the timing of further activity, or even recognizing that a new business or division needs to be created to exploit the potential of the idea.

When there is a recognition that the concept is valuable and falls within the scope of the strategic objectives of the organization, but there is less clear information about what the final outcome of developing the idea will be, then *judgement* and experience need to be brought to bear on the process of deciding whether or not to progress. At a technical level, peer review processes can be valuable in bringing other perspectives in to assess the concept. Rules of thumb are often adopted, based on what has tended to work in similar situations in the past.

The final situation is when neither the value of the concept to the organization, nor the outcome of further development activity is clear. The latter may be a consequence of the former. Perhaps the concept is truly 'off the wall' and involves trying things that no-one has experience of. Then the outcome and potential cannot be easily anticipated. *Intuitive decision-making* processes are unavoidable in this case. We often hesitate to rely on intuition as the basis of a decision to invest resources into developing a concept, but intuition is often reliable because it is derived from tacit patterns of experience. The discomfort occurs because the patterns are too complex to easily make explicit and allow us to see the logic behind them (McKenzie, 1996).

 Signpost   See *Competence Area 2: Deciding* to find out more about the role of tacit knowledge in intuitive decision-making and ways this capability can be developed.

We can see the application of three of these approaches to assessing the value of knowledge in the way Microsoft approached software development (Cusumano, 2001). Microsoft tried to stay flexible and entrepreneurial by 'scaling-up' a loosely-structured small-team style of product development as it grew into a global operation. Many small parallel teams evolved individual product features and were free to innovate, as long as they synchronized their changes frequently so that product components all worked together. Interdependent components needed to be developed which were difficult to define accurately in the early stages of the development cycle, so the ability to both co-ordinate and allow creativity was needed.

Judgement – a complete functional specification was not created at the outset of a development activity. The specifications were allowed to evolve with features being added or removed on the basis of experimentation and testing. A few metrics were used to track daily progress and the patterns compared with previous development experience to help decide when to move forward in a project. Products were introduced that were 'good enough' rather than perfect, with some features and 'bug fixes' being introduced in later releases.

Bargaining – product teams tested features as they built them, including bringing in customers to try prototypes. By developing and testing the code in parallel, uncertainties about the value of new ideas could be quickly resolved. Many small teams working in parallel on aspects of the design stayed in regular communication to debate design ideas.

Formal planning – product managers defined the goals (or vision) for a new product, based on knowledge of the market, their understanding of the needs of users and the product development investment plans of the company. The programme manager could then write an outline functional specification to allow schedules and staffing to be organized. 'Fixing' the project resources by limiting the people allocated to it and the time allowed for development acted to focus creative efforts in the most valuable areas.

Edvinsson (2000b) has suggested that part of the process of assessing the value of new knowledge is to move quickly through the *externalization* phase of the knowledge spiral. He uses the term 'rapid prototyping' to suggest that developing the means to put knowledge into practice at the same time as refining the concept is the most rapid way of assessing value. Working on a controlled scale is a way of quickly and inexpensively confirming intuition. The pace of change in the external environment means that the capability to carry out rapid prototyping of new concepts has become a source of competitive advantage.

The final way that we can create the conditions for knowledge creation to flourish is through the people management practices that are adopted in our organizations.

Align people management practices to encourage knowledge exploration

The human resource management practices that encourage knowledge creation are those which promote creativity and risk-taking. Table 1.1 shows what this means for important aspects of managing people.

An example of a company that has used people management practices to develop a culture that emphasizes innovation is Quidnunc, a custom software development firm that won a Most Admired Knowledge Enterprise Award (Mellor, 1998). Quidnunc valued intellect above experience due to the rate of change of technology experienced in its industry, and therefore adopted recruitment practices that attracted graduates straight from college. Their appraisal process was used to overcome the barriers often seen between chargeable work and knowledge-related activities in professional services companies. Six-monthly appraisals included a focus on what the employee had learned and what contribution he or she had made to knowledge sharing. Career progression was tied into the acquisition of knowledge so employees were constantly seeking experience in new techniques. Individual employees took responsibility for gaining new knowledge by contacting resource and project managers and asking to be allocated to work that would offer development opportunities. Individuals also maintained intranet home pages cataloguing their skills, and an 'I want to . . .' section of the intranet that acted as an electronic marketplace. At an organizational level, metrics were maintained to track the number of skills per fee-earner and the number of projects in any month that made use of new tools, technology or techniques.

Now we have looked at what we can do to pay attention to creating new knowledge resources, we will move on to look at how we can generate value from current knowledge resources.

Table 1.1	Managing people to create the climate for developing new knowledge (based on Bierly III and Daly, 2002)
Recruitment	• Moderate external hiring (including, for example, from academic institutions or geographic areas where relevant entrepreneurial firms are situated) to bring in new ideas and deepen knowledge in strategically important areas. This increases diversity.
Selection	• Assess whether individuals tend to experiment and be non-conforming in their approach to work. This encourages autonomy. • Look for people who are comfortable with taking risks.
Training and development	• Use mentoring to support people in managing risk. • Enhance expertise in strategically important areas. This builds judgement. • Promote a culture that values creative thinking and analysis to build the context for creative socialization. • Develop management skills in facilitation and feedback. This improves bargaining capability and collaborative working. • Encourage participation in relevant external development opportunities such as conferences, industry fora, working groups, etc.
Performance management	• Adopt results-oriented appraisal systems that emphasize valuable outcomes, rather than how work is undertaken. • Recognize team and individual knowledge sharing. This emphasizes individual contribution and the combination of ideas. • Encourage the acquisition of knowledge and skills that are of value to the firm. • Negotiate long-term goals that require significant personal development.
Reward	• Establish compensation practices that attract talented individuals (probably involving customised packages). • Reward innovation and appropriate risk-taking. • Provide challenging work, clear recognition for contributions and flexibility in working patterns.
Job descriptions	• Adopt loose job definitions that provide opportunities for people to engage in activities that interest them, use and develop their specialist knowledge and experiment with new ideas. This can provide 'slack in the system'.
Team structure	• Build cross-functional teams in which integrative and communication skills have been developed. This increases the range of ideas available to the team.

Paying attention to existing knowledge: knowledge exploitation

The second element of our balance in this chapter is the effective use of the existing knowledge resources available to our organizations. Exploiting these resources can improve efficiency and reduce costs, so delivering short-term returns and increasing the chance of surviving today's competitive pressures.

Identify what existing knowledge is strategically valuable

We will start by looking at what knowledge resources we should be exploiting for competitive advantage. Zack (2002) suggests that if an organization has more knowledge than is needed to execute its strategy (there is an internal knowledge opportunity), or more knowledge than most players in the industry (an external knowledge opportunity), then one important area of strategic choice would be how to become an efficient knowledge exploiter. This means actively seeking to apply the knowledge within the same or across other competitive niches. An example of such a strategic choice was that made by Dow Chemicals, which increased annual licensing revenues by $100m by reviewing its patents and deciding the best way of gaining from the knowledge that it had developed.

 Signpost See *Competence Area 4: Connecting* to find out about the approaches that Dow Chemicals adopted to exploit their knowledge resources that had been protected by patents.

Even without an untapped library of patents, an organization that leverages its knowledge resources more effectively than its competitors gains a potential source of advantage. Leveraging knowledge resources involves accessing, combining and applying them to improve the efficiency of an organization and ensure continuous improvement in its products and processes.

All organizations reach a stage of development and size when business processes are needed to co-ordinate activities and ensure consistency and coherence in what gets done (Brown and Duguid, 2001a). Diverse knowledge resources are distributed around any organization and need to be effectively integrated to support strategic and operational objectives. Sufficient co-ordination is needed to make sure that the right knowledge is in the right place at the right time and the recipient is able to understand and apply it to add value to the decisions he or she is making. Generally, developing the capability to share and transfer knowledge effectively has been the second stage in most organizations' knowledge management evolution (the first being capturing knowledge and the third being generating new knowledge) (von Krogh, 1999). This is not surprising because it is easier to recognize the value of existing knowledge since the link to operational or strategic objectives is more direct and the returns are quicker to realize.

In the remainder of this section, we will look at where existing knowledge resources can be found and how these stocks can be maintained and replenished. We will also look at the conditions that need to be in place to allow knowledge to flow to where it is needed to deliver value. Standardization, technology, culture and people management practices are all important enablers of knowledge flows in our organizations. Figure 1.5 shows how the elements of this section fit together using the analogy of knowledge stocks and flows.

Build knowledge stocks

We will start by looking at how knowledge stocks are built and replenished over time. Having just looked at the processes by which new knowledge is generated in organizations, we cannot ignore their ultimate contribution to available knowledge stocks. This *generative learning*, the processes of continuous experimentation and willingness to think outside the accepted limitations of a problem that are characteristics of new knowledge creation, is different from *adaptive learning*, which also enhances knowledge stocks (Senge, 1990). Adaptive learning focuses primarily on responding to and coping with feedback from the current context by making incremental improvements.

Knowledge stocks are replenished and refined through various sorts of adaptive learning activities. Here we will look at how to capture feedback from significant actions and events and integrate it into our organizations, supplementing it with continuous improvement processes so that adaptive learning becomes an integral part of the culture and operation.

Significant actions and events

Knowledge can be developed through learning before, during and after significant organizational actions and events. What is meant by 'significant' is a matter of choice. As an example, Hewlett Packard Consulting expected learning opportunities to be generated from all project engagements and so they integrated knowledge practices into the entire project lifecycle process. At the project proposal stage, consultants accessed online resources relating to similar projects or customer engagements. Milestone reviews during the project captured on-going reflections and at the end of the project the Project Manager invited everyone who had participated in the project to review what should be learned from it.

In general, there is a checklist of things worth thinking about when designing systems to learn from significant events (Baird and Henderson, 2001).

Learning before action   Anticipating an event focuses attention on the particular knowledge needed to be successful. Steps include:

- Accessing databases, intranets and other electronic sources of information that relate to the event. Use these to inform planning and selection between options.
- Taking time to simulate the event, walk through possible scenarios and draw upon the experience of the team in exploring a range of 'what ifs'.
- Consulting with colleagues who have experienced similar events in the past.

Figure 1.5   The mechanisms involved in knowledge exploitation: maintaining the stocks and enabling the flows

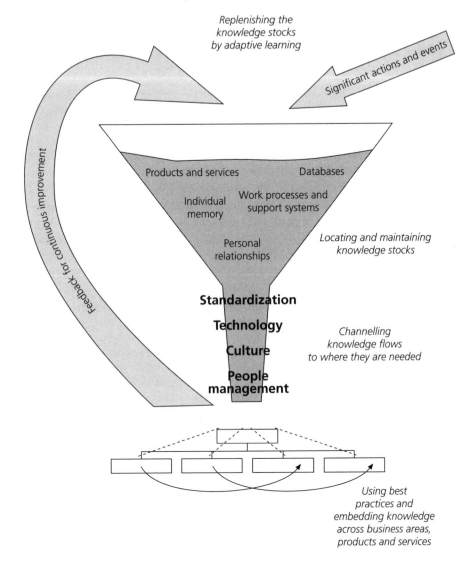

Learning during action   Those closest to the event are in the best position to see what is happening and how things could be immediately improved. The challenge is to retain that knowledge for future benefit, not just make short-term adjustments. The US Army (1993) developed a 5-step process, which teams apply regularly during an engagement in order to learn as they go. Following the procedure they ask:

Step 1: What was the intention?

Step 2: What happened?

Step 3: Based on our experience what have we learned?

Step 4: What do we do now?

Step 5: Whom do we tell about it?

Adopting a similar approach involves building in time for structured reflection during events.

Learning after action   As soon as possible after the end of an event, all involved need to reflect on what was successful and what they would do differently in the future. Activities to do this could include:

- Bringing everyone together to follow a structured process of integrating everyone's perspectives on what happened. An external facilitator who wasn't directly involved can be useful.

- Working with a Learning Observer, a specialist (often in the specific topic as well as in the process of capturing learning) who can work with the team to draw out the most significant findings, particularly those that may otherwise remain tacit. He or she may also have responsibility for ensuring that the findings are drawn to the attention of others in the organization who should know about them.

- Documenting key points and ensuring they are captured in a searchable electronic format for others to access in the future.

One organization that successfully adopted processes for learning from significant events was the petroleum and petrochemicals group BP (Collison and Parcell, 2001). Whenever a team faced a significant technical or commercial challenge they adopted what was called a Peer Assist process. People from around the world were formally invited to assist their colleagues by sharing insights and experience from similar situations. Teams undertaking major projects like building gas production facilities in the Sahara Desert, or undertaking the refurbishment of an oil drilling platform, invited people who had been involved in similar activities elsewhere in the world to take a few days to review plans with them, provide suggestions and offer advice. Significant savings were achieved from this sharing of experience, because the organization was able to bring to bear dispersed learning from around the world to avoid known pitfalls and generate solutions.

An example of the use of Learning Observers was a Hewlett Packard initiative called KnowledgeLinks (Stewart, 1997). In this programme a dedicated department (the Product Process Organization) acted as a go-between, collecting knowledge from one Hewlett Packard business and translating it so another business unit could see how to apply it. One-to-one consulting support was provided to help the receiving organization exploit the ideas. Over time, major topics that mattered to all Hewlett Packard businesses were identified. These became the basis of an online version of KnowledgeLinks accessible to everyone on the internal Web servers. This incorporated stories that captured the essence of a project or programme.

Continuous improvement

The concept of continuous improvement has been an integral component of the Total Quality Management movement. In knowledge management terms, we need to think about how we can tap into the intelligent reflection of knowledge workers during their day-to-day activities to increase the knowledge resources of our organizations. One essential feature of any continuous improvement system is that people need to feel that their ideas will be taken seriously. Beyond this, there are various different ways of encouraging people to contribute and rewarding them for doing so. Three of the many approaches that have been adopted are suggestion schemes, databases and communities of practice. Below are examples of companies that have achieved some success with each. How centralized or decentralized the processes are to keep track of idea evaluation varies with the organizational culture.

Effective suggestion schemes   The UK telecommunications firm BT developed a system called 'BT Ideas' using purpose designed technology applications to encourage, collect and distribute suggestions (Lakin, 2001). The system operated as a brokerage service between employees who had the ideas and those who needed them. Both those who generated the ideas and the recipients who evaluated and adopted them were treated as customers of the system. Performance measures were used to track their satisfaction. Ideas were also actively sought around targeted problem areas that had been identified as business priorities. The reward for a successful idea was a share in the benefits; either 10 per cent of any savings or 10 per cent of the additional income generated, both up to a given ceiling. Information overload within the system was reduced by two mechanisms. First, by only accepting contributions from outside a proposer's own work area. Second, by opening ideas databases to potential contributors so they could check whether their idea had already been submitted. High profile communications activities were used to publicly recognize those involved in contributing and evaluating the ideas.

Publishing to shared databases   The Xerox 'Eureka' project collected, validated and distributed technicians' solutions to photocopier repair problems across the world (Wright, 1999). Xerox found that the pace of technology developments and new product releases meant it was hard to keep photocopier manuals up to date. Through the Eureka project, engineers could quickly share problem-solving tips beyond the network of immediate work colleagues. The approach was designed to fit as closely as possible with existing work practices and to be credible and acceptable to those using it. Individuals who generated solutions to repair problems submitted a 'tip' describing the problem, its apparent cause and the method used to fix it. The name of the author was associated with that tip in the system. Once submitted, the tip was quickly validated by one of a trusted group of field engineers and that person's name was also linked to the tip. It could then be accessed on site via the laptop computers used by the field engineers.

Communities of practice   The Ford Motor Company Best Practice Replication Process (eBPR) used the company intranet to collect and share working practices around the world (Kwiecien and Wolford, 2001). It facilitated the effective operation of and connections between communities of practice that had grown organically around groups of people doing similar work in different countries. Proven practices were shared, rather than unproven ideas, and the community of practice always quantified or qualified the value added to the business by the practice. Each community set its own guidelines for value, level of detail and types of media to use. A small central team provided the technology infrastructure and guidance on how to launch and sustain a community, but responsibility for making the process work was embedded into the daily work of the members of the communities of practice themselves. The person who first identified the best practice was named and this offered recognition amongst peers around the world.

 See *Competence Area 3: Learning* to find out how to create the conditions for communities of practice to flourish.

Maintain knowledge repositories

We now need to think about where an organization's knowledge stocks can be found. By looking at what had been learned from many projects and where knowledge had migrated in various organizations, five general forms of knowledge repositories have been identified (Cross, 2000).

Individual memory

Individuals retain both explicit and tacit knowledge generated from their day-to-day experiences in delivering the products and services of the company and participating in the processes that maintain the functioning of the firm. Social interactions transfer this knowledge between employees.

Personal relationships

Most people turn to colleagues rather than databases to find information and advice. Collaborative working practices establish reciprocity and trust to support the development of relationships. Interaction builds a shared understanding of each person's knowledge base so that future requests can be targeted appropriately. Increasingly, relationships stretch across traditional boundaries in networked organizations. The pattern of relationships reflects the history of the company and acts as an intangible asset that is difficult for competitors to copy.

Databases

Technology advances allow intranets and groupware products to be used extensively as the repositories of the explicit knowledge resources of an organization. Four primary resources to manage explicit (codified) knowledge have been identified: repositories designed to reflect the structure and content of the knowledge; refineries for acquiring, refining, storing, retrieving, distributing and presenting knowledge; organizational roles to execute and manage the refining process; and information technologies to support those repositories and processes (Zack, 1999).

Work processes and support systems

The history of an organization determines the design of its work processes and support systems. Knowledge becomes embedded in practices that define how to get things done to meet customers needs, processes to control running expenses, co-ordinate employees and others who help the organization to function. The way an organization functions is a unique representation of the pattern of its earlier decisions and choices. The more these processes can be standardized and codified the easier they are to transfer to other parts of an organization. However there are two risks in codifying these knowledge 'recipes'. First, they may be more easily copied by competitors; and second, formalizing them may make it harder to change them so they may become out of date and unrepresentative of what is actually needed.

Products and services

The products and services an organization offers are a tangible representation of what it knows. They also determine what people pay attention to in terms of training and experiential learning opportunities.

It is helpful to think about organizational memory as more than a passive storage process. If we think of it instead as an aspect of *remembering*, we capture the active and constructive nature of the process individuals go through to use memories (Bannon and Kuutti, 1996). This shifts the emphasis away from one-off capture towards producing and storing information in ways that can be interpreted and understood by other people in different settings. To be re-usable, the information needs to be infused with meaning that can be interpreted appropriately by various people. This requires the careful use of language and prior creation of shared contexts where relationships have formed to allow people to communicate more effectively. Standardization of terminology through common taxonomy structures can also be helpful.

 See *Competence Area 3: Learning* to find out more about the processes involved in developing shared meaning in organizations.

Enable knowledge to flow

Once we have built up relevant knowledge stocks, we then need to help the knowledge flow to where it is are needed. There are four enabling conditions that support knowledge flows: standardization of interfaces and practices;

technologies to support the management and co-ordination of knowledge resources; a culture of trust and openness that encourages knowledge sharing behaviours; and an integrated and coherent set of people management practices. We will look at practical approaches to each in turn.

Standardization

Standardization involves recognizing that there are many boundaries within our organizations and the networks within which they operate (functional, structural, cultural and national). For knowledge to flow across these boundaries, there need to be appropriate 'translation mechanisms'. Rules, procedures, taxonomies and operating policies are standardization mechanisms that can be used to co-ordinate the flow of knowledge.

Take the example of the development of new electronics products. To produce a mobile phone, printed circuit boards will probably be designed and laid out by a specialist firm; these will be produced by a PCB manufacturer and then combined with other components by a phone manufacturer. The mobile phone needs to be able to transmit and receive signals from base stations produced by cellular infrastructure manufacturers, running on a network operated by a network operator, who needs to be able to collect data from the network in order to bill customers. Computer-assisted design and development (CADD), computer-integrated manufacturing (CIM) and electronic data integration (EDI) allow firms to embed the co-ordination of various development activities involved into the product development process. These 'quick-connect' technologies have standardized interfaces that transfer information between interrelated processes to streamline communication and achieve efficient co-ordination among (possibly several) contributing organizations (Sanchez, 1996). In this case, technology provides the standardization mechanism for sharing learning and knowledge across organizational boundaries, which is key to improving design capability.

Another example is the use of rules and procedures as an efficient way of converting tacit knowledge into readily comprehensible explicit knowledge (Grant, 2002). For example, it is not efficient for Safety Managers to teach every production worker all they know about safety. They can integrate relevant knowledge into the manufacturing processes by establishing rules and procedures that standardize working practices.

Technology

Technology solutions are frequently used to provide tools and techniques to capture, create, structure, communicate and effectively make use of knowledge resources. Existing technologies offer organizations a way to improve their efficiency and effectiveness mainly through explicit knowledge sharing. There are two general approaches to getting knowledge to where it can be better exploited: pushing it and pulling it. Pushing it out to where it is needed runs the risk that there may be different perceptions of value between the sender and receiver, but reduces the risk that users don't pull it because they 'don't know what they don't know'.

Leveraging knowledge across a global organization can become a reality when technology is selected and managed carefully in support of real business objectives. A study by Cranfield School of Management and Microsoft (2000), looking at the potential of technology in supporting knowledge exploitation, found that there was evidence of a shift towards richer technology environments that can support the management and sharing of complex content and more tacit knowledge. Using technology to exploit the tacit knowledge resources of the organization involves connecting people and supporting collaborative working. Many organizations have adopted 'Yellow Pages' type systems that connect people through 'adverts' explaining what they know. BP designed their 'Connect' system to include rich information about employees. People were actively encouraged to add valuable content about what they were currently working on, what they had worked on in the past, the subjects they were happy to be contacted about, and the help they would like from others (Collison and Parcell, 2001: 111). Helping selected people to input information at the launch ensured that good quality examples were available for others to follow. Individuals each had their own 'marketing' page on the system and were responsible for maintaining the accuracy of the information.

A contrasting approach was that adopted by Egon Zehnder International (a global executive search firm). Using data that was already being collected to manage assignments in a customized data warehouse, they developed an application to interrogate the pattern of inputs recorded as users went about their everyday work (Haddon, 2002). Users were inputting details of people, companies, business sectors and functions. They enhanced the system so that in a two-click process, the software could help others to find out 'who knows what about company X?' or, 'who best knows this industry or business sector?' Answers were generated based on which users had most frequently or most recently recorded information related to the subject of the enquiry. Links to e-mail addresses and telephone information allowed rapid contact to be made with the appropriate colleague from elsewhere in the organization. This is an excellent example of embedding the ability to connect people into the existing procedures and practices of an organization.

Technology helps knowledge flow between widely separated locations, but standardized procedures become even more important when there are large differences between the contexts in which people are working, that is, when there are many barriers to effective collaboration.

 Signpost See *Competence Area 5: Relating* to see how to recognize and manage different types of collaboration.

Culture

The third enabler of effective knowledge flows is the culture of an organization. Culture influences the behaviours that are central to knowledge creating, sharing and application in four main ways (De Long and Fahey, 2000):

- It shapes assumptions about what knowledge is and which knowledge is worth managing.
- It defines the relationship between individual and organizational knowledge; that is, who is expected to control specific knowledge, who must share it and who can hoard it.
- It creates the context for social interaction that determines how knowledge will be used in particular situations.
- It shapes the process by which knowledge is created, verified and distributed in organizations.

 Signpost In *Competence Area 2: Deciding* we look at what influences the development of organizational culture.

Culture can also create three common reasons why people feel reluctant to share knowledge or use the knowledge of others (Greengard, 1998):

- The belief that sharing their best ideas with others will slow down their own progression in the organization.
- A reluctance to use other people's ideas because it makes them look less competent.
- It encourages people to act as if they know best.

So, what does a culture look like in which there is effective knowledge exploitation? Detailed benchmarking studies by the American Productivity and Quality Center (APQC, 1999) pointed to the cultural factors that are present in best-practice organizations which 'draw people in to be interested in, excited about, and motivated to share their own knowledge and build on the ideas of others'.

The benchmark organizations exhibited a variety of practices. For example, the business and information technology consulting firm American Management Systems adopted collaboration based on knowledge sharing as a core organizational value and made it a criterion for promotion. At National Semiconductor, a high proportion of the company's leaders were involved in championing knowledge sharing initiatives. In the Ford Motor Company, everyone in the organization used mechanisms such as intranets, video-conferencing, discussion forums and best practice networks to share knowledge. In general, the factors present in the cultures of benchmark organizations could be summarized as follows:

- Knowledge was shared to solve practical business problems or achieve specific objectives: the outcome of sharing was clearly understood.
- People saw the connection between sharing knowledge and the purpose of the business.
- Knowledge sharing was closely linked to a core value of the organization.

- The style of each knowledge sharing process or activity was consistent with the style in which other things happened in the organization.

- Strong management and peer pressure encouraged people to help each other and to collaborate.

- Knowledge sharing was integrated into normal work by embedding it into routine processes or by holding visible knowledge-sharing events.

- Management support was appropriate for the scale of the overall effort to share knowledge.

- Informal networks were supported without needing to be formalized.

- Both formal and informal networks of people were facilitated to ensure that people actively participated.

- Reward and recognition were aligned with knowledge sharing practices.

In the next section we look at some of the people management practices that will support the development of this kind of culture.

Aligning people management practices to knowledge objectives

Earlier we looked at the people management practices that encouraged knowledge creation. The approach to human resources management that supports knowledge exploitation is subtly different in practice, but has a significantly different impact. Now practices are needed that focus efforts on continuously improving our organizations' products and processes. Increasing employee participation at all levels is needed to provide the source of practical knowledge this requires. Table 1.2 shows what this means for important aspects of managing people: the main differences from the practices that encourage knowledge creation are highlighted in bold type.

Buckman Laboratories, a manufacturer of speciality chemicals, is widely recognized for its excellent knowledge management practices having won Most Admired Knowledge Enterprise Awards on several occasions. Bob Buckman, the CEO and Chairman who led many of the initiatives, believed that much of that success came from the company's investments in its people; furthermore, the company adopted many of the practices we have been looking at. High visibility incentives were used to encourage active use of the knowledge-sharing technology systems when they were first introduced. Anyone not contributing to the system received a note from a senior manager enquiring whether he/she needed assistance in order to be able to use it effectively. As a global company, people were encouraged to contribute to knowledge-sharing systems in their own language and the company paid for translators to make relevant materials more widely available. People were promoted based on how much knowledge they shared and there has been significant investment in a Learning Centre to deliver high-quality education and training to employees anytime, anywhere around the world.

Table 1.2	Managing people to create the climate for exploiting existing knowledge (based on Bierly III and Daly, 2002)
Recruitment	• Hire **internally** whenever possible to exploit the existing knowledge of the employees and use their networks and relationships to promote knowledge sharing.
Selection	• Assess a potential employee's disposition to produce high-quality work and **follow procedures**. • Look for **interpersonal skills** that support teamwork and the ability to communicate effectively.
Training and development	• Use **on-the-job training** to transfer tacit knowledge between employees. • Use job rotation and shadowing to extend knowledge exchanges and build relationships. • Include programmes to emphasize communication skills and the abilities involved in sharing knowledge with others. • Adopt a relatively **formal** approach to on-going training in new technologies and present this in-house to demonstrate the connection with existing activities. • Use standardized training (including, possibly, e-learning) to support the rapid adoption of new process innovations that have been identified.
Performance management	• Design appraisal systems that are concerned with **how results are achieved**. • Recognize and reward **incremental improvement** and the efficient use of resources. • Set **shorter-term goals** to encourage more rapid action. • Combine individual and team goals to support knowledge sharing behaviours.
Reward	• Tie pay to performance of both individual employees and teams. • Ensure there is particular recognition for high levels of employee participation and engagement.

Signpost   See *Competence Area 2: Deciding* to find out how Buckman Laboratories' code of ethics has created shared values that have aligned the operation of divisions around the world.

Now that we have looked at what is involved in creating value today from existing knowledge resources, we will look at the issues that arise when we try to combine this with our earlier view of what was involved in generating a sustainable future by creating new knowledge.

Two sources of tension make it difficult to simultaneously exploit existing knowledge and create new knowledge

Creating new knowledge (knowledge exploration) is the basis of innovation and offers the promise of sustainable success in the future from new products and services. Existing knowledge resources deliver value today when we develop and spread best practices and continuously improve products and services in response to customer feedback (knowledge exploitation). So what is the problem with paying attention to both? Surely our organizations need to be both innovative and efficient? The answer is that of course both are needed, but in reality it is difficult to excel at both at the same time. Progress with one or the other is likely to reach a certain limit beyond which it is hard to proceed unless efforts are made to overcome the tension that success with one creates for the other. We can identify two sources of this tension.

1. Organizational processes to develop each form of capability can send conflicting messages to individuals Incentives and structures put in place to support knowledge exploration and knowledge exploitation are not always mutually supportive. This is particularly apparent in the people management processes we have been looking at. For example, recruitment and selection practices differ according to which sort of capability the organization needs and a single individual may not be able to fulfil both sorts of selection criteria. Also, time for different types of training and development opportunities is limited, specific managers place different emphases on aspects of appraisal and incentives, and job descriptions may encourage the wrong sort of behaviour in any given context, particularly if one individual is working across teams or projects with different objectives.

2. Embedded knowledge gets in the way of new knowledge We can understand what this means by looking at the consequences of increasing success in knowledge exploration and knowledge exploitation in turn.

Success in knowledge exploration comes when a fluid and flexible environment encourages interplay between tacit knowledge and explicit knowledge across individuals and groups. Pockets of people with high levels of specialized knowledge are needed to generate new ideas beyond what is generally known about the subject. Such specialization carries a risk if the effort and investments in exploring new subjects is not widely used within an organization. The expertise required to evaluate the potential of new knowledge becomes too specialized and decision-making can only be based on judgement or intuition. In the end, an organization becomes trapped in trying one thing after another, or exploring interesting but unproductive avenues, without spending enough time to make any initiative worthwhile by exploiting to the full the knowledge that has been created.

In contrast, *success in exploiting existing knowledge resources* requires sufficient structure and discipline to ensure best practices are widely adopted. The more successful we are at exploiting knowledge the more we are likely to reinforce the preference for financial returns from investments in knowledge exploitation, because they are more certain and immediate. This emphasizes a short-term perspective on the value of knowledge and tends to encourage people to favour existing ways of doing things. An excessive focus on refining existing knowledge can limit an organization's ability to adapt to changing circumstances. It loses flexibility, because its knowledge resources become too specific, ultimately reaching a point where significant sunk costs make radical change appear too costly to contemplate.

We can look at this tension in terms of the different environments that are needed (fluid versus disciplined), or the different timescales for the delivery of value (potential value in the future versus delivered value today). At a more fundamental level, we can see these in terms of what has been learned already (through refining existing knowledge) getting in the way of accepting new ways of doing things. Our organizations need to 'unlearn' or discard existing knowledge before new knowledge can be accepted. This is not easy, because knowledge tends to become embedded in products and routine processes that shape our habits and limit our activities. When knowledge becomes embedded in the mental models of individuals or dominant logic of groups it acts as a form of short-hand for those involved to collectively make sense of the world and understand their place in it. It restricts what we perceive to be important and worth paying attention to; it creates limits on the decisions that we consider to be acceptable. Embedded ways of looking at things can easily prevent an organization from responding to what have been called 'disruptive' new technologies: radically different products or services that create entirely new markets (Christensen and Overdorf, 2000). Deeply embedded perspectives are the source of resistance to change and make 'unlearning' far from straightforward.

 Signpost

In *Competence Area 2: Deciding* we look in more depth at how mental models and dominant logic influence decision-making.

We started this chapter by arguing that resources and capabilities, in particular knowledge resources and the capability to leverage them, are sources of competitive advantage. However, we also have to recognize that what are core capabilities in one context can become core rigidities in another. It is useful to reflect on Theodore Levitt's comment that, 'nothing characterizes the successful organization so much as its willingness to abandon what has been long successful' (Levitt, 1988).

In the next section, we identify elements that can help our organizations to maintain the best on-going balance between knowledge exploration and exploitation. We suggest ways in which standardization can enhance flexibility and explain why adopting best practices can improve the standard of innovation. In other words, we explore how each side of the tension between exploration and exploitation can be turned into a complementary activity. Finally, we argue that collaboration is at the root of both knowledge exploration and exploitation. If it can be encouraged through the ways that people are managed and jobs designed, we create the generic conditions that allow our organizations to pay attention to both aspects of the tension together.

Resolve the tension through structure, competence and commitment

We have reached the conclusion that knowledge exploitation and exploration are not mutually exclusive, although they are hard to optimize at the same time. We have to find an appropriate balance between the two because exploration provides the 'knowledge capital to propel the company into new niches' while exploitation provides the 'financial capital to fuel successive rounds of innovation and exploration' (Zack, 2002: 263)

In finding the balance, we need to recognize that the value from each may be returned over different timescales, as well as from different parts of organizations (Zack, 2002). If different timescales are involved, then we may need to use organizational memory systems (for example, human- or technology-based) to manage the delays between developing and applying new knowledge and also between successive rounds of knowledge development investments. If exploration and exploitation occur in different organizational locations, we may require well-developed internal transfer capabilities to support knowledge flows between the two. The flows between functions such as research and development, manufacturing, sales and marketing, and customer service are particularly important.

We saw at the beginning of this chapter that knowledge creates value when it is transferred and converted within and between the people and structures that are the heart of an organization. The challenge is to co-ordinate and link the transfer and conversion processes associated with both exploitation and exploration, while overcoming the resistance caused by clinging to existing knowledge embedded in products, routines, systems, processes or mental models.

Convert individual competence to internal structure

Leif Edvinsson has suggested that one of the predominant objectives of organizations should be to set out to convert human capital to structural capital (Edvinsson, 2000a), or in terms of the families of knowledge resources that we looked at earlier, to translate individual competence to internal structure. Then it becomes a resource available to more parts of the organization for current exploitation and a basic knowledge 'building block' for others to develop in the future. Losing essential foundation level knowledge resources when people leave the organization can be a setback to knowledge creation as knowledge is built cumulatively and advanced knowledge needs prior absorption of basic principles and concepts.

Signpost See *Competence Area 4: Connecting* to find a more in-depth discussion of absorptive capacity.

Losing people can also weaken the advantage to be gained from knowledge exploitation as valuable knowledge may 'leak' to competitors.

Converting individual competence to internal structure can lead to an improvement in both knowledge exploitation and knowledge exploration. Embedding expertise and best practices into internal operating practices and products 'raises the bar' for future knowledge creation activities, as well as making them an unconscious operational competence that improves exploitation. Then we can pay attention to features that differentiate the product or process, rather than its basic core elements.

We can illustrate what we mean with an example from new product design. By adopting platform designs for families of products (such as cars), the strategically important knowledge is embedded in the internal structure of the organization through the design and manufacturing practices that are adopted across multiple teams. Volkswagen and General Motors have adopted this approach, creating families of vehicles based on common structures, engines and components. This leverages the knowledge that has been developed over time in these areas, but also offers two other benefits (Sanchez and Collins, 2001):

1. Standardization increases flexibility Standardization at a lower level of the system (that is, the basic platform) creates flexibility at higher levels (that is, design features to meet the needs of niche customers). By reducing the time, cost and difficulty in creating the basics of a new design, more attention can be paid to creating innovative features. In general, standardizing components and interfaces of products and services greatly increases the flexibility in generating new products and services.

2. Discipline enhances creativity New product innovation can be improved by following well-defined rules for the creative design process. Then designers can:

- Combine things in new ways by following a set of rules. This is creative improvisation within current capabilities.
- Create new sets of rules for combining things to bring about new possibilities for improvising. Effectively these are creative transformations to new sets of capabilities.

In general, we suggest that being good at exploiting the knowledge resources of our organizations means ensuring that best practices are widely adopted, that good ideas are shared and that contributions are recognized and valued. All of these things demonstrate that our organizations expect the best of people. Creating a culture of excellence in exploiting the knowledge resources of our organizations (in other words, raising the bar for the level of performance that is expected), allows us to compete at a higher level. Then, when people think of new ways of doing things, they are building on the best existing knowledge (the baseline of their absorptive capacity starts at an optimum level). In addition, the more widely dispersed the existing knowledge is, the more possible connections people can make to generate new ideas. When they see that good ideas are put into practice, they are more likely to be motivated to contribute further. The activities of exploration and exploitation become mutually supportive. The cycle of value generation is self-sustaining: good exploitation should lead to good new knowledge development, if it is undertaken with the intention of inspiring intelligent people, rather than controlling incapable workers.

Box 1.3

An aside
Bach wrote a series of Two and Three Part Inventions to help his son, and then later other students, learn to play the piano. Each *inventione*, or little idea, is a discovery from which a larger whole grows, as the learner follows a journey that refines the essence of the idea to reveal 'what matters'. Each has two or three fairly simple themes that are repeatedly refined and reinterpreted, resulting in what has been called 'a perfect balance of form'. Bach described his intention as being to give apprentice musicians a foretaste for composition that would inspire them to find their own ways of creating similar experiences. His examples of excellence teach the structural elements of composition, as well as inspire the creative talents of other musicians (BBC, 2002).

Invest in a climate that values competence and commitment

To optimize both knowledge exploitation and the development of new knowledge we need to create a climate in which people are inspired by good practice and motivated by effective knowledge-sharing to create new solutions. We need to ensure that people are not threatened by change and feel secure in their role and the recognition of their contribution. To achieve this, it is important that workers access and contribute to databases, engage enthusiastically in discussions with colleagues, participate in communities of practice and seek to develop their expertise for both their own benefit and that of the organization; in summary, they actively and constructively collaborate with colleagues.

Signpost See *Competence Area 3: Learning* to find out how knowledge workers are increasingly motivated to stay with employers, based on the expectation that their competence (and therefore future marketability with other employers) will be maintained.

Competence and commitment are the two vital complementary components of human intellectual capital (Ulrich, 1998). People management processes are the tools for creating a culture that encourages individual commitment and collaborative behaviour, and sources and develops the right competences. For an organization to be effective at developing new knowledge and getting the most from existing knowledge, its people management practices have to support the behaviours associated with both sets of knowledge practices (Bierly III and Daly, 2002). In particular, high employee participation needs to be encouraged, while job descriptions need to be loose and flexible.

The two areas that may find it difficult to achieve the required balance are training and performance management. Less formal training (allowing more experimentation) and a long-term results-focused approach to performance management (appraisal, compensation and goal setting) encourage the development of new knowledge. In contrast, formal training to embed efficient practices and a short-term approach to performance management that recognizes means are as important as ends, encourages the exploitation of existing knowledge. To implement both sets of practices simultaneously can be difficult and confusing for people. The alternatives are to apply different practices in different parts of the organization, or to tailor practices to uniquely motivate each individual. The overall approach to human resources management needs to be very flexible and capable of resolving the complexity and the potential conflict that can arise when varying practices are adopted. The maturity of organizational culture and practices required to make this work and the confidence in the equity of mixed approaches that each person must feel, may be the reasons why so many organizations have found it difficult to develop the capability to both develop new knowledge and exploit existing knowledge effectively. Yet businesses are still trying, because both are essential.

This balanced approach is summed up in the published Human Resources Management aims of the global technology and business consultancy firm CGE&Y (Nimmy, 2001):

> Our people's needs and wants govern our value proposition – we challenge and enable them to:
>
> Create: not just do their job, but also innovate and seek new ways.
>
> Connect: not just excel on their own, but also team up with fellow professionals.
>
> Evolve: not just deliver top quality, but also constantly learn and adapt.

Summary

In this chapter we set out to understand how knowledge helps us compete and be successful today and in the future. We started with a number of questions:

▶

How does the way knowledge is harnessed make an organization more successful?
How is new knowledge created?
Which knowledge should we focus our attention on?
How can existing knowledge create more value?
What makes it hard to shift the knowledge emphasis of an organization?
Which people management practices make a difference?

To answer these questions we looked at how knowledge is a critical resource available to an organization and how it varies over time. The capability to simultaneously develop and leverage this resource is both a source of competitive advantage today and the basis for a sustainable future. Value creation lies in the transfer and conversion of knowledge between three families of knowledge resources: the competence of employees, the experience of organizing and co-ordinating activities to deliver products and services, and the relationships that have developed with the outside world. We saw that knowledge can regenerate our organizations if we explore and learn new ways of doing things, while at the same time exploiting what we have already learned.

Paying attention to creating new knowledge involves:

- Creating the right conditions for new knowledge to be generated: clear organizational intention, individual autonomy, fluctuation and creative chaos, redundancy or resource slack and sufficient variety to stimulate change.
- Evaluating the new knowledge consistently against the value drivers of the organization.
- Developing the capability for rapid prototyping to quickly show the value of new concepts.
- Adopting people management practices that promote creativity and risk-taking.

Paying attention to exploiting existing knowledge involves:

- Building knowledge stocks by
  - learning before, during and after significant events;
  - supporting continuous improvement through effective suggestion schemes, databases and communities of practice.
- Maintaining various forms of organizational memory.
- Enabling knowledge to flow across the organization through
  - standardization of interfaces and practices;
  - technologies to support the management and co-ordination of knowledge resources;

▶

▶

- – a culture of trust and openness that encourages knowledge sharing.
- Adopting people management practices that encourage the adoption of good practices and knowledge-sharing behaviours.

Optimizing both knowledge creation and knowledge exploitation at the same time is made more difficult because some of these processes are not mutually supportive and also because existing knowledge gets in the way of new knowledge. Knowledge that is firmly embedded in products and processes creates a barrier to changes in accepted practices. It also traps the organization in a dominant logic that prevents the value of new knowledge being recognized. The ability to 'unlearn' is needed in order to move in a new direction.

The capability to optimize both the way new knowledge is developed and the way existing knowledge is exploited rests on the capability to convert knowledge from the insights and competences of individuals (the source of new knowledge) to structures, processes, products and systems that allow the value to be exploited. We have seen that we can use standardization to increase flexibility and discipline to enhance creativity.

The competence and commitment of people needs to be nurtured in an environment where excellence is an inspiration and driver. The way that people are managed is the basis for creating a culture that supports collaboration, which is the underpinning characteristic of both knowledge exploitation and the development of new knowledge. People management practices that support this encourage high levels of employee participation. Flexible organizational structures and job descriptions need to be used to build the capacity for continuous change into the culture. In this way, both current value can be delivered from knowledge and its future potential value can be nurtured.

References

Amit, R. and Schoemaker, P. J. (1993) 'Strategic assets and organizational rent', *Strategic Management Journal*, 14: 33–46.

APQC (1999) 'Creating a Knowledge-Sharing Culture', American Productivity and Quality Center, Consortium Benchmarking, Houston, Texas.

Baird, L. and Henderson, J. C. (2001) *The Knowledge Engine*. San Francisco: Berrett-Koehler Publishers Inc.

Bannon, L. J. and Kuutti, K. (1996) 'Shifting perspectives on organizational memory: from storage to active remembering', 29th Hawaii International Conference on System Sciences, Hawaii.

Barney, J. (1991) 'Firm resources and sustained competitive advantage', *Journal of Management* 17(1): 99–120.

BBC (2002) Bach Inventions http://www.bbc.co.uk/radio3/classical/discover.shtml (accessed 21 November 2002).

Bierly III, P. E. and Daly, P. (2002) 'Aligning human resource management practices and knowledge strategies', in *The Strategic Management of Intellectual Capital and Organizational Knowledge* (eds. C.W. Choo and N. Bontis). New York: Oxford University Press, 277–95.

Blackler, F. (1995) 'Knowledge, knowledge work and organizations: an overview and interpretation', *Organization Studies* 16(6): 1021–46.

Brown, J. and Duguid, P. (2001a) 'Creativity versus structure: a useful tension', *MIT Sloan Management Review* 42(4): 93–4.

Brown, J. and Duguid, P. (2001b) 'Knowledge and organization: a social-practice perspective', *Organization Science* 12(2): 198–213.

Christensen, C. M. and Overdorf, M. (2000) 'Meeting the challenge of disruptive change', *Harvard Business Review* 78(2): 66–76.

Collison, C. and Parcell, G. (2001) *Learning to Fly*. Oxford: Capstone Publishing Ltd.

Cranfield School of Management and Microsoft (2000) *Releasing the value of knowledge*. Report K453KM. Survey of UK industry.

Cross, R. (2000) 'Technology is not enough: improving performance by building organizational memory', *Sloan Management Review* 41(3): 69–78.

Crossan, M. M. and Holland, J. (2002) 'Leveraging knowledge through leadership of organizational learning', in *The Strategic Management of Intellectual Capital and Organizational Knowledge* (eds C.W. Choo and N. Bontis). New York: Oxford University Press, 711–23.

Cusumano, M. A. (2001) 'Focusing creativity', in *Knowledge Emergence* (eds I. Nonaka and T. Nishiguchi). New York: Oxford University Press:, 111–23.

De Long, D. W. and Fahey, L. (2000) 'Diagnosing cultural barriers to knowledge management', *The Academy of Management Executive* 14(4): 113–27.

Dell, M. (2002) 'Inspiring innovation: don't fear failure', *Harvard Business Review*, 80(8): 41.

Earl, M. and Hopwood, A. (1980) 'From management information to information management', in *Information Systems Environment* (eds H. C. Lucas, F. F. Land, T. J. Lincoln and K. Supper), IFIP Working Conference Proceedings, August 1980. Amsterdam: North-Holland Publishing Company.

Edvinsson, L. (2000a) 'Latest Developments in Knowledge Management', KM Forum, Henley Management College, UK.

Edvinsson, L. (2000b) 'Welcome to the Henley KM Forum', Henley KM Forum Launch Meeting, Henley Management College, UK.

Graham, A. and Pizzo, V. (1996) 'The Learning Organization: Managing Knowledge for Business Success', The Economist Intelligence Unit, New York.

Grant, R. M. (1991) 'The resource-based theory of competitive advantage: implications for strategy formulation', *California Management Review*, 33(3): 114–35.

Grant, R. M. (1996) 'Toward a knowledge-based theory of the firm', *Strategic Management Journal* 17(Winter Special Issue): 109–22.

Grant, R. M. (2002) 'The knowledge-based view of the firm', in *The Strategic Management of Intellectual Capital and Organizational Knowledge* (eds C.W. Choo and N. Bontis). New York: Oxford University Press, 133–48.

Greengard, S. (1998) 'Will your culture support KM?' *Workforce* 77(10): 93–5.

Haddon, H. (2002) 'Creating a compass to reveal knowledge', *Knowledge Management in Practice Series. Report Number 2.4*, Henley Knowledge Management Forum.

Kwiecien, S. and Wolford, D. (2001) 'Gaining real value through best-practice replication', *Knowledge Management Review*, 4(1): 12–15.

Lakin, S. (2001) 'BT's approach to ideas management', *Knowledge Management Review* 4(1): 24–8.

Levitt, T. (1988) 'The innovating organization', *Harvard Business Review* 66(1): 7.

March, J. (1991) 'Exploration and exploitation in organizational learning', *Organization Science* 2(1): 71–87.

Maula, M. (2000) 'The senses and memory of a firm – implications of autopoiesis theory for knowledge management', *Journal of Knowledge Management* 4(2): 157.

McKenzie, J. (1996) *Paradox: The Next Strategic Dimension*. Maidenhead: McGraw Hill.

Mellor, V. (1998) 'Balancing knowledge creation with high growth', *Knowledge Management Review* 1(5): 28–31.

Mintzberg, H. (1994) 'The fall and rise of strategic planning', *Harvard Business Review*, Jan–Feb: 107–14.

Nonaka, I. (1991) 'The knowledge creating company', *Harvard Business Review* Nov–Dec: 96–104.

Nonaka, I. (1994) 'A dynamic theory of organizational knowledge creation', *Organization Science* 5(1): 14–37.

Nonaka, I. and Konno, N. (1998) 'The concept of "ba" building a foundation for knowledge creation', *California Management Review* 40(3): 40–54.

Nonaka, I. and Takeuchi, H. (1995) *The Knowledge Creating Company*. New York: Oxford University Press.

Quinn, J. (1980) 'Managing strategic change',*Sloan Management Review*, 21(4): 3–20.

Rumelt, R. (1991) 'How much does industry matter?', *Strategic Management Journal*, 12: 167–85.

Sanchez, R. (1996) ' "Quick-connect" technologies for product creation', in *Dynamics of Competence Based Competition* (eds R. Sanchez, A. Heene and H. Thomas), pp. 299–322. Oxford: Elsevier Science Ltd.

Sanchez, R. and Collins, R. P. (2001) 'Competing – and learning – in modular markets', *Long Range Planning*, 34(6): 645–67.

Senge, P. (1990) *The Fifth Discipline*. London: Century Business.

Skapinker, M. (2002) 'The change agenda'. London: CIPD.

Spender, J. (1996) 'Making knowledge the basis of a dynamic theory of the firm', *Strategic Management Journal* 17(Winter Special Issue): 45–62.

Stewart, T. A. (1997) *Intellectual Capital: The New Wealth of Organizations*. New York: Doubleday.

Sveiby, K.-E. (2001) 'A knowledge-based theory of the firm to guide strategy formulation', *Journal of Intellectual Capital* 2(4): 344–58.

Toffler, A. (1990) *Powershift: Knowledge, Wealth and Violence at the Edge of the 21st Century*. New York: Bantam.

Ulrich, D. (1998) 'Intellectual capital = competence × commitment', *Sloan Management Review* 39(2): 15–26.

US Army (1993) *A Leader's Guide to After Action Reviews*. Washington, DC: U.S. Army.

von Krogh, G. (1999) 'Developing a knowledge-based theory of the firm', www.dialogonleadership.org/vonkrogh-1999 (accessed 3 September 2002).

Weick, K. E. (1989) 'Theory construction as disciplined imagination', *Academy of Management Review* 14(4): 516–31.

Whittington, R. (1993) *What Is Strategy and Does It Matter?* London: Routledge.

Wright, P. (1999) 'Leveraging frontline knowledge for smarter service', *Knowledge Management Review* 1(6): 4–5.

Zack, M. (1999) 'Managing codified knowledge', *Sloan Management Review* 40(4): 45–58.

Zack, M. (2002) 'Developing a knowledge strategy', in *The Strategic Management of Intellectual Capital and Organizational Knowledge* (eds C.W. Choo and N. Bontis). New York: Oxford University Press, 255–76.

2 Second Competence Area
Deciding

Business Challenges

- How can better knowledge management lead to better decision-making?

- How do we actually make decisions?

- How can we make sure that we have access to different points of view to improve our decisions?

- How can we make sure that the decisions that everyone makes, no matter where they are in the organization, are sufficiently consistent?

Introduction

In our second competence area, we set out to understand what is involved in using knowledge resources to improve decision-making. In the face of rapid change and high levels of uncertainty, individual employees have to take many quick decisions on a daily basis that cumulatively affect the fate of their organizations. Somehow we need a way to ensure that these decisions are based on the best available knowledge and do not work against one another. Our starting point will be to ask how decisions are made in organizations. This will then help us see how knowledge resources can be used to enable more effective decision-making in an increasingly unpredictable environment.

In understanding more about how effective decisions get made, it is important to recognize that our organizations are now compelled to draw upon a wider range of knowledge sources and points of view in order to comprehend the complex and unpredictable forces shaping their environment. That is why organizations often find themselves operating as a part of interconnected networks of diverse individuals and other organizations. Networks give cost-effective access to essential knowledge and different perspectives, which bring a fuller sense of the world. We need competence in integrating these diverse points of view into organizational decision-making processes so we can challenge the accepted view about how things should be done.

Signpost In *Competence Area 5: Relating* we look at how to design and manage a network of different kinds of relationships.

Diverse points of view inevitably create differences of opinion. This is further aggravated by the fact that we must increasingly distribute decision-making authority to increase speed and flexibility. Yet, to keep decisions aligned, those asked to make the decisions need a shared perspective about what matters: which business to be in and which not to; how to do business and how not to; and how to relate to each other and how not to. Without this harmonizing view, decisions become fragmented and even contradictory. By appreciating some of the mechanisms involved in developing a sense of identity and purpose, both as an individual and as part of a group, we start to identify practical ways to build a shared view of what matters. This increases the degree of alignment and allows employees and other partners to take effective decisions on a distributed basis.

However, in reality we all know that issues of power, hidden agendas and conflicting objectives make alignment difficult, even more so when different points of view have been deliberately encouraged. So how can we benefit from *both* bringing in diverse knowledge resources to challenge thinking *and* aligned energy and effort, so that our organizations' resources are not wastefully fragmented? We end this chapter by suggesting that one way is to develop leadership behaviours in everyone associated with an organization. By this we mean that each person, through understanding and identifying with the values of the organization, accepts personal accountability for his/her performance and impact on the performance of others, and engages in continuous learning to maintain a relevant knowledge base from which to make decisions that are consistent with the purpose and objectives of the organization.

How do we make decisions?

We can define decision-making as choices between and commitment to courses of action. Three limitations that 'come with the territory' of being human (Simon, 1957; 1976) prevent us ever making totally rational decisions:

- The mental skills, habits, reflexes and assumptions we develop over time.
- Our personal values or conceptions of purpose which may not be aligned with organization goals.
- The extent of knowledge and information that we possess and can bring to bear on decisions.

Much of this is tacit knowledge, frequently unknown to others and sometimes even unconscious to ourselves. To improve the quality and consistency of decision-making, we need to look at how such limitations develop and how they can be influenced.

So, what is the link between knowledge and decision-making? To answer this we need to return to the definition of knowledge (Sveiby, 2002) as both:

1 *justified true belief* – 'know what' or 'know that', which provides the raw material for deciding what to do and includes facts, assumptions and values; and

2 *the capacity to act* – 'know how', derived from resources such as procedures, rules and mental and physical abilities. This is the knowledge base that we draw on to take action.

Clearly, knowing what to do and knowing how to do it work together as a basis for decision-making, so we need to look at each in more detail.

Knowing what to do

If knowing what to do involves assumptions and values as well as facts, then how can different people in our organizations share these so as to make consistent decisions? Sharing facts is relatively simple, as we have already seen. When we start looking at how assumptions develop and subsequently influence choices, the picture is less clear. In making any decision, we each draw upon our experience to assess how to deal with the situation we are facing. We search for ideas until we find one that gives us sufficient confidence to follow the course of action it suggests (Choi, 1993; Lissack, 1997). Over time, preconceptions about how to handle particular categories of situations develop into a paradigm or mental model (a set of beliefs or assumptions about the world) that we rarely question.

People who live and work together often come to share a similar model of the world. Their shared paradigm strongly influences the solutions that they adopt and the decisions that they make. In organizations, the terms dominant logic (Bettis and Prahalad, 1995; Prahalad and Bettis, 1986) or strategic logic (Sanchez and Thomas, 1996) have been coined to describe the collective rationale for decisions. This set of shared assumptions often goes unquestioned. It is also widely recognized that such commonly-held assumptions tend to act as filters, screening out information that does not fit as irrelevant. Dominant logic is effectively a patterned response learned through experience. It simplifies and speeds decision-making by assuming that the future environment will be very similar to the past environment. See Box 2.1 for more about the emergence of dominant logic.

So, our capability to evaluate new options and take advantage of diversity in choices and plans for action are both grounded in and limited by these individual and collective perceptions of the world. These preconceptions also become embedded in the way we design systems and the way we manage people.

The exact interpretation given to the dominant logic will be similar but not identical for each individual, division, function and project team in an organization because each will interpret the overarching logic through the filter

Box 2.1

Dominant logic as an emergent property of the organization

Organizations are often described as complex systems with the innate ability to adapt with their environments. Complex systems adapt and learn either through random mutation or by sharing part of their model with others in a process of recombination. For example, DNA is the model of human form. Small adaptations occur through mutation of the genetic code whereas large-scale change occurs when half of the DNA of the mother combines with a different half from the father: thus the human species as a system can adapt and learn. In general, the behaviour of complex adaptive systems emerges from the interaction of many independent 'agents' as they self-organize in configurations that are beneficial to each individual agent. The diversity and density of the connections between agents affects the behaviour of the system. When the balance is right, new 'emergent properties' appear at the system level that are not present in any of the individual sub-elements. Emergent properties usually, though not always, help the system to survive. In organizations, we can interpret 'agents' as individual people and social groups that interact with one another. Their interactions act to shape their own responses and decisions as well as the responses and decisions of those they are interacting with. At the organizational level, the emergent properties of their interactions affect the outcome of decision-making.

▶

of how they see other aspects of the world. This can make it difficult for an organization to achieve concerted action and coherence in the decisions everyone makes (von Krogh and Roos, 1996).

As dominant logic is an emergent phenomenon, it has no static state. However, we need any shifts to remain appropriate and relevant to the conditions that our organization faces.

> Organizations' environments are largely invented by organizations themselves. Organizations select their environments from a range of alternatives, then they subjectively perceive the environments they inhabit. The processes of both selection and perception are unreflective, disorderly, incremental, and strongly influenced by social norms and customs.
>
> *Starbuck, 1976: 1069*

As these reflections suggest, perceptions that are self-created can be changed, but the process will be messy, rely heavily on social processes and take place slowly through each decision that is made.

Figure 2.1 shows the stages involved in decision-making and the tensions that challenge alignment across an organization at each step.

Once decisions have been implemented, the consequences are likely to impact some aspect of the competitive environment, producing further new

Signpost   See *Competence Area 3: Learning* for more about complex adaptive systems.

Emergent properties of organizations that arise from this pattern of interactions include political coalitions and shared values. Dominant logic is also an emergent property. It is collective tacit knowledge about what is 'in' and what is 'out'. In this role, it both supports action by providing a form of short-hand to speed decision-making and keeps coherence by establishing a commonly understood basis for decisions. This 'inherently results in "adaptive ability", so long as changes in the underlying logic are not necessary' (Bettis and Prahalad, 1995).

The dominant logic acts as a locally-optimized response to the environment and creates a kind of equilibrium. However, as changes in conditions invalidate the current dominant logic, an organization must develop a new dominant logic quickly and unlearn the old one if it is to survive. The longer the organization has been in equilibrium, the harder it is to unlearn. Also, the greater the difference between the previous environment and the new one, the more difficult it is to create the necessary shifts in thinking.

Signpost   In *Competence Area 1: Competing* we saw that unlearning is a difficult process. Emotional attachment to investments in knowledge and expertise block the acceptance of new knowledge and new ways of doing things.

Figure 2.1   The factors and tensions involved in achieving distributed decision-making that can evolve as the environment changes (based on Choo, 1996)

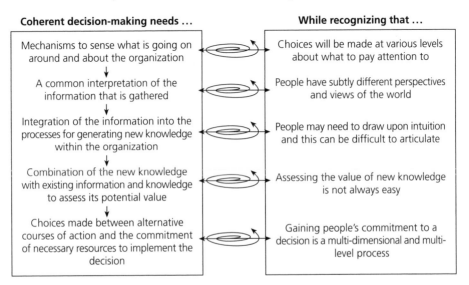

information to be sensed and adapted to. It is a self-perpetuating spiral of assumptions, decisions and outcomes that creates new conditions to challenge existing assumptions. Each step is deeply embedded in dynamic social processes. Inevitably, the process will not develop entirely smoothly and there will be interruptions and iterations. This is further complicated by the fact that in highly complex systems such as organizations, small interventions can have significance far beyond what would be suggested by linear cause and effect relationships. So, the outcome of a decision, however well-reasoned through the left-hand side of Figure 2.1, is unlikely to be what was originally intended. Small interpretative differences on the right-hand side of Figure 2.1 can translate into large distortions in outcome.

General Motors is one organization that recognized the need for a more sophisticated approach to decision-making that would help keep underlying assumptions up-to-date and relevant (Coles, 2000). It began to document important decisions and monitored their subsequent effectiveness. Analysing and reflecting on the reasons for deviations from the plan provided valuable learning opportunities. The procedural elements of the General Motors approach included:

- Making it easy to *access relevant experience* – this did not mean more repositories for papers and reports, but focusing on connecting people so that they could talk to each other.
- *Recording key decisions* – including the information used, the dialogue that took place between the decision-makers about the strategic context, underlying assumptions, commitments made and so on. These were not necessarily made public, but used by the original decision-makers so that they could reflect on how the outcome related to their original intent.
- Using impartial third-party individuals to *monitor the implementation* of decisions.
- *Analyzing* reports on the outcome of decisions, determining areas for improvement, implementing these, measuring the impact and then institutionalizing the change. Learning Observers worked with leaders to capture the entire group's perspective of the events.
- Integrating an *intelligence function* to scan for early warnings about anything that could impact current decisions. This also provided insights into reasons why the implementation of previous decisions was not as envisaged.

General Motors tackled the impact of social forces upon the adoption and targeted value from the procedures by:

- *Purposefulness* – the purpose of the approach was clearly communicated as being
  - to reduce the gap in the organization's performance between agreed goals and what was actually achieved;
  - to help those making decisions to make better ones.

- *Discipline* – developing a structured system helped ensure improvement actually happened, rather than the translation of learning to action remaining simply a desirable, but unachieved, goal.

- *Responsiveness* – information was made available at the time decision-makers needed it, and key learning was organized around steps of work processes so that it was easily recognized as valuable.

- *Engagement* – by working with decision-makers to find out what they needed to close performance gaps, how they wanted their decisions to be tracked and in what form they wanted feedback, individuals were drawn into the process and were prepared to act on the findings.

- *Credibility* – respected and experienced employees were involved in supporting the processes.

For assumptions in our organizations to remain relevant and valid, we need to collect and process information from the outside world, perceive it in a common way and integrate it consistently into our collective decision-making processes. Yet, as Figure 2.1 shows, for each step there is something that makes it hard to do this. Later in this chapter, we consider how to manage this cycle of collecting and integrating new ideas, aligning collective decision-making and resolving the tensions that arise as a consequence of the process.

Before that, we need to think about the second aspect of knowing what to do: shared values. The values we share with other members of our organizations are different from the dominant logic, but they are an equally important component of what is known as 'collective mind', or the cognitive infrastructure of our organizations. We can think of the sense of identity that we share with other members of our organizations as coming from the values and beliefs that we create and actualize in our interactions with others (Stacey, 2001: 168). How we behave together and what we jointly believe matters; they contribute to both a shared sense of the identity of our organizations and the level of coherence of our collective decision-making.

Identification is the process through which we see ourselves as one with another person or group of people. We adopt the values or standards of others as a comparative frame of reference. We tend not to act in a manner which threatens our perception of our identity and we make sense of our own actions and those of others in terms of whether they reinforce our sense of identity or not. Although we are always looking for ways to define our identity, by its very nature it cannot be pinned down because it emerges and is reinvented through our on-going interactions with each other.

For an organization, identity is 'that which members believe to be central, enduring and distinctive about their organization . . . what is perceived by members to be of an enduring or continuing nature linking the present organization with the past (and presumably the future)' (Albert and Whetton, 1985). It evolves slowly and 'identity will always be somewhat unclear and people will always want to talk about it' (Lissack and Roos, 2001). It both places a limit on what the members of an organization pay attention to and also what they consider to be

Box 2.2

Organizational identity

There are three perspectives on the nature of organizational identity (Oliver and Roos, 2000):

(i) Identity is stable and slowly changing and appears the same no matter who is looking at it. This means that it can be uncovered and used.

(ii) Identity is a continual 'work in progress' and people and groups in the organization have to negotiate to reach shared meaning, which includes embedded tacit knowledge.

(iii) Group identity has little rhyme or reason. Power differences at different times mean that perspective shifts as groups compete for dominance.

Although apparently contradictory, all are valid perspectives. Which we use depends on the slant we take on the idea of identity. There can be a core of organizational identity (i) which stays recognizable to everyone over time; the edges are likely to be subtly blurred and continuously developing as a result of renegotiating values and meaning (ii); and within the mess and detail of day-to-day decision-making filtered through many group dominant logics there may seem to be little that apparently contributes to a coherent identity (iii), until the accumulated effect is viewed on the larger scale.

By acknowledging all these views as valid, we can understand how a sense of identity can contribute towards a shared view of the world and how to act within it, whilst still allowing for change.

The development of a sense of identity, or shared self-concept, is one facet of the 'collective mind' or cognitive infrastructure that enables members of an organization to jointly make sense of the environment, integrate their knowledge and commit to action. In addition to the idea of self-concept, there are three other components of 'collective mind' (Merali, 2001). These are:

- The *roles* people take on and the way these determine how they interact.
- The *relationships* between individuals that determine the content and structure of knowledge networks to share and diffuse ideas.
- The *total collection of interconnected beliefs and the perceptions that form the dominant logic* and shape the way people collectively make sense of the environment.

All the components are mutually dependent and need to be maintained in harmony if organizational members are to know what to do and there is to be 'wisdom in action' (Merali, 2001). Lack of harmony results in a waste of organizational energy and can undermine the sustainability of an organization's existence. These connections are illustrated in Figure 2.2.

▶

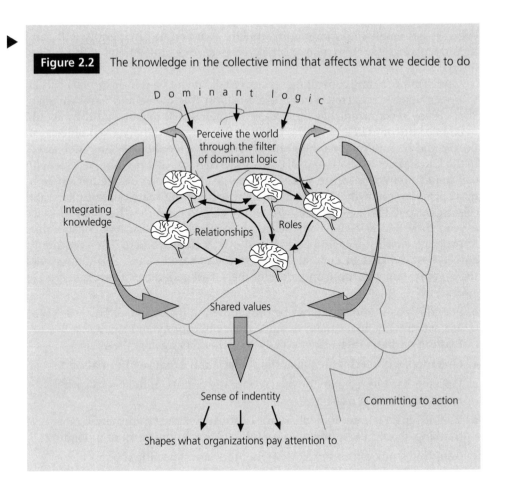

Figure 2.2 The knowledge in the collective mind that affects what we decide to do

acceptable alternative courses of action. See Box 2.2 to find out more about how organizational identity fits with other components of 'collective mind'.

Although individuals and groups within our organizations can and do change, there tends to be a general pattern of activities that remains largely the same. This happens as a result of various forms of 'glue' that tie the levels of our organization together and allow it to reassert its identity in the changing environment. Assumptions and values form part of that 'glue'.

A shared sense of organizational identity also establishes a commonly-held perception of the boundary of an organization. Clear boundaries of our organizations in a physical sense (where it is situated), or contractual sense (who are employees), make it easier for us to know with whom we need to identify. Yet, increasingly, these are absent in many of our organizations. Networked, virtual and some other newly-developing organizational forms may make it harder for us to have a clear sense of the identity of our organizations, and, in particular, what they represent (Weick, 1999). In these new forms of organization evolving in complex environments, making shared values and beliefs explicit becomes extremely important as an attractor that people can identify with, and a guide against which to align distributed decisions and actions with those of others.

One firm providing consulting services to the oil and gas industry has chosen to operate as a completely virtual organization (McKenzie and van Winkelen, 2001). They recognized that the nature of their work meant that they would need to be distributed around the world, so they decided that a fixed office location would be superfluous; their only shared space would be a computer server in the UK. Each consultant had all of the tools they needed to communicate with colleagues anywhere in the world. Sometimes they worked together on common projects; often they worked alone co-ordinating teams of suppliers and clients. Despite the fact that they were only able to meet together once or twice a year, they had a very strong sense of corporate identity and collaborative knowledge sharing was embedded in the way they worked. The consultants agreed that the keys to their success were their shared values and the sense of the organization's purpose and identity these had generated. These emerged as a result of:

- Spending six months together before launching the business. This was seen as a worthwhile investment to agree their philosophy and shared values. Existing partners then screened any new member against these.
- Openness with each other, including salary and expense information.
- Working hard to recreate the open company culture in their relationships with clients and suppliers.
- Establishing a common database for capturing explicit information and thinking about how it might be useful to others at the point of uploading.
- Adopting a mix of communication methods and selecting the most appropriate medium for the problem in hand.

Another example is the global computer manufacturing and services firm, Hewlett Packard. The company became well-known for the way the values and management principles that form the 'HP Way' created a strong sense of corporate identity. Commitment to personal autonomy and decentralization, to teamwork and egalitarianism, and to fair dealing and trusting each other became fundamental aspects of the culture. Through employee selection and promotion decisions, induction and training programmes, appraisal and mentoring processes, HP employees were helped to see what the HP Way meant in terms of their relationships with others and for the day-to-day practice of their jobs.

So far we have been looking at the influences on 'knowing what to do'. Now we will look at what influences the 'knowing how to do it' part of effective decision-making.

Knowing how to do it

Knowing how to act draws on expertise that we develop over time through learning how to respond to particular situations. It may also involve following explicit and implicit rules that determine what is acceptable and unacceptable. National and organizational culture implicitly places limits on what we perceive to be acceptable; laws and codes of ethics make some of these limits on our behaviour explicit. To improve consistency and productivity, our organizations also prepare procedures manuals and contingency plans, train people to follow them and use performance management tools like appraisals and reward systems to ensure conformity.

We can refer to past decisions to help us make future ones if there is agreement in principle about how to handle such situations and the consequences of the decision are reasonably certain (Stacey, 1999). To support these decisions, information technology can be used to collect and analyze data, plans can be drawn up and progress monitored during implementation. Frequently, most of the knowledge that needs to be drawn upon can be made explicit and efforts can be made to codify this and make it available across our organizations.

The beverage distribution company Heineken USA consciously set out on a five-year journey to use knowledge to improve decision-making. The knowledge management team defined their mission as being to 'combine the resources of technology, research and analysis to provide Heineken USA employees with the right tools to make decisions closer to the customer' (Chase, 2002).

Throughout, the Heineken USA team viewed knowledge as a strategic asset that results in and supports action. The main focus was to turn information into actionable know-how that could be transferred to key decision-makers to improve business performance. Initiatives were introduced in phases. They started with ways to better disseminate explicit know-how. Early on they built a technological infrastructure to provide sales and marketing teams and senior managers with relevant consumer, business information and knowledge to help them make more informed decisions. The latter phases included managing internal research and external providers of data and analysis to produce business insights on, for example, the purchasing patterns of ethnic groups, the effectiveness of advertising and promotion initiatives and the price sensitivity of consumers. Enterprise-wide decision support tools were made available to non-technical people so they could access, report and analyze information from a variety of storage systems across the organization. They integrated both external and internal data sources to ensure they were managed in a coherent way. Advanced modelling and analysis including simulation tools were also planned. The knowledge management team saw itself as responsible for driving 'the creation of knowledge by combining fact-based analysis with the dissemination of consumer, customer and employee information and experiences'.

Heineken USA measured the return on their investment in knowledge-based activities in terms of the difference it made to effectiveness of the decisions of customer-facing teams and senior managers:

- Speed of knowledge transfer – more rapid and more straightforward access to the information and knowledge needed for meaningful action.

- Integration of internal and external information sources – reduced duplication leading to lower costs in maintaining the information.

- Improved retention of expertise within the organization and more effective decision-making to support collaboration between employees, customers and network partners.
- A better knowledge of consumer behaviour and the overall business environment resulting in a more efficient market investment strategy.
- Increased sales and improved profitability.

These initiatives combined effective design and application of technology with content management, market research and business analysis into an integrated approach to support decision-makers in knowing how to act more effectively.

This example illustrates the contribution of effective management of explicit knowledge in knowing how to act. Now we move on to consider the contribution tacit knowledge can make. Intuition is a particularly important aspect of knowing how to act and is the way we access our tacit knowledge. Described as 'direct knowing, immediate understanding, learning without the conscious use of reasoning, or making a choice without formal analysis' (Behling and Eckel, 1991), intuition forms a connection between our subconscious and conscious mind (Anthony et al., 1993). We draw on tacit knowledge to make sense of our actions when we use experience gained from handling problems that have arisen in our jobs in the past. Intuition is know-how formed from tacit patterns of experience. It is a unique human ability that allows us to develop a sufficient answer from insufficient information or data. In that respect, it is particularly useful in fluid and uncertain situations.

In practice, we often use intuition when we make strategic decisions because they are generally future-oriented, highly uncertain, complex and lacking in information. More structured and analytical processes are not appropriate. In this context, our ability to 'discern patterns in reality that are suggestive of information within [our] experience but not readily accessible as ordered thought functions' (Brockmann and Anthony, 1998), effectively to use human insight rather than analysis, becomes an important decision-making option. The intuitive decisions of experienced senior management teams with a well-developed 'collective mind', have been shown to be more effective than decisions based solely on rational or analytical techniques.

Our ability to use tacit knowledge and intuition for effective decision-making is built on repeated practice (Brockmann and Anthony, 1998). Herbert Simon (1987) provides a useful pointer as to why developmental experiences are so important in this process. He describes intuition and judgment as 'analyses frozen into habit and into the capacity for rapid response through recognition'. Habits of response are learned through repeated practice and reinforcement so that they are embedded in automatic patterns of behaviour and thinking. The fire service, police and army develop intuitive decision-making skills through rigorous training and rehearsing in realistic scenarios.

In a complex and changing competitive environment, it is no longer always appropriate for the senior managers of our organizations to be the primary decision-makers: often they sit at a level far removed from day-to-day practicalities. The responsibility for the content of decisions has to move closer to the customer and other stakeholders in the organization, otherwise the issues and concerns will be filtered and reinterpreted as they are communicated through the hierarchy. Senior managers do, however, remain responsible for framing the organizational context that facilitates intuitive decision-making. Decision-making will become part of the remit of more people in our organizations and intuition will be key, particularly for those who are facing demanding customers and who need to act quickly despite ambiguity.

The challenge for our organizations is to ensure that initiatives like customer care programmes, development training and secondments give people the practical experience needed to build their capacity for intuitive decision-making.

Undeniably, there are risks in making decisions intuitively. Individuals can become overconfident and may conveniently forget when intuitive decisions didn't work out. Reflection (self-checking) is a necessary process to avoid these pitfalls. Experienced CEOs often confer with trusted advisers who were not involved in the original discussion when they are uneasy about a decision (Hayashi, 2001). We need to institute practices in our organizations that encourage reflection at all levels, provide time to reflect and create an environment where mistakes do not engender blame, but stimulate a genuine desire to understand and learn. These are necessary complements to intuitive decision-making.

Having looked at the contribution of know-what and know-how to decision-making in general, we will now follow two specific themes. Both of these are important for our organizations, although, as we will see later, optimizing both at the same time is not straightforward. Firstly, we will look at how to access and integrate diverse knowledge resources into the decision-making processes of our organizations. Secondly, we will look at how to create the conditions for decision-making to be sufficiently aligned and consistent, even when it is distributed across the organization.

Paying attention to the diversity of information and knowledge that we use for decision-making

Why do we need diverse information and knowledge to improve the quality of our decisions? One answer lies in our earlier discussion where we saw that as individuals and as groups, our mental models and dominant logic constrain how we see the world. We need the stimulus of different perspectives to avoid the trap of 'groupthink', a collective bias that distorts our interpretation of signals and trends. Ingrained mental models limit what we each consider to be important, so we might not even notice some indications about changes in the pattern of competitive activity or customer requirements, even if they are crucial to our future success. Many overlapping signals from a range of external sources are more likely to show up on the corporate 'radar screen', particularly if we have people with diverse experience within the organization to help interpret them.

We should also bear in mind the idea of 'requisite variety' or 'requisite diversity' (Ashby, 1956). To be able to respond and adapt appropriately to the challenges of its external environment, the level of diversity inside an organization should match the variety and complexity of outside conditions. Our organizations are facing more and more external complexity, so greater diversity of information and individual knowledge and experience is necessary to comprehend what is happening around us and enable us to make better decisions.

In *Competence Area 1: Competing* we saw that requisite variety is one of the conditions that enables effective organizational knowledge creation.

In the following sections, we will look at two possible means of increasing the variety of our organization's knowledge resources: systematically extending access to external information sources and perspectives, and enlarging the range of knowledge and expertise available within the organization.

Access diverse external information sources and perspectives

Information flowing across the external boundaries of our organizations is the raw material to enhance know-what and know-how. We can collect and analyze market and competitor data so that we know what is the most profitable business to invest in. We can work collaboratively with partners and participate in external communities to develop and transfer advanced skills and abilities across our organization. Figure 2.3 shows how technology, networks, communities, and partnership relationships give access to different sorts of information and knowledge outside the organization's boundaries.

To see what these ideas mean in practice, we will look at two examples of companies that are getting value from such approaches. We start with Customer Relationship Management (CRM) systems. Most organizations find their vital information sources are distributed across a mixture of legacy technology systems. By overlaying integrative solutions they can make accessible a broader range of pertinent facts for the task in hand. Chase Manhattan, the US-based global bank, adopted this overlay approach to developing a Relationship Management System (Lotus Consulting, 1998). They combined customer information from one system with the knowledge of those responsible for the relationships and then mixed it with product knowledge and material about the bank's own policies. The system could present the information in a variety of ways, which allowed the managers to make better decisions in terms of the bottom-line impact for the bank. The fact that attention was drawn to the most appropriate products also improved perceptions of customer service, which in turn led to even stronger relationships.

Figure 2.3 Accessing diverse knowledge resources from outside the organization

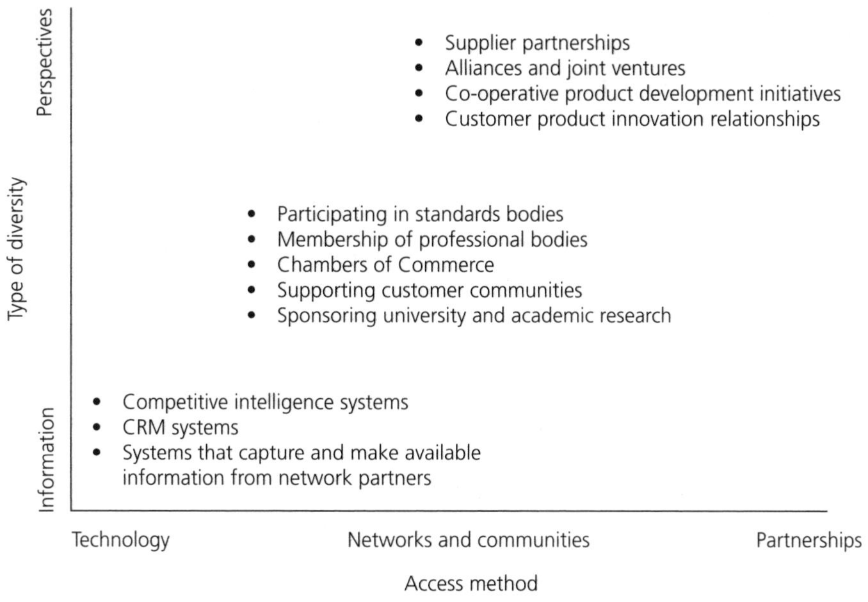

Type of diversity

Perspectives
- Supplier partnerships
- Alliances and joint ventures
- Co-operative product development initiatives
- Customer product innovation relationships

- Participating in standards bodies
- Membership of professional bodies
- Chambers of Commerce
- Supporting customer communities
- Sponsoring university and academic research

Information
- Competitive intelligence systems
- CRM systems
- Systems that capture and make available information from network partners

Technology · · · Networks and communities · · · Partnerships

Access method

Even closer relationships are needed for co-operative product development initiatives. Dupont created a knowledge and technology transfer network involving Research and Development directors, representatives from all their business units, joint venture partners and central Research and Development laboratories (Skyrme, 1998). They found that co-operating on product development activities could produce more worthwhile discoveries, as well as saving time and costs, because there was more opportunity to make new connections between ideas. Co-operation was based on the following six principles:

- *Strategic selection of projects*: the development method (acquisition, in-house development, partnership, etc) was chosen based on an assessment of the potential return and an assessment of their own strengths.

- *Selecting partners based on key criteria*: criteria such as relevant competency, level of commitment and perceived trustworthiness were important.

- *Matching projects with partners*: relationships needed to be mutually beneficial by meshing complementary competencies and matching interests.

- *Effective project management*: everyone needed a clear understanding of the goals.

- *A strong and respected business champion*: someone needed to ensure that the pace was maintained, cultural diversity was respected, etc.

- *Effective communication and networking*: local support infrastructures needed to be provided and attention paid to face-to-face communication.

Signpost In *Competence Area 5: Relating* we will look in more depth at the partnership perspectives at the top right of Figure 2.3 and see how to co-ordinate an appropriate mix of relationships with external individuals and organizations. Close relationships are needed for valuable tacit knowledge to be transferred. Looser associations allow information and explicit knowledge to be exchanged.

The broader knowledge resources and perspectives needed to keep decision-making relevant come from outside our organizations; however, there are things we can do from within to increase the diversity of available knowledge.

Increase the diversity of knowledge available inside the organization

Investments in formal training, education and job-based experience underpin any attempt to diversify an organization's knowledge base. Yet when conditions become more uncertain, these are often the first activities to be scaled down. Employee learning can be seen either as a cost to be reduced, or a resource to be developed. In environments of increasing complexity, the opportunity cost of scaling down knowledge diversification may be higher than the short-term cost of providing it.

Signpost See *Competence Area 3: Learning* to see how to design effective learning opportunities for employees.

Many organizations have also recognized the value of deliberately encouraging diversity of gender, race and background in their employees. Hewlett Packard uses the Internet to declare its belief publicly in the link between diversity in the workforce and business value through the following statement (HP, 2002):

At HP, we believe that diversity and inclusion are key drivers of creativity, innovation and invention. Throughout the world, we are putting our differences to work to connect everyone to the power of technology in the marketplace, workplace and community.

The value proposition for diversity is very clear:

- Diversity drives creativity.
- Creativity drives invention.
- Invention drives profitability and business success.

What the words mean to us:

diversity

Diversity is the existence of many unique individuals in the workplace, marketplace and community. This includes men and women from different nations, cultures, ethnic groups, generations, backgrounds, skills, abilities and all the other unique differences that make each of us who we are.

inclusion

Inclusion means a work environment where everyone has an opportunity to fully participate in creating business success and where each person is valued for his or her distinctive skills, experiences and perspectives. Inclusion is also about creating a global community where HP connects everyone and everything through our products, services and our winning workforce.

(Used with permission. Content is the property of Hewlett-Packard Company www.hp.com)

However, even when we have diversified workforces in our organizations, the actual pattern of interpersonal relationships may not reflect that diversity. So the desired assortment of perspectives and knowledge may still not be brought to bear on decisions.

Social Network Analysis is a useful tool for exposing the actual pattern of knowledge flows in an organization (Cross *et al.,* 2001; Cross and Prusak, 2002; Parker, Cross and Walsh, 2001). By asking people a few questions such as, 'to get your work done, with whom do you regularly communicate?' it is possible to map how information and knowledge are really flowing and where the blockages may be. Research based on Social Network Analysis has shown that effective relationships can be distinguished from ineffective ones based on:

- Whether we know enough about what another person knows to judge when to turn to them for help.
- Being able to reach that person when we need them.
- The willingness of the person we seek out to engage with us in solving our problem, rather than just flooding us with information.
- How safe we feel in the relationship to be creative and learn.

Often, mapping relationships against one or more of these dimensions reveals a disproportionate reliance on a few key individuals in a network, with others on the periphery representing an under-utilized resource for the group. There are always some people who regularly act as conduits for information between groups and networks. Having too few of these 'boundary spanners' stifles incoming diversity. Other people often stand out as being particularly valuable in brokering relationships, even though they themselves don't have the information required. Helping them share their skills with others can be profitable.

By mapping these knowledge flows, we are better able to judge where they may be inadequate and instigate initiatives to improve them. We can deliberately integrate relatively isolated experts into internal projects to raise other people's awareness of their skills and experience. New communication methods can be introduced to get those on the periphery more involved and we can make concerted efforts to reduce reliance on a few individuals. The pattern may also indicate underlying political tensions that can be diffused by targeted change initiatives.

The research and development firm Aventis Pharmaceuticals relies heavily on globally dispersed teams to produce new therapeutic drugs and vaccines. They used Social Network Analysis to identify who was connected with whom across the organization. This gave them a baseline 'status' of their networks against which they could measure changes over time as various initiatives were introduced (Rush, 2002). They were able to see gaps that needed to be filled and also recognized areas of strong interaction that would benefit from support and recognition. They analyzed patterns of communication and whether people knew about the knowledge bases of colleagues elsewhere. They were pleased to find that many people were actively sharing their knowledge and reaching out to seek knowledge from others. These findings were combined with interviews to assess the benefits to the organization that could come from more effective networks. As a result they were able to design specific interventions that exploited strengths and overcame weaknesses to best support the teams.

The arguments for diversifying the knowledge inputs to decision-making are strong, but we must avoid falling into the trap of confusion and indecisiveness by stimulating too many ideas and solutions. How can we produce sufficient alignment in the decisions made by people distributed across our organizations?

Paying attention to aligning decisions

The second aspect of good decision-making in our organizations is for everyone to have a clear understanding about what matters, so that decisions are harmonized across all levels of our organization and reflect the current view of what collectively we know.

How does this happen? Each of us makes decisions moment by moment and as independent, thinking, self-aware individuals we have choices about the actions we take. How can a group of such people who are geographically distributed, operating in different time zones and from different national cultures, choose to make decisions consistently with one another? Perhaps more importantly, how can this be influenced and improved through knowledge management practices?

It may not be obvious how higher order patterns of coherent collective action emerge from individual actions, but it does happen. In some situations, such as the flight deck of an aircraft carrier, it is particularly important that there is high reliability in the pattern of joint activities. In such complicated and demanding environments, individuals need to make reliable decisions that fit seamlessly into a coherent pattern of joint activities so they act as if they are guided by a 'collective mind'. Research suggests that in these situations two things happen: there is a 'struggle for alertness' and individual responses are guided by 'heedful interrelating' (Weick and Roberts, 1993).

Is this state of alertness and mindful interaction achievable in other situations? Do our organizations need the same level of concern for decision reliability? The flight deck of an aircraft carrier may be an extreme example, but if we accept that the complexity of the business operating environment is increasing, then to achieve high reliability and prevent people from pulling our organizations in too many directions at once, everyone does need to be more alert to the situation and more heedful of what others are doing. Otherwise, the complexity will produce greater contradictions, more misunderstandings and mistakes. Increasingly, our tasks are heavily dependent on the work of colleagues elsewhere, either because of the nature of the market being addressed, the product being developed or the technology being used. Yet the order in which the tasks are undertaken still needs to remain flexible to respond appropriately to varying demands from different stakeholders. To co-ordinate this type of interdependency we have to shift the emphasis away from incremental hierarchical decision-making where one person collects all the information, makes a decision and tells others what to do. Instead, we need to move towards the reliable performance of our 'collective mind', which means organizing for 'controlled information processing, mindful attention and heedful action' until attentiveness to work and the needs of colleagues become ingrained behaviours (Weick and Roberts, 1993).

Reflection on how we pay attention to our work and how we relate to others and appreciate their needs provides some pointers for how we can influence the consistency of decisions and direct energy towards a common purpose.

Improve attentiveness to work and the needs of others

Even in similar situations, people do not pay equal attention to their work or the needs of others. This is because in each situation we are affected by three potentially conflicting characteristics (Tsoukas, 1996):

Our own disposition – the mental patterns of perception, appreciation and action we have acquired from past social interactions, which we uniquely bring to bear on each particular situation. Disposition includes the mental models we have developed to explain the world around us and to provide a form of short-hand for choosing how to act.

The demands of the role – the social expectations we have to live up to in order to fulfil a particular role. Both formal and informal expectations influence and constrain our actions.

Context – the characteristics and demands of the specific situation that we are facing.

From moment to moment, these three factors work together to influence attentive behaviour. Others may have some control over what expectations are associated with our role, but we bring our disposition with us and our unique characteristics may or may not suit the context, creating comfort or discomfort in our role. The context is continuously shaped by local circumstances that can neither be fully known beforehand, nor fully understood by anyone who is not there at the time. This has led to the suggestion that management is 'an open-ended process of co-ordinating purposeful individuals, whose actions stem from applying their unique interpretations to the local circumstances confronting them' (Tsoukas, 1996).

In practice, situations are not totally open-ended. The number of variations in the patterns of our actions is limited when we work for an organization. In most situations, there are some explicit guidelines to follow and we all refer back to a tacit and unarticulated background of common understanding about how to act (also known as 'common knowledge' (Spender, 2002)). In general, we pay better attention to our work when (Weick and Roberts, 1993):

- We are naturally disposed to act with attentiveness, alertness and care.
- Our conduct takes into account the expectations of others.

No-one can *control* our attentiveness because we all approach tasks based on our disposition and our knowledge of how to handle our role in the situations we find ourselves in. However, attentiveness can be changed by influencing the climate in which we take action.

These ideas are closely linked to work that identifies care as an important enabling characteristic for knowledge creation (von Krogh, Ichijo and Nonaka, 2000: Ch. 3). This suggests 'to care for others is to help them learn; to increase their awareness of important events and consequences; to nurture their personal knowledge while sharing their insights'.

However, care is a feature of our individual disposition, so we must question how much external interventions can directly impact the collective display of care. Intuitively, it seems reasonable to argue that if our disposition develops through past social interactions then, to some extent, the current social environment will also influence it. If social conditions are consistent over time, it should be possible to create new patterns of collective behaviour and adjust perceptions of the sort of behaviour that is expected. In general, it has been found that modelling, articulating, rewarding and otherwise reinforcing and paying attention to desirable behaviours can influence the emergence of new patterns of action in groups of people. Table 2.1 suggests some ways to encourage behaviours that affect the level of care manifested in organizations.

We can see some of these ideas in practice in Advanced Cardiovascular Systems (ACS), a medical device manufacturer owned by the pharmaceutical firm Eli Lilly (Graham, 2002). Their CEO realized that although the company results looked good, it was still performing at a sub-optimal level. Performance was being badly undermined by internal disagreements and a culture of blame. She set out to establish practices that would lead to open and honest communication and foster a sense of personal accountability. The approach that was adopted can be described in terms of the features of a high-care organization:

Mutual trust – employee 'town hall' meetings were used to talk about issues that had previously only been discussed in management meetings. Any question was allowed from any employee and those closest to the activity answered it so they were clearly accountable to their peers.

Active empathy – each executive was assigned a coach drawn from non-managerial ranks. These coaches were trained to gather information from the workforce about executives' openness and honesty. They provided feedback and helped close the gap between what actually mattered to employees and what senior managers thought would matter to them.

Access to help – employees were encouraged to feel responsible for helping to solve the organization's problems. Direct appeals were made for help when unforeseen circumstances meant that extra effort was needed. Management demonstrated that they would listen and respond to the needs of employees who provided this help (such as supporting the additional child-care arrangements needed).

Lenience in judgement – internal issues were confronted in a non-judgemental way. For example, despite the short-term cost, product development was closed down while a new approach was designed that would end the persistent problem of the manufacturing department claiming that R&D designed products that couldn't be built and the R&D department claiming that manufacturing were unwilling to integrate new technologies.

Courage – the senior management team offered each other clear feedback on performance with suggestions for improvement. This was undertaken as a regular group exercise and acted as a 'powerful tool for building mutual accountability and honest communication'.

The CEO summed up the benefits of this approach in the following statement: 'in the process of becoming comfortable with honesty, we learned to respond quickly to internal and external changes. And in the transformation, we dramatically improved our chances of ongoing success'.

We have suggested that care is an important aspect of our attentiveness at work and our appreciation of the needs of others. However, the ways in which activities are tied together determines the effects they produce (Weick and Roberts, 1993). We therefore need to look in more detail at how our relationships with others connect our actions and drive the alignment of our decisions. How can we influence the style and strength of the 'glue' that ties our activities to those of other members of the organization, to keep them in line with the overall purpose and objectives of the organization?

Increase the level of mutual interdependence

Again we need to start with individuals. Every act each of us takes is based on an unarticulated background that we take for granted (unquestioned mental models and interpretations given to words and gestures in the light of past experience). 'It is when we lack a common background that we are forced to articulate the background, and explain it to ourselves and to others' (Tsoukas, 1996).

Table 2.1 Moving to a high-care organization (based on von Krogh, Ichijo and Nonaka, 2000)

Dimension of care	Why it's important	Key characteristics	Ways to influence the development of a high-care organization
Mutual trust	• Compensates for lack of knowledge about motives, interests etc. • Allows belief that teaching and recommendations will be used in the best possible way.	• Must be reciprocal • Strongly depends on consistency of behaviour over time.	• Create maps that make explicit what people or teams are expected to achieve, what resources they would be expected to draw upon and what both the outcomes and learning are expected to be. • Design jobs for mutual dependence.
Active empathy	• Allows assessment and understanding of what someone else really needs. • Accepts and respects emotional issues.	• Conversations need to take the form of dialogue rather than advocacy for a point of view.	• Train people in active listening techniques. • Value those who demonstrate empathy.
Access to help	• Professionals expected to grow through both increasing their own expertise and their accessibility to others.	• Requires both the inclination to help and ensuring the availability of that help. • Expects that everyone has a teaching role.	• Train people in how to teach others and develop their facilitation skills. • Include recognition for providing help in performance management systems.

		• Ensure stories of how giving and receiving help has contributed to success are widely talked about. • After action reviews encouraged and the findings widely shared. • 'Slack' built into plans to allow time for learning.
Lenience in judgement	• Acknowledges the value of experimentation	• Mistakes tolerated as the knowledge development process progresses.
Courage	• Accepts and offers feedback during experimentation and development.	• Honesty and openness in seeing the strengths and weaknesses of own and others' ideas. • Adoption of 360-degree feedback in the appraisal processes. • Risks in developing new ideas encouraged through the budgeting and promotion processes.

The collective unarticulated background has been called common knowledge (Spender, 2002). It relates to self-awareness and the ability to make sense of the world. Background common knowledge acts to integrate the knowledge we normally think of as organizational knowledge, the 'material inputs, performance objectives, transformation processes and resources, market segments, distribution channels and so forth ... the stuff that can be identified, either explicitly or as skilled performance'.

Background common knowledge changes with context, is emergent, self-regulating and self-sustaining. Although unarticulated, it determines the strength and style of the ties between our activities and those of others. It determines what is acceptable, establishes the meaning we give to the words and actions of others and as such relates to an emergent understanding of group identity.

Here we face circular thinking: common knowledge emerges from our relationships with others, yet the nature of the relationships depends on the common knowledge that exists between us. So what can we pay attention to if we want to influence this? We suggest that we can make a difference to both relationships and the level of common knowledge by paying attention to the density of connections within the organization through the level of mutual interdependence that is designed into work activities. We also need to adopt consistent explicit methods of co-ordination and help members of the organization develop their interpersonal skills so that they can communicate effectively and develop the level of shared common understanding.

Table 2.2 suggests some practical approaches that can make a difference to the interdependence of activities and the levels of common knowledge in the organization. Many of these are explored in more detail in other chapters of this book.

Again, we can look at an example to see how some of these approaches have been used to help align decisions in practice. General Motors recognized the inevitable difficulties in communication between different individuals, teams and functions and adopted the Dialogue Decision Process (DDP) to 'sort through the different perspectives, mental models, lexicons, and political biases that exist in the company' (Barabba and Pudar, 1998). DDP was a disciplined way of structuring dialogues between the group responsible for reaching a decision and those responsible for implementing the resulting action plan. One group was called the Decision Review Board: this represented the different functions and was formed from people with the authority to allocate resources. The other group was the Core Team representing the people who had a stake in the implementation of the decision. The dialogue between the two groups followed four sequential stages:

Framing the problem – recognizing that each person saw things differently, this step set out to ensure everyone was looking at the same issues. The output was a clear and comprehensive description of the problem, its scope, the underlying assumptions and the values-based decision criteria that would be applied.

Table 2.2   Increasing the level of interdependence in an organization

Influencing the interdependence of activities and the level of common knowledge	Practical approaches
Increase the density of connections between activities	• 'Yellow pages' systems that show who to talk to for help and advice. • Develop Communities of Practice and work to 'join up' the communities too. • Design physical and virtual workspaces to reduce functional silos.
Increase levels of mutual dependence between people	• Design work around cross-functional teams. • Encourage job rotations and cross-functional movement of staff. • Develop mentoring programmes across organizational boundaries. • Make intranets open access to all and ensure that the navigation is intuitively easy for people outside particular disciplines.
Design explicit methods of co-ordinating tasks to support alignment with the organizational purpose	• Focus on connections that matter: ensure that the connection points between the people who interface directly with the customer and those involved in product or market development are particularly effective. • Clarify expectations for those involved in activities that reach across organizational boundaries – work to build trust between work groups as well as within them. • Define standards and actively support the adoption of best practice methods. • Build in 'human' as well as 'machine' interactions between groups and individuals and allow time for these.
Develop interpersonal skills	• Provide formal training and coaching to help people develop their communication and interpersonal relationship skills. • Adopt 360-degree appraisal practices to provide constructive feedback on how effective individuals are in using those skills.
Communicate what matters most	• Talk about organizational values at every opportunity and integrate them into performance management and reward systems. Create the opportunity for everyone to build a common understanding about what they mean in terms of acceptable and unacceptable actions. • Talk about organizational objectives openly, continuously and consistently. Do not ignore dissent; deal with issues as they arise by engaging in meaningful dialogue across the organization about how to act to support the objectives. • Value openness; encourage those who talk constructively about what isn't working and what has gone wrong.
Develop the common language of the organization	• Engage in dialogue about strategy and how to meet objectives to integrate it into everyone's job. • Use story-telling to share real experiences of successes and failures. • Talk openly about what it means to be part of the company.

Developing alternatives – the purpose was to make clear the range of viable solutions to the problem. These could challenge common assumptions about what was acceptable or possible, but needed to respect the 'frame' that had been agreed. The starting point was the default decision that would have been pursued had the DDP not been followed. The final decision could then be assessed in terms of the incremental value added by the team effort. Groups with different perspectives could think through their ideas and the DDP provided the basis for communicating potentially conflicting solutions.

Conducting the analysis – a risk and return analysis of each alternative was undertaken based on a model of value constructed for the exercise. The models were constructed to show the uncertainties in the data and build a common understanding about which data and elements of the decision were critical for the solution.

Establishing connection - the final stage was a dialogue resulting in a new alternative that combined the best elements of each of the alternatives, the underlying rationale for the recommended solution and a commitment to allocate resources.

This approach was not viewed as a way of finding the single 'right' answer, but 'increasing the chances that decision-makers would identify a solution that was better than the existing alternative choices'.

The way we choose to design our organizations influences the extent of the interdependence between activities. The density and nature of these connections between activities determines how much environmental complexity the 'collective mind' can comprehend (Weick and Roberts, 1993). Comprehension improves when systems and structures to access and incorporate sources of organizational memory into activities are designed to:

1 *Connect across longer timescales*: bringing more know-how from the past to inform current practices that are then extrapolated further into the future.

2 *Connect more activities*: designing interdependent activities that connect earlier and later stages of task sequences.

3 *Connect more levels of experience*: mix newcomers (with new perspectives) with experienced people (who have ingrained views of the world).

 Signpost In *Competence Area 1: Competing* we saw that there are five main repositories of organizational memory: individual memory; relationships; databases; work processes and support systems; products and services.

Networks and other new forms of organizational structure are increasingly appropriate for an organization operating in a complex environment because they encourage more connections between activities than traditional hierarchical or rigid structures. However, although more connections potentially increases the capacity to make sense of the environment, the social processes between those who are involved in the activities make the difference in realizing that capacity. Everyone has to be attentive to the task in hand and the needs of their colleagues.

These ideas associated with attentiveness and care for others are closely linked to the components of the 'collective mind'. Earlier in this chapter we argued that the intrinsic values underpinning the development of a shared sense of identity between the members of an organization affect the coherence of decision-making. Values act as boundaries on the choices available to us when we make decisions; they lead us to comply with shared norms of behaviour and they determine the mutual expectations we have of each other. They are prescriptive but not narrowly so, which empowers people to take decisions in isolation from one another, but still feel confident of their grounding. The breadth of the boundaries created by values influences the level of comprehension of the corporate 'collective mind' and therefore the degree of complexity that we will be able to deal with together.

The one-paragraph Employee Handbook of Nordstrom has been highlighted as an example of creating freedom within boundaries (Kinsey Goman, 2003):

> Welcome to Nordstrom. We're glad to have you with our company. Our number one goal is to provide outstanding customer service. Set both your personal and professional goals high. We have great confidence in your ability to achieve them. Nordstrom rules: Rule No. 1 – Use your good judgment in all situations. There will be no additional rules. Please feel free to ask your department manager, store manager or division general manager any question at any time.

Kinsey Goman points out that despite inviting everyone to rely solely on good judgement when making decisions, Nordstrom's workforce does not disintegrate into thousands of employees 'doing their own random thing'. Nordstrom's secret lies in stressing its primary corporate value – outstanding customer service – and then liberating employees in service of that value.

Buckman Laboratories, winner of the Most Admired Knowledge Enterprise Award in 2000, is another organization that has thought deeply about how values act as intrinsic boundaries by creating a sense of identity that helps shape the decisions of its employees. The company used an organization-wide consultation process to develop a Code of Ethics. Once in place, this helped people to trust each other and collaborate more effectively. Bob Buckman was the CEO who led this initiative. He has likened the organization to a ship and the Code of Ethics to the waterline – if you damage the ship below the line, you can sink it (Buckman, 2001). That is why breaching the Code was made a dismissable offence. The full Code of Ethics is reproduced below:

Buckman Laboratories: Our Code of Ethics

Because we are separated – by many miles, by diversity of cultures and languages – we at Buckman need a clear understanding of the basic principles by which we will operate our company. These are:

- That the company is make up of individuals – each of whom has different capabilities and potentials – all of which are necessary to the success of the company.
- That we acknowledge that individuality by treating each other with dignity and respect – striving to maintain continuous and positive communications among all of us.
- That we will recognise and reward the contributions and accomplishments of each individual.
- That we will continually plan for the future so that we can control our destiny instead of letting events overtake us.
- That we maintain our policy of providing work for all individuals, no matter what the prevailing business conditions may be.
- That we make all our decisions in the light of what is right for the good of the whole company rather than what is expedient in a given situation.
- That our customers are the only reason for the existence of our company. To serve them properly, we must supply products and services which provide economic benefit over and above their cost.
- That to provide high quality products and services, we must make 'Creativity for our Customers' a reality in everything we do.
- That we must use the highest ethics to guide our business dealings to ensure that we are always proud to be a part of Buckman Laboratories.
- That we will discharge the responsibilities of corporate and individual citizenship to earn and maintain the respect of the community.

As individuals and as a company we must endeavour to uphold these standards so that we may be respected as persons and as an organization.

(Used by permission – Buckman Laboratories)

The Buckman Laboratories Code of Ethics has been part of the operation of the company for several years and has had a demonstrable impact on the culture and knowledge-sharing practices. Recent detailed and extensive empirical research into 'the values, beliefs and assumptions that influence the behaviours and the willingness to share knowledge' (called the collaborative climate by the researchers) found that Buckman employees rated their climate higher than that of any other organization studied (Sveiby and Simons, 2002).

Agreeing a workable code of ethics takes time and mutual discussion. Many of the ideas in this section are equally applicable to relationships that span the boundaries of an organization, although realizing them is a greater challenge. How can we build relationships based on shared understanding and common values to a sufficient degree for knowledge to flow and for there to be consistency in the actions when the various parties are not internal to the organization? More importantly, how do we determine the best mix of tight and loose associations that warrants the investment of our efforts in developing and maintaining these relationships?

See *Competence Area 5: Relating* for a discussion of building the right forms of social capital with network partners to support effective collaboration.

For now, we need to move on to think about the consequences of increasing diversity on our ability to sustain alignment in decision-making.

People, power and politics are sources of tension between diversity and alignment

So far, we have looked at the contribution of knowledge diversity to good decision-making and at the importance of aligning decisions across organizational levels. We have seen that the more complex the external environment, the more the members of an organization need diverse information sources and perspectives to comprehend their surroundings *and* ways to hold themselves together as a coherent entity.

Here we look at the realities involved in optimizing both of these two desirable elements of decision-making at the same time. We might imagine that the more diverse the backgrounds of the people involved, the harder it is for trust to develop and for there to be sufficient background common knowledge for communication to be easy. The opportunity for mixed messages increases, value systems may differ at a fundamental level and we find that as a result there can be a tendency for our organizations to shift towards an emphasis on individualism, which, as we have seen, reduces our collective capacity to deal with complexity in the environment.

Introducing people from diverse backgrounds at either the team or organizational level can magnify the likelihood of including individuals with multiple and often competing demands upon the levels of their commitment. They may be members of several groups, both within the organization (perhaps multiple project teams, quality initiatives, functional groupings, management teams etc) and in the external community (perhaps social and interest based activities). Relationship, family and caring responsibilities add another dimension. Personal needs may conflict with organizational needs; for example, heavy work commitments conflict with family responsibilities. Conflicts of allegiance cause 'resentment, illness, inefficiency and poor decisions' (McKenzie, 1996). A subliminal resistance can then obstruct the alignment of these individuals with the organizational objectives.

However, we do need to be willing to bring into the organization people who do not think like ourselves; in the past we might have called them mavericks, troublemakers, non-conformists, etc. We can no longer afford to 'clone' our workforce by rigorously recruiting against a tight competency framework. We need to choose people who will think differently, but still encourage them to channel their energy so as to achieve some form of coherent outcome for the organization.

Signpost

In *Competence Area 1: Competing* we saw how recruitment and selection decisions can be used to increase diversity and improve knowledge creation in our organizations.

Power imbalances inevitably emerge within any human system and deliberately increasing the level of diversity within the system can magnify this effect. New organizational forms and changes in social norms have shifted the emphasis from power that is based on position and role, yet 'people aren't skilled in the "unofficial" processes of power and influence needed to supplement formal authority' (Pfeffer, 1992). Organizations end up with a situation in which it becomes difficult to take any meaningful action. Decisions relating to innovation in processes may be particularly problematic because they almost invariably threaten the status quo: innovation is 'an inherently political activity'.

In our organizations, we may find that there is a large gap between knowing that something is important and actually doing it. For example, if we look at the transfer of best practices, rather than being a rational process in which people recognize the benefits and are keen to adopt better ways of working, self-generated barriers to adoption often occur, created consciously or unconsciously by the people involved. Gaining commitment to action (the basis of effective decision-making) is rarely as straightforward as we hope or expect. It has been pointed out that in many organizations there is a 'knowing–doing' gap and transforming knowledge into organizational action is at least as important as other aspects of knowledge creation and management (Pfeffer, 1999).

See Box 2.3 for a possible explanation of why this happens as a result of the 'shadow system' that exists in all human social situations.

In the next section, we identify a unifying element that can support the stretch between drawing on diverse knowledge resources as the input to decision-making and generating cohesion and alignment in the patterns of action that are actually undertaken across our organizations. We suggest that since individuals acting in specific local contexts increasingly make important decisions, we need to develop their capacity to resolve this tension closest to the point of action. We describe this capacity in terms of leadership behaviours. These behaviours are manifest in several ways. Through accepting accountability for their own performance, individuals are attentive to their own work and the needs of others. Through identifying with the values of the organization, they are able to draw on their understanding of what matters to the business to make appropriate decisions. Through recognizing the need to draw upon diverse perspectives to understand a changing world, they actively seek to learn and to keep their knowledge base relevant.

Resolve the tension through leadership

Our focus in this section is on 'leadership' as a set of behaviours, not on 'leaders' as a set of individuals. We are not suggesting that there is no role for the Board of the company, just that the emphasis needs to shift away from leadership by a

---

Box 2.3

The organizational shadow system

We can perhaps explain the political impact of increasing the level of diversity within the organization if we recognize that in any situation, we tend to develop spontaneous and informal links with others beyond the 'legitimate' system, that is, outside the range of people we would be expected to relate to for the tasks we are engaged in. These 'unauthorized' connections constitute a network that is a kind of shadow of the legitimate system. Through these informal, social and political links we develop localized rules for interacting with each other (CMC, 1996). Increase employee diversity and we increase the complexity of the shadow system.

Self-organizing processes occur to make this shadow system naturally coherent and this complex web of social, political and psychological interactions exists in tension with the legitimate system (Stacey, 1996). The shadow system responses are very non-linear, making it very difficult to identify what levers will produce organizational change because links between cause and effect are lost. We tend to design change initiatives within the legitimate system and take no account of the shadow system. However, the shadow system similarly pulls against the alignment of organizational decision-making.

Once we accept that we have limited ability to influence the tension between the legitimate system and the shadow system, then we realize that we have few direct 'tools' to help us optimize the balance between drawing upon diverse perspectives *and* achieving coherence in action. We can only 'fan' what is happening, not control it.

---

few with followership by the many, towards leadership behaviours being expressed by all. Everything that we have been looking at in this chapter relates to moving to the point where the knowledge of everyone involved with our organizations is made available voluntarily, collectively integrated and drawn upon in the decisions that deal both with today's issues and shape the ongoing renewal of the identity of the organization. The new model becomes one of 'integrating thinking and acting at all levels' (Capra, 1997).

In a complex environment, we saw earlier that there needs to be 'requisite diversity' within the organization to be able to read all of the signals and make sense of the pattern of activities. Hence, if a single leader really directs, he or she limits the capacity of the organization to comprehend its environment. Managers need to create conditions in which there can be relevant behaviours, without somehow identifying the outcome in advance (McKelvey, 1999).

Is this approach to leadership practical? There is certainly evidence of a trend in this direction and recognition that the world we are now operating in needs a radical shift in the way we design and function within our organizations.

However, many companies are still in the early stages of finding out how to be successful in this environment. In looking at twenty companies trying to transform themselves to meet the challenges of the new economy, most were struggling to achieve the 'speed, flexibility and continuous self-renewal' required (Bartlett and Ghoshal, 2002). But it was clear that the role of those at the top was shifting from deciding the content of specific strategies to framing an organizational context that 'creates a sense of purpose and integrates and injects meaning' such that more decision-making could be 'bottom-up'. In addition to competing for product markets or technical expertise, competitive strategy now includes 'competing for the hearts, minds and dreams of exceptional people'.

In many countries, there are also social changes affecting what people expect from work, which are driving changes in the way companies need to function. 'Today's employees are more questioning and demanding. They are confident enough to air their concerns, grievances and aspirations. If they were customers, we would call them sophisticated.' (Ridderstrale and Nordstrom, 2000: 204).

The sources of these new employee attitudes and behaviours are many and varied, reflecting the changes in societal expectations over the past three decades. One of the growing trends in Western Europe has been the growth in self-employment and new forms of contract (such as part-time, short-term, annual hours). Charles Handy, author of numerous books on management and the changing nature of work, reflected on the relationship between large organizations (which he termed old or new elephants) and independent operators working for themselves or in a partnership (termed fleas). He explains that the metaphor of elephants and fleas emerged from trying 'to explain why large organizations needed irritant individuals or groups to introduce the innovations and ideas essential to their survival' (Handy, 2001: 6). Perhaps we should think about requisite variety as having a sufficient number of fleas!

Handy recognized that the requirement for organizations to be flexible means that they can no longer guarantee careers, lifelong employment, secure pensions or many of the other traditional benefits of the employer–employee relationship. As a consequence, 'Loyalty these days is first to oneself and one's future, secondly to one's team or project and only lastly to the organization'. Yet, . . . 'businesses are now worried that life outside the organization is becoming so attractive to free and independent spirits that there is a real danger of losing their best and most innovative people. They didn't intend flexibility to go that far'.

In a related vein, a new moral contract between companies and employees has been suggested (Ghoshal and Bartlett, 2000). Life-long employment was a feature of a more stable competitive environment. Yet, 'the alternative of a free-market hire-and-fire regime is not a viable replacement' as it does not deliver the trust and teamwork needed for innovation and collaborative knowledge-sharing. Instead, we need each employee to take responsibility for their own performance and engage in continuous learning to support their performance as the environment changes. In exchange, as the company can no longer offer employment security, it offers enhanced employability by providing the environment and opportunities for skill and development, protecting job flexibility whether it is within the company or outside it.

As well as being the basis for attracting, motivating and retaining knowledge workers, learning is the basis for organizational growth and sustainability in a changing environment.

 Signpost   In *Competence Area 3: Learning* we will see how support for communities of practice enables optimization of both individual and organizational learning.

So, the traditional roles of managers and leaders need to change. The term 'middle leaders' (Frohman, 2000) has been used to describe the roles of those who:

- Help their people understand what they each value as individuals.
- Enable people to see the link between their goals and the organization's goals.
- Encourage people who are curious, take initiative and responsibility, and possess a healthy irreverence for the status quo.

This transition is well described in a Conference Board Report (Hackett, 2000): 'Leadership is changing from personal and interpersonal to relational, from dominance to meaning making. And leadership development is changing from preparing the leader to exercise power to increasing the capacity of the community to work smarter through collaboration'. The report quotes the example of W. L Gore, the innovative materials and technology company, which uses four operating principles to underpin this kind of relational leadership:

1   The *freedom principle* that encourages individual growth in terms of knowledge, skill and scope of responsibilities.

2   The *waterline principle* that allows for mistakes in areas 'above the waterline' by discouraging blame and encouraging learning from them. Ethical standards and values define the waterline and freedom to 'shoot below the waterline' is not supported as this can 'sink the ship'.

3   The *commitment principle* says that those associated with the organization are expected to keep their commitments (the basis of trust and effective relationships).

4   The *fairness principle* that sets a standard of fair play and equitable treatment in relationships with others, including customers, suppliers and other partners.

The company believes that these principles support their view that leadership is expected of everyone.

Increasingly, there is a view that some organizational forms limit the ability of individuals to exhibit the behaviours we are looking at here. Hierarchy and traditional structure are seen to place restrictions on individuals, particularly their expression of leadership behaviours and creativity. In contrast, leadership is allowed to emerge if we move to a new model that sees organizations as a network of relationships in which individuals and organizations co-evolve (Owen, 2001).

Signpost In *Competence Area 5: Relating* we will see how to design and maintain a network of knowledge-based relationships.

The network or web organization that is based on these relationships has been described as having a circular rather than a pyramid structure. Through relationships across the network and in the communities of practice in which people participate, work has a purpose, meaning and direction and there is a sense of shared identity. Required behaviours are enabled rather than constricted, including 'leadership . . . and other changes in behaviour such as flexibility, creativity, cooperation, self-actualization and learning' (Owen, 2001). This form of organization can flex, regroup and re-shape to co-evolve with the environment. Everyone sees a pattern in the actions taken and the decisions made, rather than from structures imposed through an organization chart.

To transform organizations towards this form, the following steps are recommended (Owen, 2001):

Widespread dialogue within the organization that challenges assumptions and collectively explores values. This process must engage everyone who is to be part of the new form – this is not something that can be undertaken by a few and communicated through team briefings. New shared mental models are developed through building the background common language about how to operate together and in the world.

Establishing the *purpose* of the organization (making money isn't sufficient, it doesn't create meaning or purpose at the level of shared identity).

Using large-scale events to involve everyone and shift the focus to *relationships and interconnections*. Trust in the senior management/Board keeps them at the centre even when hierarchy has lost importance, so these individuals must demonstrate integrity.

Focusing on the *performance of teams* and allowing them to regulate themselves as far as possible.

Developing the *leadership potential of individuals* through providing role models, telling stories of the leadership behaviours of others, participation in action learning sets, encouraging self-reflection, coaching and mentoring.

An example of this kind of transformation process is provided in Hubert Saint-Onge's description of shaping tacit knowledge at the Canadian Imperial Bank of Commerce (Saint-Onge, 1996). Group sessions were used to systematically surface individually- or collectively-held assumptions about how to deal with the business, customers or employees, making explicit the beliefs that underlay these assumptions, then determining how these beliefs and values needed to change in order to accomplish objectives in the new business environment.

Our vision is to create a dynamic forum where everyone is a leader. We will achieve this vision through learning: individual learning at all levels of the organization, team learning that focuses on aligning mindsets and transferring knowledge and skills, organizational learning that seeks alignment and facilitates the evolution of our corporate culture toward the full realization of a performance-oriented environment, and customer learning that offers customers an avenue for input on changing needs and an opportunity to become an integral part of our total learning process.

Saint-Onge, 1996

In this chapter, we set out to address the question of how the knowledge resources within our organizations can be used to enable more effective decision-making. We can encompass all the facets of the answer to this question under the heading of 'organizational culture'. A shared sense of identity amongst those involved with the organization, the integration of diverse perspectives, alignment of diverse actions, understanding how to act, the dimensions of care, shared values as boundaries to action, the style and nature of relationships between people, and the development of leadership behaviours; these are all elements of a culture in which people understand what matters and make use of and contribute to the knowledge resources of the organization (be they explicit or tacit) because they see the point of doing so.

Human nature, power and politics are unarguably realities of organizational life. However, the more we try to constrain and control individual action, the less the emergent 'collective mind' of our organizations can comprehend the complex environment we have to operate within. More than anything, we have to pay attention to the *culture* of our organizations: a culture in which thinking and reflection are valued, in which differences are welcomed and dialogue is the tool used to stimulate engaged participation in producing the best possible outcomes by everyone.

Summary

We have looked at how knowledge can be used to support rapid distributed decision-making so that we can respond to demanding customers and global competition. We started with a number of questions:

How can better knowledge management lead to better decision-making?
How do we actually make decisions?
How can we make sure that we have access to different points of view to improve our decisions?
How can we make sure that the decisions everyone makes, no matter where they are in the organization, are sufficiently consistent?

To answer these, we looked at how knowledge contributes to decision-making in two ways:

1. Knowing what to do

Ideas such as mental models, dominant logic and strategic logic were discussed to show that for both individuals and organizations, our perspective

▶

of the world determines what we pay attention to, what we see as important and what alternatives we consider to be feasible. The shared perception of the identity of our organizations is an important influence on ways in which we jointly make sense of our actions.

2. Knowing how to do it

The rules for how to act are made explicit through procedures and guidelines, manuals and plans. Intuition is a method for making decisions in some complex situations and the capacity for intuitive decision-making needs to be developed more widely.

We then saw that effective decision-making involves access to both diverse knowledge resources and aligning the decisions that are made across our organizations. Paying attention to the diversity of information and knowledge that we use for decision-making involves:

- Accessing diverse external information sources and perspectives by using technology, networks, communities and partnership relationships to reach across the organization's boundaries.
- Increasing the diversity of knowledge available within the organization through training and policies that increase the diversity of the people we employ.

Paying attention to aligning decisions involves:

- Developing the conditions that encourage individuals to be attentive to their work and to the needs of colleagues: demonstrating care, meeting expectations, increasing mutual dependency and cultivating sufficient common background knowledge.
- Setting boundaries for decision-making based on intrinsic factors such as values and ethics.

We need to pay attention to both of these forces simultaneously. However, we recognize that it is difficult to optimize both at the same time because issues of power and politics can be exacerbated by the combination.

Informal social and political relationships can result in the emergence of a 'knowing–doing' gap (Pfeffer, 1999); the gap between knowing something is important and actually doing it. Organizational energy is dissipated through lack of coherence resulting from divergent interests. Direct interventions from individual senior managers to control this tension do not work, since a pre-defined intention will narrow the perspective of the 'collective mind' and its ability to comprehend complex environmental factors. The solution is to stimulate the self-organizing potential of the organization by developing the leadership potential of all members to allow them to resolve the tensions in the local context of the decisions that need to be made.

▶   A co-evolutionary contract between knowledge workers and organizations based on learning provides the basis for a new form of employment relationship that offers long-term value to both parties in a changing environment. Traditional management and leadership roles are evolving towards supporting individuals to make sense of their work and environment and enabling collaborative relationships to be effective, so that actions are appropriate and knowledge resources are enhanced. Rigid hierarchical structures constrain the evolution of leadership potential. New network and web forms are a more effective way of building the capacity to make decisions in complex environments. However, in these forms, it is even more important to pay attention to achieving coherence through a shared sense of identity that is derived from a common view of what matters.

Using knowledge to improve decision-making depends on the culture of an organization and this chapter has presented a view of the elements of culture, how it emerges and how it can be influenced.

References

Albert, S. and Whetton, D. (1985) 'Organizational identity', in *Research in Organizational Behavior* (eds L. L. Cummings and B. M. Staw). Greenwich, CT: JAI Press, 263–95.

Anthony, W., Bennett, R., Maddox, E. and Wheatley, W. (1993) 'Picturing the future: using mental imagery to enrich strategic environmental assessment', *Academy of Management Executive*, 7(2): 43–56.

Ashby, W. R. (1956) *An Introduction to Cybernetics*. London: Chapman and Hall.

Barabba, V. P. and Pudar, N. (1998) 'The dialogue decision process at General Motors', *Knowledge Management Review*, 1(1): 14–19.

Bartlett, C. and Ghoshal, S. (2002) 'Building competitive advantage through people: human not financial capital must be the starting point and ongoing foundation of a successful strategy', *MIT Sloan Management Review* 43(2): 34–41.

Behling, O. and Eckel, N. (1991) 'Making sense out of intuition', *Academy of Management Executive* 5(1): 46–54.

Bettis, R. and Prahalad, C. (1995) 'The dominant logic: retrospective and extension', *Strategic Management Journal*, 16: 5–14.

Brockmann, E. and Anthony, W. (1998) 'The influence of tacit knowledge and collective mind on strategic planning', *Journal of Managerial Issues*, 10(2): 204–22.

Buckman, R. H. (2001) 'Building a strategy around knowledge', 1st Annual Conference, Henley KM Forum, Henley Management College, UK.

Capra, F. (1997) *The Web of Life*, New York: HarperCollins.

Chase, C. (2002) 'Turning knowledge into action at Heineken USA', *KM Review* 5(2): 22–5.

Choi, Y. B. (1993) *Paradigms and Conventions: Uncertainty, Decision Making and Entrepreneurship*. Ann Arbor, MI: University of Michigan Press.

Choo, C. (1996) 'The knowing organization: how organizations use information to construct meaning, create knowledge and make decisions', *International Journal of Information Management* 16(5): 329–40.

CMC (1996) 'A brief survey of complexity science and how it is being used in relation to organisations and their management', *Complexity and Management Papers, Number 8*, Complexity and Management Centre, University of Hertfordshire, Hertford.

Coles, W. (2000) 'Learning from our mistakes: The General Motors story', *KM Review* 1(12): 14–19.

Cross, R., Parker, A., Prusak, L. and Borgatti, S. P. (2001) 'Supporting knowledge creation and sharing in social networks', *Organizational Dynamics*, 30(2): 100–20.

Cross, R. and Prusak, L. (2002) 'The people who make organizations go – or stop', *Harvard Business Review* 80(6): 104–12.

Frohman, A. (2000) 'Middle leadership', *Executive Excellence* 17(12): 6.

Ghoshal, S. and Bartlett, C. (2000) *The Individualized Corporation*. London: Random House Business Books.

Graham, G. L. (2002) 'If you want honesty, break some rules', *Harvard Business Review* 80(4): 42–7.

Hackett, B. (2000) 'Beyond knowledge management: new ways to work and learn', *Report 1262–00–RR*, The Conference Board, New York.

Handy, C. (2001) *The Elephant and the Flea*. London: Hutchinson.

Hayashi, A. M. (2001) 'When to trust your gut', *Harvard Business Review* 79(2): 59–65.

HP (2002) www.hp.com (accessed 13 August 2002).

Kinsey Goman, C. (2003) Business as usual http://www.linkageinc.com/newsletter/archives/od/carol_goman_change_1002.shtml (accessed 23 January 2003).

Lissack, M. (1997) 'Of chaos and complexity: managerial insights from a new science', *Management Decision* 35(3–4): 205–18.

Lissack, M. and Roos, J. (2001) 'Be coherent, not visionary', *Long Range Planning*, 34: 53–70.

Lotus Consulting (1998) 'Relationship management at Chase Manhattan', *Knowledge Management Review*, 1(2): 16–21.

McKelvey, B. (1999) 'Panel discussion. The gurus speak: complexity and organizations', *Emergence* 1(1): 73–91.

McKenzie, J. (1996) *Paradox: The Next Strategic Dimension*. Maidenhead: McGraw Hill.

McKenzie, J. and van Winkelen, C. (2001) 'Exploring e-collaboration space', 1st Annual Conference, Henley KM Forum, Henley Management College, UK.

Merali, Y. (2001) 'Building and developing capabilities: a cognitive congruence framework', in *Knowledge Management and Organizational Competence* (ed. Ron Sanchez). New York: Oxford University Press.

Oliver, D. and Roos, J. (2000) *Striking a Balance: Complexity and Knowledge Landscapes*. Maidenhead: McGraw-Hill.

Owen, H. (2001) *Unleashing Leaders*. Chichester: John Wiley.

Parker, A., Cross, R. and Walsh, D. (2001) 'Improving collaboration with social network analysis', *Knowledge Management Review* 4(2): 24–8.

Pfeffer, J. (1992) *Managing with Power: Politics and Influence in Organizations*. Boston, MA: Harvard Business School Press.

Pfeffer, J. (1999) 'Knowing "what" to do is not enough: turning knowledge into action', *California Management Review*, 42(1): 83–108.

Prahalad, C. and Bettis, R. (1986) 'The dominant logic: a new link between diversity and performance', *Strategic Management Journal* 7: 486–501.

Ridderstrale, J. and Nordstrom, K. (2000) *Funky Business*. Harlow: Pearson Education Ltd.

Rush, D. (2002) 'Measuring connectivity at Aventis Pharmaceuticals', *KM Review* 5(2): 10–13.

Saint-Onge, H. (1996) 'Tacit knowledge: the key to the strategic alignment of intellectual capital', *Strategy and Leadership* 24(2): 10–14.

Sanchez, R. and Thomas, H. (1996). *Dynamics of Competence-based Competition*. Oxford: Elsevier Pergamon.

Simon, H. (1957) *Models of Man: Social and Rational*. New York: John Wiley.

Simon, H. (1976) *A Study of Decision Making Processes in Administrative Organization*, 3rd edn. New York: Free Press.

Simon, H. (1987) 'Making management decisions: the role of intuition and emotion', *The Academy of Management Executive* 1(1): 57–64.

Skyrme, D. (1998) Creativity is not innovation, I3 Update No. 17. http://www.skyrme.com/updates/u17.htm#virtual (accessed 6 December 2002).

Spender, J. (2002) 'Knowledge management, uncertainty, and an emergent theory of the firm', in *The Strategic Management of Intellectual Capital and Organizational Knowledge* (eds C. W. Choo and N. Bontis). New York: Oxford University Press, pp. 149–62.

Stacey, R. (1996) *Complexity and Creativity in Organizations*. Berrett-Koehler: San Francisco, CA.

Stacey, R. (1999) *Strategic Management and Organizational Dynamics: The Challenge of Complexity*, 3rd edn. New York: Financial Times Prentice Hall.

Stacey, R. (2001) *Complex Responsive Processes in Organizations*. London: Routledge.

Starbuck, W. (1976) 'Organizations and their environments', in *Handbook of Industrial and Organizational Psychology* (ed. M. D. Dunnette). Chicago: Rand McNally, pp. 1069–1123.

Sveiby, K.-E. (2002) 'Creating knowledge focused strategies – good and bad practices', 2nd Annual Conference, Henley KM Forum, Henley Management College, UK.

Sveiby, K.-E. and Simons, R. (2002) 'Collaborative climate and effectiveness of knowledge work – an empirical study', www.sveiby.com (accessed 30 July 2002).

Tsoukas, H. (1996) 'The firm as a distributed knowledge system: a constructivist approach', *Strategic Management Journal* 17(Winter Special Edition): 11–25.

von Krogh, G., Ichijo, K. and Nonaka, I. (2000) *Enabling Knowledge Creation: How to Unlock the Mystery of Tacit Knowledge and Release the Power of Innovation*. Oxford: Oxford University Press.

von Krogh, G. and Roos, J. (1996) 'A tale of the unfinished', *Strategic Management Journal* 17: 729–37.

Weick, K. E. (1999) 'Sensemaking as an organizational dimension of global change', in *The Human Dimensions of Global Change* (eds J. Dutton and D. Cooperrider). Thousand Oaks, CA: Sage Publications.

Weick, K. E. and Roberts, K. (1993) 'Collective mind in organizations: heedful interrelating on flight decks', *Administrative Science Quarterly* 38(3): 357–81.

3 Third Competence Area
Learning

Introduction

Learning is our third area of knowledge competence. Even though learning is integral to the activities in all the competence areas in this book, from the way we compete and decide, to our openness to the environment, our relationships with customers and other organizations and the indicators we use to monitor our actions, we have made it a separate area of competence simply because of the difference it makes to business performance.

Some organizations (and individuals) learn more successfully than others. We believe an increased sensitivity to the key features of the learning process can help develop this competence area. In this chapter, we will explore some conceptual aspects of learning and suggest a range of practical approaches to enhance individual and organizational learning. As with the rest of the book, we avoid going straight to the 'how to' lists because there isn't a single recipe that anyone can, or should, pick up and use. We have to understand *why* each approach can make a difference to develop a sound rationale for *when, where* and *how* to use it effectively.

Although we will draw upon ideas from organizational learning, the learning organization and the learning processes of individuals, the underlying principles are grounded in complexity theory which provides a way of looking at how systems of living, thinking individuals interrelate and why interactions between people and groups of people give rise to unexpected, creative and sometimes surprising behaviour.

Some people regard the idea of an organization learning with scepticism, pointing out that when people leave the building at night, there is nothing left of an organization to do the learning. Yet if this were the case, why would one organization be any different to another operating under largely the same conditions? We all experience real differences between similar firms, both as customers dealing with them and as employees working in them. On the whole, organizations in the same market space have the same access to people with largely the same mix of education and experience. We suggest that one thing that leads to persistent differences between them is the subtle variation in the way each enables people to learn, interact, communicate their thinking and collectively make sense of the signals from the outside world.

If we want to influence these subtle variations, we have to know more about what the process of learning involves at three levels: individuals, groups and organizations. Specifically, we have to recognize that knowledge (the input and outcome of learning) is 'sticky' and can be blocked from flowing within each level and between the different levels. In an organizational setting, communities of practice provide a mechanism for reducing stickiness. By appreciating why, we start to identify practical suggestions for how to make a difference in our organizations.

Developing our common language to learn about learning: knowledge landscapes

In this chapter, we adopt the metaphor of 'knowledge landscapes' developed by David Oliver and Johan Roos (Oliver and Roos, 2000). As they point out, metaphors allow us to convey a vast array of information easily and succinctly, a concept central to our discussion later in this chapter. This metaphor is helpful, as we all tend to find it easy to relate the idea of learning to climbing a hill. A knowledge landscape is made up of small mounds, hillocks and varying sized peaks, the heights of each representing the extent of our knowledge about something, the range representing the breadth. As we start to imagine what our own knowledge landscape might look like and how that affects the landscapes of the groups and organizations we belong to, it raises questions that are related to learning. Can we see a distant horizon because the landscape is an undulating range of small and middle-sized hills (giving a broad general understanding of lots of topics)? Or is the horizon obstructed by the towering peaks of our refined expertise, which make it hard for others to follow? Knowledge landscapes are spaces of possibilities, shaped by ignorance (the valleys), expertise (the peaks) and capability (the hills and undulations). By thinking about how the landscapes develop and what we might be able to do to influence their development, we can start to appreciate what shape the landscape needs to be to suit our environment and objectives.

What is learning?

The paths that we take across our knowledge landscapes are 'knowledge trails'. Our senses (or the intelligence gathering functions of our organizations) are continually feeding us data as we progress along a knowledge trail. We categorize this input and use the information generated to make increasingly fine distinctions about the topic we are exploring. Each distinction is a fork in the path, which may take us a step higher up a knowledge peak. When we take one fork, we exclude the other. Making finer and finer distinctions is what constitutes specialization. Commercially, some forks can lead to blind alleys, even though they still take us further up the specialization peak. Knowing which fork is a worthwhile distinction and which is a blind alley is valuable learning in itself.

Knowledge development or learning happens when we take a journey across the knowledge landscape. We will think about the nature of that journey for ourselves as individuals first of all. The way we explain the steps of the journey depends on what we think knowledge is. So, before we proceed any further, it is important to clarify what we believe about the nature of knowledge (see Ventzin, von Krogh and Roos, 1998; von Krogh, Roos and Slocum, 1994 for a more detailed discussion of these ideas).

A process of uncovering a reality that is out there waiting to be found?

Let us start by thinking about learning as an attempt to making increasingly accurate representations of the world around us. If we view the environment as pre-ordained and available to everyone to understand in the same way, then we will tend to focus our learning efforts on collecting and assimilating information in order to understand it better. We will compare new information with our previously acquired mental models and frames of reference and try to adjust our internal picture of the world closer to an actual reality. Any perceptions that cannot be categorized easily are handled by re-configuring a mental model until we reach a comfortable state of equilibrium again, based on a mix of views that explain the world we find ourselves in. Alternatively, we reject the perceptions as invalid. The more data that we gather, the closer we should get to an accurate representation of reality (Schramm, 2002). In this scenario, more exposure to information sources and a guide to help us find the information are all that we need to learn. Our brains are like sponges waiting to be filled with information.

Thinking about learning in this way, as a process of increasing our level of understanding about the world around us, means that cognitive psychology adequately explains the steps we take to learn from our experiences of being in the world. It describes how we examine the information we have collected through our senses and if it is interesting enough we transfer it to our short-term memory. We then interrogate our long-term memory to see if there is any meaningful related knowledge. If so, the new stimulus is integrated into this and we learn, that is, new knowledge is created (Matlin, 1994; Moon, 2002).

At the level of organizations, this view of knowledge corresponds to what has been called the technical view of organizational learning (Easterby-Smith and Araujo, 1999; Huber, 1991). Identifying, collecting and redistributing information are the basis for developing new knowledge. Therefore, gathering and sharing data and information will be the main focus of developmental activities and knowledge transfer between individuals and groups across our organizations (learning processes) will depend on the effectiveness of information management systems such as databases and manuals.

The next step in this orientation to learning is to focus on connecting people to further refine knowledge. Our organizations act as networks of connections and the strength and persistence of local relationships is the basis for capturing knowledge. Again, there is an assumption of an objective reality, but now different experts collect information about parts of the representation of the world the organization exists within and the local nature of the network determines how this is jointly combined into knowledge of 'reality out there'.

This way of looking at learning and knowledge has already taken us a long way down a rational path towards improving knowledge development in our organizations. We can build better databases, deploy more people to collect information to fill them up and design 'yellow pages' systems to show who knows what.

However, we need to ask if this is satisfactory and sufficient to explain what each of us experiences in our working lives. If I have the same information at my disposal, how likely is it that I will make sense of it and act upon it in the same way as my colleague at the next desk (particularly in a non-routine situation where I am not simply following a procedure)? Does this information processing view of knowledge development take account of my intuitive, individualistic view of the world? Does it account for the differences between organizations that can all buy the same large, fast databases and employ people with similar experience and education? Why is it so hard to change the behaviour of individuals or the culture of organizations even when the logical reasons to do so seem obvious and overwhelming?

A process of constructing reality by creating meaning in each context?

What if reality is not out there waiting to be found? What if the mental act of perceiving knowledge (which is the Everyman dictionary definition of cognition) is a creative act rather than a descriptive one? Then learning becomes a process of extracting *meaning* from our experiences, activities, ideas and feelings. The way we make sense of information becomes highly context-dependent and the knowledge we develop is subjective and depends on many more factors than the quality of the information that we are presented with or the people who are trying to guide us through it.

What do we mean by 'knowledge' in this view? Knowledge is no longer an abstract entity to be searched for, but interpretation cultivated through the

Box 3.1

How living systems maintain their place in the world

As thinking, reflecting, imaginative and totally unique individuals, how can we be described in systems terms? Certainly we are different from the simplistic feedback systems that control, for example, the central heating or air-conditioning in our homes. Our mental capacity is more flexible, more dynamic and more infinitely variable than a simple programme. Similarly, when we work with others, there is the potential for something creative and insightful to emerge from the combination of each person's unique knowledge and perspectives. We need a way to characterize this social system. How about when groups of groups come together and try to make sense of each other's ideas, align their intentions and communicate their ideas (for example in organizations or networks of organizations)? What gives that system the capability to make sense of its world?

Individuals, groups and networks can all be described as living systems and the biologists Maturana and Varela recognized that the fundamental feature of living systems is that they are 'characterised by their continual self-production' (Maturana and Varela, 1980; 1992). The term used to describe this process is autopoiesis (from the Greek, *auto* – self, *poiein* – to make, produce, conceptualize) and it is a concept that has had an impact in many fields, including the theory of knowledge of social systems and organizations (Luhmann, 1986; von Krogh, Roos and Slocum, 1994; von Krogh and Vicari, 1993). An autopoietic system:

● Has a boundary that is self-created and defines its identity, so it can set itself apart from the world in its own way.

▶

process of living and uniquely construed at each level of the social system – be that in our own heads, or in the small and large groups to which we belong. See Box 3.1 for a discussion of why this is consistent with how living systems in general view their world.

As individuals, our knowledge landscape is not an open playing field that we can explore at will. It is a landscape that is coloured and shaped by our journey across it so far, and where we are standing now determines what we see and what we choose to be relevant. Knowledge may allow us to make distinctions about our observations en route, but it also determines what trail we explore next and what we notice (von Krogh, Roos and Slocum, 1994).

Signpost We saw in *Competence Area 2: Deciding* how the mental models of individuals and the dominant logic of organizations determine which options are considered feasible and acceptable in decision-making.

▶ • Has an internal model of itself and its world, so there are natural limits to its capacity to perceive the world.

As Arthur Battram writes,

> In a very real sense, all living systems, from IBM to E. Coli 'imagine' themselves and their world. This concept challenges the very core of our sense of reality: we experience the world as something solid 'out there', yet Maturana and Varela tell us that we never really experience a world 'out there'. What we experience is our model of the world 'in here', based on its interpretation of data from 'out there'. They also point out that we cannot know what we don't know.
>
> *Battram, 1996: 231*

So although we are 'open' to data from outside our system, our internal structure is complex and forms the basis for determining our response to that data. We are conservative and respond to maintain our sense of self, so data will be ignored if our internal model is not interested in the input. Applying this to the knowledge landscape metaphor, this means that the space of possibilities is not infinite because on our journey across the landscape we tend to sense the parts of the world that add increasingly fine distinctions about something that matters to us in preference to signals that are alien to our thinking. So learning is more likely to be self-referential and everyone's learning is different (we are autonomous).

These ideas are developed further in Box 3.2, where we look at the interdependencies between living systems.

There are some far-reaching consequences if we adopt this perspective on knowledge. Once we categorize individuals, groups and organizations as systems of meaning-making and knowledge as a 'chameleon-like' property of that system, rather than a discrete but abstract object, we need to ask ourselves two questions:

1 Is it possible to associate individual and organizational learning?
2 What can we do to influence the knowledge development process at the level of individuals, groups or organizations?

To answer these questions, we need to start by deciding whether individuals (as systems) create meaning in the same way as social groups. Individuals primarily create meaning through the use of language; 'languaging' is the general term to describe the emergence of meaning as a result of linguistic distinctions (von Krogh, Roos and Slocum, 1994). Distinctions are, as we saw earlier, forks in the trail up a peak on a knowledge landscape. Languaging is the common process for constantly refining meaning in both individuals and social groups. In individuals it is the medium of consciousness; in groups it is the medium of communication. The result in both is the continuous refinement of self-knowledge, but 'in interacting with other individuals, in the social system, a different meaning may arise around the same object or concept, and the new meaning which holds true for the group may not exactly hold true for the individual' (Magalhaes, 1998: 107).

The commonality of this underlying process and the difference it produces at different scales (that is the individual group and organization) is vital evidence of the criticality of socialization in diffusing individual knowledge across an organization (so addressing our first question, which was how to connect individual and organizational knowledge). We can also deduce that the way individuals generate new knowledge (learn) by making new distinctions is similar to the way groups and organizations generate new knowledge. It is just a matter of scale. This similarity means that whatever processes we use at one level are likely to produce similar learning effects at other levels, so consistent attention to the tools of languaging and meaning-making may be the catalyst for self reenforcing knowledge diffusion (von Krogh and Roos, 1995).

With this perspective on knowledge, we can also start to appreciate why – even with equal access to the same information – individuals and organizations never respond in the same way. Languaging and meaning-making drives differences in observable behaviour between people and between organizations in the same kind of environment. With three levels of activity in the space of possibilities (individuals, groups and organizations), all linked by the forces of emergence, the final shape of the knowledge landscape for one organization cannot help but be very different from another. Knowledge landscapes at each level are always more than the sum of the landscapes at the lower levels (Oliver and Roos, 2000). We look at why this is in more detail in Box 3.2.

The height of a peak on our knowledge landscape is directly dependent on the extent of our tacit knowledge. Rather like an iceberg, 90 per cent of tacit knowledge lies hidden below the surface of our consciousness. It is that densely-packed part of our own understanding, or that of the groups we belong to, that accumulates over time as a result of experience, but stays for the most part hidden and is only ever partially exposed (McKenzie and Potter, 2002). The deeper the tacit knowledge, the harder it is to put into words and the more languaging is likely to distort any attempt to exchange tacit understanding.

Collective tacit knowledge is an emergent property of social groups that often arises without a conscious languaging process being involved. Cultural assumptions of what is right and wrong can influence the way groups, organizations and even nations respond in the same way to certain situations, but they often remain unspoken. Common sense, myths and traditions of unknown origin coalesce into 'the way things are done around here' without anyone actually spelling them out (Baumard, 1999). Basically this means that the store of

Box 3.2

How complex adaptive systems interact with their world
This is really the opposite face of the autopoiesis discussion in Box 3.1. Living systems are both self-regenerating and constantly adaptive. As Battram points out:

> The difference is about focus. When the focus is on the system as a single entity, we need to be aware of autopoiesis; when we focus on a system as a complex adaptive system, we need to be aware of the interactions of the individual elements of the system which give rise to emergent behaviour.
>
> *Battram, 1996: 37*

So, for example in decision-making, we need to pay attention to autopoietic forces for alignment of behaviour across the organization, whereas for knowledge development and learning we need to pay attention to the forces that enable adaptive behaviour.

Figure 3.1   Facets of complex systems

In autopoietic systems the component elements are dynamically active, but they abide by an internal model that holds them together

Complex adaptive systems reach out towards new sources of enlightenment and nourishment by branching and refining distinctions at the periphery

▶

We established in Box 3.1 that autopoiesis means the urge to stay consistent and includes a definition of boundary and separateness from the environment. In contrast, complex adaptive systems are driven to change by innate mechanisms that naturally engender learning. They have an urge to explore outwards (see Figure 3.1).

'Complex' refers to 'a state where the details cannot be understood but the whole (or general result) can be understood by the ability to make patterns' (Battram, 1996: 20).

An 'adaptive system' is one that appears to be 'adaptively intelligent' – constantly seeing and imagining patterns, testing ideas, acting upon them, discarding them again – always evolving and learning (Battram, 1996: 33).

Complex adaptive systems always exhibit emergent properties: properties that could not be predicted by looking at the elements the system is made up of. For example, if we dissect a human 'system' into its component organs, we cannot isolate the property of 'life'.

Individuals, groups, organizations and networks of organizations are like a nested set of complex systems and they are all interactive. They adapt and evolve by self-organizing and learning triggered by the various points of contact with their environments as illustrated in Figure 3.2.

This interdependence between them means that the evolution of one cannot be separated from the evolution of the other; in other words, they are co-evolving and in the process of co-evolution new knowledge emerges at the highest level out of the linkages between them (Oliver and Roos, 2000). ▶

collective tacit knowledge is diffused amongst individuals and only becomes apparent when that group works together towards a common end.

So we are now in a position to answer the second question we set ourselves: how can we influence the knowledge development process (learning) at the level of individuals, groups or organizations? We have seen that we need to encourage the creation of common forms of meaning by individuals. We also need to encourage socialization based on different forms of languaging processes that consistently build the connections between each individual's interpretations, group level distinctions and organizational knowledge. Finally, we need to encourage the emergence of strong collective tacit knowledge as a basis for interpretation through shared meaning at an intuitive level.

Viewing reality as something we co-create and categorizing individuals, groups and organizations as systems of meaning-making is very different to the way many of us have been looking at the world. It offers an entirely different perspective (or lens) on why we struggle to communicate and learn together. It also helps us to find new ways of influencing these endeavours and to see patterns emerging in the trends of what we are paying attention to in our organizations. We will move on now to what this means in practice, firstly at the level of individuals and then at the level of our organizations.

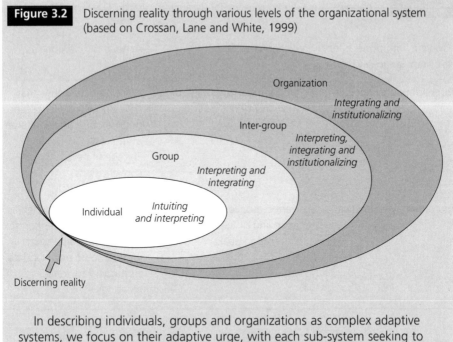

▶ **Figure 3.2** Discerning reality through various levels of the organizational system (based on Crossan, Lane and White, 1999)

In describing individuals, groups and organizations as complex adaptive systems, we focus on their adaptive urge, with each sub-system seeking to improve in response the ever-changing signals being received from the environment. Each sub-system is driven to learn and improve relative to others that it perceives as similar.

Paying attention to individual learning

Returning to the metaphor of knowledge landscapes, how can we each take action to influence the shape of our own landscapes? Some suggestions are summarized in Table 3.1.

We also need to think about how we can support individual knowledge development in our organizations. We will look at three approaches to facilitate individual employee learning by enabling them to create meaning from their experiences at work:

- training
- 'on the job' learning
- tacit knowledge exchange.

Design meaningful training experiences

In thinking about how to design effective learning experiences for employees – for example, training courses or education programmes – we have to think about the implications of learning as knowledge construction (Moon, 2002; Schramm, 2002):

| Table 3.1 | Changing our own knowledge landscapes (based on Oliver and Roos, 2000) |
| | |

Problem with position on the knowledge landscape	General solution	Actions for individuals
Too narrow a perspective	Broaden horizons by adding new knowledge peaks	Participate in groups that have knowledge landscapes outside our immediate area of interest. Engage in new conversations. Read more widely.
Too broad a perspective	Narrow horizons by removing or ignoring knowledge peaks	Focus and reduce generalist interests. Limit attention to inputs from some sources (reduce some news update, stop going to some meetings etc).

- If learning is a search for meaning it must start with the issues around which students are actively trying to construct meaning.
- Meaning requires understanding wholes as well as parts.
- In order to teach well, we must understand the mental models that students use to perceive the world and the assumptions they make to support those models.
- To learn effectively, students need to interact with the environment in which the learning is to be applied so that the context from which they create meaning is relevant (Dewey, 1916/1966).

The learning process involves the reorganization and reconstruction of experience, which takes place in a social setting. Language acts as a mediation tool both in the form of the 'internal' thought processes and dialogues through which individuals make sense of their experience and reflect on it, and as an 'external' communication process with others (Elkjaer, 1999: 86).

These insights provide useful guidelines for us when we design training and education programmes (Johanssen, 1994):

- Make the experience multi-dimensional, providing multiple representations of real situations, thereby avoiding over-simplification.
- Encourage learner construction of knowledge, rather than remembering by rote.
- Emphasize meaningful, authentic, contextualized tasks that are anchored in real-world or case-based settings.

- Encourage thoughtful reflection.
- Emphasize collaboration instead of competition.

The implementation of many of these guidelines is evident in the approaches adopted by the Unipart Group of Companies, a logistics and distribution organization that also manufactures automotive parts for several leading car firms (Conway and Whittingham, 2001). Three major knowledge management initiatives were all geared towards supporting the company's commitment to continuous learning, with their intranet having an almost total focus on learning and being used as a 'connecting tissue' between these initiatives.

The first of these initiatives was the Unipart approach to quality circles called 'Our Contribution Counts' which empowered all employees to set up circles to solve the challenges they faced in their jobs. Circles were commonly formed across company boundaries and this was encouraged by training everyone in common problem-solving techniques, support from facilitators and a central register allowing each circle to access relevant materials from other circles to avoid duplication. This collaborative approach to learning relied on the high level of senior management commitment to continuous improvement.

In 1993, Unipart established the 'Unipart U', a company university to train and develop people from all the business divisions. More than 260 courses were developed and these were practical enough to allow the participants to apply 'this morning's learning to this afternoon's job'. Unipart staff and managers taught the courses and this emphasized the relevance of the material. A particular feature of the approach included feeding the contributions from employees on each course back into working practices. The intranet also provided a platform for the development of the 'virtual U' which allowed employees to access modules as they needed them to help tackle their jobs, rather than having to attend courses. Unipart found that this use of e-learning resulted in a deeper level of learning as each person customized the way they used the materials to best suit their own needs. They also found that they could ensure that people really understood core concepts and key terms, by building in multiple-choice questions that stopped progression until the correct understanding had been demonstrated (in contrast, in a classroom situation, people could be too embarrassed to say that they did not understand). This agreement on important elements of shared language was seen as essential for effective knowledge-sharing.

The third initiative was called the Faculty on the Floor. This allowed employees to work on production-related problems within custom-built learning centres. These were located on the shopfloor and made the latest technology and tools available to everyone. The Faculty on the Floor became an integral part of daily activities by being used for team meetings and problem-solving activities, as well as being a training facility. A key objective was to create an environment for continuous learning and problem-solving, allowing the latest knowledge to be shared quickly.

Unipart has blended individual learning with recognition of the importance of social interaction in supporting the learning process. It has been shown that working with more experienced peers helps develop higher levels of understanding (Vygostky, 1978), and learning also takes place vicariously through observing others and taking note of the consequences of their actions (Bandura, 1971).

These examples of learning through meaningful contextualized tasks and social collaborative activities point the way to the importance of real 'on the job' learning as the most important source of knowledge development for individual employees.

Create structured opportunities for 'on-the-job' learning

Jean Lave and Etienne Wenger set out to explore the relevance of apprenticeship forms of learning to today's workplace. They used their research to develop a more general understanding of adult learning within the context of work practice (Lave and Wenger, 1991). They concluded that learning arises from engaging in and contributing to practice. From an employer's point of view, this means engaging people in meaningful practices and providing access to resources that enhance the opportunity for employees to participate in different ways.

They coined the term 'legitimate peripheral participation' to describe the experience of working with a learning objective, rather than working where the only focus is on achieving a task output (Lave and Wenger, 1991). The involvement of a more experienced individual was as much to legitimize the participation of the learner as to actually provide teaching. Based on anecdotal observation and speculation, it was noted that where peers and near-peers worked together in this way knowledge could develop exceedingly rapidly and effectively.

This form of participation by the learner is essentially about allowing them to develop the language needed to understand the working practices. In other words, to give them the language 'tools' so they can create meaning from their experience. 'For newcomers then the purpose is not to learn *from* talk as a substitute for legitimate peripheral participation; it is to learn *to* talk as a key to legitimate peripheral participation' (Lave and Wenger 1991: 109; original emphasis).

Based on these ideas, our organizations can adopt a range of practical approaches to improve learning from on-the-job experiences.

Engaging People in Meaningful Practice:

- Meaningful means from the point of view of the learner – so engage in *constructive dialogue* to understand the motivations, drivers, ambitions and goals of individuals. These change over time so on-going dialogue is essential.
- Communicate the *relevance* and importance of individual jobs to achieving the purpose of the organization. Make the link clear and explicit and check understanding.

Providing Resources that Enhance Participation:

- *Mentoring* – provide support for individuals to make sense of the organization and how to be successful within it.

- *Coaching* – support reflection on learning through practice and help individuals identify 'gaps' in their understanding.
- Support *peer group networks* of learners; graduate entry cohorts, supervisor or management development learning sets, professional examination study groups, etc.

Looking first at an example of a mentoring initiative, Microsoft designed a programme that was focused on helping people to engage in meaningful work. Mentoring was used to give two hundred of their top staff the time and space to reflect, review their options and make more considered decisions (Glover, 2002). People were helped to focus on the challenges they faced, the choices that were open to them and the consequences of each choice, together with creative solutions or conclusions that they could adopt. Both internal and external mentors were used, with the latter being valued as clearly independent and offering different perspectives. Considerable care was taken to match the mentor and mentee, so that they were sufficiently like-minded. The company believed that the programme helped retain high-performance employees because it enabled people to realize their aspirations, often finding a way of doing this within the company rather than necessarily feeling that they had to leave to do so. It tapped into the meaning that they were looking for from work, enabled this to be articulated and then followed through, whilst also acknowledging and balancing outside work priorities.

In contrast, a coaching programme with a more deliberate intention of increasing company performance was the 'Super Skill Transfer' initiative for sales professionals at the pharmaceutical company Nippon Roche (Nomura and Ogiwara, 2002). A number of medical representatives were identified who consistently performed at a high level. Although they found it hard to describe what they were doing that allowed them to be so effective, they were each partnered with two medical representatives who performed at a more average level, and then accompanied them on visits to customers. The higher-performing representatives were encouraged to engage in non-judgmental dialogue; for example, about the way to approach doctors when they wanted to explain the value of a new drug. In this way, they transferred their tacit knowledge about how to be more effective. The intention was to help people see other ways of doing their jobs by finding new ways of making sense of the situations that they faced on a daily basis. It was concluded that the programme had enriched individual knowledge, whilst significantly improving the overall productivity of the entire sales force.

Moving on to the third suggestion of creating peer group networks of learners, an approach that is frequently used is action learning. This is based on individuals working on real problems that are amenable to having action taken on them (Moorby, 2002). Each individual identifies a problem, owns it and identifies the steps needed to resolve it. An action learning 'set' is formed from a group of people all working on their problems in parallel, and individuals learn by questioning their own and others' proposed actions. Regular communication between set members is used to report progress and reflect on what has been learned. As an example, the UK-based building firm Westbury has used action learning as an integral element of its senior management development programme (Carrington, 2002). A consistent learning need amongst managers had been identified as the ability to influence others. A programme was designed which included a workshop on 'impact and influence'. This required the participants to bring real business issues and allowed them to practice different approaches to resolving the problems. Over the following two months the participants practiced their skills within their real job environments and then returned to describe what they had learned and show this had brought financial benefits for the firm. The learning sets continued to meet regularly after this event so individuals could continue the learning process through dialogue with their colleagues. This approach was integrally linked to the work practices of the participants and was designed to support individuals in making sense of new ways of resolving their problems by collaborating with supportive colleagues. It also demonstrated the direct link between individual jobs and the performance of the organization by emphasizing the financial benefits that had been achieved from the new approaches.

Facilitating action learning sets is one way in which organizations can support individuals in the 'practices' in which they participate through their jobs to gain experience. Later in this chapter, we will also look at how our organizations can create the conditions for 'communities of practice' to flourish.

Mentoring, coaching and action learning sets all to some extent balance individual learning with social participation. It is interesting to note that too strong an emphasis on social participation as the basis of effective learning has been criticized. An important element needs to be our own purposeful engagement in the process and our reflection on the experience (Elkjaer, 1999). This is particularly important for the development of tacit knowledge.

Understand the limitations of language in tacit knowledge exchange

In addition to the training, education and experience-based learning that we have just been looking at, we also need to look at the special case of developing individuals through others passing on the benefit of their own experience. It could be argued that thinking of knowledge in terms of the meaning that has been attributed to contextualized experience should lead us to the conclusion that knowledge cannot be transferred from one person to another, particularly tacit knowledge, as by definition this is hard to put into words (Polanyi, 1958; 1966). However, we suggest that some level of exchange (rather than transfer) is possible and we can create conditions that help the process.

The traditional model of tacit knowledge exchange is based on the relationship between master and apprentice. Let us look at what happens when we find ourselves in this position. Having developed our expertise over many years in many different situations, we may try to put into words (make explicit) what we have learned to less-experienced colleagues who work with us. We will probably find that, more often than not, it is the demonstration of a practice that transfers the meaning. Implicitly, we are the giver of the knowledge and we hope that others will be receivers for it.

For the exchange to be successful, we have to design a process that will make our knowledge accessible to the receivers. However, the receivers have no way of accessing the many situations in which we have refined our knowledge. The receivers absorb as much as possible of our explanations and demonstrations, with the level of understanding that is actually achieved being conditioned by their existing tacit knowledge and the contextual background. They then try to internalize the understanding through practice. Mentally, they are reshaping our knowledge to fit their current context (Dixon, 2002).

These interactions will inevitably generate questions, which require tailored answers. Mentally, we as the givers are also refining our knowledge as a result of the languaging process involved in articulating our experience. In this way, we are encouraged to reflect on our own knowledge and may learn something new as a result of making explicit what had previously been tacit. We are unlikely to be conscious of the full range of tacit knowledge that we have because it is so deeply internalized that it is an instinctive part of our behaviour. This means we do not even try to put it into words and to explain it to ourselves, let alone others. If we do not perceive something, we do not invest much effort in reflecting upon its value and drawing it out into the open (Haldin-Herrgard, 2000).

Although it is the basis for conveying facts, language can also pose a significant obstacle to this communication process. If our tacit knowledge is held in non-verbal form, then we have to find the precise words required to express our understanding. Often, the more expertise we have, the more difficult it is for us to put our understanding into simple language that is accessible to others. In general, experts tend to talk in words that convey complex constructs to colleagues engaged in the same type of work practice, but the meaning is impenetrable to others who lack the experience that gave the words the same connotations (Haldin-Herrgard, 2000; Swap *et al.*, 2001).

Clearly, we cannot transfer our tacit knowledge intact, like an artefact. The relevance of the input, the timeliness and the context in which it is received all affect the efficiency of the exchange process. For the receiver, internalizing tacit knowledge takes time and repetitive experience. Reflection is essential to the process of integrating the new ideas with existing knowledge.

The process is difficult enough with colleagues that work closely with us, but at least we can then judge more easily whether there is evidence of learning and change our approach accordingly to help them build their understanding of the subject. However, increasingly we need to try to exchange tacit knowledge with colleagues around the world. Is it possible to exchange tacit knowledge virtually? Inevitably, separation between people creates contextual obstacles to the exchange. For example, virtual working limits us to using only one or two of our five senses; feedback is limited and slow or non-existent; and the lack of a common physical environment and competing distractions undermines our own involvement and active engagement, as well as that of the person with whom we are trying to exchange knowledge (McKenzie and Potter, 2002).

If there is a high level of rapport between us and we are both sufficiently motivated, we can overcome some of these limitations. Empathy and trust between us tends to increase the sense of social obligation and help sustain the extra effort required in a virtual setting. In general, tacit knowledge is more likely to be exchanged between individuals, particularly virtually, when the following guidelines have been followed:

- *Rapport* has been built before progressing to the task that requires knowledge to be exchanged. For example, virtual social activities and informal communication spaces have been designed and used.
- The *motivations* of both the giver and the receiver have been aligned so that they both engage actively in the process.
- Conscious effort has been invested in *communicating* effectively, including using as many different ways to communicate as possible. Appropriate language has been used at different stages, with reflection on whether it is enabling or blocking the development of understanding. Regular feedback has been provided and the communications paced, recognizing the time to pause and the time to move on. Particular attention has been paid to developing interpersonal skills, such as recognizing and responding effectively to the needs of others, and displaying patience and adaptability in the communication processes adopted.
- *Time* has not been over-compressed. *Reflection* has been recognized as a key element of building tacit knowledge, and time has been allowed for each new fact to be reconciled with existing knowledge.

The effort needed to exchange tacit knowledge depends on all these factors: the levels of rapport, the motivation of the giver and receiver of knowledge, the effectiveness of the communication techniques; and the time available. These factors are interdependent and when one is less than ideal, the others need to be adjusted to compensate.

Paying attention to organizational learning

Having looked at how the learning of individuals can be supported, we now move our focus to the collective learning processes of social groups, in particular of organizations. Returning to our metaphor of knowledge landscapes, suggestions for ways in which those making strategic decisions can shape the landscapes of organizations are given in Table 3.2.

 Signpost In *Competence Area 4: Connecting* we look at how to change the permeability of the boundaries of our organizations to adjust the flow of knowledge in both directions as the basis for shaping the knowledge landscapes.

Table 3.2 Changing the knowledge landscape of organizations (based on Oliver and Roos, 2000)

Problem with position on the knowledge landscape	General solution	Actions for organizational decision-makers
Too narrow a perspective	Broaden horizons by adding new knowledge peaks	Mergers Acquisitions Alliances Parallel groups of products addressing similar markets. Maintaining a network of knowledge-sharing relationships
Too broad a perspective	Narrow horizons by removing or ignoring knowledge peaks	Split up businesses Divest operations Streamline product lines Tighten the organizational structure

The challenge for our organizations today is to find the right balance between these perspectives, depending on the competitive environment and the objectives we are pursuing:

> in order to thrive in knowledge landscapes, we have to balance between the two opposing risks of over specialization and over generalization. That trade-off – broadening and narrowing our horizons – is critical to simultaneously adapting to and shaping our business environments in a complex world.
>
> *Oliver and Roos, 2000: 84*

Signpost In *Competence Area 1: Competing* we looked at what leads to the risk of over-specialization or over-generalization. We saw how to balance 'adaptive' learning that refines distinctions to exploit existing knowledge resources with 'generative' learning that develops new distinctions to broaden the range of our knowledge resources.

Narrowing and broadening perspectives are all relatively high-level objectives that depend on linking a number of organizational processes and the actions of many individuals. In this chapter we are drilling down into the concept of learning at a much more detailed level, so we can appreciate the conditions and the style of interacting needed to make these things effective.

Earlier in this chapter we saw that we can influence knowledge development (learning) at the level of the social groups in our organizations by paying attention to languaging and socialization processes; these are the most effective means to convert individual knowledge to organizational knowledge. We also saw that collective tacit knowledge provides the context for learning. We can now draw these ideas together and see that organizational learning will depend heavily on the use of language and facilitating effective knowledge connections between people (von Krogh, Roos and Slocum, 1994). Firstly, we will look at the organizational processes that use language effectively, then at ways of creating the right kind of shared context for relationships to form so shared meaning can emerge in groups.

Employ the tools of organizational languaging

There are three powerful ways of using language to promote shared systems of meaning within our organizations: dialogue, stories and metaphor.

1. Dialogue

> The ability to explore the space of possibility can be found in an organization's ability to engage in dialogue.
>
> *McMaster, 1996*

For both individuals and organizations, current knowledge landscapes limit imagination of the possibilities that exist over the horizon. If language is both the way we construct our view of reality and the vehicle for communicating that to others, then communication is also to the route to imagining other realities and possibilities.

Dialogue is a special kind of communication. It is conversation that requires us to listen, think and reflect at the same time. Dialogue is about emergence: the articulation of new and previously hidden meanings and understandings (Battram, 1996). The differences between dialogue and discussion are summarized in Table 3.3.

Guidelines for achieving productive dialogue can be adapted to many organizational situations such as one-to-one conversations, team meetings and large group change programmes. The fundamental requirement is for participants to work at suspending assumptions and try to see the issue from other perspectives. Rules may be used to ensure open and honest participation, but it is undoubtedly best if the participants develop these themselves. Examples are:

- Respect the person who 'holds the context', that is, the person who is closest to the issue and can keep a focus to the exchange.
- Suspend the tendency to judge.
- Treat everyone's view as equally valid.

Several organizations have found that the principles of dialogue can be used to make large group events more effective. GE introduced three-day-long off-site 'Workout' sessions where people from different levels of the organization came together to work on ideas (Boone, 2001). The goal was to give people time and space to reflect on how they could do their jobs better, with a safe environment where suggestions and observations would be welcomed. Senior management joined the group on the last day to provide rapid feedback on the ideas

Table 3.3	Comparing the characteristics of dialogue and discussion (Battram, 1998)

Dialogue	Discussion
Starts with listening	Starts with talking
Direction emerges	Direction is pre-conceived
Focuses on insights	Focuses on differences of opinion
Generates ideas	Generates conflict
Synthesizes options	Analyzes options
Encourages reflection	Encourages quick thinking
Prefers 'sub-optimal' solutions	Looks for one best way

that had been generated. These 'mega conversations' were intended to spark creativity and good planning; flexible physical space and experienced facilitators were needed to create the conditions for these events to be successful. In general, well-structured events can generate ideas and solve problems much more quickly than would be the case using conventional communication channels.

 Signpost In *Competence Area 2: Deciding* we saw how large group events can be used to build a shared sense of organizational identity and support the development of widespread leadership behaviour.

2. Stories

Stephen Denning, who refined the use of stories as a means of creating the impetus for change within the World Bank, has suggested that narratives are a powerful way of capturing and communicating the essence of highly complex situations and environments (Denning, 2001a). The fact that narratives are not mathematically precise and full of fuzzy qualitative relationships, seems to be a key to their success in enabling us to cope with the complexity of our organizations and the world around us. Denning suggests that although narrative only acts as an analogy for most purposes (in the same way as equations or maps are forms of analogies), as descriptions of complex systems and situations they have considerable accuracy. Storytelling is a powerful knowledge-sharing vehicle. A well-crafted story includes lots of 'hooks' for the listener, so they can apply the ideas to their own situation, make connections, and see the point of a new way of thinking.

Denning describes good organizational stories as having five key characteristics (2001b):

Endurance: the stories go on through decades.

Salience: they have punch and emotional power.

Sense-making: they explain something.

Comfort: the story resonates with something people have experienced.

Authenticity: people trust the story-teller and believe the story.

Denning coined the phrase 'springboard stories' to describe those stories that help others take an imaginative leap into the space of new possibilities. In this way, stories can be used in organizations to stimulate change, to convince people of what you want them to believe, to gain commitment and loyalty and to transfer knowledge. Although Denning accepts that some people are natural story-tellers, he suggests that it is a technique everyone can learn.

3. Metaphor

Metaphors link ideas so new knowledge can emerge. They are relevant to any situation that requires both new thinking and reflection on past experience. In a complex world, the impossibility of comprehensive description is resolved by making sense through pattern recognition. Metaphors provide the language to describe those patterns and communicate their meaning. We need to remember that 'language creates reality', so the metaphors we adopt generate the perception of reality for ourselves and for the people with whom we are communicating.

Dave Snowden of IBM has suggested that metaphors are useful way of communicating what knowledge management is about, without the need to resort to complex formal definitions that try to capture the interdependencies and subtleties of the subject (Snowden, 1999). He has used a metaphor that compares the use of a London street map with the use of a London taxi to navigate around the city. The street map represents the collation of large amounts of data into a codified information object that allows individuals to navigate without specialized training. However, using the map whilst driving slows the journey and it is hard to respond to uncertain situations such as road closures or accidents. In contrast, using a London taxi driver brings the benefit of access to an intuitive understanding of how to use the data from the map in practice. Change and uncertainty that arises in the journey can be handled adaptively and responsively. Snowden suggests that this metaphor can be helpful in early communications about knowledge management; for example, by asking whether a problem needs a 'map' or a 'taxi' at first and later transitioning back to the words 'information' and 'knowledge', but now with confidence that there is a consistent meaning being attributed to them.

Design shared contexts to enable effective relationships to develop

Our second consideration in paying attention to organizational learning involves finding ways of creating different kinds of shared context in which relationships can form and shared meaning can develop. This helps knowledge connections to be made within and between 'levels', that is, between individuals, groups and the organization. A useful term to describe the idea of shared space or shared context is the Japanese word *Ba* (Nonaka and Konno, 1998; Nonaka, Toyama and Konno, 2000; Ray and Little, 2001).

When we have created links between our own mental, virtual or physical context and that of other involved colleagues, we have established a *Ba* space. The more links there are, the stronger the shared context and the easier the communication process can be. The quality of those links needs to change over time and different qualities take priority at different times, depending on the complexity of the process needed to develop shared understanding. The concept of *Ba* has been applied to the process used to explain the way knowledge develops in our organizations as a continuous dialogue between tacit and explicit knowledge (Nonaka, 1991).

 Signpost In *Competence Area 1: Competing* we looked at Nonaka's four modes of knowledge creation and how they can be managed in organizations to form a continuous cycle.

Figure 3.3 shows the *Ba* spaces that correspond to the socialization, externalization, combination and internalization stages of the knowledge creation cycle.

Conditions in each *Ba* space need to be different to enable the appropriate level of relationship connections to form and the range of knowledge linkages to be made. The creation of innovative organizational knowledge requires all of these conditions to exist and to operate synergistically. The behaviours and resources that support the creation of these spaces are as follows:

Figure 3.3 *Ba* and the knowledge creation spiral (based on Nonaka and Konno, 1998)

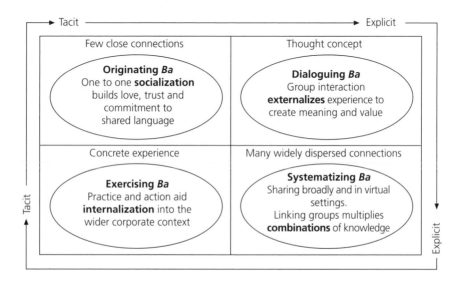

Originating Ba requires mutual understanding, empathy, interpersonal sensitivity and the other qualities of emotional intelligence. This supports the socialization stage, where connections are made between people to explore the meanings about the particular knowledge area that they have each created through their own experience and insights.

 In *Competence Area 2: Deciding* we saw that a similar set of conditions supports the emergence of a high-care environment in which people are attentive to work and the needs of others.

Dialoguing Ba requires advanced communication skills to enable people to understand one another. Versatility with language, the use of accessible terminology, the avoidance of jargon, rich evocative expressions that convey meaning at different levels, metaphors, analogies, pictures and music may all be relevant. This is the externalization stage of the cycle where a collective meaning of the knowledge being explored is negotiated and made explicit.

Systematizing Ba requires free-flowing two-way communication methods that disseminate explicit information broadly and collect other explicit feedback to associate with it. Groupware, databases, networks and mailings, as well as seminars, lectures, workshops and meetings are all useful ways of generating this context. In this combination stage, explicit knowledge from a wider community is drawn upon to refine the knowledge and integrate it into the organizational level collective system of meaning and view of what is considered feasible and acceptable. Once knowledge can be standardized and codified into a format that is easy to connect, it is easier to produce creative combinations.

Exercising Ba needs to provide the time and the space to experiment and to put into action the knowledge that has emerged from all the other *Ba* activities. Jointly building competence through transforming the knowledge that has been developed into a 'capacity to act' generates collective tacit knowledge that provides the foundation for future activity and the continuation of the cycle.

How can these ideas be put into practice? One organization that set out to create the conditions for Originating *Ba* is Kao Corporation, a Japanese manufacturer and distributor of cosmetics and household and industrial products. The company grew through creating innovative products and paid particular attention to creating an environment in which researchers could share ideas to spark creative thinking (Nomura and Ogiwara, 2002). It deliberately set out to reduce the physical and psychological barriers between people with different kinds of expertise. Researchers from different disciplines worked next to each other in large rooms. It also arranged for those working on fundamental research to be situated next to those working on related product development. Creativity-stimulating discussions were encouraged through informal, active interactions between people as they carried out their work. The company believed that by making the latest knowledge and ideas visible, creative dialogue became a natural process.

In addition to thinking about *Ba* spaces when knowledge creation is important, it is also useful to think about their relevance in situations in which existing knowledge has to be brought together quickly. In the fast-moving customer-focused environment of the Japanese office supply company ASKUL, the physical environment has been used to allow people to quickly gather together when a problem arises (Nomura and Ogiwara, 2002). The business was built around a commitment to deliver their products within a day. This has driven a similar focus on resolving all customer problems by the next day. The company designed its headquarters so that the call centre that received inquiries and complaints from customers was at the very heart of the building. The desks of the President and various supporting functions surrounded it, demonstrating the importance of this point of contact with customers to the business. When a problem arose, the people who had relevant knowledge could be quickly identified and collected together. This 'just-in-time' approach to knowledge management succeeded because of the way physical space was used, as well as because people were encouraged to be proactive in solving problems and changing existing practices, that is, they were given sufficient autonomy and mental 'space' to work out how best to meet customers' needs.

We now need to look at how to combine our efforts to pay attention to individual learning with those that pay attention to organizational learning. However, knowledge does not always flow smoothly between individuals, groups and organizations, and this can reduce learning potential at all levels, as we shall see in the next section.

Knowledge stickiness is a source of tension between individual and organizational learning

We have looked at how to support both individual and collective learning in our organizations. Earlier we saw that the link between them is the process of 'languaging', a term used to describe the on-going process of generating meaning through making linguistic distinctions to progress up a peak on our knowledge landscape. So far we have seen how language is used to make knowledge connections. Now we need to look at the potential problems that language can also create for us.

In exploring how individuals learn through participation in meaningful practice, for example through 'on-the-job' learning, we saw that work groups develop a shared language to talk about their activities, standards and experiences. Now, we also recognize that the language of expertise can act as a barrier that excludes others who do not share that language. If we invest in developing pockets of expertise, without an appropriate balance of investment in transferring this to organizational level learning, we risk valuable knowledge residing largely in the heads of a few individuals and not being leveraged collectively for business success. We need to balance our attention to developing the expertise of individuals with attention to collective learning so that we can make business decisions that are appropriate in complex and fast-moving competitive environments.

Thinking a little more deeply about the language of expertise points us towards a way of managing this balance. Within an area of shared work practice, a system of meaning is communicated through a common language that allows knowledge to develop and be embedded in the practice. It is not necessarily the case that this knowledge domain boundary sits within the formal boundary of the organization. For example, professionals such as scientists, engineers, doctors and nurses often consider themselves to be part of a wide external community. This mismatch of boundaries has given rise to the idea of 'sticky' and 'leaky' knowledge. Knowledge can leak from our organizations where practices are shared with outsiders and it can stick in certain places within our organizations where practice is not shared sufficiently to allow effective communication (Brown and Duguid, 2001).

Our challenge is to co-ordinate the development and application of knowledge across practice boundaries that lie within our organizations, so reducing stickiness, whilst managing the leakage of knowledge outside them.

 See *Competence Area 1: Competing* to see how other factors, such as lack of standardization, ineffective people management processes or use of technology and an unsupportive culture can also prevent knowledge from flowing around an organization.

 See *Competence Area 4: Connecting* to find out how to design organizational boundaries that have the right level of knowledge permeability.

The problem of stickiness was highlighted in a study of a series of knowledge transfer projects. Using project success indicators, such as on-time and on-budget delivery and a satisfied recipient, it was possible to identify the specific factors that made knowledge sufficiently sticky to significantly impact the success of the project (Szulanski, 1996). The main reasons were:

- The inability of the recipient to accept the data as meaningful.
- Data which needed more effort to collect than appeared to be worth investing.
- Data which did not appear to be something that needed to be paid attention to.
- Data which required the dismantling of a peak on the recipient's knowledge landscape before a new peak could be constructed.

It was concluded that knowledge stickiness was mainly associated with characteristics of the situation (context), rather than with any inherent characteristics of the type of knowledge involved. However, tacit knowledge can be very sticky simply because of the difficulty of transferring years of experience and practice through the limits of time, words and relationships.

So, the question we need to address is how can we encourage both individual learning and organizational learning to be dynamic and relevant, whilst avoiding the problems of knowledge sticking in the heads of individuals or within isolated groups which stops it being accessible to others who may benefit from it?

A parallel challenge can be seen from the perspective of the individual. Self-actualization is believed to be a strong source of workplace motivation (Maslow, 1943) and is a consequence of continuously developing and improving ourselves through a self-directed, inquisitive and creative approach to learning (Antonacopoulou, 1999). However, there can be a source of conflict between self-actualization and self-fulfilment, which are psychological needs, and our need to belong, feel secure and be accepted by a social group (our social needs). Often we adopt a role, portray an image or limit our participation in activities in recognition of the political realities of our organizations and the consequences for our social acceptability if we pursue certain knowledge paths. Power and politics in the organization effectively act to constrain our receptivity to knowledge through reducing our motivation and these social barriers are another form of stickiness that stops knowledge from flowing around the organization. Effort is needed to ensure that the factors that motivate individuals to engage in learning initiatives are recognized. Aligning the value to individuals and the organization from learning initiatives is necessary if they are to deliver the anticipated results.

Signpost In *Competence Area 2: Deciding* we saw that power and politics are a source of tension in our organizations and create a gap between knowing what is needed and what is actually done.

A solution to these sources of tension is also to pay attention to learning in the groups that form around the knowledge-based practices of the organization. Increasingly, there is a view that groups defined by a knowledge domain associated with a work practice play an essential role in stewarding and developing that knowledge (see, for example, Brown and Duguid, 1991; Wenger, 1998; Wenger, McDermott and Snyder, 2002). By actively enabling and supporting these communities of practice and paying particular attention to co-ordinating knowledge flows across multiple communities of practice, we deliberately focus our efforts on reducing the problems caused by knowledge stickiness, social barriers to knowledge flows and individual motivation.

Supporting and co-ordinating multiple communities of practice allows our organizations to:

- Create the context for the development of relationships (*Ba spaces*), overcoming social barriers to knowledge flow and creating the conditions for a shared language to develop.
- Address knowledge stickiness and ensure that the knowledge can be accessed beyond the boundaries of the community of practice that generated it.

- Leverage the organization's investment in the learning of individuals by enabling them to integrate that learning with those of others who participate in a similar practice area.
- Focus the investment in organizational learning approaches on integrating communities of practice.
- Enable the emergence of new perspectives and creative solutions by providing mechanisms to link different 'systems of meaning making' (individuals, groups and organization).

We will move on to look at practical approaches to supporting and co-ordinating communities of practice to achieve these objectives.

Resolve the tension through communities of practice

A useful definition of communities of practice is :

> Groups of people who come together to share and to learn from one another face-to-face and virtually. They are held together by a common interest in body of knowledge and are driven by a desire and need to share problems, experiences, insights, templates, tools and best practices. Community members deepen their knowledge by interacting on an ongoing basis.
>
> *Hubert, Newhouse and Vestal, 2001*

Characteristics that support this definition are (van Winkelen and Ramsell, 2003):

- A community of practice may be designed (intentional) or emergent.
- Knowledge is shared in the community of practice based on relationships with others, rather than direct transactions. Hence interaction involves an emotional as well as an intellectual component.
- A community of practice is largely a collection of volunteers.
- A community of practice does not have a hierarchical management system and is largely self-organizing.
- A strong community of practice will stay together in the face of obstacles.

An individual's motivation to participate in a community of practice and an organization's willingness to support that community both stem from an expectation that it will deliver a particular value. This suggests that there are two broad principles involved in building effective communities of practice:

1 Sustaining the delivery of value from that community for both individuals and the organization.
2 Aligning the value drivers for individuals with those for the organization.

It has been found that for individuals there is a cyclical relationship with anticipation of value driving the initial motivation to participate in the community of practice, and delivery of value sustaining participation. The sources of motivation and value vary between individuals and a range of sources that have been identified are summarized in Table 3.4 (van Winkelen and Ramsell, 2002).

By examining the factors that underpinned communities of practice that were considered to be effective and comparing them with those that were considered to be ineffective, four drivers have been found to encourage the required alignment between the delivery of value for individuals and organizations.

An appropriate subject area. Subjects that are new to the organization, topical or relevant to particular business objectives are particularly suitable. The subject area needs to be something that people will pay attention to and perceive to be meaningful.

A clear purpose. A clear purpose legitimizes both the participation in the community of practice by individuals and the commitment of organizational support. The purpose directs attention to be paid to that knowledge area.

The fulfilment of certain roles. A pro-active and respected leader is essential to generate energy and enthusiasm in the community of practice. This may not be the most senior person and in this situation, the group may give them implicit authority. It is also useful to note that (Wenger, McDermott and Snyder, 2002):

- Subject-matter experts add credibility and are needed by the community of practice, but may be peripheral to the main activities.

- Roles change over time depending on the way that the community of practice evolves.

- The number of formalized roles may depend on the size of the community of practice.

Table 3.4   Categories of motivation and value for individuals participating in communities of practice

Intellectual (cognitive)	Emotional (affective)
Develop own expertise	Satisfaction from helping others
Awareness of opportunities across the organization	Recognition and kudos
	Increased confidence
Understand different perspectives	Build relationships/network
High return on effort involved	Greater sense of belonging
Sense of achievement	
Improve status	**Means to an end (instrumental)**
Increase influence	Improve pay/benefits due to better company or personal performance
Improve ability to get the job done	
Share with others with similar interests	

- Roles help create a sense of belonging for individuals and give the community of practice an identity of its own.

The fulfilment of appropriate roles both legitimizes participation in the community of practice and can ensure that some participants (possibly through previous experience or formal training) have appropriate knowledge landscapes to allow them to make sense of the activities going on in the community of practice and therefore focus and guide them.

Appropriate organizational support. If the fulfilment of appropriate roles is about putting the right people in place (with training if necessary), appropriate organizational support takes the form of processes to integrate communities into other business activities and technology to support communication and collaboration. Under this broad umbrella, a wide variety of approaches are being adopted by organizations. For example, the financial services company Abbey National has used Social Network Analysis (Cross *et al.*, 2001) to help 'kick-start' informal communities that wanted to develop their activities, and the computer service firm Unisys provided a web portal for communities to use once they were established. This offered threaded messaging, document management and chat facilities.

Having identified four factors that drive alignment and the sustained delivery of value, two more general factors (enablers) have been shown to be present in effective communities and absent in less effective ones.

A culture of trust and openness. A culture of trust and openness may be either an external environmental factor that acts as an enabler of effectiveness, or a consequence of the presence of effective communities of practice.

 Signpost In *Competence Area 2: Deciding* we saw how various elements contribute to developing a culture in which people make use of and contribute to the knowledge resources of the organization.

Organizational acquiescence. Organizational acquiescence towards the community of practice may be active or passive. The minimum requirement is a willingness to tolerate these forms of working and to allow individuals sufficient time and any necessary resources to participate.

Understanding that these drivers and enablers generate alignment and the delivery of value for both participants and our organizations helps us identify various ways in which to create, support or sustain communities of practice. However, context remains a key consideration in identifying the ingredients of a 'recipe' to be adopted by any particular organization. What is desirable and acceptable in one organization could be undesirable and unacceptable in another. These differences have been illustrated by the observation that Abbey National employees were used to a structured approach to working and needed the same when it came to participation in communities. In contrast, QinetiQ employees (a UK-based research and development organization) were used to a culture of independence and individualism and resisted structure and direction in attempts to manage communities centrally. Clearly, the approach to supporting communities needs to be consistent with the prevailing business paradigm of our organizations.

Many companies have seen the potential benefit of the community model for connecting people across their organizations. Often, flexible approaches are adopted, with support being given to groups that range from true communities of practice to others that could also be described as networks (groups with a less strong sense of identity), or distributed work groups (with a strong project or task focus) (Wenger and Snyder, 2000). Increasingly, intranet-based technology is being used to support the formation of distributed communities. In this situation, most of the communication and collaboration is likely to be electronic rather than through direct meetings between people and, as we saw earlier, this may limit the transfer of tacit knowledge that is possible within these communities.

One group of companies that set out to create a range of different types of virtual community, including communities of practice, was St. Paul. This is a global organization providing insurance products and services. It recognized that its commercial success depended on the expertise of its people and, as a global operation, extensive knowledge-sharing activities in various forms were needed to develop that expertise to a consistent level in all countries (Owens and Thompson, 2001).

St. Paul launched an intranet site called the Knowledge Exchange to provide tools and processes for online virtual communities, allowing people to share expertise and experience to solve work problems. We can map their approach onto the four enablers and two drivers of effective communities that we have just described:

An appropriate subject area. St. Paul deliberately set out to support several types of virtual community and the nature of the community determined the subject that they focused on and the objective of their interaction:

- *Community of practice* – voluntary groups of people coming together because of their shared interest in the subject and a desire to further their knowledge about it for the benefit of the business. For example, globally-dispersed people who were involved in insurance products relating to workers' compensation had been struggling to connect with colleagues from across the company.
- *Centre of expertise* – experts about a highly-specialized knowledge area appointed by management to be a resource for the company. These acted as a hub for employees wishing to find out about the topic.
- *Work groups* – people from the same department with a shared responsibility for a product or service.
- *Project teams* – cross-functional groups responsible for a time-specific project. Secure discussion areas and document sharing facilities supported collaboration.

- *Virtual classroom community* – an online collaborative platform enabling the exchange of ideas after the completion of classroom-based learning activities.

A clear purpose. St. Paul emphasized the purpose of the virtual communities as tools to get useful work completed more effectively. The purpose and relevance of each community was made clear so that participation was not perceived to be additional work.

The fulfilment of certain roles. In the St. Paul communities, the facilitator was termed the 'mayor' and this role was seen to be the key to the success of the community. They found that the mayor needed to be respected for his/her expertise in the community's knowledge domain and also needed sufficient skills in motivating and leading others in a virtual environment.

Appropriate organizational support. The supporting technology was designed to be easy to use and it took less than 30 seconds to set up the community. Coaching and online resources were available to help the community as it established itself.

A culture of trust and openness. Sharing news, documents and questions and answers around important issues was used to build trust and openness. Community participants were encouraged to post personal information such as photographs and family information to help build relationships.

Organizational acquiescence. The corporate level appointment of a Chief Knowledge Officer with responsibility for learning and knowledge management across businesses and geographical boundaries demonstrated business level commitment to knowledge-sharing. The virtual communities were integrated into a portfolio of other learning-based initiatives including the St. Paul University and an online resource centre for education and learning information. Senior management support was active rather than passive, encouraged through revised leadership competencies for senior managers including 'seeking and sharing knowledge'.

The St. Paul Companies recognized the importance of connecting communities, with the Chief Knowledge Officer observing, 'inter-community collaboration is the mark of a truly powerful knowledge exchange system'. As we saw earlier, if communities of practice are to act as the bridge between individual and organizational learning, particular attention needs to be paid to finding ways of connecting them, rather than allowing them to become a new form of knowledge silo with the shared language of the community becoming a barrier to understanding and learning by others.

Connecting communities by spanning the boundaries creates a 'constellation' of communities (Wenger, 1998). Practical ways in which this can be encouraged include (Ward, 2000):

- Defining 'boundary spanner' roles such as knowledge and relationship brokers.
- Building communities of practice amongst the people who have the boundary spanner roles.

- Making the collective documented knowledge of all the communities visible to everyone and making it easy to access through effective cross-referencing and search systems.

- Multi-community activities such as meetings and conferences based around themes that reach across community boundaries.

- Common documents and facilitating technology and processes that act as something tangible that are shared by all the communities.

- Shared norms and principles relating to standards of communication and knowledge quality that have been jointly developed by the communities and are collectively co-ordinated.

- Common efforts or causes that leverage the passions of multiple communities.

Unisys is a company that designed their knowledge management strategy around the formation of a constellation of communities (van Winkelen and Ramsell, 2002). They established a structured process to integrate new communities into their global network of communities from the outset. Knowledge managers worked with groups of people interested in potentially forming a community around a specific topic. They negotiated the 'outcomes' desired by each group of stakeholders and synthesized these into a set of 'community outcomes' that defined what the community would exist to do. This became the basis for deciding on the support the community needed and provided a clear basis for relating the new community to those that already existed. Common technology support was then available to community members to allow them to run virtual workshops, manage documents and communicate formally and informally. Wherever possible, community initiatives were integrated into existing company programmes, emphasizing their contribution to key business objectives.

It is useful to reflect on another valuable outcome from using communities of practice as the mechanism to leverage and connect both individual and organizational learning: they offer the opportunity to increase the job satisfaction of knowledge workers and therefore to retain them within our organizations.

 Signpost In *Competence Area 2: Deciding* we saw how offering the opportunity to learn is the basis for attracting, motivating and retaining knowledge workers.

As individuals develop greater awareness of their own worth in the knowledge economy and recognize that inevitably they must take responsibility for their own career and future, they will increasingly add into their own decision-making process consideration of the opportunity a potential work experience offers to learn and allow them to retain their own market value in the future. Organizations that can offer the opportunity to participate in a leading community of practice in the professional knowledge domains of their workers now appear particularly attractive (Wenger, McDermott and Snyder, 2002). Being within the company forms the basis for staying ahead in the discipline and this is the source of future individual 'marketability'. The pace of change and the rate of development of new knowledge mean that it has become too difficult for individuals to do this independently.

Participating in workplace communities of practice offers individuals the opportunity to map their own knowledge landscape onto that of our organizations. Individual, group and organization knowledge landscapes all co-evolve dynamically when the conditions are created for knowledge to flow between them and when knowledge peaks emerge from new knowledge connections. In the next chapter, we move 'up' a level and look at how to connect the knowledge landscapes of our organizations with those of others in our industry.

Summary

In this chapter we have looked at how to increase the competence of our organizations in supporting effective learning processes. We started with a series of questions:

How do we learn?

How can we help individuals to make sense of their work and learn from it?

How can we create an environment in which groups of people can learn collectively?

How can we stop knowledge sticking in pockets of expertise, rather than flowing more widely throughout the organization?

To appreciate where to invest management attention and resources in developing competence in learning, we adopted the metaphor of knowledge landscapes as a way of describing the breadth and extent of the knowledge base of individuals and of our organizations. We also needed to adopt a point of view about what learning involves. Three important insights emerged:

1   Individuals, groups and organizations are distinct levels in an interconnected system of mutual meaning-making.
2   Language is the mechanism that mediates learning.
3   Knowledge is embodied in individuals and embedded in the practices of social groups. Knowledge represents meaning in a context and is refined through increasingly precise linguistic distinctions.

We looked at supporting learning by individuals in our organizations, as well as supporting collective learning. Paying attention to individual learning involves:

- Designing training and education programmes that encourage the learner to construct their own understanding through meaningful, authentic, contextualized activities.
- Supporting 'on-the-job' learning through engaging people in meaningful work practices and providing resources to enhance their active participation (such as mentoring, coaching and peer group networks).
- Supporting tacit knowledge exchange through recognizing the importance of building rapport, improving communication processes and building in time for reflection.

Paying attention to organizational learning involves:

- Developing a shared language to communicate what matters through the use of dialogue, stories and metaphors.
- Developing ways of creating shared contexts in which relationships can form and shared meaning can be developed. These contexts will have different characteristics depending on what is trying to be achieved. The concept of *Ba* spaces (originating, dialoguing, systematizing and exercising) is helpful in appreciating what these characteristics are.

We also appreciated the 'stickiness' of knowledge that comes from both the highly-specific language that experts develop to communicate their ideas with each other, and from the social barriers and lack of motivation that block individuals from learning. By paying attention to the development and co-ordination of communities of practice, managers can address knowledge stickiness, leverage the investment in individual learning by enabling them to integrate the knowledge they have developed with those of others in the practice area, and focus investments in organizational learning more effectively.

Ways in which effective communities of practice can be supported include:

1 Sustaining the delivery of value from the community for both individuals and the organization.
2 Aligning the motivations by which individuals participate with those for the organization.

These will be helped by:

- an appropriate subject area for the community
- a clear purpose
- the fulfilment of certain roles
- appropriate organizational support.

However, to know what these mean in terms of practical interventions we need to understand:

▶
- the culture of the organization
- the extent of the organizational acquiescence for the community way of working
- the business paradigm.

    Competence in learning means successfully mapping the knowledge landscapes of individuals and communities of practice onto that of the organization, and creating the conditions for knowledge to flow between them and new knowledge peaks to emerge in response to the changing competitive environment.

References

Antonacopoulou, E. (1999) 'Developing learning managers within learning organizations: the case of three major retail banks', in *Organizational Learning and the Learning Organization: Developments in Theory and Practice* (eds M. Easterby-Smith, L. Araujo and J. Burgoyne). London: Sage.

Bandura, A. (1971) *Social Learning Theory*. New York: General Learning Press.

Battram, A. (1996) *Navigating Complexity*. London: The Industrial Society.

Battram, A. (1998) 'Key concepts in learning from complexity'. GLEA Conference, 1–12.

Baumard, P. (1999) *Tacit Knowledge in Organizations*. London: Sage.

Boone, M. E. (2001) 'Opening a dialogue with the whole organization', *Knowledge Management Review* 4(4): 26–9.

Brown, J. and Duguid, P. (1991) 'Organisational learning and communities of practice: towards a unified view of working, learning and innovating', *Organizational Science* 2(1): 40–57.

Brown, J. and Duguid, P. (2001) 'Knowledge and organization: a social-practice perspective', *Organization Science*, 12(2): 198–213.

Carrington, L. (2002) 'House proud', *People Management* 8(24): 36–8.

Conway, B. and Whittingham, V. (2001) 'Managing knowledge and learning at Unipart', *Knowledge Management Review* 4(3), 14–17.

Cross, R., Parker, A., Prusak, L. and Borgatti, S. P. (2001) 'Knowing what we know: supporting knowledge creation and sharing in social networks', *Organizational Dynamics* 30(2): 100–20.

Crossan, M. M., Lane, H. W. and White, R. E. (1999) 'An organizational learning framework: from intuition to institution', *Academy of Management Review* 24(3): 522.

Denning, S. (2001a) *The Springboard: How Storytelling Ignites Action in Knowledge-Era Organizations*. Boston: Butterworth Heinemann.

Denning, S. (2001b) 'Storytelling: further perspectives', 1st Annual Conference, Henley KM Forum, Henley Management College, UK.

Dewey, J. (1916/1966) *Democracy and Education: An Introduction to the Philosophy of Education*. New York: The Free Press.

Dixon, N. (2002) 'The neglected receiver of knowledge sharing', *Ivey Business Journal* 66(4): 35–40.

Easterby-Smith, M. and Araujo, L. (1999) 'Organizational learning: current debates and opportunities', in *Organizational Learning and the Learning Organization: Developments in Theory and Practice* (eds M. Easterby-Smith, J. Burgoyne and L. Araujo). London: Sage.

Elkjaer, B. (1999) 'In search of a social learning theory', in *Organizational Learning and the Learning Organization* (eds M. Easterby-Smith, L. Araujo and J. Burgoyne). London: Sage, 75–91.

Glover, C. (2002) 'Good for the soul', *People Management* 8(14): 29–31.

Haldin-Herrgard, T. (2000) 'Difficulties in diffusion of tacit knowledge in organizations', *Journal of Intellectual Capital* 1(4): 357–65.

Huber, G. (1991) 'Organizational Learning: the contributing processes and the literature', *Organizational Science* 2(1): 88–115.

Hubert, C., Newhouse, B. and Vestal, W. (2001) 'Building and sustaining communities of practice', Next-Generation Knowledge Management: Enabling Business Processes, Houston, USA.

Johanssen, D. (1994) 'Thinking technology: toward a constructivist design model', *Educational Technology* 34(4): 34–7.

Lave, J. and Wenger, E. (1991) *Situated Learning: Legitimate Peripheral Participation*. Cambridge: Cambridge University Press.

Luhmann, N. (1986) 'The autopoiesis of social systems', in *Sociocybernetic Paradoxes* (eds F. Geyer and J. van der Zouwen) Beverly Hills, CA: Sage, 172–92.

Magalhaes, R. (1998) 'Organizational knowledge and learning', in *Knowing in Firms* (eds G. von Krogh, J. Roos and D. Kleine), London: Sage.

Maslow, A. H. (1943) 'A theory of human motivation', *Psychological Review* 50: 370–96.

Matlin, M. (1994) *Cognition*. Forth Worth, TX: Harcourt Brace College Publishers.

Maturana, H. and Varela, F. (1980) *Autopoiesis and Cognition*. London: Reid.

Maturana, H. and Varela, F. (1992) *The Tree of Knowledge*. Boston: Shambhala.

McKenzie, J. and Potter, R. (2002) 'Understanding the enabling conditions for virtual tacit knowledge exchange', 2nd Annual Conference, Henley KM Forum, Henley Management College, UK.

McMaster, M. (1996) *The Intelligence Advantage: Organizing for Complexity*. Boston: Butterworth-Heinemann.

Moon, S. (2002) 'Learning Models', Henley Management College, Henley, UK.

Moorby, E. (2002) 'Action learning for practitioners and managers', http://www.cipd.co.uk/Infosource/Training/Actionlearningforpractitionersandmanagers.asp (accessed 24 December 2002).

Nomura, T. and Ogiwara, N. (2002) 'Building knowledge-centred organizations', *KM Review* 5(4): 16–19.

Nonaka, I. (1991) 'The knowledge creating company', *Harvard Business Review*, Nov/Dec: 96–104.

Nonaka, I. and Konno, N. (1998) 'The concept of "ba" building a foundation for knowledge creation', *California Management Review* 40(3): 40–54.

Nonaka, I., Toyama, R. and Konno, N. (2000) SECI, ba and leadership: a unified model of dynamic knowledge creation', *Long Range Planning* 33(1): 5–34.

Oliver, D. and Roos, J. (2000) *Striking a Balance: Complexity and Knowledge Landscapes*. Maidenhead: McGraw-Hill.

Owens, D. and Thompson, E. (2001) 'Fusing learning and knowledge at the St. Paul Companies', *Knowledge Management Review* 4(3): 24–9.

Polanyi, M. (1958) *Personal Knowledge: Towards a Post-Critical Philosophy*. Chicago: University of Chicago Press.

Polanyi, M. (1966) *The Tacit Dimension*. London: Routledge and Kegan Paul.

Ray, T. and Little, S. (2001) 'Communication and context: collective tacit knowledge and practice in Japan's workplace ba, *Creativity and Innovation* 10(3): 154–64.

Schramm, J. (2002) 'How do people learn?' London: CIPD.

Snowden, D. (1999) 'Three metaphors, two stories and a picture', *Knowledge Management Review* 1(7): 30–3.

Swap, W., Leonard, D., Shields, M. and Abrams, L. (2001) 'Using mentoring and story telling to transfer knowledge in the workplace', *Journal of Management Information Systems* 18(1): 95–114.

Szulanski, G. (1996) 'Exploring internal stickiness: impediments to the transfer of best practice within the firm', *Strategic Management Journal* 17: 27–43.

van Winkelen, C. and Ramsell, P. (2002) 'Building effective communities', 2nd Annual Conference, Henley KM Forum, Henley Management College, UK.

van Winkelen, C. and Ramsell, P. (2003) 'Aligning value is key to designing communities', *Knowledge Management Review* 5(6): 20–3.

Ventzin, M., von Krogh, G. and Roos, J. (1998) 'Future research into knowledge management', in *Knowing in Firms: Understanding, Managing and Measuring Knowledge* (eds G. von Krogh, J. Roos and D. Kleine), London: Sage.

von Krogh, G. and Roos, J. (1995) *Organizational Epistemology*. Basingstoke: Macmillan.

von Krogh, G., Roos, J. and Slocum, K. (1994) 'An essay on corporate epistemology', *Strategic Management Journal* 15: 53–71.

von Krogh, G. and Vicari, S. (1993) 'An autopoiesis approach to experimental strategic learning', in *Implementing Strategic Processes: Change, Learning and Co-operation* (eds P Lorange, B Chakrvarthy, J. Roos and A. Van de Ven). London: Blackwell, 394–410.

Vygostky, L. (1978) *Mind in Society*, Cambridge, MA: Harvard University Press.

Ward, A. (2000) 'Getting strategic value from constellations of communities', *Strategy and Leadership* 28(2): 4–9.

Wenger, E. (1998) *Communities of Practice: Learning, Meaning and Identity*. Cambridge: Cambridge University Press.

Wenger, E., McDermott, R. and Snyder, W. M. (2002) *Cultivating Communities of Practice*. Boston, MA: Harvard Business School Publishing.

Wenger, E. and Snyder, W. (2000) 'Communities of practice: the organizational frontier', *Harvard Business Review* 78(1): 139–45.

4 Fourth Competence Area
Connecting

Business Challenges

- How can knowledge be a source of influence internally and externally?

- How permeable should organizational boundaries be to knowledge flows?

- Can we use our knowledge to influence the competitive conditions for others?

- What knowledge is critical to protect?

- How do we know which new ideas to absorb?

Introduction

In the first three competence areas, we have been examining the dilemmas that occur primarily inside the Knowledgeable Organization. Clearly it is vital to manage the tensions in knowledge-based activities shaping competitive choices, decision-making and the way we cultivate learning. Yet, although we have identified many practical ways to tap into the potential value of organizational knowledge, focusing on internal choices is not sufficient on its own to assure survival. If competing, deciding and learning are to generate value, they must be linked inextricably to knowledge activity outside the existing boundaries of the firm so we can access knowledge that we cannot create ourselves and shape the competitive environment. This is the subject of our next two competence areas: Connecting and Relating.

The economic environment has changed. Our starting point is to consider why knowledge can create value in more ways than the tangible physical and financial resources that we are used to managing. We will also reconsider where and how we actually establish the boundaries of an organization in the context of knowledge as the main economic driver. How much knowledge can and should flow in and out of our organizations to create value?

Signpost

In *Competence Area 1: Competing* we saw how knowledge can be a source of competitive advantage and how the 'knowledge-based view of the firm' argues that organizations exist primarily to integrate and co-ordinate knowledge into goods and services on a competitive basis.

If the firm is a mechanism for turning knowledge into market value, there are some basic characteristics of knowledge we cannot ignore. One is the fact that, unlike money, knowledge is a commodity that is not in limited supply and generally others can use it at the same time as we do. Competitors and potential new industry entrants have relatively equal opportunities to exploit knowledge resources and combine them into innovative business opportunities. This activity constantly changes the current value of the knowledge base that everyone has. It also provides an opportunity to actively shape conditions for our own organizations and for others, by strategically evaluating knowledge flows around the competitive environment.

In a modern economy where knowledge is the primary source of value creation, an effective knowledge-based strategy needs to focus on more than just tracking our knowledge capabilities against those of our competitors. It should provide insights into how our organizations can both actively shape external knowledge forces and absorb external knowledge to influence internal choices. We need ways to decide how much knowledge from outside our organizations to integrate into our products and services and how much of our own knowledge to disaggregate and share.

The key question is how to capture real environmental influence? When external conditions change, internally-focused knowledge initiatives that help us use what we know more efficiently may only allow us to do the wrong thing 'righter' (Barabba, Pourdehnad and Ackoff, 2002). The cycles of excellence and sudden demise, historically experienced by some organizations, are often caused by clinging to outdated expertise, or because of ignorance of the patterns of external knowledge development. Our organizations need to embed processes and capabilities that help us make sense of the changing knowledge environment. Inevitably this may have a profound effect on the current view of its purpose and identity. The mission, vision, objectives and strategy that normally set the boundaries of our activities may need to evolve too.

Once it was recognized that learning faster than competitors would be the only source of future competitive advantage (De Geus, 1988), learning became a strategic priority for many organizations. In that scenario, delivering above average market returns requires a learning capability that is more than simply innovating faster than the competition. The speed of innovation cannot escalate infinitely. Superior learning capability is about gaining a strategic influence on the dynamics of the knowledge landscape. This is achieved by selectively channelling the right knowledge from the environment into our organizations, whilst simultaneously feeding internal knowledge out to actively shape environmental conditions.

As we open up our organizations to more inward and outward knowledge flows, it seems important to understand how to establish a meaningful boundary with the outside world (Spender, 1996). We need some way to distinguish 'what is in and what is out' in knowledge terms, so that our organizations have meaning and coherence for those associated with them. This may mean rethinking what we mean by boundary. If we define the firm 'as a structure of relationships for creating knowledge, where human experience is a starting point of this process' (von Krogh and Grand, 2002), we have to accept that this boundary is not going to be limited by the legal boundaries of a PLC, partnership or independent trader. Human experience is diverse, far-reaching and constantly changing. Knowledge is fragmented and diffused and creates differential value in different contexts. The boundary of our organizations is really only constrained by the richness of knowledge resources that we seek to integrate for value. Much of that richness is accessible through relationships, whether these are internal or across organizational borders. So in the context of efficient value generation, a knowledge-based strategy also has to include some means of evaluating the kinds of knowledge-generating relationships we need to become involved with. The product of our thinking in this chapter should be an identification of where we need relationships. The following chapter will look at how to manage the external element of those relationships for greatest value.

In the knowledge economy, we suggest that competence to act intelligently in the face of uncertain conditions comes from paying strategic attention to the connections that create knowledge flows into and out of the organization. We need to consciously manage the permeability of our organizations' boundaries to ensure knowledge flows fit our strategic needs. Remembering that flows can take place in both directions, this gives us two key strategic questions to be answered in this chapter:

1 *Outside-In* – How much knowledge can reasonably and efficiently be absorbed from outside and effectively integrated into our organizations to generate greater market value?

2 *Inside-Out* – What influence can be exerted on external conditions by releasing and/or restricting flows of knowledge from inside our organizations into the external environment?

A better understanding of ways to adapt these two flows will help us set the knowledge boundaries of our organizations by focusing strategic knowledge investments to fit activity in the wider business context. Thriving in the knowledge economy needs both capabilities. This only happens if we are consciously aware of the need to develop a unique and flexible strategy to adjust the rate of knowledge flowing in and out of the business to match the level of turbulence in the external competitive environment. Strategy becomes an active process of connecting knowledge flows across the boundaries of our organizations.

Extending our common language: fitness on knowledge landscapes

In this chapter we will continue to use and develop the metaphor of knowledge landscapes that we introduced in Chapter 3 (Oliver and Roos, 2000).

Signpost

In *Competence Area 3: Learning* we looked at how learning changes the shape of both individual and organizational knowledge landscapes. The heights of peaks on the landscapes represent the extent of knowledge about something and the range of the peaks represents the breadth of capability.

Here we will be considering the knowledge landscapes of whole industries, rather than individual organizations. We can look at each landscape as a space of possibilities. Peaks and valleys represent areas of expertise and ignorance respectively. Some organizations dominate certain peaks, but even from the top of these, there are many peaks in the whole terrain that they are not able to see. The higher they have climbed, the greater the depth of knowledge underneath them. Much of this knowledge will have become tacit through long experience. Such knowledge becomes deeply embedded in the organizational context and so is very hard to change. This limits the ability of an organization to compete for different market opportunities (although, equally, it is hard for others to copy).

To reach a peak, an organization has followed a particular learning path by constantly refining its knowledge in context. Specialization has meant appreciating finer and finer distinctions within the subject area. As it nears the real top of a peak, the climb (improvement) becomes harder because there are fewer paths to choose from in terms of further refinements to existing knowledge. As others follow, organizations that find the climb too difficult will fail, but competitors who are similarly thriving in the industry will also be close to the top of a peak. Gradually, the refinements all competitors can make become less valuable and little new knowledge develops, so turbulence in the competitive landscape lessens. The only route to the next major change is through recombination: connecting knowledge from completely different domains to produce something so radically new that it invalidates existing competencies.

We can illustrate this latter situation with an example. National Cash Register, a market leader in the manufacture of mechanical shop tills, faced radical upheaval when electronics capability enabled competitors to emerge, who could produce machines that both registered the cash being paid and captured the data on the daily store takings. At first, the company found it hard to foresee all the benefits of the new technology. It was also difficult to see how to translate its entire knowledge base from one set of competencies to a totally new technology. Moving to electronic registration across its entire product range was a major undertaking, requiring deliberate unlearning and abandonment of what had historically been valuable markets. In time the company was successful and regained its strong market position.

The route that competitors take up each peak on the landscape gives them a unique perspective on a particular area of knowledge. Some routes upwards may be more difficult, producing less value initially but greater value later because the outlook from that side of the peak to other knowledge peaks may have better prospects. Some firms may climb rugged peaks faster because they are 'fitter'. Fitness on knowledge landscapes means having a greater capacity to absorb and act upon new input, because prior knowledge and experience helps progression upwards.

Sometimes the path a firm has chosen leads to a blind alley and sometimes it can be difficult to go back once committed to a route. This leads to path dependency, where commitment to one route precludes exploration of others and narrows the possible perspective on the landscape.

If we think of the landscape as the combined relative value of different areas of knowledge within a domain of commercial activity, then the survival of an organization depends on its ability to recognize and explore the main areas of associated knowledge, but only conquer the peaks where they can deliver most value. Of course others are exploring and climbing too. In taking one path across the space of possibilities, an organization inevitably ignores other routes. This limits its perspective and ability to respond to other signals from the environment. Relative to the competition, an organization's position may be higher or lower in different areas, but by co-operating, it may be possible to raise the 'fitness level' of both companies. How valuable the areas of peak expertise are relative to the competition determines how capable an organization is to survive in the current situation. How well it can explore the knowledge terrain determines how fit it is to thrive overall in the knowledge economy.

How can knowledge be a source of influence?

Since the dynamics of knowledge exchange are very different from those we have been accustomed to in traditional market transactions, we need to start by clarifying the characteristics of knowledge that are the background for strategy design. Our starting point is to recognize that knowledge does not work like money as an economic instrument. Competing through the value of ideas and information, rather than fixed assets and tangible inventory, leads to the means of organizational production being far less stable and much less logically analyzable in terms of cause and effect. Unpredictability has clear implications for economic value generation.

Unlike the money supply, knowledge is not constrained; in fact, the more knowledge is used, the more it multiplies. We know more about the universe, the atom, and the human genetic code than ever before, but it still seems that there is more to learn. It has even been suggested that 'by the year 2010 all of the world's codified knowledge will double every 11 hours' (Bontis, 2001).

No single organization is ever likely to come near to a monopoly on information and knowledge. The inability for anyone to have perfect information and complete knowledge means that economically, adopting a traditional insular, market-driven competitive approach may deliver less overall value than collaborative activity. See Box 4.1 if you are interested in finding out more about how knowledge challenges conventional economic assumptions.

Raw material in the form of data and information becomes valuable knowledge when it is organized in context and linked with complementary knowledge, although each firm may interpret incoming information differently. Whilst the potential for valuable knowledge being created may be infinite, in practice the extent of effective processing capability limits the realization of value that is achieved.

At the business level, if we accept that each individual's knowledge is in a constant state of flux, changing day-by-day as a result of interaction with others and the experience they are gaining in different contexts, then we can see that there can never be a steady state of organizational knowledge assets. Although

Box 4.1

The dynamics of knowledge challenge economic assumptions

In 1990, Alvin Toffler wrote an insightful and comprehensive analysis of the social, commercial and technological impact of knowledge as an economic driver. He suggested that knowledge alters the dynamics of power because, unlike physical force or monetary wealth as sources of influence, knowledge is accessible to the weak and the poor, as well as the rich and the strong. Translated into information, knowledge can be made to flow freely so that anyone can use it to cajole and to bring others to their way of thinking and it does not get used up in the process. The more knowledge is shared, the more it grows. As a result, power is more diffused and its effects are more unpredictable. For example, we see individuals spontaneously unite to form a coherent pressure group that can exert a significant influence on the choices an organization can make.

Having knowledge can both amplify the effect of limited wealth or operational capability, as well as enhance performance efficiency by saving money or unnecessary effort. So knowledge is a versatile resource when used in combination with other complementary tangible assets. It also grows when combined with other knowledge to increase potential. The more we know, the more we can know, creating endless possibilities and infinite diversity.

In some contexts, knowledge is sticky and hard to transfer, which makes the process costly. The master–apprentice relationship is a typical example. In other circumstances knowledge can flow easily. Knowledge codified into a computer programme is costly to develop but cheap to replicate and transfer around the world (Grant, 2002). The difference between sticky and free-flowing knowledge depends on how easy it is to codify the knowledge and how much transferable expertise depends on localized collective knowledge in practice (Spender, 2002).

this continuously developing knowledge base creates infinite potential, it is hard to predict – or even retrospectively make sense of – how knowledge translates into business results.

Within any industry, it also hard to foresee how the potential of ideas and knowledge will translate into reality. Will there be sustainable returns from a particular innovation? Will an idea be adopted or ignored? Often, this depends on how well it fits with legacy knowledge that is precious to the organizations in the industry. The 'not invented here' syndrome can be very powerful. Generally, less that 10 per cent of ideas translate into profitable activity and this is further reduced by competitive activity, which can make new ideas redundant before they can deliver value. For example, at the present time, research into fuel cell technology is rapidly moving down several alternative routes. The type of cell that is ultimately adopted is likely to generate huge returns for its owners if the potential value of the technology can be realized in many different markets. However, there are large risks for investors developing the industry, because those knowledge advances that are rejected will incur similar development costs, but potentially have little commercial value.

With such uncertainty associated with knowledge assets, a flexible response that spreads risk is a key capability for firms in a knowledge economy. We must try to make sense of the various developments in the light of past history and future potential. Timing is critical in the development and application of any knowledge.

At an industry level, although knowledge is a versatile and accessible resource, its characteristics can also have disadvantages. From a control perspective, we need to remember that knowledge is not consumed with use. In most cases the same knowledge can be used to advantageous ends as well as damaging ones. It is important to take steps to ensure that detrimental use does not spread further than we would like, and we do this by protecting knowledge that can be used to undermine the security of our position.

This all leads to the conclusion that we cannot afford to be mentally cut off from knowledge activity outside the current boundaries of our organizations. Meaningful strategic decisions about our knowledge base can only be taken in the context of the knowledge developments of others travelling across the same knowledge landscape and we must remember that many of our competitors may be in distant parts of the world. If others are more active in research than we are, then we are at risk of becoming 'less fit' to progress across the landscape than they are. Their responsiveness to environmental changes is likely to be higher and their flexibility greater.

However, there needs to be a trade-off if we do not want to be overwhelmed by too much knowledge. Learning is a costly process and no business can afford to internalize all the knowledge it might need. Complex products like airplanes, for example, are massive agglomerations of technical knowledge, the cost of which could not reasonably be amortised over the production capacity of one corporation (Brusoni, Prencipe and Pavitt, 2001).

Reflecting on these economic characteristics of knowledge, we can identify three ways in which we can gain influence from connecting knowledge flows across the boundaries of our organizations. First, simultaneous possession of knowledge offers the potential of increasing returns; second, the knowledge base of an industry co-evolves, so collaboration can increase the success of all; finally, increasing absorptive capacity means that the more knowledge we have, the more we can take on board and the more value we can generate. We will look at each of these mechanisms in turn.

Some knowledge activities produce increasing returns

Knowledge that can flow easily can sometimes produce greater value if we deliberately release control over it. Put simply, increasing returns is based on the idea of a positive feedback system, a kind of a snowball effect. The bigger or more knowledgeable the organization, the more knowledge it can accrue. Alternatively, the more an organization dissipates knowledge, the more value that knowledge can potentially create. See Box 4.2 for a discussion of the economic basis for the idea of increasing returns.

The implications are important. First, the more an organization uses knowledge and skills, the more likely it is that it will become even more knowledgeable and effective. Second, first-mover advantages can produce significant value if the first organization to have the knowledge makes it widely available and can lock customers or suppliers into a particular way of operating. Early wide-scale usage can lead to long-term advantage, which can subsequently be re-enforced through incremental innovations in the future.

The concept of increasing returns has a number of implications for knowledge-based strategies.

Making learning a priority increases business potential. Companies with a reputation for investing in people and their individual knowledge reap returns above and beyond the value generating potential of each individual because the firm becomes better placed to retain and recruit the most knowledgeable people. Increasing returns apply to learning. The more we learn, the more we can learn.

 Signpost In *Competence Area 3: Learning* we saw that knowledge workers are attracted by the opportunity to develop their expertise through participation in progressive communities of practice.

Knowledge generation may be expensive, but reproduction is cheap and easy. The usual pattern of returns on investment in tangible assets is an increase followed by a steady decline. This can be replaced by a continuous upward trend for knowledge products such as software since the cost of producing each incremental item reduces to near zero. This allows us to play with different time scales for return on investment. If the product increases in desirability as more people have it, then increasing returns can lead to 'snowballing'. The upward trend does assume that sufficient protection of the initial investment is possible so that the product cannot be copied without some form of royalty payment, a problem which the music industry is currently grappling with. Increasing returns combined with protection can amplify the benefits of knowledge exploitation.

Box 4.2

Increasing returns: getting more from owning less

The idea of increasing returns is based on the opposite premise to traditional economic assumptions about decreasing returns. Decreasing returns assumes that raw material supply is limited and the means to produce it have a limited life. Marketplaces are efficient ways of distributing such scarce resources.

Traditionally, an organization has expected to serve its survival interests best by protecting its assets and capturing large market shares as quickly as possible. The idea is to maximize profits before decreasing utility of a product, competitor's copies or a decline in the means of production reduces the returns from a particular activity to uneconomic levels and the market declines. Classical economics assumes markets move to an equilibrium point because people respond predictably and identically so action and reaction can be rationally determined.

None of these assumptions apply specifically to knowledge, although some may apply to knowledge in combination with tangible assets. A basic principle of the increasing returns concept is that value does not come from discrete tangible products but from the accumulation of intangible benefits over time. It also arises because of what are called network effects. This is when the benefits gained from using basic information and knowledge multiply as more people use it (for example, e-mail technology became more useful as more people got email accounts). Given the ease and speed with which information and some knowledge can travel across the globe, value can snowball when users attract more users.

Taking advantage of the increasing returns principle is a four-step process (Arthur, 1990):

- Target an underdeveloped market.
- Create initial leverage of the value of the knowledge by making it widely accessible to others at low costs.
- Connect 'autonomous agents' that is, the users, consumers and other potentially interested parties, who may exploit and add to the knowledge, amplifying the positive feedback loop.
- Lock everyone in until usage becomes the standard.

Microsoft is the most commonly cited example of the benefits of increasing returns. The Microsoft Windows™ operating system has become ubiquitous and the company reaps the returns of the activities of many other firms that develop applications that run on its system (Aley, 1996).

Sometimes knowledge can prove to be more valuable if you give it away. A well-known example of the value of making knowledge available in order to set the industry standard is the case of domestic video recorders. Sony protected the 'know-how' around their Betamax video technology, whereas VHS technology was available to anyone to produce under licence. More users of VHS video machines led to more demand for VHS films recorded onto videotapes. The availability of this format of videotaped film led to more demand for VHS recorders. This was a form of positive amplifying feedback that resulted in the establishment of an industry standard, despite many people believing that the Betamax technology was superior. Increasing returns applies to strategic knowledge-sharing.

Detrimental knowledge flows as fast as positive knowledge. If value is generated through the independent and unpredictable action of thinking (autonomous people responding to knowledge flows), then it follows that the flows can escalate to produce detrimental knowledge about a business, as well as positive perceptions. For example, a dissatisfied customer-user group communicating with one another through access to the Internet can quickly destroy brand value. Strategically, we need to take rapid action to minimize the increasing returns to competitors from flows of damaging knowledge about our organizations' products or services. Fortunately, research suggests that a prompt and empathetic response to dissatisfaction can actually work in our favour in the long term. Satisfying once dissatisfied customers can generate strong customer loyalty.

Trust and relationships are essential mechanisms to co-ordinate and regulate knowledge flows. Markets regulate flows of resources through price, but as we have seen, increasing returns suggests that lowering the price can sometimes produce greater long-term value from knowledge flows. Hierarchical structures in organizations tend to regulate resource flows in the firm through authority, but in the case of knowledge, concentrating access to knowledge constrains the ability of the firm to respond to rapidly changing external market conditions.

 In *Competence Area 2: Deciding* we saw that diverse knowledge resources need to be widely accessible throughout the organization for effective distributed decision-making.

Knowledge works best in an open environment where trust regulates the flow and individual people assess and monitor the utility of these flows based on their willingness to trust the source or the recipient. There can be both decreasing and increasing returns to trust (Adler, 2001). Valuable trust tends to build over a long period of time in relationships that develop based on shared values rather than contractual commitment. The increasing returns to trust and relationships take the form of exponentially increasing tacit knowledge-sharing. Decreasing returns take over if the trust is fragile and uncertainty blocks knowledge-sharing behaviours.

 In *Competence Area 5: Relating* we see that enduring alliances depend on trust. Sustaining increasing returns from this sort of social capital is central to the value an alliance can deliver.

Co-evolving knowledge shapes environmental conditions

To understand co-evolution we need to return to our metaphor of the fitness of organizations progressing across the knowledge landscapes of their industries. So far we have described these landscapes as if they are relatively static, slowly changing as organizations learn and develop new knowledge peaks. In reality, the contours are continuously shifting, changing the basis for decision-making and constantly unsettling apparently well-formed strategies.

Knowledge has an important impact on an organization's ability to perform successfully, but that performance is also intimately connected to the knowledge dynamics at the industry level (Sanchez, 2002) and the country level (Lewin, Long and Carroll, 1999). Strategic thinking in the knowledge economy involves finding a way of balancing on a highly unstable knowledge landscape co-created through the behaviour of the players in an industry, often on a global scale. See Box 4.3 to find out more about co-evolution as a mechanism behind the 'survival of the fittest'.

Box 4.3

Understanding co-evolution as a factor in 'survival of the fittest'
The landscape metaphor is well established as a way of understanding complex flows of resources amongst interdependent and competing species in nature. Scientists use the notion of fitness landscapes to map and simulate the effect of relationships on the performance of biological systems; for example, how the interaction between populations of different animals affects the survival rate of each (Oliver and Roos, 2000). From this they have learned much about how populations evolve together. Generally, the fate of one species cannot be dissociated from the development of another and they co-evolve, becoming fitter or not so fit as a result of their interactions.

Co-evolution has been described as a powerful form of learning, but at the system rather than individual level (Battram, 1998). We can apply the idea to organizations since there is a level of mutual adaptation that occurs during the learning activity of different organizations, even though the intentions of each are not the same. The impact of collective action is seen in the rate of technological or knowledge-based change that we have to respond to. Survival depends on the intelligence of our response to developments and whether this increases our fitness to progress on the knowledge landscape relative to others.

Unfortunately, even if we do this well, the idea of 'survival of the fittest' does not mean that our own organizations will actually survive, simply that the industry will perform better as a whole. On a more positive note, the fitter an industry becomes, the less rugged the landscape that we each have to traverse, because there is less that can make a real difference.

The more knowledge activity there is in an industry, the harder it is to explore comprehensively the space of possibilities, identify where the gaps are and decide how long the returns from knowledge exploitation will be sustainable. A complex interactive pattern of forces shapes an organization's ability to deliver value from knowledge resources. The purpose of strategy is to see the pattern in what is happening and take action to intervene in the knowledge flows that are creating these patterns. We need to plan for a continuous journey across a shifting knowledge landscape in a kind of adaptive walk, learning as we go and adjusting to the turbulence.

Studies show that thriving organizations adjust the level of innovative activity and new knowledge creation to match the rate of change in the environment (Brown and Eisenhardt, 1997). The more unbounded external knowledge activity there is, the faster we have to adapt to our neighbour's activity; sometimes those neighbours may not even be competing directly yet.

Signpost In *Competence Area 1: Competing* we saw that long-term survival depends on combining enough knowledge exploitation to sustain current viability, with enough knowledge exploration and radical innovation to ensure future viability.

What co-evolution tells us is that the balance between knowledge exploitation and knowledge exploration activities needs to be adjusted depending on the overall level of knowledge development in the industry and in associated technologies. How willing we are to explore the knowledge landscape depends on the intensity of the external triggers and where they come from (Zahra and George, 2002). A crisis tends to trigger greater willingness to explore, acquire and internalize external knowledge than do gradual external developments (Kim, 1988). Government policy is likely to be perceived as a greater force for change than unco-ordinated consumer opinion, although active and co-ordinated consumer demand can be a very powerful trigger. It also depends on the relative cost of coming down from one knowledge peak and climbing up another, the cost of unlearning being quite high in complex products because knowledge is often interrelated. If responses to triggers remain instinctive, our organizations risk being slow and unfit to respond to significant threats. Conscious awareness of the issues as we make strategic plans is a first step to avoiding the pitfalls.

There are a number of implications to keep in mind as we develop knowledge-based strategies:

- The knowledge landscape is far larger than we can ever explore alone.
- The route we choose affects the view we have of the world and indeed the view we can have of it.
- We are often unaware of what there is still to know because local peaks can obscure our view.
- Fitness relative to others can be assessed by how many knowledge peaks we have efficiently integrated into business activity.

- Capturing any knowledge peak will only provide temporary dominance.
- The faster the knowledge landscape is changing, the faster we need to cross the landscape to survive and the fitter we will become.
- The fitter we are and the faster we learn, the better able we are to influence the knowledge landscape.
- The fitter we are, the more attractive we will be to others, so the less we may have to invest internally to enhance our access to new knowledge.
- The members of our landscape evolve together as a result of mutual interaction, and these interactions simultaneously change the landscape.

Later in this chapter we will look at a matrix that prompts us to systematically explore the knowledge landscape.

It is worth noting that co-evolutionary effects can also apply inside organizations when communities of practice interact to redefine their collective knowledge landscape.

In *Competence Area 3: Learning* we saw that communities of practice can be used to connect the knowledge landscapes of individual employees with those of an organization. We also saw the importance of connecting communities of practice to create 'constellations'.

Different types of knowledge lead to different rates of co-evolution. Peaks based on explicit knowledge are relatively easy to climb. In contrast, tacit knowledge cannot be readily codified and progressing up a peak that is based on tacit knowledge takes time and considerable investment. Ultimately, however, tacit knowledge provides greater potential for long-term business value because it tends to be more widely applicable to different circumstances, creates greater differentiation and is easier to protect (Boisot, 1998).

Building absorptive capacity increases competitive fitness

To notice and assimilate new knowledge, we need to be able to see its relevance. Looking at external knowledge, we need to see the connection between its potential and the way we realize value from knowledge within our organizations. Making these connections can only happen if our organizations have the right knowledge base on which to build. The broader the internal knowledge landscape, the more connections we can make outside, but ultimately the more expensive it becomes to integrate more new connections.

The steps we can take across our knowledge landscape are influenced by the relevance of our past experience, the perspectives that we have from where we are and the spare resources we have available to allow us to explore. Fitness to climb a knowledge peak depends on absorptive capacity. This is both the level of prior related knowledge and the capacity to recognize and accept new connections, which together shape our ability to absorb new knowledge. In general, absorptive capacity gives our organizations evolutionary and discriminatory capability. It works best when supported by a foundation of common knowledge: the shared meaning, language, beliefs and values that simplify the communication processes between people.

 Signpost   In *Competence Area 2: Deciding* we saw that we all have unarticulated background knowledge that we take for granted. This 'common knowledge' determines what we see as acceptable and creates a basis for the meaning that we give to the words and actions of others.

There are two key facets of absorptive capacity (Zahra and George, 2002).

Potential – the acquisition and assimilation of potentially useful knowledge. This process is usually triggered by internal or external stimuli such as crises, performance failures, technology shifts or government policy. Acquisition is largely at the level of explicit knowledge, though assimilation requires some tacit knowledge. Potential absorptive capacity produces breadth of perspective, depends on opportunistic strategy, competitive intelligence that can be translated into realizable change and a strong learning culture. Enhancing it is important for the innovative orientation that is part of competing effectively.

Realized – the realization of knowledge value by transforming potential knowledge into operational capability. Long-term returns are realized through efficient knowledge exploitation requiring extensive tacit knowledge and the development of core competencies that can be translated into distinctive operational capabilities to deliver competitive advantage. Realizing value from this aspect of absorptive capacity requires strong social integration mechanisms and the reduction of structural, cultural and behavioural barriers that might hinder knowledge integration.

In Figure 4.1 we can see how these two facets of absorptive capacity influence the internal knowledge landscape of our organizations and also create the capacity to influence the knowledge landscape of the industry.

The balance of strategic investment between potential and realized absorptive capacity depends on our organizational contexts. The balance needs to take into account:

- The cost of building absorptive capacity relative to the potential for market returns.
- Competitors' activity in building absorptive capacity (their learning capability).
- The strength of the dominant logic within the business and how that pushes us towards consistency and unity, rather than turmoil, during change.
- The need to secure or protect against uncertainty and risk.

The most efficient use of knowledge is when the internal knowledge domains of our organizations fit perfectly with the knowledge needed for products and

Figure 4.1 Absorptive capacity as a source of influence (adapted from Zahra and George, 2002)

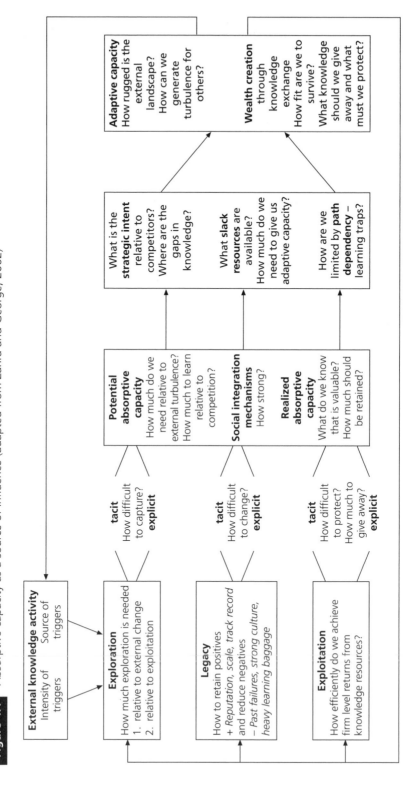

services, with no overlap or under-utilization or wastage of knowledge (Grant, 2002). Clearly, that is an ideal that may be hard to achieve, but nevertheless strategically it is an important objective.

Integrating the sources of influence

Having looked at three ways in which knowledge is a source of internal and external influence in the knowledge economy, we can now see that making commercial sense of knowledge flows is a cyclical process that requires us to proactively integrate knowledge into our organization, retrospectively notice actions and outcomes that work well, and finally interpret them to create meaning (Sanchez, 2002) through the cycle of competing, deciding and learning described in earlier chapters. We have summarized these ideas in Figure 4.2.

Doing this well requires calculated discrimination regarding which knowledge flows to allow into our organizations, as well as calculated judgments regarding which knowledge to dissipate outside. The basis for this calculation is what knowledge the business can and should absorb to optimize business value, together with which knowledge to dissipate to leverage the potential of increasing returns or shape competitive relationships.

Figure 4.2   The knowledge activities of firms in the knowledge economy

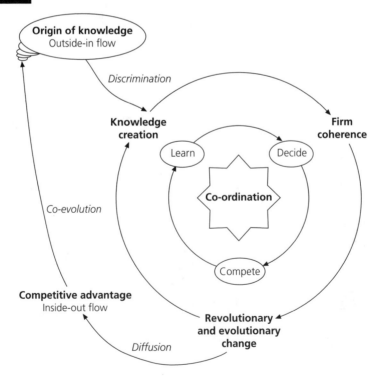

We can distil these ideas down into four areas of strategic focus represented in the boxes of Figure 4.3. In the right-hand column, we think about what is as yet unknown to our organizations that has potential to deliver value when we:

1 Improve competitive status by reducing the blind spots.
2 Innovate through products and services that expand into untapped markets.

In the left-hand column we consider what value can be generated from what is already known to our organizations when we:

3 Protect knowledge that can earn more by keeping it inside the business, either because it is unique or because it is superior to that of competitors.
4 Deliberately dissipate it to enable the development of complementary products, establish dominant standards or capture critical user mass, taking advantage of network effects and increasing returns.

Together these form 'The Window of Knowledge Opportunities' that can be used to evolve and review strategies targeted at translating knowledge into value. Evaluating knowledge competence through the panes of this window allows us to prioritize strategic investments that are appropriate for thriving in the knowledge economy.

Figure 4.3   The Window of Knowledge Opportunities

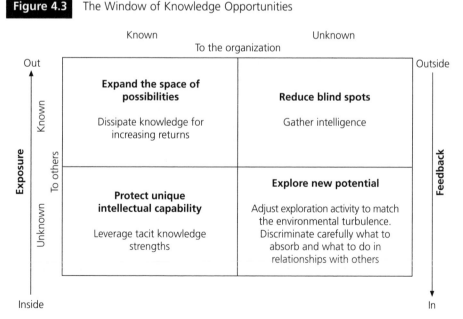

Returning to the two strategic questions that we set earlier, we can use 'The Window of Knowledge Opportunities' to understand what we need to do in practice to pay attention to:

Outside-in knowledge flows (the two right-hand panes of the window). What can our organizations do to develop appropriate discrimination so that we integrate the most valuable feedback from the knowledge economy into business operations?

Inside-out knowledge flows (the two left-hand panes of the window). What can our organizations do to control dissipative activity so we can actively influence external conditions in our favour?

We will now look at each of these flows in turn, starting with the knowledge flow from outside the organization inwards.

Paying strategic attention to 'outside-in' knowledge flows

If strategy is about charting a course to achieve a superior position in a competitive knowledge landscape and that landscape is shaped by the sum of the knowledge activity of all players in the industry, then mapping the terrain is a good place for us to start. This helps us to know what knowledge is available externally and how it fits with internal capabilities (Huizing and Wim, 2002; Zack, 2002). We can then make more informed decisions about our knowledge investments.

Mapping the terrain often starts with mapping what our organization already knows, but it should extend to mapping competitors' knowledge too if it is going to highlight real gaps. A knowledge audit is a useful starting point, as long as we keep in mind that we will never be able to produce a complete picture.

 Signpost

In *Competence Area 1: Competing* we saw that mapping the core, advanced and innovative knowledge resources of our organizations can be a useful starting point to identify internal and external knowledge gaps.

Having identified some of the most obvious knowledge gaps, we need to access external knowledge where it already exists but is currently unknown within our organizations: effectively this is a current blind spot. We also need to develop new knowledge, possibly in collaboration with others, to fill knowledge gaps that have significant value creating potential. We will start by looking at how to reduce the likelihood of important external knowledge lying in a blind spot area and then move on to look at exploring new knowledge potential.

Reduce blind spots

Blind spots are the areas of knowledge that are known to others but which we do not know, or even recognize as valuable and worth knowing. Three things cause blind spots:

1 Too much introspection and overconfidence.

2 Insufficient absorptive capacity to notice or act on what might be important.

3 Too little environmental scanning.

Remedying the first requires a change of dominant logic and culture while remedying the second requires organizational development and a learning environment. We have already explored these areas in depth earlier in the book.

 In *Competence Area 2: Deciding* we saw how dominant logic and culture affect an organization's ability to recognize the importance of external information. We also saw some ways in which these can both be adjusted over time.

 In *Competence Area 3: Learning* we explored ways to encourage the development of a learning environment.

The third can be resolved by putting in place appropriate mechanisms to increase environmental scanning. Table 4.1 shows the three main approaches that can make a difference to our organizations.

Introducing external knowledge to challenge current thinking is also important for building potential absorptive capacity. It helps us notice patterns in what is becoming important to customers and competitors and prevent us developing blind spots in the future. Ways to do this include:

Adopting competitive technologies. Companies in rapidly changing technology businesses may need deliberately to set up development projects that present direct challenges to existing products, even through they could potentially destroy current market strengths. For example, Hewlett Packard set up an inkjet printer division despite having a strong laser printer business.

Comparing practices. Benchmarking and best practice audits challenge thinking about processes and supply chain management. Employing people who have worked for competitors can provide insights into where a company is vulnerable and where competitors have limited knowledge, though ethical and legal considerations are also important here.

Collecting intelligence about competitors. Competitor intelligence focusing on what competitors know, rather on what they do or are planning to do is particularly useful (Zack, 2002). We can challenge complacent thinking in our organizations by linking the output of competitor intelligence activities with the learning from customer relationship management systems and relating these to our knowledge strategies.

Participating in intelligence networks. The more turbulent the economic environment, the more connections we need with the outside world to keep up-to-date. Participating widely in external fora such as industry associations, communities of interest and trade fairs helps create an intelligence network (Huizing and Wim, 2002). Additionally, various forms of alliances, such as joint

Table 4.1 Scanning for blind spots

Potential blind spot	Mechanisms to increase environmental scanning	Example
Customers and markets	• Build strong relationships with customers and channel their feedback to the creative part of the organization to identify unfulfilled needs and new opportunities.	Host online customer communities that are facilitated by R&D personnel with a brief to look for new ideas. DoCoMo, Japan's largest mobile telephone carrier, used customer communities as one key element in the development of its 'i'mode' strategy (moving the market from portable phones to information terminals) (Kodama, 2002).
Suppliers and other stakeholders	• Strengthen links to key suppliers and involve them in R&D. • Establish shareholder groups and link communities of interest across companies.	Toshiba maintained an active network and association of validated suppliers with the deliberate intent that knowledge sharing should alter strategy (Skyrme, 1988).
Macro and competitive environment trends	• Systematic evaluation of political, economic, social, technological and environmental changes. • Formalize competitor intelligence activities. • Active membership of market intelligence networks and industry fora.	SmithKlineBeecham created an online library that gave research scientists instant access to market updates, patent scanning and environmentally relevant data (Skyrme, 1988). Lincoln Re, a medical insurance provider in the US, scanned research in the medical arena to gain early signals of anything that may affect mortality and risk management in their products (Zack, 2002).

ventures or contractual relationships with consultants, academics and external knowledge workers, provide new perspectives.

 Signpost   In *Competence Area 5: Relating* we will look at how to use loose associations with many organizations to provide access to a broad range of knowledge resources.

External knowledge creates value only when it is applied, that is, translated from potential to realized absorptive capacity (Zahra and George, 2002). Once we have acknowledged the potential of what has been assimilated from outside, the efficiency with which it can be integrated is important. This depends on both the scope of the existing knowledge foundation on which the new knowledge will be built and on the flexibility of our organizations in reconfiguring embedded practices and processes to respond to the new knowledge. Blind spots will persist if we are too busy to take on new ideas, or too tied up in refining our existing knowledge to make time to reflect on the value of new ideas. Training, coaching and mentoring can all be used to develop the absorptive capacity of individuals in the organization, increasing their ability to makes sense of and recognize the importance of new knowledge.

The second way knowledge flows into our organizations and becomes a source of influence on our activities is a consequence of opportunistic prospecting to find valuable untapped knowledge domains.

Explore for potentially valuable new knowledge

Scanning for knowledge that is new to our organizations and to others in the industry is difficult and tends to have highly unpredictable results. Rather than incrementally developing knowledge peaks, it involves taking large leaps into new areas of the industry knowledge landscape. This capability depends on correlating ideas and combining knowledge from diverse sources into novel business opportunities.

 Signpost   In *Competence Area 1: Competing* we saw that in general the knowledge creation cycle involves progressive conversion of tacit knowledge to explicit knowledge and back again as insights are shared, articulated, evaluated and prototypes developed.

There are some tools that we can use to help develop our capability to draw upon external knowledge in this way.

Data mining. Data mining is a scientific way of finding patterns in volumes of data. Retailers with loyalty cards, credit card companies and Internet-based businesses such as Amazon all have a wealth of data about customers' purchases and tastes. Data mining offers the opportunity to generate insights that perhaps customers individually are not even aware of. Such insights can lead to new products or services.

Identifying missing markets. Missing markets exist where there is no established link between potential suppliers willing to supply at an acceptable price and customers willing to pay that price. Brainstorming can be used to determine how new configurations of suppliers and customers could serve a currently unfulfilled need (Borg, 2001).

Scenario planning. Scenario planning is a way of prospectively making sense of knowledge potential by exploring alternative futures in an orderly manner. Scenarios are plausible and internally consistent stories about possible futures that enable an organization to react more quickly and adapt faster to changes in the knowledge landscape because possible responses have been foreseen. The oil company Shell was an early user of scenarios. They developed two types: framework scenarios that produced far-ranging stories about potential background activities of stakeholders in the oil, gas and chemical industry; and project scenarios that explored in more depth issues such as the impact of possible wars (Stopford, 2001). Scenarios act as a valuable challenge to organizational dominant logic, creating openness to change and generating new ideas by showing the potential impact of trends.

Collaborative innovation. Participating in joint ventures and other forms of alliances with partners who have complementary knowledge creates the opportunity for new knowledge to be created and spreads investment risk.

Technology scanning. Strategic threats come from technological discontinuities in peripheral markets or ones outside the industry (Utterback, 1994). Regularly reviewing patent applications can provide early warning signals, as can participating in technology fora to help understand the implications of the key trends.

Paying attention to the organizational context for knowledge exploration is also important. Historically, positive experiences of innovation create a climate in which people are more open to new ideas. Negative experiences encourage reactivity or passivity. Some years ago, the food producer Heinz had a run of unsuccessful innovations (McKenzie and Reynolds, 1997). For several years, fear of making more costly mistakes led them to abandon the search for new opportunities. When the market suddenly became highly competitive with the introduction of value brands of baked beans, they recognized that innovation was vital to survival. Their first steps were very tentative and significantly constrained by the legacy of past experience. The climate was not conducive to rapid innovation and getting investment funds to translate the new ideas into manufactured products was something of an uphill struggle.

Core rigidities develop from such experiences and can limit the way we prospectively make sense of the world. Signals from outside will be either rejected as irrelevant or incorrectly interpreted when filtered through the prejudice of past experience. For example, if a knowledge peak was costly or painful to command, there will be more resistance to letting it go.

 Signpost In *Competence Area 1: Competing* we saw how core capabilities in one context can become core rigidities in another. Unlearning is difficult as existing knowledge gets in the way of new knowledge.

Studies of firms in the computer industry provide evidence of the problems this can cause (Afuah, 2001). When workstation technology moved from CISC microprocessors (complex instruction sets designed to minimize slow expensive memory usage) to a RISC microprocessor architecture (simpler, reduced instructions sets designed to be faster and more flexible), DEC (Digital Equipment Corporation) were so focused on the value of past knowledge that they ignored a vital market opportunity. Technological expertise had become a core rigidity rather than a competitive advantage. Both their CISC workstation group and the CISC microprocessor group denied the potential benefits of RISC. Business processes and routines were so embedded in the old technology which both groups had developed, that they discounted the advantages of processors with simple instruction sets over complex instruction sets. They also ignored vital intelligence about the other changes in the market, for example, the activities of Sun Microsystems and Hewlett Packard. It was not until DEC started to lose loyal customers to Sun's RISC technology that they took notice of the signals.

Sun's strategy was particularly successful because it combined the decision to internalize knowledge about new microprocessor technology with the opportunity to leverage the benefits of increasing returns. Having designed the SPARC (Scalable Processor Architecture) microprocessor, they licensed the knowledge to anyone who wanted to make chips. Subsequently, they created an independent business to license the workstation technology to other manufacturers. In so doing, they created a sort of consortium, which had several value-creating benefits. Members could tap into the learning of other members because their workstations were compatible. The more members with compatible workstations there were, the more attractive it was for software developers to write applications for these workstations and hence the more valuable workstations became to customers.

Although DEC ultimately developed its own very fast microprocessor, which had the advantage of incorporating learning from others' mistakes, the firm never regained its market position in the face of Sun's more effective knowledge strategy (Afuah, 2001).

Develop the capacity to discriminate

An important aspect of paying attention to the flow of external knowledge into our organizations is the capability to discriminate what to absorb. Sufficient stability is needed to prevent any organization being torn apart by too much novelty. Discrimination is necessary to sustain a sense of organizational identity, but in a turbulent market place the form of that identity needs to be evaluated strategically rather than created accidentally by core rigidities.

Two broad approaches to discrimination have been suggested (Stopford, 2001):

Action driven to test the market response to ideas. Experiments, R&D investments and commitments designed to pro-actively influence the external environment in a particular way, such as educating clients, advertising or forming alliances to protect a market area.

Belief-driven to assess the fit internally. Evaluation of the possible opportunity against the collection of shared beliefs, values and social capital that determine the operation of an organization.

How an organization chooses to do this very much depends on the path it has taken to where it is now. Simultaneous evaluation on both fronts is a good way to detect the strength of signals and find patterns in external activities.

It has also been suggested that adopting a marketing orientation is one way of combining the flexibility to adopt new opportunities with the need to protect organizational identity (Christensen 1995). Using brand and reputation to discriminate 'what's in' and 'what's out' of the organization allows for a more fluid and commercially relevant boundary to our organizations.

Brand may be a rather nebulous concept, but it can have a powerful drawing power providing a tightly encapsulated representation of what an organization knows best about:

> Brands have tangible and intangible characteristics. They simplify decision-making and provide security in consumer choice concerning the quality of the product, value for money and consistency. They also have emotional characteristics which appeal to the self-image of consumers and their aspirations and fantasies. Brand 'personalities' accumulate over time, and are embedded in particular cultures or associated with a particular set of values, such as heritage or images associated with a certain region or country.
>
> *Da Silva Lopes, 2002*

Building brand recognition has had a particularly marked effect in the alcoholic beverage industry. Loyal customers have built up strong emotional attachments to favourite brands over many years, making it hard to change drinking patterns and market share. The result is that individual brands have become almost a commodity, an intangible asset that can be traded to increase organizational value. Diageo, the company formed in 1997 as a result of the merger of Guinness and Grand Metropolitan, provides us with a clear example of how brands can be used to decide 'what is in' and 'what is out'.

Diageo made brands the basis of the competitive advantage of the company, effectively the core of a knowledge-based strategy. The company set out with the intent of leveraging 'an ability to build global drinks brands and it created an organization that allowed it to extract value from that ability' (Birkinshaw, 2002).

That intent initially drove its acquisitions and divestiture strategy; for example, it bought the drinks company Seagram and sold Pilsbury and Burger King, both food companies. It established a 'Diageo way of Brand Building' based on deep knowledge of consumer needs and the deliberate structuring of the whole organization around the expertise and potential required to build brands. The strategy was to launch the brands in lead markets (US, UK, Ireland and Spain) and test the consistency of the brand image, roll them out into fourteen 'key' markets and then, if successful, to areas they dubbed as 'venture' markets. The success of this approach is evidenced in the new Ready to Drink (RTD) brands, such as Smirnoff Ice, which by 2002 had sold fifteen billion bottles, most of which have taken share away from the beer market – traditionally a place where the original Smirnoff Vodka could not compete.

The practical approaches that we have discussed in this section are familiar to many organizations. However, we suggest that seeing them in the context of strategic action to influence the rate of 'outside-in' knowledge flow is possibly a new perspective. We need to reorient strategic thinking in our organizations towards how much external knowledge to absorb and discuss widely how much influence to allow it to have in triggering internal change. We have seen that developing this area of competence may mean long-held assumptions that are no longer relevant need to be abandoned and knowledge that has delivered significant returns in the past has to be updated.

Paying strategic attention to 'inside-out' knowledge flows

Now we will move on to look at how our organizations can adjust knowledge flows from inside to outside to shape the pattern of activities in the competitive environment.

> A critical skill for the knowledge-based firm will be to know what to share and what to hold on to. Recognizing when knowledge should be actively diffused to outsiders rather than hoarded, when it can be used to extend the firm's organizational reach beyond its boundaries will become an important source of competitive advantage.
>
> *Boisot, 1998*

We are now focusing on what is involved in evaluating knowledge through the left-hand panes in The Window of Knowledge Opportunities (Figure 4.3). These represent knowledge that is known to our organizations, but which may or may not be known to our competitors. We will start by looking at the opportunities that come from dissipating organizational knowledge widely and then move on to look at the situations when it is more appropriate to protect knowledge and stop it becoming known to others.

Identify knowledge that could be worth more if you give it away

Generally, we know that organizations with more aggressive knowledge strategies innovate more, keep exploring opportunities and reducing their blind spots: as a result, they tend to outperform their more conservative competitors (Bierly and Chakrabati, 1996). What is even more interesting is that aggressive firms also deliberately let their knowledge flow outside the organizational boundaries to accelerate their own learning cycle (Spender, 2002).

An organization with an above-average learning capacity can turn this capability to significant advantage by leaking explicit knowledge into the marketplace and deliberately increasing turbulence on the knowledge landscape of the industry. A strong culture and an attractive working environment keep staff turnover low and ensure that its own tacit knowledge stays intact. It can also leverage its learning capability to re-absorb changes quickly as competitors respond, creating chains of products (Helfat and Raibitschek, 2002).

In general, an organization may need to be careful about how much knowledge it releases, but by leaking enough to create a 'knowledge dependency' and protecting certain knowledge in-house, it can gain significant influence in the marketplace. Organizations that franchise parts of their business, but retains dependencies in other areas are one example.

IKEA, the Swedish furniture manufacturer, has demonstrated the rapid growth potential that can come from being able to duplicate knowledge and extend its use beyond the existing boundaries of the firm (von Krogh and Cusumano, 2001). Between 1984 and 1999, sales grew by more than 600 per cent and they extended their presence into 25 countries, with 50 000 employees worldwide. This was achieved by a mix of franchising and direct investment in new stores set up from scratch with entirely new staff on greenfield sites. IKEA chose retailing as a safe area for knowledge transfer to franchisees, keeping more strategic knowledge areas in-house. The package of knowledge to be transferred was the same whether they were franchising retail activities or setting them up from scratch themselves. It involved a deliberately-balanced mix of standardization by codifying practices to exploit existing knowledge, and adaptation by changing the processes to suit the local requirements.

The knowledge transfer relied on a combination of 'black-boxing' and personal expertise. The former allowed practical knowledge to flow outwards easily, the latter mechanism became a way to ensure knowledge flowed back into the hub of operations. 'Black boxes' were:

> critical data at various levels of detail in ready-to-use form, such as written or online manuals or video presentations . . . A single black box at one level of detail may help in establishing a new subsidiary in a new territory. It might include checklists on choosing a site, using legal counsel, selecting and training personnel, laying out a store and purchasing manuals. A box at another level might include detailed instructions on how to service clients outside business hours or how to set up a store-maintenance program.
>
> *von Krogh and Cusumano, 2001*

To replicate its recipe across Europe, the company set up a dedicated expansion group whose task was to buy land, hire people and co-ordinate the construction of the new outlet and its decor. Once the major construction was complete, a first-year operations group would take over. Their task was to co-ordinate training and store opening and to get things running. Finally, IKEA would hand over to a local in-country organization to continue running the business. Although initially most senior managers remained Swedish or spoke the mother tongue, IKEA also gradually trained local managers in some areas.

IKEA used a group known as the 'Knowledge Marines', as a central human repository of know-how about international expansion. The Knowledge Marines became the custodians of entrepreneurial knowledge developed at each new site. Their job was to make this accessible to all new operations. Gradually, they learned to 'black box' key know-how.

Spreading the corporate vision was also seen as another key element of success. Local employees would be given some formal training in that area, but critically the CEO drove this, devoting a lot of effort to communicating the vision, visiting new stores, seeing store operations first-hand and discussing improvements to local procedures.

Whilst the 'black box' approach worked in most countries around Europe, the diversity of markets imposed some limitations on the standardized franchising approach. When IKEA tried to transfer the expertise to the United States they found that tastes and shopping habits were sufficiently different to require significant adjustments and further learning. For example, American beds were larger, as were cups, plates and cabinet drawers. However, the company was able to exploit the processes it had developed to learn quickly and it was able to adapt its designs for local markets.

Let us look at other ways in which our organizations can generate value by allowing non-strategic knowledge to flow outwards:.

Forming purchasing coalitions. Forming a coalition with other companies allows us to pool buying power and reduces supplier power. For example, American Express, Sears and IBM worked together to reduce the cost of buying medical insurance (Nalebuff and Brandenburger, 1997).

Operating outsourcing contracts. We may be better outsourcing the maintenance and development of knowledge that is not strategically critical to our organizations, or knowledge that requires significant investment to develop, but which others can provide as a generic service. It is important to decide when knowledge investments will create strategic value and when more value could be gained from investing in other options. For example, Federal Express has particularly strong logistics management capabilities. Organizations that depend on excellent distribution and tracking could invest large amounts of money and time in acquiring the knowledge necessary to manage distribution without ever achieving the same level of performance it has achieved. They might be better to outsource the capability to Federal Express to manage on their behalf and invest their own knowledge resources in areas where they can generate more value.

Buying-in complex component knowledge. In high-technology industries such as aircraft manufacture, the complexity of each component requires intense specialization. Buying-in much of the component-level manufacturing expertise and retaining knowledge of systems integration often generates more value. To ensure continued viability in these circumstances, it is important to retain more knowledge than is actually directly applied in core technology areas to manage the risk in co-ordinating the product development and allow future innovation (Brusoni, Prencipe and Pavitt, 2001).

As we saw earlier, when we looked at the mechanisms by which knowledge is a source of influence, the returns from knowledge can be amplified by managing the flows appropriately. Important conditions are that the supply of knowledge that generates value is not finite or scarce, transactions are not discrete and the transfer cost is minimal (Vandermerwe, 1997). There are several ways to generate greater value in the long-term by releasing knowledge for less than present market value. Often, these require decisions to be taken at a more strategic level within our organizations.

Establishing customer loyalty. We may deliberately accept lower margins in the short-term, in exchange for accumulating knowledge that will help build a strong relationship with our customers. The initial lower margins may bring greater returns in the long-term because the customer develops sufficient loyalty to make repeat business an attractive option. The banking industry has adopted this sort of strategy, accepting lower margins on entry-level products bought by students and young people and giving them good service to build loyalty and make the high-value sales more likely in the future. Even charitable organizations are using this sort of approach to manage their income flows. The cost of the first mailing to a potential donor usually significantly exceeds the initial returns, but over the life of the relationship the costs get progressively less and the returns much greater because of loyalty (Sargeant and McKenzie, 1999).

At a different customer level, Citibank has measured the number of points of contact it has with corporate customers (Vandermerwe, 1997). Contrary to expectations, it found that the more products a customer took in different regions and countries, the more value it got over time. Customer switching costs were lower, returns from global brand growth were higher and the customers tended to take progressively higher-added-value products. There were certain predictable acceleration points where the relationship intensity started to produce disproportionately high returns, at disproportionately low cost. Ultimately, the relationship became self-sustaining. It was worthwhile for Citibank to invest in moving customers towards these acceleration points. To achieve these sorts of increasing returns, we need knowledge about customer preferences and patterns of spending.

Identifying complementary products. Rather than selling products in isolation to gain market share, we can integrate our knowledge offerings with those of other organizations to jointly dominate a market space. Success comes from providing an integrated experience for the customer. As an example, the car manufacturer Mercedes linked with the Swiss watch manufacturer SWATCH to leverage both brands by promoting the SmartCar, a compact runabout vehicle for urban dwellers (Vandermerwe, 1997). From this straightforward product development, extensions to the product added even more value and attractiveness; for example, a larger Mercedes for holidays to accommodate more people and luggage and Smart Centres that provided information and services to SmartCar users.

Linking complementary products can also expand the size of the market space overall. For example, Starbucks joined forces with Barnes and Noble because it was recognized that they had common customers who would place additional value on being able to purchase books and coffee together. Similarly, Intel and Microsoft have integrated their complementary products. Advances in the Intel chip made Microsoft's Windows™ operating system more effective. Advances in Windows™ software encouraged people to upgrade to faster machines that were based on the next generation of the Intel chipset.

Driving common standards. Prevalence in the way of doing things can increase the market space. Citibank chose to limit access for its customers to its own ATM machines when they were a new innovation in the marketplace. Other banks did not, which made them more attractive to customers seeking many points to access their money. Citibank's ATM product became far less attractive as a result (Vandermerwe, 1997).

Co-operatively competing. Co-opetition (co-operative competition) changes the rules of business to create a larger market space for everyone to share, rather than apportioning the existing market space through directly competitive activity (Nalebuff and Brandenburger, 1997).

An example is Columbia South Carolina's local newspaper, *The State*. The newspaper was finding it hard to compete locally against *USA Today* in terms of weekly circulation. All the traditional competitive options such as adding colour, reducing prices or including more local news had failed and the business was still losing money. It turned out that the best option was to actually print *USA Today* alongside *The State*. This was possible because the Sunday issue of *The State* took 50 per cent more capacity than the weekday edition, so for most of the week half of the production facilities were unused. The value achieved by both organizations was increased by this cooperative competition (Nalebuff and Brandenburger, 1997).

Future pricing. Pricing today based on the economies of scale that will be generated by future sales of a product is a potentially risky approach, but one which can create new market opportunities. For example, when Hewlett Packard launched colour inkjet printers for the consumer market, they were accused of anti-competitive practices by setting the price too low. They successfully proved that they had calculated the price based on future anticipated volumes of product sales that would cover their investment costs in the long-term, rather than immediately. They were prepared to risk pricing at this level based on their view that a lower priced product would generate a new market for cheap colour domestic printing.

The value net of any organization is the network of stakeholders between whom value is exchanged through the operation of the business: 'A value network generates economic value through complex dynamic exchanges between one or more enterprises, its customers, suppliers, strategic partners, and the community' (Allee, 2000).

Opportunities for increasing returns can arise from making knowledge available to any member of the value net of our organizations. A number of examples of this are shown in Figure 4.4. The ability of an organization to maintain a position at the hub of its value net depends on the centrality of the knowledge that is protected rather than made available and its position relative to others in the network.

 Signpost See *Competence Area 5: Relating* where we look at how an organization's position in the network affects the value that can be gained from knowledge activities.

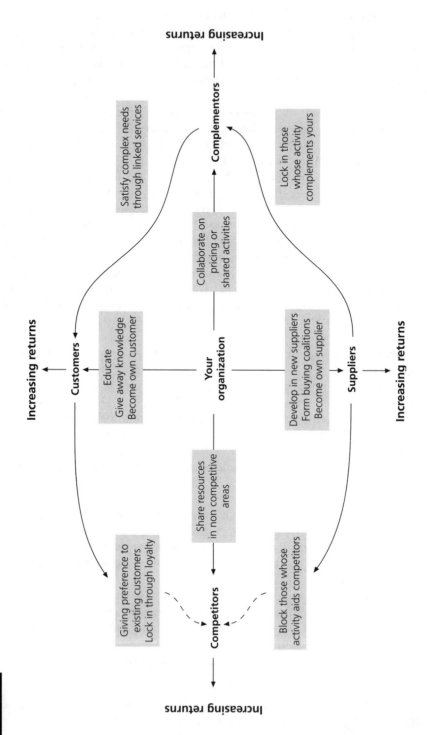

Figure 4.4 Generating increasing returns in the value net

The concept of increasing returns has generally been used to describe obser-vations of economic activity in technology and direct knowledge industries, but there is growing evidence of mild increasing returns in service and manufactur-ing industries too, if they have a significant knowledge emphasis. The US airline industry has gained increasing returns from the domination of the hub and spoke system of airports by guaranteeing and conveniently scheduling linkages between flights in a particular hub, predisposing customers to choose to fly with a particular airline for their whole journey (Arthur, 1996). Similarly, by dominat-ing the airline ticket booking mechanism, the SABRE booking system generated increasing returns for its owner, American Airlines. Insurance companies, finan-cial service providers and retailers all receive mild benefits from increasing returns when the benefits of being part of a user network make it unattractive for customers to change and when the size of the user base gives the service provider a customization advantage over its rivals.

However, there is always the risk of giving too much knowledge away. Faced with the threat from Apple, IBM rushed to launch a personal computer onto the market quickly. Abandoning a policy of internal development, they outsourced chip design to Intel and production of the operating platform to Microsoft. In addition, they allowed other manufacturers to produce IBM clone PCs. The result was undoubtedly greater returns for all, but IBM did not get the biggest share. Intel and Microsoft gained far greater rewards because they developed knowledge that many others in the market now needed.

This leads us to our next consideration: when and how to protect valuable knowledge.

Protect valuable knowledge

In general, intellectual property can be difficult to protect, as the US software industry has found to its cost. It has been estimated that the industry loses around 25 per cent of its annual revenues as a result of pirate copying of soft-ware applications. The music industry is facing similar problems. Once codified and digitized into software, the knowledge becomes harder to protect. Although codifying knowledge is beneficial if we want to diffuse it more widely for inter-nal use or take advantage of the potential for increasing returns, we have to be aware of the risks involved. By making it explicit and easily accessible, it can 'leak' to where we do not want it to be (Boisot, 1998).

Some types of knowledge are easier to protect than others, as shown in Table 4.2. This would suggest that the software and music industry might be better to protect added value service and support revenues, rather than system and dig-itized code, because these are likely to include elements of more 'sticky' tacit knowledge. Points of integration with other software may also prove more dif-ficult to copy and embedded translation codes can add a level of security to music distribution.

Table 4.2   Relative knowledge fluidity and associated protection mechanisms

Type of knowledge	Description	Protection issues
Individual tacit knowledge (Polanyi, 1966)	Developed through experience and hard to put into words, or even detect, until a situation arises that requires its use.	Protected by good people management policies to motivate and retain employees.
'Sticky' collective tacit knowledge (Szulanski, 1996)	Knowledge embedded in social structures about how to act in particular situations.	Protected by the fact that it is distributed throughout a collection of people. Damaged if social structures are disrupted.
'Leaky' explicit knowledge (Szulanski, 1996)	Knowledge that is explicit and inherently mobile.	Protected through mechanisms that incur costs (Huizing and Wim, 2002), such as patents, trademarks, copyright, confidentiality clauses in employee contracts and computer security systems.

 Signpost   In *Competence Area 3: Learning* we looked at how knowledge can 'leak' across the boundaries of our organizations when it is based on jargon, tools and techniques that are common to external communities.

Patent and copyright trademarks do give some legal protection for explicit knowledge that has been codified. However, the cost of maintenance can be high, particularly if there is a tendency to protect ideas 'just in case'. Dow Chemicals is one example of a company that gained significant value from paying attention to patent maintenance (Rivette and Kline, 2000).

In 1993, Gordon Petrash became the Director of Intellectual Asset Management for Dow Chemicals. At the time the company was maintaining approximately 30 000 patents. Petrash started by identifying the knowledge that was important for Dow's business and evaluating competitors' strategies and knowledge assets. The portfolio of patents was then organized and classified.

Petrash found that no-one had been responsible for commercializing or licensing patent usage. This meant that patents were filed to protect a new discovery, although often the new discovery was not used to generate revenue. Some patents had high potential value if used properly, but were not being exploited because the right people didn't know about them. It was found that the lifetime cost of maintaining each patent could be $250 000.

With a database of patents and designated responsibility for managing their potential, it became much easier to realize the full value of the intellectual assets, including deciding which ones to abandon. Releasing unusable patents saved about $1 million in the first 18 months. Some were even offered free to universities, which meant they could be written off against tax as charitable donations.

There were also far greater rewards than the cost savings. Once Dow knew what they knew, they could maximize the use of that knowledge. By identifying gaps in their portfolio, they could invest more strategically in research and development. They could also leverage more value from the knowledge they chose to protect. By combining patents they could make products that were more difficult to copy. Licensing patents in collaborative relationships with other companies enabled them to protect their position in the market by excluding avenues for others to pursue. The net effect of a reasoned knowledge protection strategy was a significant contribution to bottom line returns.

However, we do need to recognize that in addition to protecting knowledge, sometimes registering patents can also result in knowledge leaking away. Publicising the codified knowledge and research citations in patent documents gives away important clues and can make it obvious to others that it is worth exploring the same knowledge domains. Some organizations choose to avoid the patenting process for this very reason.

Others use multiple patent strategies to reduce the 'leakiness' of knowledge by increasing the complexity for potential competitors trying to replicate patented knowledge. Determined competitors can still overcome these, but higher levels of investment are required. An example of this was the development of plain paper photocopying technology. Xerox had safeguarded its early dominance in plain paper photocopying by protecting the process with multiple patents. Senior managers at Canon set research engineers the goal of developing a plain paper copier that did not infringe these patents. Although they were later to market, they eventually produced a smaller and simpler copier based on different technology that allowed the machines to be used in local office environments, rather than central copying departments.

We have seen that tacit knowledge is often considered to be more valuable knowledge and it also may be easier to protect because it does not easily flow across the boundaries of our organizations. For this reason, organizations often keep their core knowledge fluid and tacit within the heads of their people (Sanchez, 2002). For example, the McKinsey and Bain Consulting firms use the expertise of their consultants rather than predefined methodologies and solutions to create high value-added customized solutions to customer problems.

 Signpost

In *Competence Area 3: Learning* we saw that tacit knowledge exchange is a difficult process requiring personal rapport, motivation and well developed communication skills.

Tacit knowledge that is deeply rooted in collective thinking and cultural values is probably the most difficult to copy.

Signpost In *Competence Area 2: Deciding* we saw that Buckman Laboratories developed a code of ethics that has resulted in a particularly strong collaborative culture. Knowledge-sharing in that organization has resulted in new products and services and strong financial performance over many years.

However, individual tacit knowledge can also be difficult to retain. If an experienced individual leaves the company, then their tacit knowledge leaves with them. Talent retention through good people management practices is one important means of protecting tacit knowledge. Work shadowing to diffuse tacit knowledge more broadly also protects the knowledge without requiring it to be codified. Clearly this can be costly, but for critical expertise it is a way for our organizations to retain value if employees leave.

Successful knowledge strategies concentrate knowledge protection efforts where they are likely to have most effect, at least cost. The choice about which knowledge to protect needs to be constantly reviewed. There are likely to be only a few aspects of knowledge that must always remain proprietary and need constant protection. Protecting other knowledge beyond its useful life may lead our organizations to be trapped in old ways of operating or produce inferior value from knowledge resources.

One intangible asset that is likely to need particular protection is a strong and positive brand image. This is derived from the widely-held perception of the range of values and capabilities that the organization represents. Brand could be viewed as the external manifestation of all the strategically valuable knowledge recipes that are leveraged by an organization and which influence the buying decisions of its customers. Clearly, if the influence is positive, the knowledge that supports that brand image is something that should be protected.

Overall, the safest position for an organization is to develop a blend of corporate capabilities and reputation built on long-lasting relationships with loyal

Figure 4.5 Routes around The Window of Knowledge Opportunities

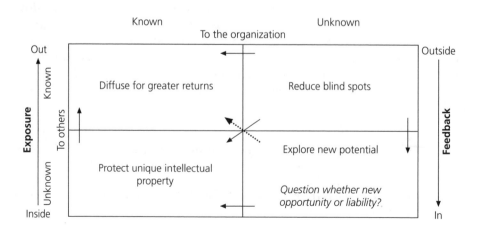

customers and suppliers who understand what the business stands for. This should be combined with alliances with firms and knowledge workers who have capabilities that can be leveraged collaboratively. Such a mix is extremely hard to replicate because of the time and experience that have been invested. It is deeply reliant on 'sticky' collective tacit knowledge. Chapparal Steel, often cited as a model example of a learning organization, actively shares their product knowledge with other members of the industry. The CEO is untroubled that opening the doors of the company to others will reduce its value because he firmly believes that they will never be able to replicate the underpinning tacit common knowledge that holds the firm together and makes it an effective learning community (Garvin, 1993).

Dynamically adjusting knowledge flows in both directions is a source of tension

As we can see from Figure 4.5 there are a variety of ways to help us decide which knowledge should flow from the 'outside-in' and which should flow from the 'inside-out' across the boundaries of our organizations. Tension arises because the effort we need to invest in each area varies with the level of turbulence in the outside environment and the level of internal resistance to doing something different.

The arrows in Figure 4.5 indicate potential strategic routes to explore the various opportunities. The first priority for any organization is to identify its blind spots, since this is where competitive threats are most likely to come from. With a clear idea of the knowledge in use across the industry, we are then in a better position to ask whether our organizations should be developing that knowledge too. Do we have the absorptive capacity to realize value from the knowledge, is it cost effective to develop it and would it fit with other areas of expertise within our organizations? The more turbulent the environment the more likely there are to be 'holes' in our vision and the more our organization is at risk. Unfortunately in this scenario, the knowledge that is currently being exploited is not yet obviously redundant, so significant effort may be invested to protect it despite its decreasing utility.

The next step depends very much on the strategic balance between knowledge exploitation and knowledge exploration that our organizations need to adopt. If exploitation is a higher priority than exploration, because the market is relatively stable, then we need to evaluate existing knowledge against the potential for increasing returns and the cost and benefits of protection. Generally, to be vertically integrated into an old technology is not a good value generating strategy if the market is mature and under threat from radical new technology developments. In this scenario, it may be better to either divest old knowledge or find a way to use resources to better advantage by giving knowledge away to customers, or outsourcing expertise to others in the market. 'As firms pursue both incremental and discontinuous change, they may be better off being vertically integrated into the major components that drive the discontinuity and better off not being vertically integrated into the components that drive the incremental change' (Afuah, 2001).

Clearly, decisions about which knowledge to protect and which to release will depend on the dynamics of the external environment. Of course, as we have already argued, the exploration of completely new opportunities must not be ignored. There must be some activity in the bottom right-hand pane of 'The Window of Knowledge Opportunities'. Once new opportunities have been identified and evaluated in terms of potential fit with the identity and purpose of our organizations, there is a further decision to be made. Should the knowledge be released quickly to gain first mover advantages and lock users in, or should it initially stay within the firm's boundaries and only be released later in the produce or service life cycle?

To reap the rewards of increasing returns, it is recommended that we (Arthur, 1996):

- Read the feedback from the market environment – what are customer needs, distribution channels and rival products? Where could these be connected to create self re-enforcing patterns of behaviour?
- Keep track of the ecology in which the firm exists – the web of relationships to which a firm belongs can act as an amplifier that delivers increasing returns, so it makes sense to manage that web pro-actively.
- Be prepared to play for the long term – generating increasing returns requires high-quality technology, fine timing to catch the market in the early stages, pricing that sacrifices current profits for future returns, courage and determination.
- Foresee the next wave – increasing returns dissolve when they are washed away by the next wave of technological change. Keeping an eye out for the next cycle of change is an essential part of strategy.

Dynamically adjusting all these flows simultaneously can be a source of tension, particularly when many of the elements do not lie within the control of our organization. The flow of knowledge from outside the organization to the inside is probably most easily adjusted by ramping up exploratory activity, but it is not necessarily easy to translate it into value-generating innovations, given the inertia caused by existing ways of doing things. Certainly, influence on the external competitive environment is not totally within the control of any one organization.

Absorbing too much knowledge from the outside without questioning its relevance and value means that we are unlikely to have the capacity to integrate it efficiently. Organizational time and financial resources will be wasted. An appropriate level of discrimination is needed to recognize and integrate the most valuable knowledge and highlight the key gaps between current performance and future opportunities.

An unmanaged approach to the diffusion of knowledge from inside our organizations to the outside risks excessive exposure and lost opportunities to generate value. An appropriate level of diffusion means that we moderate the flow to exert appropriate influence on external conditions, either by restricting access to particular knowledge, or by dissipating it to generate more value.

An organization's strategic capability to manage knowledge effectively depends on whether the permeability of its boundary has been set to the right level for the environmental conditions and whether there is the flexibility to adjust it as required. It also involves recognizing that the boundary cannot be fixed in one place or form due to the evolving nature of knowledge itself. These issues are captured in Figure 4.6.

There is no easy way to for us to resolve the tension between the bi-directional flows, but there is evidence that it is worth monitoring the level of organizational activities in each of the four areas, so that strategies can be adjusted where there are obvious weaknesses. The final element in developing competence in Connecting shows why we need to recognize the importance of matching the flow rates to the level of turbulence in the knowledge landscape

Figure 4.6   Forces affecting the boundary of an organization

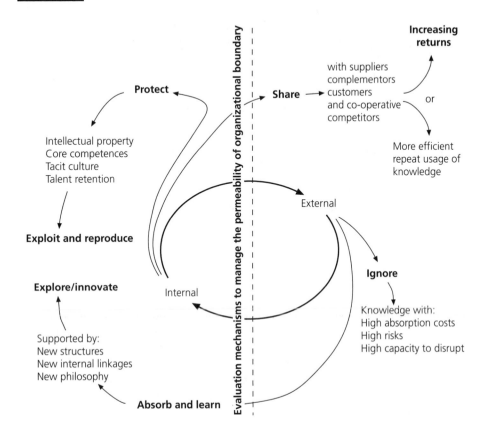

of our industry. This requires patience, determination, open communication and trust, as well as a clear strategic definition of the purpose and identity of our organizations.

Resolve the tension through adapting boundary permeability to suit environmental turbulence

The more turbulent the environment, the greater the inward flow of knowledge needed to identify patterns and trends, but the narrower the knowledge domain we need to exploit. The organization's technological competences should dictate where to focus. By narrowing our focus to areas where change is strategically critical, we increase its intensity so we are more likely to spot relevant threats and opportunities.

At the other end of the spectrum, the more stable the environment, the more potential there is for outward flow of knowledge to create competitive advantage in terms of first mover advantage. However, it is more difficult to identify the knowledge domains we need to exploit in order to achieve superior business performance, because most of our competitors will also have covered the knowledge domains in our immediate vicinity and have reached similar heights on comparable knowledge peaks. Therefore, we must explore more broadly to find the knowledge that makes a difference (Sidhu, Jijssen and Commandeur, 2000).

A survey of firms in turbulent markets such as information technology and telecommunications, and stable markets like paint and varnish, lubricants, pneumatic and hydraulic equipment identified the following issues:

- When the environment is turbulent, it is easier to monitor external knowledge activity if an organization has focused competencies in a narrow knowledge domain.

- When the environment is stable, it is advisable to monitor industries producing substitute products for competitive threats and potential expansions and an organization needs to have a reasonably broad knowledge range in order to thrive. However, breadth must be carefully managed because as the range increases, it becomes more difficult to monitor potential substitutes and generate value on all fronts.

However, one thing is clear, whatever the external conditions, making explicit the range of the knowledge domain to focus on is positively associated with superior business performance in a market space. A clear definition of boundaries, in terms of what knowledge domains an organization covers, helps it identify which external signals to pay attention to. It also provides clarity in the minds of stakeholders as to the organizational purpose and identity and helps align the efforts of diverse parts of the organization (Sidhu, Jijssen and Commandeur, 2000).

Realistically, we cannot expect to define precisely which knowledge is needed at which time, but we can plan and monitor the mechanisms we have identified in this chapter. Paying strategic attention to these areas allows us to consciously adapt the rate of knowledge flowing in and out of the business to suit the turbulence in the external environment (Brown and Eisenhardt, 1997). The value of reviewing events in this way is that we can deliberately look for knowledge-based strategies that are appropriate for current conditions. Looking at the knowledge economy through 'The Window of Knowledge Opportunities' provides both feedback (which gives us insight into the actions of others) and foresight (we can foresee potential consequences of the protecting and releasing knowledge) to help us moderate the flows in the future.

 Signpost See *Competence Area 6: Monitoring* to find out about other ways of monitoring the effectiveness of knowledge investments.

What is involved in deliberately adopting appropriate knowledge-based strategies? The balance that we set between innovation activities (exploration and new knowledge creation) and protection activities (exploiting proprietary knowledge internally) depends on how much turbulence there is in our competitive environment (Matusik and Hill, 1998). Matching knowledge-based strategies to changing competitive conditions means that we need to recognize that different characteristics are important at different times. In particular different strategies require:

- Different emphases on potential and realized absorptive capacity.
- Different levels of slack resources to respond effectively to knowledge inflows.
- More or less attention paid to the integrative effects of social capital and common knowledge.
- Different protection mechanisms and diffusion strategies.
- Different capabilities for gaining intelligence and knowledge discrimination.
- An appreciation of different kinds of opportunities to get value from increasing returns.

In Table 4.3 we summarize the characteristics of knowledge-based strategies that are appropriate to four levels of environmental turbulence.

Challenge and Break-out (see table) as strategic options are also likely to require radical changes to the structure of our organizations, with potentially significant impact on the form and nature of the boundaries.

In addition to deliberately adopting knowledge-based strategies that suit the industry conditions, we should also be expecting to flex the boundaries of our organizations by paying attention to different forms of external relationships. Flexing the boundaries of our organizations builds capacity to respond to turbulence.

Table 4.3 Strategic knowledge fitness relative to the environment

Option	Choice	Organizational knowledge strategy requirements	Environmental fitness
Survive	Let the market decide the fate of the organization, protect existing position as far as possible (Huizing and Wim, 2002). Acceptable in a relatively stable environment.	• Medium Realized Absorptive Capacity. • Low slack resources. • Low intelligence gathering. • Low discrimination. • High protection. • Low diffusion.	Low learning fitness is acceptable in stable environments.
Thrive	Consolidate niche and grow through incremental exploration. Use increasing returns to exploit technical knowledge (Lewin, Long and Carroll, 1999). Fine for a moderately changing environment.	• High Realized Absorptive Capacity. • High social capital. • Low slack resources. • Medium discrimination. • Medium diffusion. • Medium intelligence. • Medium protection.	Average learning fitness needed for steadily evolving environments.

Challenge	Innovate continuously. Destabilize market by accelerating the learning cycle for others and triggering hyper-competition (Lewin, Long and Carroll, 1999; Spender, 2002). Needed in a rapidly changing environment	• High Potential and Realized Absorptive Capacity. • High social capital. • High slack resources. • High diffusion. • High intelligence gathering. • High discrimination.	High learning fitness used strategically to create strong turbulence in environment
Break-out	Abandon niche and pursue new directions: explore aggressively (Spender, 2002). Large leaps across the knowledge landscape are risky. Use alliances and joint ventures to reduce exploration risk. Needed to move beyond the existing environment	• High Potential Absorptive Capacity • Low social capital • High slack resources • High intelligence gathering	Extreme learning fitness

Signpost See *Competence Area 5: Relating* to find out more about different organizational forms and how they relate to operating within in a network of knowledge-sharing relationships.

We started this chapter by arguing that the main purpose of an organization in the knowledge economy is to integrate and co-ordinate knowledge better than the marketplace. It does this by accumulating private knowledge (collective tacit knowledge, common knowledge, routines, processes, patents and capabilities) that creates the context in which public knowledge (explicit expertise and best practices) can be applied more efficiently and effectively. An effective knowledge-based strategy aims to make better commercial sense of the mix of public and private knowledge than others by managing the knowledge that flows into and out of the firm.

By implication, the rate of knowledge flowing back and forth across the boundaries of our organizations varies according to how active others are in knowledge creation and application. Effectively this determines the turbulence of the knowledge landscape of our industry. Hence, our organizational strategies should pay attention to growing or contracting our knowledge boundaries, flexing in and out to accommodate the various changes. This means changing what we specialize in over time, in parallel with the rate of knowledge change in the industry.

The most effective way of doing this is by constantly adjusting the network of connections in our value net. These are the conduits for knowledge creation and application and allow us to respond more intelligently to our environmental conditions. As we shall see in the next chapter, networks of organizations are important for gaining access to new knowledge, although a critical factor is managing the level of conflicting constraints they may also create.

Summary

In this chapter we have moved our attention to the external environment and looked at how to build competence in managing the flows of knowledge across the boundaries of our organizations. We began with a series of questions:

How can knowledge be a source of influence internally and externally?

How permeable should organizational boundaries be to knowledge flows?

Can we use our knowledge to influence the competitive conditions for others?

What knowledge is critical to protect?

How do we know which new ideas to absorb?

We started to answer them by looking at the characteristics of knowledge that make it different to other physical assets. Based on the economic characteristics of knowledge, we saw that there are three ways in which we can connect knowledge flows across the boundaries of our organizations for internal and external influence:

1   Knowledge multiplies with use, offering the potential of increasing returns.

2   The knowledge in an industry develops through co-evolution so collaboration can increases the success of all.

3   We need to actively develop absorptive capacity so that we are better at amplifying the effects of knowledge flows than our competitors.

'The Window of Knowledge Opportunities' was created to show how to use these characteristics to develop practical approaches to two strategic questions:

Outside-In – How much knowledge can reasonably and efficiently be absorbed from outside and integrated into the firm to generate greater market value?

Inside-Out – What influence can be exerted on external conditions by releasing and/or restricting flows of knowledge from inside the business into the external environment?

Paying attention to 'outside-in' knowledge flows involves:

●   Reducing blind spots by environmental scanning and challenging current thinking within the organization to enhance potential absorptive capacity; for example, by adopting competing technologies, benchmarking practices, collecting intelligence about competitors and participating in industry networks.

●   Exploring new knowledge domains by correlating ideas and combining knowledge; for example through data mining, identifying missing markets, scenario planning and collaborative innovation projects.

Effective ways of discriminating which flows of knowledge to allow into our organizations are also needed to produce stability and maintain our knowledge-based identity. Brand and reputation may be one important discrimination mechanism, recognizing patterns in external trends is another.

Paying attention to 'inside-out' knowledge flows involves:

●   Identifying which knowledge could be more valuable by giving it away. For non-strategic knowledge, this may involve participating in purchasing coalitions or establishing outsourcing contracts. For strategic knowledge, there may be opportunities to amplify its value by releasing it to establish customer loyalty, complement another firm's product or service, drive the adoption of common standards or co-operatively compete with another organization.

▶

▶ • Protecting valuable knowledge in appropriate ways. Explicit knowledge may best be protected through patent and copyright law, though this may also make it visible to competitors. Retaining the tacit knowledge of individuals requires good people management practices. Embedded collective tacit knowledge is the most effective form of protection.

Successfully paying attention to both knowledge flows is difficult because they need to be dynamically adjusted in both directions. Too much knowledge flowing into the organization indiscriminately creates the risk that we will waste organizational energy trying to integrate it. Too much knowledge flowing out of our organizations creates the risk of losing potential value generating opportunities. Our organizations need to develop the capability to set the permeability of our boundaries to the right level for the environmental conditions and then to adjust them flexibly as required.

In addition to using feedback and insight gained from 'The Window of Knowledge Opportunities', there are two other ways of matching the permeability of the boundary to the turbulence in the environment:

• Consciously developing knowledge-based strategies that are appropriate for the level of turbulence.

• Growing and contracting the knowledge boundary of our organizations through adjusting the number and nature of external relationships, which is the topic for our next chapter.

Developing competence in connecting knowledge flows across our organizations' boundaries depends on appreciating the dynamic nature of industry-wide knowledge landscapes and then setting out to take advantage of the space of possibilities presented by that landscape.

References

Adler, P. S. (2001) 'Market, hierarchy and trust: the knowledge economy and the future of capitalism', *Organization Science* 12(2): 215–34.

Afuah, A. (2001) 'Dynamic boundaries of the firm: are firms better off being vertically integrated in the face of technological change?' *Academy of Management Journal* 44(6): 1211–128.

Aley, J. (1996) 'The theory that made Microsoft (the theory of "increasing returns")', *Fortune* 133(8): 65–7.

Allee, V. (2000) 'Reconfiguring the value network', *Journal of Business Strategy* 21(4): 36–40.

Arthur, W. B. (1990) 'Positive feedbacks in the economy', *Scientific American* 262(2): 92–8.

Arthur, W. B. (1996) 'Increasing returns and the new world of business', *Harvard Business Review* 74(4): 100–10.

Barabba, V. P., Pourdehnad, J. and Ackoff, R. L. (2002) 'Above and beyond knowledge management', in *The Strategic Management of Intellectual Capital and Organizational Knowledge* (eds C. W. Choo and N. Bontis). Oxford: Oxford University Press.

Battram, A. (1998) *Navigating Complexity: The Essential Guide to Complexity Theory in Business and Management*. London: The Industrial Society.

Bierly, P. and Chakrabati, A. (1996) 'Generic knowledge strategies in the US pharmaceutical industry', *Strategic Management Journal* 17: 123–35.

Birkinshaw, J. (2002) 'Spirit of innovation', *Business Life* 45.

Boisot, M. H. (1998) *Knowledge Assets: Securing Competitive Advantage in the Knowledge Economy*. Oxford: Oxford University Press.

Bontis, N. (2001) 'Assessing knowledge assets: a review of the models used to measure intellectual capital', *International Journal of Management Reviews* 3(1): 41–60.

Borg, S. (2001) 'Missing Markets',London: CGEY.

Brown, S. L. and Eisenhardt, K. M. (1997) 'The art of continuous change: linking complexity theory and time-paced evolution in relentlessly shifting organization', *Administrative Science Quarterly* 42(1): 1–34.

Brusoni, S., Prencipe, A. and Pavitt, K. (2001) 'Knowledge specialization, organizational coupling and the boundaries of the firm: why do firms know more than they make?', *Administrative Science Quarterly* 46(4): 597–621.

Christensen, L. T. (1995) 'Buffering organizational identity in the marketing culture', *Organizational Studies* 16(4): 651–73.

Da Silva Lopes, T. (2002) 'Brands and the evolution of multinationals in alcoholic beverages', *Business History*, 44(3): 1–32.

De Geus, A. (1988) 'Planning as learning', *Harvard Business Review* 66(2): 70–5.

Garvin, D. A. (1993) 'Building a learning organization', *Harvard Business Review* 71(4): 78–92.

Grant, R. M. (2002) 'The knowledge based view of the firm', in *The Strategic Management of Intellectual Capital and Organizational Knowledge* (eds C. W. Choo and N. Bontis). Oxford: Oxford University Press.

Helfat, C. E. and Raibitschek, R. S. (2002) 'Product sequencing: co-evolution of knowledge, capabilities and products', in *The Strategic Management of Intellectual Capital and Organizational Knowledge* (eds C. W. Choo and N. Bontis). Oxford: Oxford University Press.

Huizing, A. and Wim, B. (2002) 'Knowledge and learning, markets and organizations', in *The Strategic Management of Intellectual Capital and Organizational Knowledge* (eds C. W. Choo and N. Bontis). Oxford: Oxford University Press.

Kim, L. (1988) 'Crisis construction and organizational learning; capability building in catching-up at Hyundai Motors', *Organization Science* 9: 506–21.

Kodama, M. (2002) 'Transforming an old economy company through strategic communities', *Long Range Planning* 35(4): 349–66.

Lewin, A. L., Long, C. P. and Carroll, T. N. (1999) 'The co-evolution of new organizational forms', *Organization Science* 10(5): 535–50.

Matusik, S. F. and Hill, C. W. L. (1998) 'The utilization of contingent work, knowledge creation and competitive advantage', *Academy of Management Review* 23: 680–97.

McKenzie, J. and Reynolds, A. (1997) 'Innovation success in the food and drink industry: maximizing opportunities and minimizing risks', Financial Times Retail and Consumer Publishing, 1–175.

Nalebuff, B. J. and Brandenburger, A. M. (1997) 'Co-opetition: Competitive and co-operative business strategies for the digital economy', *Strategy and Leadership* 25(6): 28–35.

Oliver, D. and Roos, J. (2000) *Striking a Balance. Complexity and Knowledge Landscapes*. Maidenhead: McGraw Hill.

Polanyi, M. (1966) *The Tacit Dimension*. Garden City NY: Doubleday.

Rivette, K. and Kline, D. (2000) 'Discovering new value in intellectual property', *Harvard Business Review* 78(1): 54.

Sanchez, R. (2002) 'Modular product and process architectures: frameworks for strategic organizational learning', in *The Strategic Management of Intellectual Capital and Organizational Knowledge* (eds C. W. Choo and N. Bontis). Oxford: Oxford University Press, 223–31.

Sargeant, A. and McKenzie, J. (1999) 'The life time value of donors: getting insight through CHAID', *Fund Raising Management*, 22–7.

Sidhu, J. S., Jijssen, E. J. and Commandeur, H. R. (2000) 'Business domain definition practice: does it affect organizational performance'. *Long Range Planning* 33(3): 376–401.

Skyrme, D. (1988) 'Developing a knowledge strategy', http://www.skyrme.com/pubs/articles.htm (accessed 27 November, 2002).

Spender, J. C. (1996) 'Making knowledge the basis of a dynamic theory of the firm', *Strategic Management Journal* 17(Special issue): 45–62.

Spender, J. C. (2002) 'Knowledge management, uncertainty, and an emergent theory of the firm', in *The Strategic Management of Intellectual Capital and Organizational Knowledge* (eds C. W. Choo and N. Bontis). Oxford: Oxford University Press.

Stopford, J. (2001) 'Organizational learning as guided response to market signals', in *Handbook of Organizational Learning and Knowledge* (eds M Dierkes, A. B. Antal, J. Child and I. Nonaka) Oxford: Oxford University Press, 265–81.

Szulanski, G. (1996) 'Exploring internal stickiness. impediments to the transfer of best practice within the firm', *Strategic Management Journal* 17(Special issue): 27–43.

Toffler, A. (1990) *Powershift: Knowledge, Wealth and Violence at the Edge of the 21st Century*. New York: Bantam.

Utterback, J. M. (1994) *Mastering the Dynamics of Innovation. How Companies can Seize Opportunities in the Face of Technological Change*. Cambridge, MA: Harvard Business School Press.

Vandermerwe, S. (1997) 'Increasing returns: competing for customers in a global market', *Journal of World Business*, 32(4): 333–51.

von Krogh, G. and Cusumano, M. A. (2001) 'Three strategies for managing fast growth', *Sloan Management Review* 42(2): 53–61.

von Krogh, G. and Grand, S. (2002) 'From economic theory toward a knowledge based theory of the firm', in *The Strategic Management of Intellectual Capital and Organizational Knowledge* (eds C. W. Choo and N. Bontis). Oxford: Oxford University Press.

Zack, M. (2002) 'Developing a knowledge strategy', in *The Strategic Management of Intellectual Capital and Organizational Knowledge* (eds C. W. Choo and N. Bontis). Oxford: Oxford University Press.

Zahra, S. A. and George, G. (2002) 'Absorptive capacity: a review, reconceptualization and extension', *Academy of Management Review* 27(2): 185–203.

5 Fifth Competence Area
Relating

Business Challenges

- How many connections does an organization need in its relationship network?

- How many are sustainable?

- How does relationship quality affect knowledge flow?

- How can we orchestrate our network to increase its value generating potential?

Introduction

The essence of strategy is the way a company defines its business and links together the only resources that really matter in today's economy: knowledge and relationships, or an organization's competencies and customers.

Normann and Ramirez, 1993

In the last chapter, we concluded that thriving in the knowledge economy means being well-connected to the outside environment. Specifying what we meant by 'well-connected' involved a strategic assessment of the potential returns from knowledge flowing into and out of our organizations. The outcome – a unique specification of knowledge opportunities – depended on where we had come from, where we were going and the environmental conditions we were operating in. Actually being well-connected requires different actions. It depends on carefully arranging and appropriately paying attention to the structure and quality of those relationship ties which carry the knowledge flows and help us realize the opportunities we have identified.

We can look at our organizations as webs of individuals, groups, business divisions and external bodies simultaneously creating and using knowledge. Value generation lies in how well they connect. The structure and operation of the network connections has a significant impact on our organization's ability to turn knowledge flows into real value.

'Owning' all the knowledge is not always the best value proposition in a changing world because this takes too much investment and can reduce flexibility. However, relying on relationships that are damagingly 'leaky', restrict flexibility, impede knowledge flows or distort knowledge transfer can also do more harm than good. The ability to organize and sustain a working network of knowledge-based relationships over time is a key competence area for the Knowledgeable Organization.

Designing and sustaining such a network is a significant challenge for our organizations. The more change there is in the environment, the more connections we need. However, the more connected our organizations, the more likely it is that conflicts and tensions between members of the network will impair our own strategic focus. To harness the intelligence embedded in a network of knowledge-based relationships in a meaningful way, we must also act to maintain the coherence of our own organizations by nurturing a common sense of identity and purpose.

If we look at the statistics, we quickly appreciate why paying attention to relationships has become important. In the USA at the end of the 1990s, around 55 per cent of the value of a product typically came from relationships beyond manufacturers' own boundaries (for Japan this figure was 69 per cent) and the percentage was rising (Dyer and Singh, 1998). Outsourcing markets are large (for contract electronics alone, the market was estimated at $31 billion in 1996, growing to $100 billion in 2001 (Schilling and Steensma, 2001)). Other reports on the value of external relationships suggest that collaborative associations in one form or another accounted for between 6–15 per cent of the market value of a typical company (Parkhe, 1991). Although care is needed in interpreting statistics when we do not know what is included in the umbrella term 'alliance', we can get a feel for the intense interest in collaborative associations from the fact that in 2001, each of the top 500 global companies reported being involved in an average of 60 strategic alliances and in the two years to 2001 firms reported more than 20 000 new alliances (Dyer, Kale and Singh 2001).

Benetton, Dell Computers and Sun Microsystems are often cited as excellent examples of how to generate value by positioning the firm at the centre of a network of alliances and outsourcing relationships, and each has a different approach to designing and managing their network. We will look at each in more detail later. In general, some organizations encourage members of their network to take on activities once seen as strategically sensitive and proprietary – for example innovation and design, customization and quality assurance (Lorenzoni and Baden-Fuller, 1995) – others diligently protect these competences.

In practice, it is important for our organizations to evaluate the nature of the relationships we invest in from a knowledge perspective: what knowledge do we need; how quickly do we need it; what resources are available externally; and how can our relationship network help us achieve our goals? From there, a knowledge-based strategy should focus on how best to configure the network structure, cultivate the appropriate form of trust and promote the right level of social interaction and coherence. Adopting a strategy of integrating distributed expertise can be highly effective because the relationships we form are inherently flexible. However, too much dependence on outsiders can leave our organization vulnerable to becoming a 'hollow' shell (Venkatesan, 1992) with no core capabilities of our own. Whatever form our network takes, we need a clear idea of what knowledge and expertise moulds the collective perception of the identity of our own organizations and then ensure this is adequately protected.

Achieving organizational flexibility without loss of integrity, particularly when organizational boundaries need to be fluid, requires 'dynamic capabilities' (Teece, Pisano and Shuen, 1997). We have already discussed several aspects of these dynamic capabilities in earlier chapters. They are shaped by the co-evolutionary effects of knowledge connections between our organizations and the environment *(Competence Area 4: Connecting)*. They are developed through decentralized authority structures that give local decision autonomy (*Competence Area 2: Deciding*). They require ingrained learning routines (*Competence Area 3: Learning*) and 'strategic flexibility' (Garud and Kotha, 1994; Sanchez, 1995) in people, processes and technology (*Competence Area 1: Competing*). To complete the picture, dynamic capabilities also need organizational structures that encourage recombination of knowledge through varying forms of external associations: this is the focus of the present chapter.

It is important to stress that we are not only looking to relationships with suppliers and competitors to produce knowledge flows. Knowledge in customer relationships is strategically valuable too. When the cost of cultivating a new customer is high, then the lifetime value of customer relationships becomes more important than any single sale. Knowing how to relate to and meet the needs of our customers can produce increasing returns to sales activity.

 Signpost In *Competence Area 4: Connecting* we saw that there are opportunities to amplify the returns generated through knowledge via all members of an organization's value net.

In this chapter, we look at how to develop competence in 'Relating' in order to profit from network-based knowledge opportunities. We will see how paying attention to the structure and operation of network connections gives us the ability to behave intelligently in different business conditions. Human intelligence is the product of flexible mental associations between patterns of neurons in the brain: we can view organizational intelligence as a similar pattern of associations on a different scale (Garud and Kotha, 1994). When we organize as part of a flexible network of loose and tight associations (relationships) with other knowledgeable entities, we can tap into the intelligence of a complex system of understanding. Intelligent relating is the process by which we invest profitably in sustaining networks that allow us to respond appropriately to changing environmental conditions.

How does the way we relate impact intelligence potential?

To appreciate how our organizations can foster intelligence in the knowledge economy, we need to understand how different organizational structures, network configurations and ways of forming relationships affect our access to knowledge and our ability to create new knowledge. By way of contrast, we can also reflect on the assumptions about organizational purpose and structure implicit in conventional theories of market economics (see Box 5.1).

The main difference is that in the knowledge economy, we are no longer seeking to minimize transaction costs with external bodies, but to maximize transaction value by relating efficiently and effectively. From this perspective, the firm is a mechanism for co-ordinating and integrating knowledge to produce value (Spender, 1996).

In *Competence Area 4: Connecting* we saw that knowledge is not in short supply. Therefore, price is no longer always going to be the most efficient co-ordination mechanism. Also, given that authority does not encourage knowledge to flow, hierarchies start to show limitations as the basis of organizational structures.

At this point, it is worth clarifying what we mean by various terms, simply because the plethora of terminology can cause confusion about intentions and objectives, which muddy the clarity of the decision-making process in this area of relationships.

'Alliance' can be a term that is used generically to describe a governance mechanism for a relationship between organizations, but:

> Many so-called alliances between Western companies and their Asian rivals are little more than sophisticated outsourcing arrangements. General Motors buys cars and components from Korea's Daewoo. Siemens buys computers from Fujitsu. Apple buys laser printer engines from Canon. The traffic is almost entirely one way. *De Wit and Meyer, 1999*

When Western companies enter into a relationship simply to avoid an investment risk, 'the commitment to learning is so one-sided, collaboration invariably leads to competitive compromise' (De Wit and Meyer, 1999). 'Collaboration' means to work jointly together. 'Co-operation', on the other hand, means to work together with the objective of combining, whether that be combining resources, sharing knowledge, or integrating a complex array of specialized products and components into a sophisticated final product like an airplane. At first glance the distinction may seem subtle, but it does have important implications for knowledge flows. Up until recently, most of the writing about alliances has focused on the governance structures, the motivations for entry into such arrangements and the factors affecting failure (Fischer *et al.*, 2002). Far less research has focused on the issues surrounding knowledge transfer and its impact on the relationship, despite the fact that knowledge transfer and learning are the implicit reasons behind most of the relationships.

Box 5.1

How market economics has influenced the structure of the firm
Traditionally, economists describe markets as mechanisms for efficient allocation of scarce resources. They define the firm as an efficient mechanism to reduce market transaction costs and leverage the potential for economies of scale and scope, particularly in uncertain conditions. The firm is seen as a discrete entity whose role is to compete effectively in the marketplace to deliver value. In that scenario, superior competitive position is achieved by investing in distinct resources and sustained by erecting protective barriers to entry, mobility, or comparability (Rindova and Kotha, 2001); in other words, disconnecting it from the outside world.

The firm's organizing structure is critical to this process: co-operative internal relationships are mediated through hierarchical authority; competitive external relationships are mediated through price. The customer is the ultimate arbiter rather than an integral part of the value generation process.

In a market economy, the general aim is to maintain stability through managed growth and to minimize uncertainty. Location, formal structure and contractual obligations are used to create clear boundaries that act as buffers to distinguish and protect those inside the firm from the vagaries and whims of the external situation and ensure business continuity.

A 'strategic alliance' has been defined as a 'voluntary arrangement between two or more firms involving exchange, sharing or co-development of products, technologies or services' (Fischer *et al.*, 2002; Gulati, 1998).

'Exchange', 'sharing' and 'co-development' imply a two way relationship, where both parties have an 'expectation of mutually beneficial outcomes' (Miles, Snow and Miles, 2000). We know that the range of potentially beneficial outcomes motivating initial involvement in what may be called an alliance stretches from the creation of fundamentally new markets, market entry, market development, altering market structure by creating critical mass or reducing costs to more efficient use of resources, skill enhancement, acquiring resources and risk reduction (Fischer *et al.*, 2002; Hinteruber, 2002; Johnson and Scholes, 2002; Varadarajan and Cunningham, 1995). Not all of these are aimed at *mutually* beneficial outcomes. Mutual gain requires certain specific conditions (De Wit and Meyer, 1999):

- Partners have similar strategic goals, but different competitive goals. This avoids conflicts of interest and maintains the focus on mutual prosperity from the shared activities.

- Partners can learn from each other, but simultaneously they can protect their proprietary knowledge and capabilities.

- Both partners are relatively modest players in the industry. This sustains interest in the value of long-term interdependence.

Our organizational network may contain a variety of relationships in terms of knowledge flows, ranging from one-sided relationships where the return to one partner might be predominantly either financial and tangible or strategic positioning, without convergent strategic goals or knowledge sharing; at the other end of a spectrum we have alliances that are mutually beneficial according to the criteria listed above, where the relationships will be closer and the knowledge flows more combinatory. These are what we would call co-operative relationships: strategic alliances in which both parties gain value and learn.

'Co-operation' is a special case of the general collaborative capability an organization requires to do business effectively in the knowledge economy. It is the sort of relationship in which valuable learning can occur. The legal structure and governance mechanisms in these relationships may vary from licensing agreements and franchising at the looser end, to technology sharing, consortia, joint development agreements and equity joint ventures, but the mutually beneficial outcome is growth in knowledge. Realistically, not all relationships will produce these returns. Some simply provide diverse input at a more superficial level. Overall, our organization needs to know how to manage each of the different types of relationships in its portfolio for greatest value.

The result of all this relating is that the boundaries around our organizations have become blurred: competitors co-operate, customers advise, suppliers innovate (Davis and Meyer, 1998). Business decisions cannot be isolated from the knowledge activities of others; uncertainty and ambiguity proliferate even as the world supply of knowledge expands exponentially. As these rules of competition change, so too must the rules by which we organize. Strategically, if change is rapid, it makes little sense to invest in durable knowledge resources that quickly become a constraint on flexibility and limit our ability to re-orient to new situations. In such situations it makes more sense to develop the capacity for comprehension and deftness (McGrath, MacMillan and Venkatramann, 1995). By strategically positioning our organizations at the hub of flexible networks of experts (and these may be other organizations or individuals), we can deliver more value than keeping all knowledge inside a pre-conceived boundary. According to a McKinsey report: 'Collaborative networks of suppliers, distributors, subcontractors, and customers have created far more value than their industry peers over the past half-decade and have held up more robustly in the recent market downturn.'(Singer, 2001)

Each member of our network contributes elements of intellectual capability. Knowing how to integrate the knowledge available in a network becomes a major differentiator for an organization that can do it well. When external conditions change, operating within a network gives us more options to adapt the knowledge support structure to meet new demands. We can strengthen or weaken specific relationships ties to alter knowledge flows. We can craft a more intelligent response to a new situation because we can draw on more diverse capabilities and knowledge than our organization could access alone. By supporting diversity within the fabric of the network, our organizations become more flexible, adaptable and faster at learning.

Diverse networks hold together because the quality of the relationships is explicitly managed, but diversity is cited as a major reason for the failure of many global alliances (Parkhe, 1991). Partners who are unfamiliar with the issues in 'voluntary co-operative relationships with foreign firms' often find it hard to surmount the differences associated with societal culture, national context, corporate culture, strategic direction, management assumptions practices and organizational structures. Yet diversity of knowledge is often the reason for the association.

Patterns of experience suggest that organizations develop three different types of network: over-embedded, arm's length and integrated (Uzzi, 1996). Over-embedded networks are primarily made up of co-operative relationships, close ties that are strongly underpinned by social cohesion, work on common values and trust, but often support redundant resources. Arm's length networks are primarily made up of loose ties each of which is purely focused on delivery of a particular resource, and members are not treated with any special preference. Integrated networks are a mix of the benefits of each type of relationship: 'strong ties enrich the network, while weak ties prevent the complete insulation of the network from new possibilities and innovation' (Mariotti and Delbridge, 2001). We should not think of networks as static either. Indeed they have been described 'as a process, a relational cognitive system for channelling valuable knowledge' (Mariotti and Delbridge, 2001).

To realize full value from our relationships, we first need to appreciate why they are important as the basis for intelligent organizing; then we need to know how to establish and develop different types of relationships by managing the factors that shape relationship quality. We will start by looking at social capital, a term used to describe the cumulative investments in the three most important aspects of relating: the network configuration, the collective basis for communication and the relationship qualities. The level of social capital affects the strength of the bonds we can form and the kind of knowledge that can flow. We will then move on to look at how different organizational structures allow us to operate in different ways within networks.

Social capital influences what knowledge can flow in the network

All relationships offer us ways of reducing the knowledge deficiencies of our organizations (Reid, Bussiere and Greenaway, 2001). The most valuable relationships are those that generate learning (Eneroth and Malm, 2001), but there are times when a relationship may simply fill a knowledge gap cheaper or faster than internal knowledge development. The choice of where to focus attention in a network depends on the knowledge that we are seeking and how much time and effort we have to invest in the relationship relative to the possible returns.

Social capital (Adler and Kwon, 2002) is the 'goodwill available to individuals or groups' that arises as a result of three elements:

- The *structure and configuration of the connections* between members in a network.

- The *cognitive compatibility* that develops from social interaction around shared language, narrative and common communication codes and protocols.

- The *quality of the relationship* between the members in terms of the level of trust, the type of norms, the extent of shared beliefs and the degree of obligation and mutual identification with one another.

Members of our network are likely to include individuals, project teams, communities, business units or discrete organizations. The relationships between these various member actors can span all levels. In knowledge flow terms, the connection may be individual-to-individual, individual-to-group, -team or -community, group-to-group, or individual-and-group-to-organization. The network then becomes 'a shared space of emerging relationships' or 'Ba' (Mariotti and Delbridge, 2001). This makes it a complex entity in which social capital is being simultaneously produced and damaged at various levels. The development of social capital will follow the same rules, but the degree to which it emerges and can be relied on will vary depending on the level. To earn social capital, a member must have the opportunity, the motivation and the ability to contribute to the network. Opportunity refers to the ease of access to other members of the network. Motivation can be based on deeply-ingrained beliefs about social responsibility, instrumental incentives such as individual self-interest, external pressure, or normative commitments to the common good of the particular community. Ability is the competence and knowledge resources that each can contribute. Obviously, each of these aspects will be manifested differently at each level and must be managed accordingly, but in principle the ideas summarized in Figure 5.1 are applicable across levels.

Individuals and groups will be developing different degrees of social capital in the course of their interactions around specific purposes. Organizations can influence the ease of connections, they can set the context for value generation and introduce the latent ability, but realizing the value of that ability depends on the willingness of individuals and groups to collaborate towards co-operation. If the knowledge of individuals and groups is to flow effectively, people have to be motivated to work across boundaries and share their abilities with partners. Of course, if the knowledge is easily packaged in products and services, the transfer is easier and social capital becomes somewhat less important. However, if the knowledge sharing depends heavily on communication, we must remember that initially cognitive compatibility can only develop at the individual or group level. Over the long term, if the relationship is to become closer, it is important for that sort of understanding to spread more broadly to unite the various actors in some sort of common communication pattern. Although we may codify some of the elements of structure and cognitive compatibility, ultimately the full extent of social capital at the level of inter-organizational relationships can only be the cumulative result of the various individual and group interactions over

Figure 5.1   Developing social capital (based on Nahapiet and Ghoshal, 1998; Adler and Kwon, 2002)

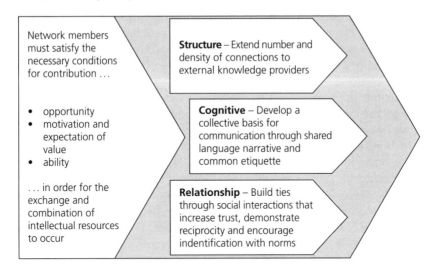

the duration of the collaborative or co-operative relationship. This makes it much harder to develop.

Social capital builds over time as a result of the structure and content of social activity that network members have engaged in. It produces benefits in terms of greater access to information, enhanced influence and increased solidarity. The stronger the social capital, the more each participant can rely on the quality, relevance and timeliness of information and the more attractive a network member will be to others who have knowledge they want to share. The amount of social capital embedded in our network relationships determines the strength of the ties between members and therefore how much knowledge we can acquire and exploit through the connections (Yli-Renko, Autio and Sapienza, 2001).

Building social capital incurs three types of costs:

- The cost of establishing the connections.
- The investment of time and money in developing ways to interact and communicate, and ways to motivate the individuals and groups to interact.
- The effort it takes to define the baseline of moral, psychological or contractual agreement on the purpose of the relationships at the various levels.

Simply establishing a web of network connections based on transactions and information exchange produces a weak form of social capital that creates potential. However, to realize more than opportunistic value, 'the more extensive the set of social links between actors, the greater the set of external resources of knowledge each actor can draw on' (Mariotti and Delbridge, 2001). The structural aspects facilitate explicit knowledge exchange. Ties get stronger as interactions are collectively interpreted and commonly understood. The cognitive dimension smoothes the process of knowledge exchange. The strongest ties depend on constantly re-affirming bonds of mutual trust and shared norms that members identify with. This takes time, sustained effort and continued motivation.

In principle, the looser our relationships, the more likely it is that we will only be able to use them to exchange explicit knowledge. However, the time and effort we have to exert to maintain these relationships will be less.

Tight bonds within our network are particularly important if we need to exchange tacit knowledge (Granovetter, 1973). Tacit knowledge tends to be 'sticky' (Szulanski, 1996), requiring frequent and dense interconnectivity in our network structure, strong social interaction between members and high levels of mutual trust to help it flow. Trust can be a facet of the organizational context as well as an aspect of individual and group relations. Perceptions of trustworthiness at both levels affect the nature of inter-organizational ties. As a facet of organizational image, trustworthiness is an antecedent that can condition any future developments in on-going relationships. It sets the context for the individual and group relations that tend to deliver the outcomes. If the strategic objective of our associations is tacit knowledge sharing, it becomes important to develop durable social capital at the different levels of individual, group and organization. The closer our inter-organizational relationships, the more tacit knowledge will be accessible as shared contexts and purposes, shared language and common experience develop. However, tight ties depend on frequent maintenance, dense interaction between participants at all levels, mutual trust, reciprocity and common beliefs at the group or organizational level. In practice there is a limit to the number of such close and binding ties our organization can properly maintain with a fixed amount of resources and without finding themselves in conflict as they try to align the demands of several close ties.

Faster access to tacit knowledge can be one benefit of relationships. Whilst it is attractive to reduce the time it would take us to develop expertise and transfer it into processes, products or services, the exchange can occur most efficiently if the tacit knowledge is packaged into some tangible form, such as a component or module, that can be accepted as a complete product without the immediate need to go around the full knowledge creation cycle.

Signpost In *Competence Area 3: Learning* we saw that full tacit knowledge exchange is difficult and at an individual level requires high levels of rapport, motivation and interpersonal and communication skills.

We have seen that being innovative is an important facet of international competitiveness in the knowledge economy and innovation is indissolubly linked to a cycle of tacit knowledge diffusion (Nonaka, 1994; Nonaka, Toyama and Konno, 2000; von Krogh, Ichijo and Nonaka, 2000).

In *Competence Area 1: Competing* we saw that the SECI knowledge creation cycle involves progressive conversion of tacit knowledge to explicit knowledge and back again.

The SECI knowledge creation cycle applies equally across networks. Logically then, if we enter into cross-boundary relationships with the specific aim of innovating and learning, we need ties that are based on a sufficiently firm foundation of collective assumptions, shared mental models and common language. We can recall that this process of knowledge creation within an organization is also aided or inhibited by the body of collective tacit assumptions, unspoken understandings and learned behaviour that influence absorptive capacity. Common understanding enhances absorptive capacity.

In *Competence Area 4: Connecting* we saw that absorptive capacity depends on a variety of factors including the level of prior related knowledge and experience. It shapes our ability to connect new knowledge to existing knowledge and internalize potential innovations.

To get full value from our network, we must also pay attention to managing the issues that affect both our individual and our organizational ability to absorb value from the relationships we forge. Otherwise internal barriers can undo the benefits of even the most extensive investment in social capital.

Let us look in more detail at how each element of social capital can be developed within our network, starting with *the structure and configuration of the connections between members*. The structure of our network affects the rate of return we can achieve from the resources available within it (Burt, 1992). Four aspects of network structure affect social capital development and the competitive position that we can achieve as a result (Gnyawali and Madhavan, 2001):

1 *The more central we are in our relationship network, the more access we have to external knowledge assets, the faster knowledge can flow and the more we can learn* (see Figure 5.2). By sitting at the hub of a relationship network, we

Figure 5.2   The organization at the centre of the network gets faster access to knowledge

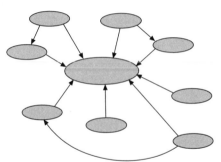

are likely to receive new information before peripheral players. This gives us more chance of first mover advantage, and an earlier opportunity to shape the competitive conditions for others. Potentially, we can also gain more prestige, which may deter others from competitive responses.

2 *The more our organizations are connected to isolated complementary players, the better positioned we are to influence information flows* and to take autonomous action that those with complementary knowledge will have to follow (see Figure 5.3). With our organizations at the hub of networks in which other players are disconnected from one another, we are well placed to influence the interpretation of information for everyone. As the central player, we are likely to get better quality input, more diverse insights and less redundancy of information than if other players in the network are closely connected.

3 *The more similarity there is between the resource profile of our network and that of a competitor, the less likely they are to confront us* because the potential for significant gains is reduced (see Figure 5.4). This hints at a possible strategy to stabilize turbulent industries where competition is escalating to damaging proportions: establish a network of knowledge-bearing relationships comparable to that of the major player.

4 *The density of our network, that is, the number of interconnections between the various players, affects knowledge flow speed and efficiency* (see Figure 5.5). Self-evidently, the more connections there are, the more chance there is to develop shared routines for information collection and distribution. In densely-connected networks, shared norms, trust and accepted ways of behaving emerge quickly and are self re-enforcing, so dense networks can be more productive than sparsely connected webs of relationships. However, damaging effects can equally escalate rapidly. Awareness of how to defuse unacceptable activities is important, as is avoiding the risk of 'group think' developing.

Figure 5.3 An organization at the centre of the network gains influence when other players are not connected to each other

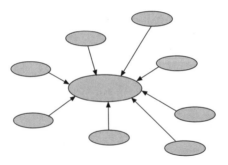

Figure 5.4 The organization with a similar network to that of the major competitor reduces the risk of confrontation

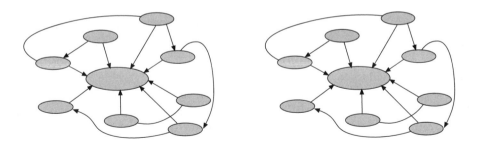

Figure 5.5 Knowledge flows more quickly and efficiently in dense networks

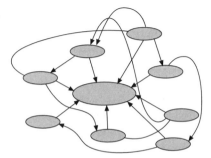

Generally, in large networks with many weak ties, the role of the central co-ordinator is to cultivate and encourage the community. In contrast, sparse networks with tight bonds take greater care in selecting and nurturing partners that fit culturally and complement their strategic goals (De Wit and Meyer, 1999).

The second element of social capital, *cognitive compatibility* develops as members of our networks come to understand our organizations and each other. The capability to communicate effectively about issues with different levels of complexity develops gradually. Most simply, data and information can be exchanged on a transactional basis through compatible systems of electronic connections. At more advanced levels, sufficient mutual understanding and communication skills develop for tacit knowledge to be exchanged between expert individuals. Over time, a shared language emerges between members of the network, which can diffuse across the organization through stories and cross-project interaction. Shared language means more than the ability to speak the same national language, it means appreciating the nuances of the sense in which words are used. As relationships develop, a common way of communicating about issues emerges. Shared experiences in solving joint problems also create the material for stories and the development of a shared history. Together, these embed collective knowledge in the network.

In *Competence Area 3: Learning* we saw that we need to pay attention to the way language is used if individual and collective learning is to be effective.

Moving on to the final element of social capital – *the quality of the relationships between the members of a network* – we find that trust is a major indicator of the way our relationships develop. There are different qualities of trust and different ways to develop it.

Trust is a complex concept that emerges as a result of the interactions of members of our network. See Box 5.2 to find out more about different forms of trust. We can make the criteria for trust explicit, as in the case of legal obligations, or leave them tacit, as in the case of reciprocal favours either between individuals or organizations. Trust can also be tacitly encapsulated in the qualities that support our brand image, or explicitly certified in an internationally recognized code of quality such as ISO 9002.

Totally tacit trust between members of our network can only be sustained between individuals or in relatively small local groups and communities. As the network grows and the interaction between different local sub-communities extends across boundaries, it usually becomes necessary to negotiate and codify some rules in order to link the communities and combine their knowledge effectively. However, the quality of trust within close relationships cannot be managed entirely by predefining rules and codes of conduct. Trust is a dynamic force that changes as close partners move further from the initial conditions, where trust was probably based on personal reputation, prior experience and/or institutional standing or negotiated agreements.

Over time, experience of partner interactions (for example, whether people live up to expectations, reciprocate favours and are transparent in their dealings) changes the basis of trust. Events outside the partnership can also cast shadows over the level of trust; for example, perceptions of individual or organizational actions outside the scope of the agreed relationship or changes in industry conditions in favour of one partner (Arino, de la Torre and Smith Ring, 2001). This process by which trust evolves and the way trust at the local level is linked to development of trust at the network level affect the ability of our own organization to tap into its networks for both innovation and access to knowledge.

A high level of trust within relationships has been shown to generate economic advantage. Trusting relationships have lower transaction costs associated with them because they reduce the need for extensive formal contracting. The risks of inequitable use of knowledge are also diminished, so less attention may need to be paid to protecting knowledge assets. Co-ordination of the activities of different parties takes less time and effort and more valuable tacit knowledge can be shared in the relationship (McKenzie and Potter, 2002; McKenzie and van Winkelen, 2001).

We may choose to deliberately decouple the elements of our network for strategic protection (Ganzaroli, 2002). The Italian clothes manufacturer, distributor and franchise-based retailer Benetton has historically operated through a

Box 5.2

The nature of trust

Trust between local members of a network and the broader global system of value creation emerges in three different forms (Ganzaroli, 2002):

- Under-socialized
- Highly socialized
- Embedded in the network structure.

Under-socialized trust is based on members making rational choices about the self-interest behind others' behaviour (in other words, I trust you because I can see it is worth your while to be trustworthy and it is in my interest to reciprocate that sort of trustworthy behaviour). Under-socialized trust can only be enforced through institutionalized mechanisms aimed at preventing or penalizing opportunistic behaviour such as:

1 Explicitly codifying the rules that define what is trustworthy and what is untrustworthy behaviour; for example, through laws and regulations.

2 Establishing a system of incentives that either formalizes evidence of trustworthiness (for example, quality awards), or penalizes untrustworthy behaviour (for example, recourse to legal fines and/or prison).

3 Appointing a 'guardian of trust' to evaluate performance against measurable standards (in the same way as a judge and jury assess action against legal criteria and an arbitration panel interpret behaviour against contractual obligations).

Highly socialized trust is based on individuals identifying with and conforming to a set of moral obligations and ethical values that become a social contract between members of a community. The development of such trust depends on dense interactions within localized strata of a community. Broader diffusion of such trust depends on reliable intermediaries; these form institutionalized linking networks that act to spread the norms and values across the strata of the community.

Trust becomes *embedded in networks* in stages. It may start out as rational calculation on the part of members joining the network, but it develops based on mutual predictability as members negotiate and execute formal commitments consistently and accurately. It matures as a result of the informal sense-making that comes from personal interactions and these establish a sort of psychological contract that binds the network together.

predominantly decoupled network of suppliers, agents and distributors, in which trust was grounded in a variety of different mechanisms.

Whilst retaining knowledge and control over strategic parts of the production process (weaving, cutting and dyeing of clothes; quality control of packaging; distribution and product design), during the 1980s Benetton established a local cluster of small- and medium-sized firms (SMEs) in Italy to manufacture the 80 per cent of its product that was labour intensive. At this local level, on-going trust was maintained through contractual relationships with a group of subcontractors (frequently owned or run by past and current employees), who agreed to work exclusively for Benetton. Most subcontractors were isolated in the network and Benetton was a communication hub, channelling most interactions down singular routes between themselves and the subcontractors (see Figure 5.3, p. 188). This local network served to keep costs down and increase production flexibility. In the 1990s the firm extended their relationship network to include new contractors abroad, which could serve their expanded global market. Once again these SME subcontractors were often set up and managed by either ex-employees or people from their Italian contractor network, but their contribution was still centrally directed.

On the distribution side, relationship ties were even weaker. Benetton relied on under-socialized trust in the form of licensing agreements to position itself at the hub of a global network of around 7000 retail franchisees. Relying on trust in the brand, licensed local entrepreneurs with little direct relationship to the parent organization became the sales outlets for Benetton products. Benetton was insulated from contact with their franchisees by a select network of 90 agents who became the intermediaries between Benetton and the market outlets. Relationships with agents were generally based on highly socialized trust because most agents were family friends or past employees. Agents initiated relationships with franchisees; under-socialized trust, which came from agents taking shares in the local stores, was used to sustain the connection. The agents diffused knowledge about new products and stimulated new franchises in the local area. However, they acted as a decoupling mechanism between Benetton and their customers, and the customers and suppliers.

Recent developments in the Benetton story show a change of network approach. The organization has moved away from the decoupled approach in order to: (a) get closer to the customer by opening their own directly owned retail outlets in the main shopping areas of big cities; (b) cultivate uniquely differentiating creative fabric ideas by establishing an international research center; and (c) link customers to suppliers through an automated logistics management process that can co-ordinate worldwide distribution of 10 million garments per month. This strategy of vertical integration has been driven by a recognition that brand equity, knowledge of consumer behaviour, innovative fabric development processes and intense knowledge of logistics should be centrally managed rather than diffused around the network (Camuffo, Romano and Vinelli, 2001).

Benetton's network strategy has provided efficiency and flexibility in knowledge exploitation, but the organization has resisted relying on its external network for innovation since it is operating within a highly competitive and creative industry. Recent changes to increase innovative capacity through better access to customer purchasing trends have stimulated innovation while retaining flexibility.

Other organizations have evolved closer network ties both to produce significant cost and efficiency benefits and to encourage innovation. In the case of Fiat, the Italian car manufacturer, close relationships between members of their supplier network were initially facilitated by codified standards of trust. Fiat established a closed network of certified local suppliers who produced to predefined standards and were therefore allowed to self-certify the quality of the parts they produced. This saved Fiat time and money, as well as guaranteeing business to the suppliers (Ganzaroli, 2002).

Over time, consistently reliable performance has formed the basis for building trust and frequent dense communication patterns helped suppliers to develop tacit understanding of Fiat's objectives. This enabled the partners to move beyond the initial under-socialized trust to a more relational form of contracting (Arino, de la Torre and Smith Ring, 2001). Suppliers became partners in the strategic development of Fiat as a company by making a considerable contribution to the design of new cars.

Fiat operates in different market conditions to Benetton. Fashions and tastes change quickly so the landscape is relatively turbulent; translating rapid innovation into acceptable products consistent with customer trust in the brand is a crucial strategic capability. Innovation in the car market is relatively slow and new knowledge is more strongly linked to knowledge of existing production capability; this makes it safer to work with a close supplier network without losing critical knowledge to the competitors. Unlike Benetton, at the distribution end of the supply chain Fiat also created a tight and interactive dealer network that could share and exchange orders; early on they linked the dealership ordering process to the supply side through a just-in-time production and sourcing system, making them a highly attractive company for suppliers to work with.

In some cases, forming loosely coupled networks that embed a mix of tacit and explicit trust at the interface between local and global networks can be advantageous. Our organizations can act as integrators using the tacit trust we have built through local one-to-one relationships to co-ordinate a variable network of specialist local enterprises in one-off contracted projects. We can extend access to this valuable network of close ties by building a reputation as a transparent intermediary able to create trustworthy linkages to a wider global network.

In other instances, communities of creation such as Sun Microsystems' Jini Project have acted like 'gated communities' that accept members under specific terms (Sawhney and Prendelli, 2000). Sun designed a networking software product to connect many different computers and output devices like TVs and printers into a single distributed network. They realized that they could not own all the expertise needed to compile such a complex software backbone into a reliable infrastructure for many customers. They formed a loosely-coupled community of source code providers to develop the product and spread the risk.

Members signed a community source licence that gave Sun some proprietary advantage, but more importantly ensured compatibility of software versions, codified the basis of trust and maintained internal coherence and cohesion. Members developed their own modifications and extensions to the software, thus encouraging innovation. Sun required only that members publicized the interfaces to these new developments so that other community members could link into them.

The codification of trust in the licensing gave Sun some flexibility to admit members on different terms. Sun provided a range of support for developers, depending on their level of integration into the network. In this case, relatively loose ties provided flexible innovation capability, while Sun's central co-ordination of the licensing agreement created a trustworthy link between dispersed members.

We can see that the three elements of social capital play different roles in loose, moderate and close relationship ties in Table 5.1.

These principles are evident in the very different network strategies that organizations have adopted. Some examples are summarized in Table 5.2.

We can now see that social capital embedded in our networks is a source of intelligence. It provides our organizations with the ability to draw on, integrate and apply knowledge stored in the various network members and so adapt to environmental conditions. The learning that arises out of the relationships can also occur at a network level too, which actually changes the environmental conditions for all players. The biotechnology industry is a case in point. The knowledge base of the industry is so complex and widely dispersed that it is almost impossible for one organization to learn alone. The interactions of the various members in the industry generate new learning that is distributed and stored across the network and changes the potential of each member to perform in their own arena: it advances the totality of knowledge that all members have

Table 5.1 The importance of each social capital element for different strengths of relationship ties

	In loose ties	In moderate ties	In close ties
Importance of configuring structure and managing the density of connections	High — based on transactional requirements and opportunistic links	Moderate – manage for reduction of conflicts of interest	High – based on strategic needs and many frequent chances to connect
Importance of cognitive compatibility	Low – based on codified rules	Moderate – based on explicit language and narrative	High – often tacit knowledge based on shared experience
Importance of quality of relationship	Low – based on under-socialized trust	Moderate – based on mix of under- and highly-socialized trust	High – based on highly socialized and network embedded trust

Table 5.2	Three very different knowledge network strategies illustrating the use of different forms of relationship ties	
Company	Activities co-ordinated and managed centrally and relationship basis	Purpose for accessing network knowledge and nature of network strategy
Toyota Car manufacture and sales (De Wit and Meyer, 1999)	Design, assembly, marketing.	• Component modules produced from primary suppliers. • Component parts produced by second tier suppliers. • Distribution undertaken through agents. Relationships based on loose ties and largely structural connections.
Genentech Biotech drugs research (De Wit and Meyer, 1999)	Technological innovation. Genentech is 'the talent scout' for Hoffman La Roche, the pharmaceutical company that owns 66 per cent of their stock (Powell, 1998).	• Production and distribution undertaken by pharmaceutical companies. • Early intelligence to feed innovation captured from universities. Most relationships for knowledge exploitation rely on loose ties. Moderate ties with universities to understand the tacit element of early intelligence.
Dell Computer assembly and sales (Quinn, 1999)	Customer knowledge and product support.	• Component design and innovation, production and software development undertaken by original equipment manufacturers. Closer relationship ties with suppliers used to co-ordinate innovation effectively and link to customer requirements. Assembly to order from industry standard components.

access to. In other words, the network as a whole becomes more intelligent (Mariotti and Delbridge, 2001).

For our organizations, the key to value generation from this web of relationships is to ensure that the returns at each node of our own networks are mutually re-enforcing. To create a sustainable and valuable network of connections we need to strategically assess the best mix of close and loose ties for the market space in which we are operating. Investments in developing social capital between organizational members of our networks are an important influence on the way we can design and manage the portfolio of ties in our network and the degree of knowledge flows and learning that can be achieved at different levels in the network. When the environmental conditions change and the returns along a particular link become less valuable, we can re-evaluate or sever that connection in favour of another more useful one.

Co-ordination mechanisms affect the flexibility and coherence of knowledge use

Our second step is to review how different mechanisms for relationship co-ordination give rise to different sorts of network structures, with different levels of flexibility and coherence. We have seen throughout this chapter that a shared sense of identity and purpose is important if members of a network are going to work together coherently, co-operate meaningfully and share knowledge effectively. Yet, the purpose of networks is to provide an organization with the flexibility to adapt to environmental turbulence. In the search to develop ways of doing both, organizations have evolved a range of structures that are appropriate to the conditions in their market space. Each networked structure creates value in a different way. Some are more suited to knowledge exploitation and others are better fitted for exploration, specifically because they support different types of knowledge to flow.

There are three mechanisms for structuring/co-ordinating relationships:

1 market/price,
2 hierarchy/authority,
3 community/trust.

Using markets and pricing to mediate interactions has limitations for knowledge co-ordination, but they are still useful. Hierarchy and authority tend to support specialization, efficiency and routine exploitation but obstruct collaboration, innovation and non-routine activities. In the quest to 'manage' knowledge, we are increasingly encouraged to move towards more communal trust-based associations. Yet trust also has its limitations. First, in some situations it may be worth betraying a trust to gain a competitive edge. Second, too much trust can blind organizations to new potential and limit innovation. For example, highly-trusted supplier networks tend to encourage stagnation because the comfort of old relationships is stronger than the attraction of new potential. Third, community and trust affect people's willingness to be accountable for an outcome over which they have no control. Fourth, unmanaged trust can allow knowledge to leak inappropriately (Norman, 2001).

Although each of the three paired co-ordination mechanisms can be mutually exclusive, if carefully implemented the complementary effects of one pair upon the other can give our organizations the ability to take advantage of otherwise contradictory benefits (Adler, 2002). Progressively more complex networked structures can be used to take advantage of mixed structural co-ordination mechanisms that satisfy more than one strategic priority and give us more flexibility to adapt to varying environmental conditions. The trade-offs are least when all three pairs of mechanisms are combined (see Table 5.3a,b,c).

As an example, the multi-divisional organizational structure evolved to introduce flexibility into large organizations and combine the efficiency benefits of hierarchical functional operations with the stimulus of market economics. Refocusing internal networks on markets can prove to be a highly-efficient way of exploiting existing knowledge, but it works less well when we try to encourage knowledge diffusion across divisions and stimulate knowledge creation. The right incentives are not in place to produce collaborative relationships. Forming communities of practice across divisional boundaries has become one option to stimulate knowledge creation internally, but accessing diverse ideas requires the ability to draw on external networks too.

In *Competence Area 3: Learning* we saw how to develop internal communities of practice to enhance learning.

To develop the right mix of loose and close relationships across divisions of one organization and across networks of many organizations, we need to select the appropriate co-ordination mechanism to achieve the desired ends. The choices we make affect how well our organization can fulfil three essential activities (Child and Gunther McGrath, 2001):

- Identifying and aligning a shared sense of purpose.
- Regulating the 'inside-out' and 'outside-in' flows of resources.
- Identifying and managing the rights, duties, functions and roles of its members.

In *Competence Area 4: Connecting* we looked at various ways in which to manage the permeability of an organization's boundary to regulate knowledge flows in both directions.

The choice of alternative ways to structure and co-ordinate internal and external relationships has become rather confusing. Tables 5.3a, 5.3b and 5.3c summarize the characteristics of the wide variety of structures that have emerged as our organizations try different strategies to achieve both flexibility in the way we relate to the outside world and a coherent sense of their own identity within a network of relationships.

Each combination has different relative strengths that affect how easy it is to identify and spread shared aims, and regulate resource flows for knowledge exploitation and innovation. Consequently, each form provides a different answer to the trade-off between maintaining both an appropriate sense of organizational identity and an appropriate level of flexibility, making it more or less suited to respond to the level of external uncertainty.

There are inevitably trade-offs. The larger networked organizational forms can rely on economies of scope as an adaptation strategy, but the bureaucratic overhead incurred to leverage knowledge to the full can outweigh the benefit if the environment is very changeable. Multi-entity networks can be more responsive and nimble in exploring new knowledge domains, but it becomes harder to encompass and harness the breadth of knowledge needed because of lack of internal coherence.

We can see from Table 5.3a that using a single pair of mechanisms (market/ price, hierarchy/authority, or community/trust) to co-ordinate relationships really only confers the ability to exploit knowledge. Selecting the pair that is most suitable depends mainly on the level of external turbulence.

In Table 5.3b, we see a combination of two pairs of mechanisms only provides greater competitive sustainability when the shared aims are internally generated (option 6). The networks of relationships cross many boundaries, but there is still a clear demarcation of organizational purpose and values or vision that pre-ordains the extent of shared identity within the network. In many circumstances, the internal cohesion may provide stronger protection against competitive threats. The advantage of this approach is that recombination of capabilities, routines and work practices for innovation may be more straightforward, but the stimulus to radical learning will be significantly less (Ciborra and Andreu, 2002).

Combining all three pairs of co-ordination mechanisms (as shown in Table 5.3c) opens up the organizational structure to more external diversity, but the basis of identity relies on the network of resources and routines being self re-enforcing and not mutually contradictory (Dyer and Singh, 1998). In these forms, our organizations can exert influence, but have less control over our shared evolution. Their unique merged identity can be hard to challenge competitively, but more difficult to maintain in the long term. The more communal the structure, the more knowledge 'spillovers' are likely. This multiplies knowledge opportunity, but makes it harder to competitively protect knowledge exchange. These complex dynamics demand that we pay more attention to the weight of investment in the three aspects of social capital in order to achieve best value from knowledge.

The permeability of the boundaries of our organizations to knowledge flows changes according to the extent of the shared aims, the main types of knowledge involved and the main means of member governance within the network: these are shown in the central three columns of each table. Ultimately, the boundaries of our organizations are defined by the choices we make about how to co-ordinate relationships (see Figure 5.6). The tension between the close ties we have and the loose associations in our network is what gives us our ability to reconfigure the organizational boundary without necessarily integrating all the required knowledge into our organizations This gives us more flexibility and more intelligence to adapt cost-effectively.

Just like a fishnet which is both strong and adaptable, as well as light and compressible, we gain the ability to support a rich 'catch' of knowledge, but the organizational boundaries can contract quickly if conditions change and the knowledge is no longer needed (Davis and Davidson, 1991).

Overall, we would argue that our organizations benefit from participating in networks of knowledge sharing relationships if (Matusik, 2002):

● Participation does not undermine the sense of identity within our organizations.

● The costs involved in maintaining the relationships do not exceed the benefits.

● There is sufficient absorptive capacity within our organizations to use the knowledge that is available.

● There is the ability to protect existing knowledge appropriately.

There are many different ways to protect knowledge in relationships. Research suggests some are more effective than others (Norman, 2001). The most effective are organizational awareness of the need for protection and 'walling off' critical knowledge. The former might include such activities as top management focusing on protecting capabilities, education about what is proprietary knowledge, appointing an information manager, contractually defining what knowledge is proprietary and what can be shared, categorizing documents for secrecy and having an alliance function to focus on protecting capabilities. The latter would include performing certain activities away from the partner and placing critical pieces of information off limits.

Patents seem to be more useful in the pharmaceutical and chemical industries than in high-tech businesses like electronics and semi-conductors. It is easier to protect the physical composition of a chemical or drug because it cannot be

Figure 5.6 The tension between loose and tight relationships defines the organizational boundary

Organizational form and boundaries emerge
from the tension created by relationships in our network

Close ties ←——————————→ Loose associations

Close ties	Loose associations
● Essential to valuable shared experience	● Provide access to distinctive know-what
● Protect against competitive threat	● Protect against uncertainty
● Allow flow of tacit knowledge	● Mainly carry codified easily-diffusable knowledge
● Require social integration	● Require systems integration
● Enable stronger market influence	● Enable responsiveness
● Re-enforce identity	● Challenge identity
● Deliver richer rewards	● Encompass diversity
● Deliver through values alignment	● Deliver through conflict management

Table 5.3a The impact of simple approaches for co-ordinating relationships upon knowledge flows, flexibility and level of internal coherence

Co-ordination mechanism	Example forms Higher trust = tighter association Low trust = loose coupling	Extent of shared aims	Main type of knowledge resource flows	Main means of member governance	Flexibility of response to external turbulence	Level of internal coherence	Suitable to exploit/ explore knowledge
1. Market/Price	**Higher Trust** *Relational contracting* (Adler, 2002).	Moderated through negotiation.	Mostly explicit, some tacit over time and embedded in products.		Moderate	Moderate	Mainly exploit. Limited new knowledge creation.
	Lower Trust *Spot Market* (Adler, 2002).	Non-existent.	Only explicit.	Contracts	High	Low	Exploit only.
2. Hierarchy/ Authority	**Higher Trust** *Enabling Bureaucracy* (Adler, 2002). *International Organization* where knowledge developed at centre and transferred overseas.	Explicit company vision and strategy critical to integration (Nonaka, 1991).	Explicit through systems Tacit through face-to-face communication.	Empowerment	Low	High	Predominantly exploit, with limited value generated from central exploration.

Overseas operations adapt and exploit parent company's abilities (Bartlett and Ghoshal 1989).

Lower Trust *Coercive Bureaucracy* (Adler, 2002).	Limited at high level	Largely explicit	Coercion through targets	Very low	Low	Exploit only
Global Organization where knowledge developed and retained at the centre. Overseas operations implement parent company strategies. (Bartlett and Ghoshal, 1989).						
3. Community/ Trust	*Clan* (Adler, 2002).	High in communities	Much tacit	Shared values and beliefs	Low	High	Exploit mainly

Table 5.3b The impact of combining two approaches for co-ordinating relationships upon knowledge flows, flexibility and level of internal coherence

Co-ordination mechanism	Example forms Higher trust = tighter association Low trust = loose coupling	Extent of shared aims	Main type of knowledge resource flows	Main means of member governance	Flexibility of response to external turbulence	Level of internal coherence	Suitable to exploit/ explore knowledge
4. Market/Price AND Hierarchy/ Authority	**Higher Trust** *Keiretsu* (Adler, 2002).	Moderate and emergent as a result of socialization and shared context.	Some tacit over time as a result of shared experience.	Membership rules, sponsorship and system for managing IPR.	Moderate	Moderate	Exploit
	Lower Trust *Multinational Corporations* (also known as MNCs & M Form). Decentralization used to create self-sufficiency in overseas operations. A mini economic network (Bartlett and Ghoshal, 1998).	Limited	Tacit developed and retained by each unit. Explicit shared opportunistically.	Internal competition.	Low	Low	Exploit
5. Market/Price AND Community/ Trust	*Open Source Movement* (Informal collaboration by	Transient shared self-interest.	Explicit	Standards. No single member owns the IPR.	High	Low	Explore

distributed experts to produce software code).

6. Hierarchy/ Authority AND Community/ Trust							
Higher Trust *Transnational Organization* Value creation from combination of specialization and interdependencies across integrated worldwide operations (Bartlett and Ghoshal, 1998).	Overarching market purpose and values.	Tacit and explicit developed together and shared worldwide.	Processes	Moderate	High	Exploit and explore
Moderate Trust *Hypertext Organization* Value creation across process levels. Combines efficiency and stability of hierarchical bureaucracy with dynamism of flat cross-functional task forces (Nonaka, 1994).	Looser coupling around organizational vision of creating relevant knowledge.	Tacit and explicit sharing across business and project levels underpinned by tacit collective level.	Self-organization around projects and interests for exploration. Processes and systems and common knowledge base for exploitation.	Moderate	Moderate	Exploit and explore

Table 5.3c The impact of a complex integration of approaches for co-ordinating relationships upon knowledge flows, flexibility and level of internal coherence

Co-ordination mechanism	Example forms Higher trust = tighter association Low trust = loose coupling	Extent of shared aims	Main type of knowledge resource flows	Main means of member governance	Flexibility of response to external turbulence	Level of internal coherence	Suitable to exploit/ explore knowledge
7. Community/ Trust AND Market/Price AND Hierarchy/ Authority	*Communities of creation* Value generation distributed and internal to the community (Sawhney and Prendelli, 2000).	Incentives to participate. Needs establishment of minimum cognitive common denominator.	Tacit interpretations within local contexts. Standardized distribution of explicit across community.	Informal. Distributed authority. IPR vested in community not individuals.	High	High	Explore

Strategic centres Major value generation centrally co-ordinated (Lorenzoni and Baden-Fuller, 1995).	Centrally co-ordinated partnering based on a vision integrating multiple capabilities for mutual learning. Trust and reciprocity are key.	The central firm develops co-ordination competence to manage long term relationships. Largely explicit and often mediated through ICT.	Brand image and effective support systems. Formal mechanisms to attract and select partners.	Moderate	High	Exploit and explore
Clusters and constellations Competing and collaborating firms within the same industry co-located geographically (Porter, 1998).	Alignment of self-interest within an industry space.	Recycling of critical know-how between members as people move jobs. This protects the knowledge within the cluster, but not individual members.	Relatively loose collaboration of self-organizing independent entities in a related market space. Repeated exchange fosters trust.	High	Low	Exploit and explore

modified and still produce the same results. In technology industries companies can 'invent around' the patent.

The least effective methods of protection in alliances are: *punitive contractual measures* like non-disclosure agreements, refusing to employ partner employees or penalties for illegal access to information; *hindering integration* by restricting information channels to one gatekeeper, refusing to share critical capabilities and placing some personnel off limits in the communication process; and *after the fact actions* like rewarding protection and reporting contact with partner personnel.

Taking all these factors into consideration, to become a Knowledgeable Organization we need to know how to pay attention to building and sustaining a network containing the right mix of loose connections and close ties, so as to maximize these returns from relationships. In that context, our knowledge strategy needs to address two questions:

1 Which members in the network add value and how many knowledge connections are sustainable given resources we have available?

2 Where would tightening co-operative knowledge-sharing ties increase value and where would looser coupling improve the knowledge generating potential of the organization as a whole?

To do this we need to know how to pay attention to forming and maintaining each type of relationship: close ties and loose connections. We will look at each in turn.

Paying attention to close relationship ties

Given the time and effort it takes to develop close relationship ties and the risks inherent in doing so (such as loss of flexibility, merged identity, 'group think', being betrayed or loss of proprietary knowledge (Reid, Bussiere and Greenaway, 2001)), it is vital that we focus on the relationships that are going to deliver the most value. Generally, 'win/win' relationships should be our objective. We might select players in our network that can contribute knowledge that is strategically critical for us, but if the relationship is not similarly advantageous for them, it is unlikely to become a close tie. When we work together on highly complex or uncertain tasks, cognitive, social and cultural compatibility becomes a high priority for developing the close ties needed to support tacit knowledge exchange.

Close relationships can be internal with employees, or external with key customers or strategic suppliers. They can also take the form of strategic alliances and joint ventures with competitors and organizations which have products or services that complement our own. We have already considered the ways in which we can develop close ties with employees, so in this chapter we will focus on external relationships.

Signpost

In *Competence Area 3: Learning* we saw that a basis for building close relationships with knowledge workers is providing the opportunity for them to continue to keep knowledge up-to-date through participating in leading communities of practice.

Some relationships will carry more 'inside-out' knowledge flows; others will support more 'outside-in' intelligence. Today, much of the value from many of the relationships is likely to be generated through interactions that are largely virtual and new forms of relationship management skills are needed. The factors which affect the closeness of any relationship are the frequency of exchange between the collaborating parties, the length of the relationship and the nature of the information being exchanged (Mariotti and Delbridge, 2001). Close ties are those in which exchange is based on some form of reciprocity, have frequent exchanges and endure for long enough for the social relations to develop sufficiently.

Practical approaches to building and maintaining close relationships involve:

- knowing how to make the relationships progressively closer;
- allocating responsibility for close relationships;
- managing problems when they arise.

We will look at each in turn.

Develop closer relationships progressively to build trust in the exchange

Often relationships progress through three stages of knowledge exchange (Venkatramann and Henderson, 1998):

1. A loose connection that builds familiarity and improves operating efficiency at a unit level.
2. Moderate connection that adds value through tightening the relationship and creating links at the organization level.
3. Strong interdependency that delivers innovation and growth through connections across members of the network.

In this section, we will look at ways of developing progressively close ties with *customers, suppliers* and *other organizations* such as competitors, organizations that offer complementary products or services, and expert sources, so that the knowledge benefits can be achieved.

Undoubtedly, it takes time to develop close ties with key *customers*. Through technological advances in Customer Relationship Management systems it has become easier to track the form and level of activities with different customers. Identifying key customers who provide a high percentage of profitable sales is now an easy first step. However, it is also worth identifying those customers with whom a closer relationship could be beneficial in terms of prestige, knowledge access or because they are particularly influential. They may be large purchasers, or have particular influence on the choices of others within the industry. Creating opportunities for interaction and listening to their feedback can produce many valuable ideas for improvement. Working with them to develop new products can reduce both the development risk and the cost of R&D. This can also help develop the loyalty and trust necessary to keep them, provided that the response to their feedback is genuine. Retaining customers by giving them better service and building their loyalty is generally more cost-effective than recruiting new customers. Table 5.4 suggests ways of developing progressively closer customer ties.

An example of a way of maintaining a loose but value-added connection to customers was Federal Express's development of a system for keeping customers informed about the location of parcels. A real-time tracking system was designed to monitor each parcel from collection, through each stage of transport and on to the point of delivery. Customers were given password-protected access to an Internet site to allow them complete visibility of the process.

A closer relationship (moderate bond) was formed through AT&T's customization of a business-to-business Internet portal application for its clients (Costello and Flar, 2000). The portal allowed clients to access customized electronically-based information on their company, their title and what features they required. It could also be used as collaboration tool between the sales team and the client, offering a shared calendar and a 'Questions and Answers' area. The portal allowed transactions such as ordering a new service or making a change to an existing one. It was recognized that successful adoption required that the information accessed provided value each time the portal was used by a client.

Even closer ties with its customers have been developed by a supplier of speciality flavours to the food industry, Bush Boake Allen (BBA) later International Flavors and Fragrances (Thomke and von Hippel, 2002). Speciality flavours are used to enhance the taste of processed foods and their development requires a high degree of customization and expertise. The company created a tool kit to allow customers to develop their own flavours, which BBA then manufactured. Correctly interpreting customers' requirements had proven to be difficult and potentially expensive, with only 5–10 per cent of flavours eventually reaching the marketplace. BBA created an Internet-based tool containing a large database of flavour profiles. The customer could select and manipulate the information from their desk and send the new design to an automated machine that manufactured a sample within a few minutes: machines could even be based on the customer's site. Tasting the flavour in combination with the other food ingredients was followed by repeated design cycles to create the required product, which BBA manufactured on the scale required.

Close bonds with *suppliers* can be developed in similar stages as shown in Table 5.5. Dell Computer Corporation has demonstrated how to integrate many of these approaches to create a network of supplier relationships (Margretta, 1998). The company sells computers directly to customers and assembles customized orders based on industry standard modular parts. The founder Michael

Table 5.4 Building knowledge-based relationships with customers

Relationship with customers	Loose connection	Moderate bond	Strong tie
Social capital investment =	*Infrastructure + interaction*	*Infrastructure + personalized interaction*	*Infrastructure + personalized interaction + trust*
Knowledge flows 'inside-out' to customers	Enable customers to experience products and services 24 hours a day, 7 days a week.	Personalize product offering to customer interests and needs. Provide customized knowledge feeds that match customers' interests. Educate customers as the more people know about your products and services the more uses they may find for them (Nalebuff and Brandenburger, 1997).	Support and actively orchestrate virtual customer communities that add value and re-enforce the trust inherent in a strong brand identity. Share knowledge about new products before release. Provide sufficient knowledge for customers to innovatively develop the product itself or applications of the product. Use reference customers in advertising to enhance brand image and external identity of the organization.
Knowledge flows 'outside-in' from customers	Collect data from interactions to establish trends and patterns. Use data mining to find the knowledge that can influence changes in products and services. Look at trends to identify customers who ought to become more closely tied into the business.	Collect and respond to feedback via Internet	Use loyal customers to critique and test products before they are ready for general launch.

Table 5.5   Building knowledge-based relationships with suppliers

Relationship with suppliers	Loose connection	Moderate bond	Strong tie
Social capital investment =	*Infrastructure + interaction*	*Infrastructure + tailored interaction that benefits supplier*	*Infrastructure + tailored interaction + trust (either codified or based on experience of performance)*
Knowledge flows 'inside-out' to suppliers	Use technology to manage information flows instead of focusing on physically managing inventory.	Become more interdependent by linking business processes more closely with those of suppliers. Help strategic suppliers understand the business better. Outsource activities based on non-core knowledge (Quinn, 1999). Lock-in suppliers who are crucial to your network by sharing product knowledge, technology and the returns from the relationship.	Build resource coalitions: clusters of producers of complementary products and services who can produce synergies by working together and sharing knowledge to supply whole experiences to customers. Share employees. Invest to help suppliers in building competence to meet required standards.
Knowledge flows 'outside-in' from suppliers	Subcontract parts of a project to assess knowledge requirements or save cost. Speed up the supply chain by sourcing knowledge compressed into modules rather than component parts.	In-source expertise through secondments, shadowing and resource sharing. Learn what customers your suppliers have and find out whether supplying them makes it more difficult to supply you. If so, either loosen the tie or give them some incentive to work more closely with you (Nalebuff and Brandenburger, 1997).	Involve key suppliers in R&D processes. Share employees.

Dell called the business model 'Virtual Integration'. A fundamental element of the approach was changing from the conventional business focus of how much inventory Dell held, to how fast it was moving. Inventory velocity has been one of the few measures that they have used and it has successfully focused efforts on working with suppliers to keep improving performance. Where suppliers were offering excellent quality, Dell was able to reach the point of zero inventories. For example, Sony manufactured monitors to such a high quality standard that Dell was able to trust that their outsourced logistics partners could simply collect them from Sony, match the monitor to the assembled computer that they had already collected from a Dell manufacturing centre and then deliver the whole order directly to the customer.

Dell developed even closer relationships with suppliers by sharing production requirements with them on a real-time basis, even hourly in some cases. This was designed to achieve the efficiencies that would be expected from information flows between departments that were internal to an organization. Michael Dell saw that Virtual Integration meant 'stitching together a business with partners that are treated as if they're inside the company'.

The effective use of communication technology was also seen by Dell as a way of increasing the value to be gained from sharing information. Design databases and methodologies have been shared with supplier partners, speeding the time to develop new products. Dell has adopted a strategy of working with as few supplier partners as possible and the relationships have lasted as long as each maintained their leadership in technology and quality.

In contrast to customer and supplier relationships, the majority of relationships with *competitors and others* do not go through the same sort of progressive steps. Generally, the relationships are either loose because they are complementary but not developmental, or they are close and take the form of an alliance or joint venture because they are based on developing a new product or market opportunity. Examples of what this means in practice are shown in Table 5.6.

Unilever's participation in establishing the Marine Stewardship Council provides us with an example of accessing the knowledge of both outside experts and competitors to support business sustainability (von Krogh, Nonaka and Aben, 2001). Unilever is a global consumer products company that produces and markets food, home and personal care products. In general, ensuring that raw material supply remains sustainable is a challenge for large food companies. As the world's largest fish processor, Unilever needed to know how to ensure a sufficient supply of fish into the future. They established the Marine Stewardship Council in conjunction with the World Wildlife Fund. The Council was an independent body. Unilever and other industry players were all able to work with the Council to understand the impact of fishery practices on consumer products and supply chains. Before this collaboration was in place, knowledge on sustainable fisheries was fragmented and scattered throughout Unilever.

An example of building an even closer relationship with an outside source of expertise was Unilever's partnership with the University of Cambridge in the UK to establish the Unilever Centre for Molecular Informatics (von Krogh, Nonaka and Aben, 2001). One objective of the Centre has been to develop

| Table 5.6 | Building knowledge-based relationships with competitors, complementors and expert sources | | |

Relationship with others	Loose connection	Moderate bond	Strong ties
Social capital investment =	*Infrastructure + interaction*	*Infrastructure + tailored interaction*	*Infrastructure + shared purpose + trust (either codified or based on cultural compatibility)*
Knowledge flows 'inside-out' to competitors/ complementors	Form buying coalitions to reduce costs to everyone. Subcontract spare capacity where competition is not viable.	Work together to establish industry standards that allow compatibility between products and services.	Enter into an alliance for strategic knowledge development.
Knowledge flows 'outside-in' from competitors/ complementors	Participate in industry working parties and standards bodies.	Allow competitors to market their products on your website to capture knowledge about their customers' interests and buying power.	Enter into an alliance for strategic knowledge development.
Knowledge flows 'outside-in' from expert sources	Participate in industry forums, conferences and exhibitions.	Employ consultants. Employee exchange schemes with academic institutions.	Invest in university research projects.

theories and tools that can be used to mine valuable knowledge from large amounts of molecular data. The research has increased the rate at which data can be screened and has allowed Unilever to speed up product development in its research and development facilities.

Create a designated function with responsibility for relationships

Strategic alliances with other organizations are ways for our organizations to develop resources and skills more quickly than we could in-house. The governance of the alliance may initially be anything from licensing arrangements or contractual consortia to equity or non-equity joint ventures for product or market development, but the intention of the alliance is to develop a close co-operation with other organizations for mutual benefit.

It is widely recognized that such alliances are not easy to manage and many fail. Even when such associations have existed for long periods of time, it can be difficult to gain sufficient value from them. However, there are ways in which we can improve the likelihood that our strategic alliances will be successful (Dyer, Kale and Singh, 2001). By examining the practices of organizations that seem to generate more value from their alliance-based knowledge connections than others, we see that an important element of their success is based on building a dedicated alliance management function.

Such a function creates a community of experts who encapsulate and harness the organizational intelligence on how to work in such close boundary-spanning relationships efficiently and effectively. They build critical know-how (Ciborra and Andreu, 2002) and become a focal point through which trust can accumulate. The returns from such an investment are significant. Enterprises that use a dedicated function have a 25 per cent higher long-term success rate with their alliances. When they announce a new alliance, these organizations also generate four times the increase in market share value than do organizations who enter alliances but leave the knowledge of managing these relationships tacit and diffused (Dyer, Kale and Singh, 2001).

Companies interpret the form of an alliance 'function' differently, but the activities are generally the same.

Evaluating potential partners. Although a potential partner may offer our organizations benefits in terms of risk-sharing, new technologies and skills, or access to new markets, there need to be reciprocal strategic goals for the partner if the relationship is to be mutually sustainable. Intensive effort is needed to understand how each partner's objectives and strategies may alter during the relationship.

Caterpillar experienced an example of an alliance in which there were dissimilar strategic objectives when they entered a joint venture with Daewoo to build forklift trucks and light construction equipment during the late 1980s. Daewoo, a large South Korean *chaebol* (conglomerate), possessed strategic ambitions to build its core competencies in heavy machinery, hydraulics, metallurgy and other related fields. Caterpillar believed it could work with Daewoo not only to gain access to emerging Far Eastern markets, but also to use Korea as a low-cost sourcing platform for machinery components. Daewoo, however, viewed Caterpillar as a provider of critical technology for component manufacturing that it could use for its own ambitious plans to enter Middle Eastern and other markets. Eventually, Caterpillar withdrew from the alliance when it realized that the costs of the relationship (creation of a new competitor) outweighed the benefits (little access to Korean, Chinese and other markets) (Lei, Slocum and Pitts, 1997).

Improving internal knowledge about alliance management. By acting as a focal point for experience, feedback and learning about what can be done to improve boundary-spanning relationships, the function is well-placed to increase knowledge about strategic alliances for the future: to plan how best to move them from collaborative to co-operative relationships. Some companies transfer this understanding through practical training workshops, roundtables and community discussions. Others choose to codify the knowledge into manuals, templates and guidelines. There are many hidden pitfalls that can undermine investment in a close relationship: capturing experience and insights into how to avoid the pitfalls is invaluable.

Concentrating external communication. Letting market analysts know about plans for new alliances and successful on-going relationships is an important part of the value generation process as it increases the value of intangibles represented in the share price. A dedicated alliance function also becomes an obvious point of contact that can act as an attractor for potential new partners.

Reducing co-ordination difficulties. When there are a variety of close relationships, it is often necessary to arbitrate between conflicting priorities for investing time, effort and other resources. Having a dedicated function makes it quicker and simpler to co-ordinate resources between initiatives and link alliance activity to other strategic decisions.

Ensuring feedback and accountability. Continuing to evaluate the performance of the relationship against objectives is important once an alliance is established. Often, there is enthusiasm at the outset for the potential offered by the relationship. However, apathy can develop unless on-going progress is monitored. Apathy makes it more difficult to withstand any area of serious conflict, and so we start on the path to alliance failure. By centralizing responsibility for alliance success, there is a focal point for evaluation. Evidence of successful performance helps overcome difficulties when they arise.

Managing exit strategies. The timely termination of an alliance that has outlived its useful contributory life is as important as the early assessment of the partnership potential. A dedicated function can review the relationship in terms of ongoing strategic value and future viability. A function that is independent of senior management involvement and the reputation of individuals introduces a much needed degree of objectivity (Inkpen and Ross, 2001). Changes in strategic orientation may also alter the rationale for the current set of close ties: a dedicated function is best positioned to review the implications of altering close ties upon the overall strategic knowledge flows.

Factors that the alliance management function needs to take into account when managing relationships include the relative status of the alliance partner, compatibility of organizational and national cultures, motivation, balance of abilities and learning opportunities, structural mechanisms for knowledge to flow and ways of building trust and rapport.

There is evidence to suggest that compatible *cultures* are particularly important to the success of alliances. Compatible cultures immediately create stronger social capital because of the familiarity of tacit assumptions, norms and beliefs. Where this does not exist, building compatibility requires considerable effort and can cause significant problems even over apparently simple things. For example, when one American company was working out the details of a joint venture with a British organization they were required to appear at a government hearing. The American organization asked the British firm to 'table' the few points that had not yet been resolved. Unfortunately in America to 'table' something means to keep it under the table, rather than to put it on the table, which is what it means in the UK. The British organization therefore raised the issues at the hearing and as a result the joint venture collapsed (Parkhe, 1991).

Societal norms pose even more obstacles to understanding, but an alliance function that can develop a sound understanding of cultural habits can manage the interactions more effectively. Often, it is impossible to overcome significant incompatibility in corporate cultures and values. If they are not explored and made explicit, it is likely that the expectations of each partner will be misaligned, the leadership styles will be too different, the reward systems will drive different performance goals and the work practices will be too difficult to reconcile.

As an example, IBM worked closely with Motorola in the field of advanced semi-conductors. Their common US ancestry and the fact that each was sharing highly-refined tacit technological and organizational competences, contributed to the success of the joint venture. IBM's alliances with Japanese partners such as Toshiba, Canon and Hitachi were less successful, partly because the translation of complex manufacturing techniques from a Japanese context to an American one was not easy, and partly because of language and culture differences (Lei, Slocum and Pitts, 1997).

Building shared *motivation* is essential for relationship quality and tacit knowledge exchange. The starting point is the commitment of both parties to the alliance. Initial commitment tends to be proportional to the possible returns, so it is important to define an equitable basis for the relationship that motivates each partner (Lei, Slocum and Pitts, 1997). Motivational drivers are likely to change over time, according to the perceived value being derived from the relationship. Sustaining motivation will depend on the level of *rapport* that can be developed between individuals. Rapport comes from such factors as mutual trust, shared language, common contextual understanding, and a mutual recognition of the potential value of the association (Nonaka, Toyama and Konno, 2000; von Krogh, Ichijo and Nonaka, 2000).

If the purpose of a strategic alliance is really learning, then it is important to pay attention to managing explicit and tacit *knowledge flows* between alliance partners. This is complex and it is often hard to disaggregate the two because organizational and technical knowledge will be tightly bound to the culture, routines and people management practices. This is when it becomes important to pay attention to the organization-specific context: the degree of social capital established at the organizational level. In this way, it becomes possible to design knowledge processes that reinforce the strengthening of the relationship.

Manage problems when they arise

There is some evidence to suggest that two major causes of alliance failure are the presence of inter-firm rivalry and the level of complexity involved in aligning operations and co-ordinating diverging interests (Park and Ungson, 2001). The ultimate returns from an alliance are often long-term and somewhat unpredictable, whereas the returns from focusing on the interests of our own organizations may be more immediate. If individual competitive interests rise above collaborative ones, there is a negative impact on trust, reputation and perceived commitment to the union. Costly and difficult communication and co-ordination processes, or incompatible operational objectives between two partners, also negatively affect the levels of trust and commitment. Logistical connections and regular interaction are unlikely to be enough on their own to hold an alliance together. It becomes extremely important to ensure that mutual understanding develops and repeated interactions re-enforce common expectations, build shared intellectual capital and affirm the 'win/win' contributions that re-enforce perceived partnership value. This sort of feedback builds 'process-based' trust, which is derived from experience of benefit.

The failure of the relationship between AT&T and Olivetti was an example of the consequences of managerially incompatible partners. Despite sound strategic reasons for the alliance based on Olivetti's global marketing capability and AT&T's advanced technology, the two partners found it impossible to work together in the long-term. The main reason was that Olivetti's management style was nimble, entrepreneurial and aggressive whereas AT&T's management style was more cautious and risk averse, with a strong emphasis on procedure (Fedor and Werther, 1996). The main factors that put an alliance at risk are:

- incompatible cultures,
- ill-connected communication structures,
- misaligned perceptions of outcome,
- short-term competitive priorities undermining perceptions of trust,
- inequity in the relationship or its perceived value,
- inequity in the rate of learning or the level of contribution,
- internal politics within one partner organization,
- any disturbance in the relative strategic positioning of either partner.

An imbalance in one or more of these dimensions can trigger damaging impressions, which seriously undermine trust and perceived benefits from a strategic alliance.

Being aware of the potential problem areas is an important first step in pre-empting them and then managing them to avoid unnecessary escalation. An organization that has built on such experience is Westminster City Council in the UK, which has 'blazed a trail in local government outsourcing' (Hammond, 2002). In July 2002, it agreed a £241 million deal with the business services company Vertex to run all its customer-facing services and related back-office processes for fifteen years. Westminster City Council drew on ten years of outsourcing experience to establish the form of the relationship. Key elements of their approach to avoid, and if necessary resolve, problems were:

- Being very clear throughout the process of evaluating bids and tenders about what the potential supplier would deliver and how they would do so.

- Establishing clear ground rules; for example, by communicating the business vision and mutual expectations.
- Drawing up a partnership code of conduct that described how each side behaved with the other.
- Setting up a partnership board that drew on senior members of each organization together with a contract review board to oversee the work.
- Putting in place technology to provide the data to monitor the contract.
- Agreeing to hold weekly meetings to evaluate the performance data and deal with problems as they arose.

The essence of all close ties lies in the communication between the people. Social Network Analysis is a powerful analytical tool, which can be applied to inter-organizational relationships to:

- identify how communication is flowing and where the crucial nodes are,
- diagnose blockages and weaknesses within a network of relationships,
- suggest points of intervention to improve collaboration and knowledge sharing (Cross, Borgatti and Parker, 2002).

 In *Competence Area 2: Deciding* we saw that Social Network Analysis can also be used to diagnose problems *within* an organization and identify opportunities to improve the flow of knowledge.

Sometimes, a strategically important group of people does not know enough about one another to use the knowledge resources of the close network to best advantage. Social Network Analysis can pinpoint the problem and identify where intervention could improve the productivity of the group. Unfortunately, the process of Social Network Analysis is time-consuming and expensive. It also may be impractical to use in many external networks.

An example of Social Network Analysis being used to build a more effective partnership was when two Fortune 500 companies, one in telecommunications and one in financial services, decided to develop a co-branded credit-card/calling card for corporate customers (Hutt *et al.*, 2000). Prior to this joint venture, the two partners had been providing mutual services to each other: the financial services company by billing telecommunications customers and the telecommunications company by supporting both voice and data transmission. Their relationship was based largely on under-socialized trust (in other words, formal transactional contracts).

Both parties could see the benefit of an alliance, but the negotiations were difficult because each side was accustomed to taking a leading stance in any relationship. It took them nine months to codify the rules for protecting their positions. In the run-up to the product launch, the need to trade customer lists caused each side to fear that their confidential information might be misused, or that the partner might become involved in similar co-branding projects with competitive rivals. Unfortunately, market pressure to launch quickly caused mistakes with customers, and disputes over logos appearing side-by-side on the card offended sensitivities in each company. Further disputes arose over who 'owned' customer service and discount policies. The different priority given to the co-branding project within each company also caused problems.

Team building exercises had only limited effect in strengthening the ties. A working off-site meeting in Florida allowed members of each company to rebuild the deteriorating relationships through social activities. Yet back at the office, the cultures and structures of each company still got in the way, making the communication process between 'opposite numbers' very complex. Frustration built and profits were modest. One year into the project, an in-depth audit of the social network supporting the relationship was conducted alongside interviews with 42 managers to collect their perceptions about trust, commitment and compatibility within the partnership. The study was able to identify:

- Where information flows were not working because of structural incompatibilities, inadequate information management policies, or insufficient personal connections.

- Where relationship patterns were strong and where essential individuals were working too much on the periphery of activities. This allowed the partners to rebalance the strength of relationships to fit the changing goals in the project and to ensure that senior individuals, who lent weight to the importance of the relationship, were communicating enough.

- Where informal communication patterns were different to the formal structure, and provided faster routes for communication, conflict resolution and learning.

Having looked at the practical considerations involved in forming and sustaining close ties within our network, we now move on to the other element of the mix of relationships that we need to develop: loose connections.

Paying attention to loose relationship connections

Close ties are not always the most valuable forms of relationship within a network. There are situations when it is better to maintain loose connections with many different organizations. For example, for relatively standard or routine activities, it is often better to develop loose associations that provide access to a wider range of information sources, triggering potential ideas for cost savings or produce or service differentiation. Many relatively loose connections with external organizations and individuals can provide our organizations with a cost-effective search mechanism for accessing diverse knowledge resources (Adler and Kwon, 2002).

 Signpost In *Competence Area 2: Deciding* we saw that diversity is important to support knowledge creation and maintain an organization's ability to respond to change in the environment.

Loose ties are ones that use contracts 'to protect each party from the self interested behaviour of others' (Mariotti and Delbridge, 2001). The relationships tend to be shorter-term and exchanges are relatively infrequent across the many individual members in the allied organizations. In Tables 5.4, 5.5 and 5.6 we saw examples of practical ways in which we can build loose connections with our customers, suppliers and other network players. We saw these as a starting point in the process of gathering sufficient information to decide whether or not we can or should invest further in the relationships to make them closer. In general, loose connections mainly support explicit knowledge exchange.

From a strategic positioning perspective, it may also be useful to create loose associations with other organizations simply to prevent them from forming relationships with our competitors. The relationships may not in themselves be directly fruitful, but may neutralize a competitive threat by blocking a knowledge combination that could be potentially damaging (Reid, Bussiere and Greenaway, 2001).

In conditions of economic downturn, we may choose to loosen ties with our employees too. Without severing the relationship completely, mechanisms such as sabbaticals, which allow the employee to travel or study, can reduce costs in the short-term. This approach retains the potential to redevelop the closer relationship in the future since loyalty and trust are maintained – both essential elements of social capital.

Outsourcing activities that are not strategically important to our organizations can be a valuable way to focus core expertise on the areas in which we make the most difference. An example of a company that outsourced routine activities was Cable and Wireless. They used outsourcing to help the human resources function become a more strategic contributor to the business (Pickard, 2002). Cable and Wireless Global was formed in 2000 from independent, international operating units. Its objective was to become a leading provider of Internet services to business companies. In 2001, they outsourced HR administration for the UK and US to Accenture HR Services. Although this was partly for financial reasons, it also allowed the separation of HR administration from HR strategy. The strategic HR function was able to adopt a more proactive role in the integration and effective operation of the business.

 Signpost In *Competence Area 4: Connecting* we saw that outsourcing can be a way of increasing value from non-strategic knowledge.

Developing the capability within our organizations to manage a range of relatively loose relationships with outsourcing companies can be useful in several ways (Quinn, 1999):

- It allows limited resources to be concentrated on areas of highest value.
- Changing the focus on internal activities can allow organizational structures to be flattened.
- Internal sources of bureaucracy can be reduced.

- Releasing resources and targeting internal efforts can increase responsiveness to customers.
- Access to new knowledge domains can be increased by exploiting the facilities and investments of outsourcing partners. It may also expose our organizations to leading edge knowledge in specific areas.
- We may be able to offer customers higher value and more flexible products and services than we could deliver alone.

In general, paying attention to loose connections in our network requires us to build the capability within our organizations to:

- *Scan the environment for opportunities* to integrate partners into the network.
- *Evaluate* potential partners on the value of their knowledge and expertise.
- *Establish connections* using both personal relationships and technology solutions. A process of streamlining communication processes needs to be created.
- *Integrate systems and processes* where necessary at the boundary between the organizations.
- *Allocate responsibility for maintaining and developing the relationship.* The main purpose will be to co-ordinate communications and resolve problems as they arise. However, it is also important to continue to monitor the value generated from the relationship and assess whether it should be strengthened or ended.

Research suggests that there are four individual leadership capabilities required to manage outsourcing relationships (Useem and Harder, 2000):

- *Strategic thinking* – knowing whether and how to gain competitive advantage from outsourcing.
- *Deal making* – the ability to broker deals in two directions, by securing the necessary services externally and making sure they are used internally.
- *Partnership governing* – overseeing the relationship to ensure it meets its objectives.
- *Managing change* – overcoming any internal resistance to the impact of outsourcing.

Organizational senior management would need to focus on delegating responsibility to local teams, streamlining processes, reviewing performance and providing training and incentives for those involved in spanning the organizational boundary and managing the loose ties.

We can look at our network of weak connections as a loosely coupled system in which 'the key to the integrity ... lies in the interplay of cognition, values and action' (Spender and Grinyer, 1996). This interplay takes place over time and changes continuously; it is distinct from the shared sense of identity forged in close relationships. It is more transactional and less trust-based, so can be managed with the appropriate explicit incentives and structural mechanisms. The starting point still needs to be some shared goal and it is important to establish some general understanding of the mutual benefits to be achieved from participating in the network. It has been found that what holds such networks together in periods of change is a sense of excitement, lots of personal commitment and a dedication to continuous improvement at all levels.

The World Bank is an organization that has actually redefined its purpose to encompass establishing and maintaining such a loosely coupled network of knowledge-sharing relationships (LaPorte, 2002). The World Bank has always offered development assistance in the form of a mix of finance and ideas to improve living standards. In 1996, the President announced that the World Bank would become the first resource anyone would contact for information and knowledge about development. This shift to emphasize the value of a systematic approach to knowledge management recognized that drawing on experience from other similar situations could influence the success of development projects and significantly impact the rate of return on World Bank-supported client investments.

The World Bank works within a network of other bodies also dedicated to development – for example, donor governments, non-governmental organizations, borrower governments and private sector groups. It set out to systematically capture and organize the knowledge and experience of staff, clients and development partners, make this knowledge available and create links between network partners. Development work takes place within the context of a complex interplay of economic, environmental and cultural factors. Engaging local stakeholders in knowledge-sharing and learning is a crucial element of adapting global knowledge to local conditions.

A basic infrastructure and set of programmes have been established to share knowledge within the World Bank and with clients and partner organizations. These have included:

- Communities of practice (both internal to the World Bank and with external individuals and groups).
- Advisory services to provide quick and easy access to resources.
- Regional and country-level programmes to provide customized information and knowledge.
- Initiatives to bring development practitioners from many organizations together, both face-to-face and virtually, to share experience and ideas.

These initiatives to improve knowledge practices within a network of loosely-connected partner organizations and individuals have been successful partly because they were aligned with the core business of the World Bank and partly because participation clearly added value to each member of the network. The integrity of the network was established through the combination of shared values within the network (all members recognized the importance of development), connecting people who benefited from building common understanding and making all the activities practically relevant.

Having looked at the practical means by which we can establish and maintain both close ties and loose connections, we now need to ask if this is sufficient to give us competence in organizing to achieve intelligence through our network of relationships. We suggest that if our organizations are to use both of these mechanisms effectively, we need additional integrative capabilities to recognize and respond to the requirements of each form of relationship.

Maintaining a dynamic mix of relationships is a source of tension

We have argued that, strategically, the networks of knowledge-based relationships of our organizations should be based on a mix of close and loose ties – the former to give depth and value to the possible knowledge exchange and the latter to give breadth and flexibility. Now we need to explore what happens if the mix is out of balance and why our goal needs to be to dynamically adjust the mix to keep it relevant for the changing environmental conditions.

 In *Competence Area 4: Connecting* we saw that changing the nature of external relationships was a way of dynamically adjusting the permeability of the boundary of our organization to knowledge flows in both directions.

We have seen that there are clear benefits from building some close relationships – for example, through various forms of strategic alliance. High social capital embedded in such relationships offers us the potential of meaningful knowledge-sharing. In general, such close bonds allow us to exchange a rich supply of worthwhile explicit and even tacit knowledge. However, there are also definite limitations. The more close ties we have, the more limited our capacity for truly independent decision-making is likely to be, the more conflict we are likely to face as we try to align with the demands of various close network partners and meet our obligations to them, the more redundancy there is in the resources tied up in the relationships (for which the opportunity cost may be high), and the more difficulty there will be to loosen the ties if the environmental conditions change.

There are benefits from the solidarity of a 'closed' network with strong social capital as this can reduce costs, alleviate the need for formal controls and make dispute resolution easier. However, there is also evidence that overly-strong social networks can promote an element of 'group think'. As well as reducing the capacity for innovation, this can also lead to unethical behaviour and conspiracies developing. A collective reduction in innovative capacity in dense networks arises because members have a much lower chance of gaining access to a unique piece of information or unique knowledge resource.

Inevitably, competitive variety within a dense and tightly-bonded network progressively reduces. Integration is a powerful source of coherence, but taken to an extreme, it can exclude potential for development and adaptation. Participating in a dense network with too many close relationships can also slow our ability to respond to significant external changes, because time to reach consensus increases exponentially with the density of the interactions between the members. However, the decision to reduce the closeness of a relationship is a hard one to make, because by their very nature close bonds are based on emotional and value-based ties.

In contrast, we have seen that many loose connections in our network are a source of diversity and creativity. These are essential if we are to differentiate ourselves competitively and adapt flexibly to changing conditions. We can choose how we use these relationships, keeping some loose indefinitely, developing others into closer bonds if there is additional value to be gained, or maintaining others for the potential they offer in the future. Their diversity, coupled with the lower level of effort and resources that we need to invest in these relationships, makes them the basis of the flexibility of our networks and of the ability of our organizations to adapt.

Yet, if all the relationships in our network are loose and based on weak ties, the network offers little potential for meaningful tacit knowledge to be exchanged and there is a risk that our organizations become 'hollow shells'. There will also be little durability under pressure and excessive fragmentation of our external network can end up being a drain on our internal co-ordination resources. The internal coherence of the network will be challenged by pressure to adapt and respond to too many incompatible agendas and values. Conflicting objectives and loyalties can develop from the different relationship priorities.

 In *Competence Area 2: Deciding* we saw that issues of power and politics are inevitable consequences of the diversity in organizations. The same happens within a diverse network of relationships.

The potential to generate high value from an extensive network of loose ties with these high co-ordinations costs is limited unless there are opportunities for increasing returns. Rather than allowing external relationships to develop opportunistically, risking the potential disadvantages of imbalance identified above, we suggest that managing a mix of value-added close and loose knowledge-based relationships should be a dynamic and conscious strategic activity. Specific expertise needs to be developed within our organizations that allows relationship options to be actively explored, selected and adjusted according to the knowledge-based strategies that we are pursuing. We also need to be able to adjust the style with which we manage each collaborative relationship to suit its specific knowledge characteristics and the potential returns. The combination of these capabilities is collaborative expertise, which actually becomes a 'dimension of competition' (Powell, 1998).

Resolve the tension through developing collaborative expertise as a competitive capability

Managing the complexity of the different kinds of knowledge-based relationships that we have been looking at has become an important capability in the knowledge economy. This is partly because the cost of failure can be high: in addition to the loss of reputation and the wasted time and effort, we may have shared valuable knowledge and reduced our options in the future. On the other side of the coin, collaborative excellence makes us an attractive potential partner and increases our options for future beneficial relationships. To develop collaborative expertise, we need to allocate responsibility for *actively managing* the relationship network, *continually evaluate* the knowledge potential and then *adapt the style* with which we manage each collaborative activity according to its specific characteristics. We will look at each of these in more detail.

Manage the relationship network as a strategic asset

We looked at aspects of this when we saw the importance of creating a specific alliance management function to build the sort of co-operative learning relationships that can increase our knowledge base. We also noted the need for developing the expertise to manage collaborative outsourcing relationships and looser ties. There are benefits in allocating responsibility to track performance of the whole relationship portfolio. We can summarize the most important responsibilities as follows (Simonin, 1997).

Identify and select the right mix of potential collaborators. Determine the knowledge we need, consider the impact of selecting one firm over another, assess their reputation in the market and their technological alignment, consider the balance of skills that they offer and the potential risk from the loss of strategically valuable information.

Negotiate beneficial terms for the collaborative or co-operative agreement. Find mutual benefits, develop a joint vision, negotiate legal, tax and financial arrangements, as well as reciprocal knowledge-based contributions.

Monitor and manage each relationship. Evaluate the contributions against expectations, enforce agreed actions without damaging the relationship, resolve conflicts and differences, build trust and renegotiate terms when external conditions change.

Terminate the relationship when it has run its course. Use judgement to time the exit of our organizations from relationships and manage the impact on competitive positioning.

Developing expertise in these areas comes through our own experience and reflection on the experience of others. Allocating specific responsibility and accountability for these processes within our organizations is important, since if experience is to develop into collaborative and co-operative expertise, we need deliberately to extract, capture and share learning (Simonin, 1997).

Evaluate knowledge potential

We can use 'The Window of Knowledge Opportunities' to evaluate the knowledge-based potential of each relationship. We need to continually re-evaluate each relationship against our strategic objectives, particularly in turbulent environments.

Signpost In *Competence Area 4: Connecting* we saw that 'The Window of Knowledge Opportunities' shown in Figure 4.3 can be used to plan strategies that translate knowledge into value by reducing blind spots, exploring new knowledge and identifying which knowledge to release and which knowledge to protect.

We can illustrate what this means using an example. Ericsson's role in initiating and developing the Bluetooth technology that enables wireless communication between mobile phones, computers and personal digital assistants (PDAs) is one example of developing relationships progressively around 'The Window of Knowledge Opportunities'. In 1993, Ericsson had the innovative idea of removing the need for cable to allow electronic devices to communicate with each other (bottom right pane of the Window). They started to develop wireless communication technology in-house, but recognized that they would need to build relationships with companies who had complementary knowledge in order to progress the project fully and quickly.

In May 1998, they launched a special interest group (SIG) involving themselves and Intel, Nokia, IBM and Toshiba, specifically to eliminate blind spots (top right pane). Intel, Nokia and Ericsson had all been working on the same idea behind the scenes, but once part of the SIG, agreed to adopt Ericsson's technology because it was the most advanced. Recognizing the opportunity for increasing returns (top left pane) by opening up the technology to a web of members, the SIG expanded to become a vast network of loose ties with 2020 organizations, all of whom signed an Adopters Agreement before the product was commercially available. By the year 2002, Bluetooth technology was a standard part in literally millions of commercial products (Eneroth and Malm, 2001).

Adapt management style to the purpose of each specific collaborative venture

Collaborative expertise also means developing the capability to adapt the style we use to manage the activities that we undertake through each relationship. We need to know the rules of working together and the way to build co-operation. This requires us to look at the specific purpose of each collaboration and the characteristics of the knowledge flows that need to be encouraged and then adapt practices accordingly.

We can use an integrative framework to assess each collaboration against three important dimensions and design practical actions accordingly:

1 the complexity of the task that is involved,
2 the barriers between people if they are to share the knowledge,
3 the quality of the relationship that exists and is needed to meet the strategic knowledge objectives.

By mapping each collaboration onto a framework representing these three parameters (see Figure 5.7), we can judge what sort of actions will help it to deliver the most value (McKenzie and van Winkelen, 2001).

A range of external relationship forms can be mapped onto this model based on the general purpose of the collaborative activities that each exists to undertake (see Figure 5.8). Looking at each dimension of collaboration in more detail:

Figure 5.7 A model of 'collaboration space' (McKenzie and van Winkelen, 2001)

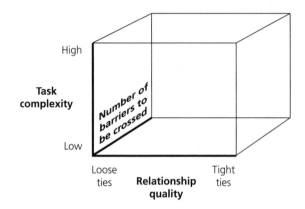

Figure 5.8 Mapping forms of external relationships onto the 'collaboration space' model

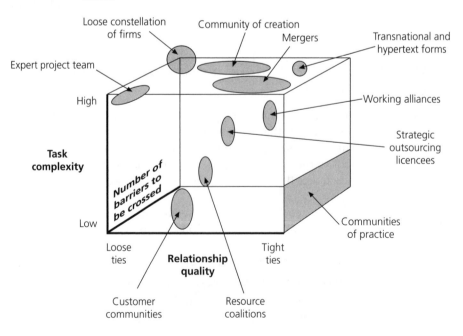

Task complexity

Most collaboration involves some form of goal or purpose. Often this means there is some task to complete. Sometimes the task is relatively straightforward; for example, based on a linear or cyclical process that can be standardized. More complex tasks are based on non-standard series of interdependent stages that need to be co-ordinated to integrate knowledge into an end-product. If the purpose of the relationship is also to generate novelty and learning, this adds another layer of complexity to the process. For example, expert project teams tend to work with high levels of task complexity.

Managing collaborations that are based on increasingly complex tasks (moving from top to bottom of the model) requires us to pay increasing attention to the *structure and configuration* aspects of social capital. Particular effort needs to be paid to ensuring that the information and communication technology adequately matches the changing needs of the task. Creating the right kinds of connections between collaborators in this way involves:

- matching technology to the task requirements,
- ensuring common access for everyone,
- establishing a communication protocol and etiquette,
- creating glossaries for common terms and templates for critical modules,
- adopting a policy of open visibility of information,
- managing information overload.

The choice of governance mechanism (whether that be contractual, financial or trust-based) will depend very much on the degree of uncertainty amongst the various partners (Gulati, 1998). It takes a long time to establish the sort of effective communication paths needed to generate mutual learning, but investing a significant amount of time and expertise in developing trust during the discussions to set up the partnering relationship can shorten the time to reaping the knowledge rewards. The discussions minimize uncertainty and reduce the complexity of the task by making expectations and motives explicit (Dodgson, 1992).

Barriers to be crossed

Building and maintaining relationships becomes more difficult as the number of barriers to be overcome in the process increases, regardless of how simple the task is. Insufficient understanding of context, language or mental and cultural orientations can create barriers to shared understanding. The more obstacles that need to be overcome for the collaborative activity to be successful, the more effort will be required to maintain the relationship in the required form.

Most organizational networks today depend extensively on virtual interactions as well as face-to-face connections. Virtual relationships increase the number of barriers to be confronted; for example, different time zones and greater cultural difference amongst participants who reside in different geographical locations and probably in different organizational contexts too. Technological barriers can also be created through incompatible systems or the need to communicate synchronously and asynchronously. In general, collaborations within loose networks of organizations tend to involve large numbers of barriers.

To overcome an increasing variety of barriers (moving from front to back of the model) requires more effort to build social capital by increasing the level of *cognitive compatibility*. Creating the right social climate in this way involves:

- making the value of the relationship explicit,
- agreeing roles and procedures to manage processes,
- employing moderators and facilitators to support electronic communications,
- training people in the nuances of cultural diversity,
- encouraging behaviours which show empathy and trust,
- making emotions explicit,
- ensuring that technology does not disempower some participants.

The quality of the relationship

This affects the type of knowledge that can flow between partners. Loose ties carry explicit information. Close ties carry tacit knowledge. Weak ties are useful for searching and transfer simple knowledge faster than close ties, but they impede the flow of complex knowledge (Hansen, 1999). Clearly then, complex partnerships, innovative alliances and communities of practice need high-quality relationships if they are to be effective. Rapport, trust and commitment all make the relationship easier and cheaper to manage.

If the nature of the collaborative activity needs high levels of tacit knowledge to be exchanged (moving from left to right across the model), then increasing attention needs to be paid to the *relationship quality* aspect of social capital. Trust needs to be fostered and common norms and values identified. Creating the right cultural climate in this way involves:

- offering shared rewards and motivational incentives,
- encouraging 'no blame' experimentation,
- encouraging social events during the relationship,
- celebrating success.

Finally, the context in which the collaboration is undertaken affects the ease with which people can cope with each of these three dimensions (Lawrence, Philips and Hardy, 1999). If external pressure is high, for example, due to a tight deadline or because the activity is strategically important, there is more incentive and opportunity to overcome the barriers, the motivation to maintain strategic relationship is stronger, and the capability in the network will be more readily accessible to complete more complex tasks. This is shown in Figure 5.9.

Figure 5.9 The effect of contextual pressure to succeed on the 'collaboration space' model

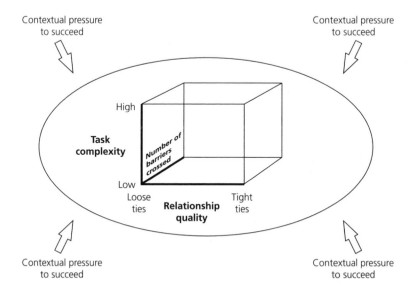

Perceived distance between points on the cube is lower
if external pressure is high

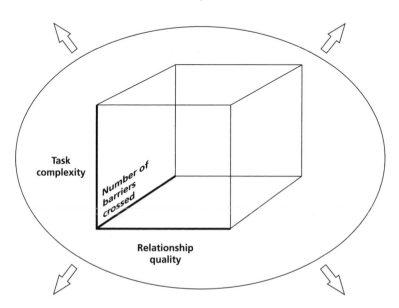

Perceived distance between points on the cube is higher
if external pressure is weak

In contrast, if there is little external pressure – for example, because the collaborative activity does not have strategic importance or the task is not seen as valuable – then each range of each dimension (metaphorically, the distances around the cube) will be perceived as larger and more difficult to traverse.

In this chapter, we have combined both a strategic and an operational perspective on how to gain value from a network of knowledge-based relationships. We have suggested ways of designing and maintaining the mix of close ties and loose connections that we need to have in our network. We have also looked at a number of ways of evaluating the effectiveness of each relationship and the design of the mix. In the next chapter, we develop these approaches to evaluation as part of an integrated approach to monitoring the value of all our knowledge-based activities.

Summary

We have continued to focus on external aspects of knowledge competence. In *Competence Area 4: Connecting* we identified that changing the nature of relationships with other organizations is a mechanism for adjusting the permeability of our organization's boundaries to knowledge flows. Here we looked at how to set up and pay appropriate attention to the relationships in our external network that carry those knowledge flows. We started with a number of questions:

How many connections does an organization need in its relationship network?

How many are sustainable?

How does relationship quality affect knowledge flow?

How can we orchestrate our network to increase its value generating potential?

The answers vary for each organization, depending on their intent and the resources used. We found two main features that impact the intelligence potential of our networks:

1 The strength and nature of social capital, or the goodwill available to individuals or groups. This arises from the structure and configuration of network connections, the cognitive compatibility between network members and the quality of relationships (shown through the level of trust and commitment).

2 The combination of the co-ordination mechanisms (price, authority and trust) we have adopted to mediate our knowledge-based relationships. Ultimately, we have to consider to what extent shared aims, governance structure and trust affect the types of knowledge flows and the coherence of activities that are needed to take advantage of these. Each

▶

structural form offers a different trade-off between the level of internal coherence we retain and our flexibility to respond to external environmental turbulence. A mix of complementary co-ordination mechanisms is important to release the full intelligence of a network.

Our knowledge strategy needs to address the questions:

1 What members in the network add value and how many knowledge connections are sustainable given the resources we have available?
2 Where would tightening co-operative knowledge-sharing ties increase value and where would looser collaborative coupling improve the knowledge generating potential of the organization as a whole?

Paying attention to close network ties involves:

- Knowing how to make relationships with customers, suppliers, competitors and other external partners progressively closer.
- Allocating responsibility for co-ordinating close relationships, particularly high-investment relationships such as alliances.
- Managing problems when they arise.

Close network ties offer the potential for meaningful knowledge flows, including tacit knowledge exchange.

Paying attention to loose network connections involves:

- Managing outsourcing relationships.
- Monitoring the performance of the relationships and identifying opportunities to generate more value from building a closer connection.
- Building leadership expertise in managing external loose relationships.

Loose network connections mainly allow information and explicit knowledge to flow. These connections create flexibility in the network and offer the opportunity to adapt.

The ability to dynamically adjust the mix of loose connections and close ties allows our organizations to respond to external environmental turbulence. However, if the mix develops opportunistically, there is a risk of too many close ties reducing access to potentially-valuable new knowledge and too many loose ties producing a fragmented and fragile network. Close ties take more investment to develop. Loose ties are not so rich in knowledge flows. It is important to manage the balance appropriately given the resources we have available in the organization. To use both of these mechanisms effectively, we need additional integrative capabilities to recognize and respond to the requirements of each form of relationship.

Collaborative expertise (including co-operative expertise as a subset) forms the basis for dynamically managing and adjusting this mix of network relationships. It is developed through:

▶

▶
- Allocating specific responsibility for actively managing external relationships.

- Continually evaluating and re-evaluating their knowledge potential using 'The Window of Knowledge Opportunities'.

- Adapting the style with which we manage each collaborative activity according to three dimensions: the complexity of the tasks involved; the number of barriers to communication that we need to overcome; and the quality of the relationships required for the knowledge that needs to flow between partners.

Developing competence in Relating offers the opportunity to form and leverage the benefits of dynamic knowledge-based networks.

References

Adler, P. (2002) 'Market hierarchy and trust: the knowledge economy and the future of capitalism', in *The Strategic Management of Intellectual Capital and Organizational Knowledge* (eds C. W. Choo and N. Bontis). Oxford: Oxford University Press.

Adler, P. and Kwon, S.-W. (2002) 'Social capital: prospects for a new concept', *Academy of Management Review* 27(1): 17–40.

Arino, A., de la Torre, J. and Smith Ring, P. (2001) 'Relational quality: managing trust in corporate alliances', *California Management Review* 44(1): 109–31.

Bartlett, C. and Ghoshal, S. (1989) *Managing Across Borders: the Transnational Solution*. London: Hutchinson.

Bartlett, C. and Ghoshal, S. (1998) 'Beyond the M-form: towards a managerial theory of the firm', in *A Strategy Reader* (ed. Susan Segal-Horn). Milton Keynes/Oxford: Open University/Blackwell, 349–81.

Burt, R. S. (1992) *Structural Holes: the Social Structure of Competition*. Cambridge, MA: Harvard University Press.

Camuffo, A., Romano, P. and Vinelli, A. (2001) 'Back to the future: Benetton transforms its global network', *Sloan Management Review* 43(1): 46–53.

Child, J. and Gunther McGrath, R. (2001) 'Organizations unfettered: organizational form in an information-intensive economy', *Academy of Management Review* 44(6): 1135–48.

Ciborra, C. U. and Andreu, R. (2002) 'Knowledge across boundaries: managing knowledge in distributed organizations', in *The Strategic Management of Intellectual Capital and Organizational Knowledge* (eds C. W. Choo and N. Bontis). Oxford: Oxford University Press.

Costello, C. A. and Flar, A. (2000) 'Applying knowledge inside and out at AT&T', *Knowledge Management Review* 3(3): 14–19.

Cross, R., Borgatti, S. P. and Parker, A. (2002) 'Making invisible work visible', *California Management Review* 44(2): 25–46.

Davis, S. and Davidson, B. (1991) *2020 Vision: Transforming Your Business Today to Succeed in Tomorrow's Economy*. New York: Simon and Schuster:.

Davis, S. and Meyer, C. (1998) *Blur: The Speed of Change in the Connected Economy*. Oxford: Capstone.

De Wit, B. and Meyer, R. (1999) *Strategy Synthesis: Resolving Strategy Paradoxes to Create Competitive Advantage*. London: Thomson Learning.

Dodgson, M. (1992) 'The strategic management of R&D collaboration', *Technology Analysis and Strategic Management* 4(3): 227–44.

Dyer, J. H., Kale, P. and Singh, H. (2001) 'How to make strategic alliances work', *Sloan Management Review* 42(4): 37–43.

Dyer, J. H. and Singh, H. (1998) 'The relational view: Co-operative strategy and sources of inter-organizational competitive advantage', *Academy of Management Review* 23(4): 660–79.

Eneroth, K. and Malm, A. (2001) 'Knowledge webs and generative relations: a network approach to developing competencies', *European Management Journal* 19(2): 174–82.

Fedor, K. J. and Werther, W. B. (1996) 'The fourth dimension: creating culturally responsive international alliances', *Organizational Dynamics* 25(2): 39–55.

Fischer, H. M., Brown, J., Porac, J. F., *et al.* (2002) 'Mobilizing knowledge in interorganizational alliances', in *The Strategic Management of Intellectual Capital and Organizational Knowledge* (eds C. W. Choo and N. Bontis). Oxford: Oxford University Press, 523–35.

Ganzaroli, A. (2002) 'Creating trust between local and global systems', PhD, Erasmus University, Rotterdam.

Garud, R. and Kotha, S. (1994) 'Using the brain as a metaphor to model flexible production systems', *Academy of Management Review* 19(4): 671–98.

Gnyawali, D. R. and Madhavan, R. (2001) 'Co-operative networks and competitive dynamics: a structural embeddedness perspective', *Academy of Management Review* 26(3): 431–45.

Granovetter, M. S. (1973) 'The strength of weak ties', *American Journal of Sociology* 78: 1360–80.

Gulati, R. (1998) 'Alliances and networks', *Strategic Management Journal* 19: 293–317.

Hammond, D. (2002) 'It shouldn't happen to a vetting', *People Management* 8(23): 32–7.

Hansen, M. T. (1999) 'The search-transfer problem: the role of weak ties in sharing knowledge across organizational sub-units', *Administrative Science Quarterly* 44(1): 82–96.

Hinteruber, A. (2002) 'Value chain orchestration in action and the case of the global agrochemical industry', *Long Range Planning* 35: 615–35.

Hutt, M. D., Stafford, E. R., Walker, B. A. and Reinegen, P. H. (2000) 'Case study: defining the social network of strategic alliances', *Sloan Management Review* 41(2): 51–62.

Inkpen, A. C. and Ross, J. (2001) 'Why do some strategic alliances persist beyond their useful life?' *California Management Review* 44(1): 132–48.

Johnson, G. and Scholes, K. (2002) *Exploring Corporate Strategy*. Harlow: Pearson Education.

LaPorte, B. (2002) 'Knowledge is currency at the World Bank', *KM Review* 5(5): 10–13.

Lawrence, T., Philips, N. and Hardy, C. (1999) 'Watching whale watching: exploring the discursive foundations of collaborative relationships', *Journal of Applied Behavioral Science* 35(4): 479–502.

Lei, D., Slocum, J. and Pitts, R. (1997) 'Building co-operative advantage: managing strategic alliances to promote organizational learning', *Journal of World Business* 32(3): 203–24.

Lorenzoni, G. and Baden-Fuller, C. (1995) 'Creating a strategic center to manage a web of partners', *California Management Review* 37(3): 146–64.

Margretta, J. (1998) 'The power of virtual integration: an interview with Dell Computer's Michael Dell', *Harvard Business Review* 76(2): 27–84.

Mariotti, F. and Delbridge, R. (2001) 'Managing portfolios of ties in interfirm networks', Nelson and Winter Conference, Aalborg Denmark.

Matusik, S. F. (2002) 'Managing public and private firm knowledge within the context of flexible firm boundaries', in *The Strategic Management of Intellectual Capital and Organizational Knowledge*, (eds C. W. Choo and N. Bontis). Oxford: Oxford University Press.

McGrath, R. G., MacMillan, I. C. and Venkatramann, S. (1995) 'Defining and developing competence: a strategic process paradigm', *Strategic Management Journal* 16: 251–76.

McKenzie, J. and Potter, R. (2002) 'Understanding the enabling conditions for virtual tacit knowledge exchange', 2nd Henley KM Forum Conference, Henley Management College, UK.

McKenzie, J. and van Winkelen, C. (2001) 'Exploring e-collaboration space', 1st Annual Henley KM Forum Conference, Henley Management College, UK.

Miles, R. E., Snow, C. C. and Miles, G. (2000) 'The future.org', *Long Range Planning* 33(3): 300–23.

Nahapiet, J. and Ghoshal, S. (1998) 'Social capital, intellectual capital and the organizational advantage', *Academy of Management Review* 23(2): 242–66.

Nalebuff, B. J. and Brandenburger, A. M. (1997) 'Co-opetition: competitive and co-operative business strategies for the digital economy', *Strategy and Leadership* 25(6): 28–35.

Nonaka, I. (1991) 'The knowledge creating company', *Harvard Business Review* Nov–Dec: 96–104.

Nonaka, I. (1994) 'A dynamic theory of organization knowledge creation', *Organization Science* 5: 14–37.

Nonaka, I., Toyama, R. and Konno, N. (2000) 'SECI Ba and leadership: a unified model of dynamic knowledge creation', *Long Range Planning* 33(1): 5–34.

Norman, P. M. (2001) 'Are your secrets safe? Knowledge protection in strategic alliances', *Business Horizons* 51–60.

Normann, R. and Ramirez, R. (1993) 'From value chain to value constellation: designing interactive strategy', *Harvard Business Review* 71: 65.

Park, S. H. and Ungson, G. R. (2001) 'Interfirm rivalry and managerial complexity: a conceptual framework of alliance failure', *Organization Science* 12(1): 37–53.

Parkhe, A. (1991) 'Interfirm diversity, organizational learning and longevity in global strategic alliances', *Journal of International Business Studies* 22: 579–601.

Pickard, J. (2002) 'A global conversion', *People Management* 8(22): 40–2.

Porter, M. (1998) 'Clusters and the new economics of competition', *Harvard Business Review* 76(6): 77–90.

Powell, W. W. (1998) 'Learning from collaboration: knowledge and networks in the biotechnology and pharmaceutical industries', *California Management Review* 40(3): 228–40.

Quinn, J. B. (1999) 'Strategic outsourcing: leveraging knowledge capabilities', *Sloan Management Review*, 40(4): 9–21.

Reid, D., Bussiere, D. and Greenaway, K. (2001) 'Alliance formation issues for knowledge-based enterprises', *International Journal of Management Reviews* 3(1): 79–100.

Rindova, V. P. and Kotha, S. (2001) 'Continuous "morphing": competing through dynamic capabilities, form and function', *Academy of Management Journal* 44(6): 1263–80.

Sanchez, R. (1995) 'Strategic flexibility in product competition', *Strategic Management Journal* 16(Summer special issue): 135–60.

Sawhney, M. and Prendelli, E. (2000) 'Communities of creation: managing distributed innovation in turbulent markets', *California Management Review* 42(4): 24–54.

Schilling, M. A. and Steensma, H. K. (2001) 'The use of modular organizational forms: an industry level analysis', *Academy of Management Journal* 44(6): 1149–68.

Simonin, B. L. (1997) 'The importance of collaborative know-how: an empirical test of the learning organization', *Academy of Management Journal* 40(5): 1150–74.

Singer, M. (2001) 'Beyond the unbundled corporation', *The McKinsey Quarterly* 3: 4–5.

Spender, J. C. (1996) 'Making knowledge the basis of a dynamic theory of the firm', *Strategic Management Journal* 17(Winter special issue): 45–62.

Spender, J. C. and Grinyer, P. H. (1996) 'Organizational renewal: deinstitutionalization and loosely coupled systems (the human side of strategic change)', *International Studies of Management and Organization* 26(1): 17–24.

Szulanski, G. (1996) 'Exploring internal stickiness: impediments to the transfer of best practice within the firm', *Strategic Management Journal* 17(10): 27–43.

Teece, D., Pisano, G. and Shuen, A. (1997) 'Dynamic capabilities and strategic management', *Strategic Management Journal* 18(7): 509–33.

Thomke, S. and von Hippel, E. (2002) 'Customers as innovators: a new way to create value', *Harvard Business Review* 80(4): 74–81.

Useem, M. and Harder, J. (2000) 'Leading laterally in company outsourcing', *Sloan Management Review* 25–36.

Uzzi, B. (1996) 'The sources and consequences of embeddedness for the economic performance of organizations', *American Sociological Review* 61: 674–98.

Varadarajan, P. R. and Cunningham, M. H. (1995) 'Strategic alliances: a synthesis of conceptual foundations', *Journal of Academy of Marketing Science* 23(4): 282.

Venkatesan, R. (1992) 'Strategic sourcing: to make or not to make', *Harvard Business Review* 70(6): 98–107.

Venkatramann, N. and Henderson, J. C. (1998) 'Real strategies for virtual organizing', *Sloan Management Review* 40(1): 33–49.

von Krogh, G., Ichijo, K. and Nonaka, I. (2000) *Enabling Knowledge Creation: how to Unlock the Mystery of Tacit Knowledge and Release the Power of Innovation*. Oxford: Oxford University Press.

von Krogh, G., Nonaka, I. and Aben, M. (2001) 'Making the most of your company's knowledge: a strategic framework', *Long Range Planning* 34(4): 421–39.

Yli-Renko, H., Autio, E. and Sapienza, H. J. (2001) 'Social capital, knowledge acquisition and knowledge exploitation in young technology based firms', *Strategic Management Journal* 22(6/7), 587–613.

6 Sixth Competence Area
Monitoring

Business Challenges

- How can we communicate the value of our intellectual capital to investors?

- How can we evaluate the current performance of intellectual capital?

- How do we know whether we have the capacity to adapt in the future?

- How do we construct a comprehensive monitor to review the balance of our intellectual capital investment and make sense of the interdependencies?

- How can we learn from the feedback a monitor gives us?

Introduction

So far we have explored five competence areas that form the basis of a knowledge-based approach to strategy and operations. There is one further competence area required for our organizations to become truly knowledgeable. We need the capability to evaluate our performance in using available knowledge now, as well as future focused indicators that tell us about our capacity to respond to changes in patterns of actions in the external environment. In other words, we need feedback. Leif Edvinsson suggests this would come from a 'navigator' (Edvinsson, 2002): a measurement system that helps us pinpoint our position on the evolving knowledge landscape.

We have seen how the actions we take in paying attention to the other five competence areas can change the configuration of our own knowledge landscape, as well as that of our organizations and industry. As the shape and horizon of the landscape changes, we need some way of assessing whether we can continue to create value in our organizations.

Signpost In *Competence Area 3: Learning* we saw that in the metaphor of knowledge landscapes, peaks represent areas of expertise and the breadth of the landscape represents the range of knowledge domains we can span.

Conventional financial and management accounts show the impact of past strategic decisions on profitability. However, an historic perspective alone is a poor 'navigator'. Financial measurements are a weak indicator of future trends. Firstly, they describe the cumulative effect of many past decisions, rather than evaluating their suitability for future conditions. Secondly, by the time signals about change register in company accounts, it is often too late to respond. In fact, conservatism in financial reporting also tends to distort triggers and warning signals, discouraging recognition of trends until their impact has been realized.

Conventional accounting systems also lack a comprehensive toolkit for evaluating and reporting the value of intangibles. Historically, accounting principles only require us to confront the issue of intangibles when a sequence of events, like a merger or acquisition, crystallizes their effects into a realized market valuation of the company. At that point, the intangibles are usually consolidated as 'goodwill' and then written off as quickly as possible so that the balance sheet returns to a representation of what can be seen and objectively verified in audit terms.

In this chapter, we set out to understand how the effect of knowledge activities in our organization can be measured and monitored to give us the necessary feedback to inform decisions about current actions and future investments. Many terms are used within this subject area; for example, intellectual asset monitoring, intellectual capital measurement and feedback on the realized and realizable value of intangibles. The definitions and differences can be complicated and subtle, so to avoid confusion we will as far as possible adopt well-known accounting conventions and consistent use of terms:

- *Assets* are the result of externally generated capital invested internally into some long-term means of revenue generation.
- *Intangibles* are the whole body of outcomes that manifest themselves as the difference between the market evaluation of company performance and the monetary values of tangible assets on the balance sheet.
- *Intangible resources* include intangible assets (such as intellectual property rights, contracts, brand value, trade secrets and databases) and individual or collective skill or competence (Hall, 1992).
- *Intellectual capital* is the sum of intellectual resources (knowledge, information, intellectual property and experience) which can be put to use to create wealth (Stewart, 1998).

There is both an external and internal motivation to measure and communicate the value of our intellectual capital. Stock markets increasingly recognize the potential value of intellectual capital through high market to book valuations, but investors often have little evidence on which to judge how wisely managers have invested intellectual capital for the future, or how efficiently the intellectual resources are currently being managed. Knowledge managers themselves are also looking for better ways to understand where to focus their efforts and how to monitor the returns that are generated from knowledge-based initiatives. Skyrme and Amidon (1997) found that when they surveyed firms about the knowledge issues that concerned them most, 43 per cent of the 431 firms they surveyed placed 'measuring the value and performance of knowledge assets' above all other issues apart from 'changing people's behaviour'.

In earlier chapters, we described an organization as a 'dynamic, evolving, quasi-autonomous system of knowledge production and application' (Spender, 1996). For the truly Knowledgeable Organization, this means we need ways of showing how dynamic actions and decisions affect our ability to evolve and thrive. Initially, we will look at how to pay attention to developing *insight* through measures that explain how we are leveraging current intellectual capital and increasing intangibles. We will then look at how to pay attention to developing enough *foresight* about an organization's capability to make sense of trends and change in response to a dynamic environment. Both perspectives (plus an additional factor to track the balance between them) come together in what we have called a Knowledgeability Monitor.

Let us start by exploring the issues that affect how we measure value from knowledge and the techniques that have been used to measure intellectual capital and intangibles.

How can we monitor the current and potential value of knowledge?

Knowledge is not tangible; it cannot be seen or touched directly. Much of the knowledge we have available to our organizations is borrowed from various sources; for example, through our relationships with individual employees and other organizations. People and relationships become valuable organizational assets when they are used in conjunction with structural assets (processes, technology and routines) to realize their potential value in the service of a specific goal.

Inevitably, any form of measurement must recognize the particular characteristics of knowledge:

Subjectivity. Knowledge has nothing more than potential value until it is put to use in a way that the market recognizes as valuable. Assessing how potential will translate into realized value is largely a subjective judgement.

Complexity. Disentangling the interdependencies between the various types of intellectual capital to estimate the contribution of specific knowledge to delivered value is very complex. Generally there is no straightforward cause and effect trail that links people, structure and relationships to the financial performance of the organization.

Comparability. Comparing the relative weighting of knowledge contributions that are measured on different scales can be difficult.

The issue of comparability becomes even more significant when we try to communicate externally. For example, how can we communicate the net effect of an estimated change in monetary value of our brand, the associated changes in customer satisfaction assessments, and growth in the percentage of sales from new products upon the current and future value generating potential of our organization? Investors want to be confident that the figures they rely on are objective, meaningful and unbiased. They also need to understand how background context and strategic intent affect the translation of potential into realized value: they need a risk assessment along with predictions. Further, the information needs to be timely (Pike, Rylander and Roos, 2002). All of this requires standards to allow reasonable comparisons of performance.

Investment decisions based on intellectual capital reports that have little standardization are difficult. Even if there is an auditable trail to link measures with value, the types of intellectual capital that are strategically important will differ from company to company. Each company will have different views on what should be measured and different measurement methods and scales. Yet too much standardization could well make the reports meaningless if the measurements are not representative of the context in which the intellectual capital has strategic value.

Disclosure also has disadvantages. Complete disclosure could give away too many secrets to competitors. Risk assessment can only be contextual and subjective, yet could lead to charges of liability if the assessment is wrong. Analysts also have limited time to assess market value, so they need simple published information to slot quickly into a valuation model without manipulation. But simplification can lose the richness of reality .

The likelihood is that intellectual capital reporting will become compulsory by 2010 at the latest. The Financial Accounting Standards Board (FASB), The Canadian Institute for Chartered Accountants (CICA), The Securities and Exchange Commission (SEC), and the International Accounting Standards Committee (IASC) are actively debating how best to incorporate intellectual capital reporting into annual reports. Sweden introduced the requirement in 2002, in recognition of the fact that intellectual capital 'simply doesn't show up on the financial radar. What investors are left with is guesswork. Guesswork can be expensive. In other words, sentiments are no substitute for fundamental insights into intellectual capital' (Edvinsson, 2002).

The basic difficulties associated with measuring the value of knowledge are:

● Often we don't know what we know and even when we do, we often undervalue it.

- Knowledge has the greatest value creating potential when combined with other knowledge. Successful recombination requires that knowledge flows to the right place at the right time.

- The same knowledge asset can generate value in many different ways depending on how it is associated with other knowledge.

We can appreciate the consequences of some of these issues by revisiting the example of Dow Chemicals and assessing the sources of value that were identified from managing their library of patents more effectively.

Signpost   In *Competence Area 4: Connecting* we saw that Dow Chemicals generated considerable value from the patents it owned by releasing some and targeting future research and development to better exploit the ones they retained.

- Dow Chemicals could put an *immediate value* on patents used in current products. However, in time, competitors would find ways of matching or exceeding the patented ideas, so the returns would eventually decrease.

- They could identify *cost savings* from not maintaining patents that had no current commercial use, but they could not know what a competitor would do with that released knowledge.

- Encouraging the combination of several patents in a product area could trigger an entirely new innovation that was hard for competitors to copy because the properties of the patented materials were interdependent. That could deliver more *durable competitive advantage*, although the potential is hard to measure.

- Although the knowledge inherent in one or more chemical patents may have positive market value, the chemical itself could have negative environmental impact. Ultimately, this could have a detrimental effect on the value of intangibles like *brand and company reputation*, as well as financial liabilities for damages.

As the last point suggests, even when we identify our stock of knowledge assets and can provide measurable evidence of it, that measure is hard to interpret in value terms because the potential of knowledge is infinite and that infinite potential can have both positive and negative outcomes.

Measurement is a form of feedback. The purpose of feedback is to enable better planning. Here timescale presents a further difficulty. The timescales we assume in our plans and calculations change as a net result of our own actions and the activities of other players in our industry. High levels of knowledge activity in a new market space contract the planning horizon, primarily because knowledge becomes out of date more quickly.

Signpost

In *Competence Area 4: Connecting* we saw that co-evolution means that there is mutual adaptation between our organizations and other players in our industries. The knowledge landscape is co-created and dynamic as a result of our actions and interactions.

It is useful to reflect on the example of the introduction of the car (Kauffman, 2000). Many industries and roles declined once cars became widely used; for example, the need for horses and grooms, stables and breeders, farriers, saddle and bridle manufacturers, carriage-makers and plough-makers all reduced. However, the appearance of the car also created a whole range of new areas of economic activity; for example, roads, petrol stations, mechanics, insurance, in-car entertainment, national motel chains, drive-through movies and drive-through food supply.

The problem of predicting how and when these long-term extinction events occur has always been considered to be too complex to devise reliable predictive mechanisms. If we could foresee them we might be able to avoid their adverse effects. Studies of how complex systems adapt are now providing some additional understanding of what we might measure. See Box 6.1 for more details.

The impact of this lack of effective prediction mechanisms shows in the instability of stock market valuations. Despite the fact that a large proportion of the market valuation of many companies is now based on intangibles, we have no effective valuation comparators to act as controlling mechanisms in the marketplace. Without sound and trusted information on which to assess the value of shares, judgments can be distorted by perception, rumour, imperfect assumptions and spin. Investors make decisions about buying or selling shares based on predictions of future worth. Distortions in the understanding that supports these predictions can lead to unsubstantiated upward and downward movements in share price and unwarranted market turbulence.

Applying this to globally-interconnected stock markets where ideas and perceptions can travel almost instantaneously, it is hardly surprising that expectations of high intangible business value in certain ventures or industries, when unsupported by measurable evidence, can produce massive but fragile 'bubbles' that burst and destroy the value of investment portfolios. It would seem reasonable to suggest that better management of investor perceptions through the provision of more information about the underlying triggers and drivers of value might have a damping effect on the fragile assumptions that create volatility in the market.

Having seen that there are benefits to be gained from attempting to assess and describe the value of intangibles, we need to look in more detail at how to measure the value generating potential of knowledge. We have already seen that the knowledge resources of the organization can be grouped into three categories: external structure, internal structure and individual competence (Sveiby, 2001). The most important knowledge within each category is summarized in Table 6.1 (see p. 243).

Box 6.1

Complexity theory and prediction

Think of an industry as a system of interacting organizations and an organization as a system of interacting individuals. There appear to be measurable relationships between the extent of change that can occur and the proportion of inputs into the system relative to the number of 'control mechanisms' (Kauffman, 2000).

In general, control mechanisms are:

- How often a majority value occurs relative to the total number of occurrences. Translating that into knowledge terms, this means the more people believe the same thing, the less likely change is to happen. From a market perspective this means that the more influence we can exert on investors' evaluation of our performance in managing intellectual capital, the more stable our share price should be.

- The number of what Kauffman terms 'canalyzing functions'. These are mechanisms that guide or channel system behaviour. They are system inputs that have one value, which is enough to guarantee the next state of a system, regardless of whatever else is being absorbed. We might translate this in knowledge terms to an incontrovertible social ethic – something that will predictably condition behaviour regardless of other knowledge influences and opportunities.

The more inputs there are to a system, the more of these sorts of stabilizing mechanisms are needed to prevent system collapse and chaos. So, one might argue that the more opportunities there are, the more social ethics we must uphold to prevent catastrophic failure in the system. If there had been more regulation to limit the creative interpretation of financial statements, we might not have seen the stock market plummet so far in 2002, following the ▶

Signpost In *Competence Area 1: Competing* we saw that the key to value creation from the knowledge resources of our organizations is the transfer and conversion of knowledge within and between these families.

In general, this kind of categorization is extremely useful in pointing us towards meaningful areas for measurement effort. A number of organizations have adapted it and applied it successfully to communicate more about how their intangible resources are sources of value. One example is Celemi, a Sweden-based company that creates and provides learning resources. They recognized that as a knowledge business, their financial statement did not represent the true value of the firm (Barchan, 1998). In 1994 they started to pay attention to key intangible assets within three categories, which map

▶ various scandals of Enron and Worldcom. If the majority of investors had believed in the ethical behaviour of corporate executives, the collapse may not have been so large and difficult to reverse. Investors are simply agents in a complex economic valuation system. As Kauffman (2000) points out, in all complex systems 'Agents that have theories of one another and act selfishly based on those theories will typically create a persistently changing pattern of actions. Therefore they persistently create a non-stationary world in which only the relatively recent past has valid data'.

If the theories each agent uses as the basis for their decisions are 'fragile', the result at the system level will be instability. How far the change spreads depends on how densely interconnected the agents are. Theories become fragile when assumptions and perceptions multiply and reasoning reaches a point where assumptions are irreconcilable and perceptions are internally inconsistent with the external evidence.

We can also apply these ideas to the rate of innovation in an organization. We can see simply that the more new innovations an organization has to absorb, the more stabilizing mechanisms it needs to hold it together. As the knowledge landscape changes, our organizations tend to be driven to look more widely for new ways to compete (Brown and Eisenhardt, 1998). Too many mergers, acquisitions, divestitures, learning alliances, internal innovations and new initiatives can overload us. Complexity theory suggests that to thrive, organizations should remain sub-critical in terms of the weight of innovation relative to the weight of mechanisms that hold them together. The rate of change must not exceed the means to evaluate it against the risks. We need feedback mechanisms that help us pick the 'winners' from the 'losers' in terms of new ideas, and restrict our exploration into ever-broader knowledge domains. As long as we have selection mechanisms that discriminate as to how much novelty can be absorbed into the system, we can adapt appropriately.

approximately to the individual competence, internal structure and external structure categories as follows:

- *Our People*: the value provided by the growth, strength and loyalty of their customer base.
- *Our Organization*: the value derived from systems, processes, creation of new products and management style.
- *Our Customers*: the value to the company provided by the growth and development of employee competencies and how well these match customer needs.

Within each category, the intangible assets were broken down into sub-sections according to whether they related to the efficiency, the stability or the growth and renewal of the organization.

Table 6.1   Measuring the most valuable knowledge assets of our organizations

Category	Most valuable knowledge	Illustrative measure (Bontis, 2002)	Desirable measurement range (Sveiby, 1997)
Individual competence	Individual tacit knowledge locked in the minds of knowledge workers.	Volume of intellect	Growth/renewal Efficiency Stability
Internal structure	• Explicit knowledge in the form of processes and procedures. • Organizational tacit knowledge embedded in the culture. • Some tangible knowledge-based resources, such as technology systems.	Efficiency of routines	Growth/renewal Efficiency Stability
External structure	Predominantly tacit knowledge embedded in the social capital sustained within the relationships	Longevity of relationships.	Growth/renewal Efficiency Stability

Each subsequent year, Celemi published their performance in each category against parameters they felt made a difference to their business. The CEO believed that this tool, which they called the Intangible Assets Monitor, helped to build stakeholder confidence in the company's ability to make effective strategic decisions. It also generated a deeper level of understanding throughout the organization about the factors driving success in their business.

Celemi has used the Intangible Assets Monitor as a leading indicator to channel efforts and move the company forward effectively and profitably. For example, by comparing trends in various indicators they have been able to quantify how hiring new people has led to reduced efficiencies. The time it took for new recruits to learn how to locate company knowledge and use internal systems, plus the investment needed by senior staff to train them, had a negative impact on performance. This feedback has been used to improve the process of initiating new recruits and to influence decisions about future rates of growth.

Skandia, an insurance and financial services company, is another Sweden-based company that has pioneered the measurement of intellectual capital. In 1995, they released a supplement to their conventional annual report and accounts called 'Visualizing Intellectual Capital' (Edvinsson, 1997; Edvinsson and Malone, 1997). This was based on an intellectual capital measurement system called the Skandia Navigator. It focused on a slightly different set of categories to those Celemi adopted, effectively combining internal and external structure at one level and then splitting it at a lower level through a simple equation structure. The design was intended to amplify renewal and development dynamics.

Intellectual Capital = Human Capital + Structural Capital *where*

Structural Capital = Customer Capital + Organizational Capital *where*

Organizational Capital = Innovation Capital + Process Capital *where*

Innovation Capital = Intellectual Property + Intangible Assets

Within each category, Skandia designed numerical indicators linked to business critical success factors. They found that 3–4 indicators were enough in each area. The Navigator was integrated into the organization's performance management system, encouraging leaders to recognize the importance of both financial and non-financial dimensions of the company.

The impact of reporting their measurements of intellectual capital to shareholders has brought Skandia significant image management benefits. Comparing Skandia's performance against 113 international companies in the same sector research showed that, over a three-year period Skandia moved from 38th to 10th place, in a ranking of intangibles (based on market to book ratios) (Strassman, 1999).

We can build on these approaches in designing what we have called a Knowledgeability Monitor. Like Celemi and Skandia, we believe that both stability and growth/renewal indicators are important, but we suggest that monitoring is more than just performance measurement. It is also a process of evaluating the organization's ability to adapt and thrive in changing conditions. The need for indicators of both stability and renewal becomes obvious when we revisit two of the characteristics of tacit knowledge.

Investments in building and accessing tacit knowledge offer the highest potential returns

Tacit knowledge takes a long time to develop but once developed it is infinitely more powerful within a given context than explicit knowledge. Tacit knowledge is the expertise and competences that develop from experience and practice over time. It leads to an intuitive insight into what to do, as well as a flexible and responsive understanding of how to do it. We need both as the basis of effective decision-making.

Within our organizations, the pattern of shared assumptions and background common knowledge about what matters and how to work together is a deeply-embedded form of tacit knowledge. It enables both the effective exploitation of our existing knowledge resources and the ability to combine ideas to create new knowledge, but it can also constrain renewal.

Tacit knowledge can lead to an inability to recognize the need to adapt to external changes

Tacit knowledge is slow to change. Although it can become a hidden constraint on an individual's or an organization's ability to adapt, or even see the need to adapt, it is a stabilizing mechanism that can offset the urge to innovate too much. Individuals establish mental models and organizations develop a dominant logic that filters the way they see the world and what they pay attention to. This aspect of tacit knowledge can create a 'blind spot' on 'The Window of Knowledge Opportunities'.

 In *Competence Area 2: Deciding* we saw that dominant logic is a response learned through experience that simplifies and speeds decision-making by assuming that the future environment will be similar to the past environment.

 In *Competence Area 4: Connecting* we used 'The Window of Knowledge Opportunities' to assess the value to be gained from knowledge flows across the boundaries of our organizations.

By looking at these two characteristics of tacit knowledge, we can conclude that our organizations need to sustain a balanced mix of knowledge resources that constantly challenge us to adapt, as well as enable us to thrive in the current environment. Both perspectives need to be incorporated into the design of a Knowlegeability Monitor. We need measures that recognize and prompt the development of current and short-term value from knowledge resources. We also need indicators to help us track the resources that give our organizations the capacity to change, including triggers to highlight the problems we could face if we simply re-enforce existing patterns by refining our current perceptions, ideas and theories beyond the point at which they are relevant. The capability for exploitation, steady adaptation and radical new approaches all need to be evaluated. A Knowledgeability Monitor must therefore contain measures of stability and change and a way to balance their effect on our overall integrity.

We have already looked at how two knowledge flows maintain the 'life' of our organizations as social systems. Now we draw upon work that suggests these knowledge flows divide into five domains of activity that are essential for any viable living system (Achterbergh and Vriens, 2002; Beer, 1985). We will use these domains to help us design a balanced Knowledgeability Monitor that reflects all the areas of competence that we have identified as essential to the Knowledgeable Organization.

Signpost In *Competence Area 1: Competing* we saw that the first flow is based on interaction with the environment and underpins learning and adaptation. The second flow accesses memories about what to do and how to do it as the basis of our survival.

In general, a viable living system is one that can 'maintain a separate existence' and reproduce through its own actions (Beer, 1979). The five domains of activity in a viable system divide into two complementary pairs linked by a control domain that manages the tension between stability and change as shown in Figure 6.1. Group A domains are the mechanisms that give a viable system its ability to change; the strength of the adaptation mechanisms needs to reflect the level of turbulence in the external environment. Group B domains are the complementary mechanisms that give the system stability, coherence, identity and the ability to resist being torn apart by that change. Control fits into both groups because its purpose is to keep the balance of new and existing activities aligned and in proportion to the needs of the system.

We can explain the concepts in the model by comparing how the ideas apply to both ourselves as human beings and to an organization. Each of the five domains is summarized in Table 6.2.

We suggest that a Knowledgeability Monitor based on these five knowledge management domains highlighted in the last column of Table 6.2 (Alertness,

Figure 6.1 Domains of a viable system (based on Beer, 1985)

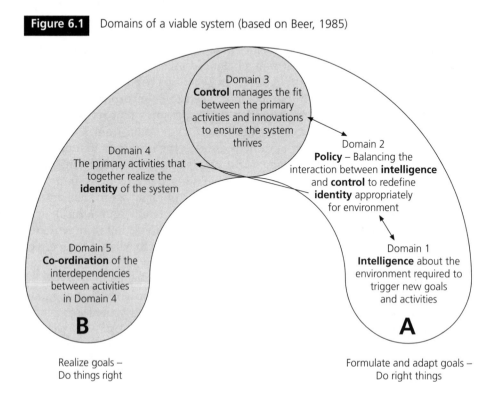

Table 6.2   Five domains of humans and organizations as viable systems

Domain	Human characteristics	Organizational characteristics
1. Change: Intelligence	The way we gather intelligence about the world through our senses (sight, smell, touch, taste, hearing).	Boundary-spanning mechanisms to gather external data about the world. These allow **Alertness**.
2. Change: Policy	Brain function to interpret sensory inputs, includes cognitive reasoning.	Mechanisms to identify trends and determine new knowledge domains to explore. These allow **Strategic Appraisal**.
3. Source of Balance: Control	DNA, which both keeps us the way we are and allows the species to innovate through recombination of half the DNA of the mother and half of the father. Also instinctive responses (fight or flight).	Legacy infrastructure and enduring culture and values and our current innovative capability. These **Control** the mix of options that can be adopted.
4. Stability: Primary Activities	Essential organs such as brain, heart, lungs, liver, kidneys, stomach and intestines.	The intellectual assets and competences available to the organization. These are the **Means to Process Intellectual Capital.**
5. Stability: Co-ordination	Endocrine system that co-ordinates the functions of organs.	Infrastructure, culture, leadership, knowledge communities, management of relationships. These are the means of **Co-ordinating** the assets to synergistically generate value.

Strategic Appraisal, Control, Means to Process Intellectual Capital and Co-ordination) will give a comprehensive overview of how well the Knowledgeable Organization is performing in the areas that are essential for it to thrive today and adapt to the future. We will identify the categories that need to be monitored within each domain. However, the detailed elements within each category must be customized to reflect the focus of the specific knowledge-based strategies that an organization is pursuing. In this chapter, we will suggest some general elements which are the starting point for design, but in practice each organization will need to tailor them to its specific context.

We will begin by looking at the domains that relate to the stability of our organizations: the Means to Process Intellectual Capital and the Co-ordination Mechanisms. Categories of the Knowledgeability Monitor based on these domains generate insights into how well knowledge is currently being leveraged. We will then move on to look at the domains that give us our capacity to recognize and respond to triggers for change: Alertness and Strategic Appraisal. Categories of the Knowledgeability Monitor based on these domains can provide foresight into emergent patterns and trends and the potential capacity of our organizations to respond. We will treat the Control domain separately, with categories of the Knowledgeability Monitor in this domain providing a way of recognising whether the balance between stability and change is being maintained appropriately.

Paying attention to gaining insight into current intellectual capital performance

The reason for monitoring current performance in leveraging intellectual capital is to provide insight into how stable our organizations are. Stability comes from our capacity to combine and apply knowledge to advantage in the environment we currently face. Categories of the Knowledgeability Monitor need to cover the *means by which we process intellectual capital* to create value and the *co-ordination mechanisms* that we use to link these into coherent action. Let us examine each in turn.

Monitor the means to process intellectual capital

A meaningful monitoring process should provide insights into our current stock of intellectual capital relative to the demands of the environment. It also needs to indicate our effectiveness in incrementally refining this. This leads us to propose elements of the Knowledgeability Monitor within four categories:

1 individual competence and organizational knowledge assets,
2 external relationships,
3 brand image,
4 patents, copyright and trademarks.

1. Individual competence and its conversion to organizational knowledge assets

The competence of individuals is the mechanism by which data and information are contextualized and converted into knowledge. Sharing that knowledge with others is the way in which competence can develop at an organizational level. Rapidly changing technology and new competitive pressures means all knowledge assets quickly become out of date. At the level of individual competence, the gap will be evident in terms of the investment in training or accessing specialist expertise to meet the requirements of new projects (McMahon and Moore, 1999). Assessing the 'stretch' required to acquire the knowledge and fill these competence gaps gives us insight into the suitability of current knowledge. It also indicates the pace of change in the environment.

There are a number of actions we can take to access and develop the knowledge of individuals and support its conversion to organizational competence:

- Attract and select employees and contract-based staff with relevant existing knowledge, the potential to apply it and a track record of developing new knowledge.
- Motivate knowledge workers using people management practices that create a comfortable climate for them to exploit and develop knowledge.

Signpost

In *Competence Area 1: Competing* we looked at how to recruit, select, train, appraise and reward people in ways that encourage them to use and develop their own and our organizations' knowledge.

- Reduce the burden of under-performing individuals through effective performance management systems.
- Develop existing employees in the light of the knowledge-based strategy.

Signpost

In *Competence Area 3: Learning* we saw how to use well-designed training, on-the-job learning, mentoring, coaching, peer-group networks and action learning initiatives to create opportunities for people to learn through constructing meaning from experience.

- Institutionalize the processes and procedures that integrate on-going learning and reflection into standard business processes.

Signpost

In *Competence Area 1: Competing* we saw how to capture learning from significant events and activities and design processes that support continuous improvement (for example, effective suggestion schemes, shared databases and communities of practices).

Elements of a Knowledgeability Monitor that could give insight into how well our organizations are leveraging these sources of knowledge might include the following:

- Track employee satisfaction as this is likely to reflect the willingness of individuals to apply their own individual competence to improve organizational performance.
- Construct an inventory of employee competencies and ensure that it is linked to the knowledge-based strategy being pursued by the organization.

- Monitor the effectiveness of the performance management and reward system in generating valuable outcomes through the application of individual and organizational knowledge assets (Dzinkowski, 2000).
- Track the financial contribution generated from activities to improve products and processes (such as after action reviews, suggestion schemes, etc).

It may be appropriate to give one particular department the responsibility for tracking and responding to these measures, or it may be better to make it the responsibility of all senior managers.

2. External relationships

Evaluating the contribution of external relationships to the performance of our organizations is important. We need to understand their value as sources of tangible returns, knowledge and intangible benefits, as well as their sustainability (Allee, 2000). Sustainable relationships are ones that provide value to both parties, although the form of value derived may not be in the same 'currency'. Three types of 'currency' can be exchanged between members of an organization's value net:

Goods, services and revenue. A traditional form of exchange in which goods and services are supplied which customers' value and payment is received to generate revenue for the suppliers.

Knowledge. For example, customers can gain value from being provided with access to information and knowledge about products and services. Suppliers of such information can use market research techniques to analyze the patterns of requests to understand customer preferences.

Intangibles. This exchange is based on benefits that are provided and returned as a result of repeated interactions, for example brand awareness and product loyalty.

A simple map of the exchange of value in the relationships of a software development business with its customers and suppliers is shown in Figure 6.2. The reason for the relationship between each organization (outsourced component development and a user-support website) is shown at the centre of the lines connecting the ovals. Each relationship is illustrated by two-way value flows. Value flows in each direction have been mapped as follows:

Outer line: the goods, services and revenue values being exchanged.

Middle line: the knowledge benefits of the relationship.

Inner line: the underlying intangible returns available.

By mapping relationships in this way, we can start to get a better picture of the value our organizations are deriving from relationships, what flows of knowledge and intangibles are contributing to strategy and where relationships are loose and where they are closer.

Signpost In *Competence Area 4: Connecting* we saw that the permeability of an organization's boundary to knowledge flows needs to be adjusted to match the turbulence in the external environment.

Figure 6.2 Mapping value flows in a software firm's relationships (adapted from Allee, 2000)

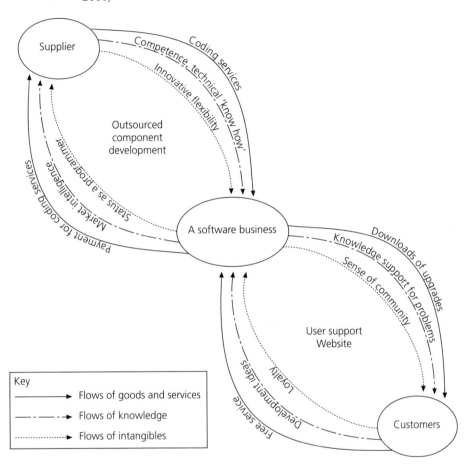

In general terms, the elements of a Knowledgeability Monitor could include:

- The value being derived from each relationship (in terms of the three types of currency discussed above).
- An assessment of the sustainability of each relationship in terms of the balance of value being derived by each party.

3. Brand image

Brand image is the external perception of the identity of our organizations: the way others conceive of what we stand for. It is more than the brand image of any individual product or service, although it can affect how attractive they seem. How we accrue this sort of intellectual capital depends on how well we communicate our espoused beliefs and values, the coherence of our product portfolio and the services and operational capabilities we deliver. Brand image is closely tied in with our reputation and as such is a critical factor affecting share price. We can enhance the value of our organization's brand by:

- Clearly communicating the value of knowledge assets and intangibles underpinning our organization's capability (the subject of the current chapter).

- Building trusting knowledge-based relationships with the customers, suppliers, partners and external bodies who play a part in our value net.

 Signpost In *Competence Area 5: Relating* we saw how to build loose connections and close ties with customers, suppliers and other organizations to create a valuable network of knowledge-based relationships.

It is hard to measure brand value consistently in monetary terms because it fluctuates with market perception. However, some companies do try. PepsiCo, the soft drinks and fast food company, developed a model to track brand equity across all of its three primary businesses – soft drinks, snack foods and quick service restaurants. The purpose of the model was to evaluate generalizable cross-category perceptions as a way to support their new strategy to develop a single brand image that would help them compete with what they defined as 'icon stature brands' such as McDonald's and Coca-Cola.

PepsiCo started by discovering the attributes that supported good brand image across all their product categories and then, through statistical analysis, they identified the key factors affecting their recognition and regard. The final model was called Equitrak™. The use of this model globally has produced several important management insights associated with transnational brand equity management and the impact of marketing and pricing on the sustainability of regard for the brand (Kish, Riskey and Kerin, 2001).

We can monitor the influences affecting image. Elements of a Knowledgeability Monitor could include:

- customer feedback collected through surveys and analysis of complaints,

- feedback provided through customer communities,

- annual cost of protecting the brand (Brooking, 1996),

- questioning the investment community about how they rate the organizational reputation (Brooking, 1996),

- Surveying customers to determine how much brand image influences new and repeat business.

4. Patents, copyright and trademarks

These intellectual assets need to be managed carefully to deliver value. Effectively, they are a way to increase the scarcity of knowledge by restricting access for others. Unfortunately, the very act of registering a patent can weaken any knowledge advantage because publication makes the findings more transparent (McGaughey, 2002).

Signpost

In *Competence Area 4: Connecting* we used 'The Window of Knowledge Opportunities' to analyze when to protect knowledge and when to share it with external organizations.

However, by combining patents in a 'recipe', the complexity of unravelling the interactions between the various patented parts makes it harder to copy the final product. It allows us to get more out of each investment in knowledge, because it is being used in more than one context. The elements of a Knowledgeability Monitor could therefore include:

- The number of products and services with more than one patent or copyrighted element embedded in them.
- The number of times any one patent is used in revenue generating products or services.

Monitor the co-ordination mechanisms linking intellectual resources

The second domain that supports organizational stability covers the mechanisms that connect and co-ordinate the intellectual capital that has been integrated into our organizations. Smooth co-ordination mechanisms make it cheaper and easier to realize value from this intellectual capital.

Co-ordination mechanisms can be seen as mediation devices that dampen 'oscillations and disruptions' to the smooth flow of resources between primary activities within the business (Achterbergh and Vriens, 2002). They determine how effectively we manage and gain value from interdependent forms of intellectual capital. We have identified five main categories of co-ordination mechanisms needed in the Knowledgeable Organization:

1 *Processes and infrastructure*: the structures that remains in the business when people go home.

2 The *culture* of the organization: the collective tacit assumptions about how things are done that guide behaviours.

3 *Communities of practice:* ways of spanning operational silos to connect, harness and leverage existing expertise for further learning.

4 *Relationship management*: the ways we manage relationships to ensure that knowledge flows are effective and learning is captured.

5 The quality of *leadership*: the effectiveness by which goals are pursued and decisions are co-ordinated.

These categories give us feedback about how well knowledge is flowing within our organizations and across the boundaries. Here we will again suggest illustrative elements to measure in each category.

1. Processes and infrastructure

Structural mechanisms are the ways in which our organizations capture and leverage the knowledge of individuals and external partners. An example of a measurable element in this category could be:

● The increases in productivity achieved through using technology to spread best practices or to connect people to share expertise.

 In *Competence Area 1: Competing* we saw how standardization through the use of rules, procedures, taxonomies and operating standards makes the flow of explicit knowledge easier. Technology can also be used to 'push' or 'pull' knowledge to where it is needed.

2. Organizational culture

The organizational culture creates the context for people to interpret their shared purpose and work effectively with the knowledge resources of the organization (be they explicit or tacit). Culture has a large impact on the performance of all knowledge-based investments.

 In *Competence Area 2: Deciding* we looked at how organizational culture emerges from the shared sense of identity, care, shared values, the style and nature of relationships between people and leadership behaviours.

Elements in this category could assess the collaborative climate of our organizations. The Collaborative Climate survey produced by Karl-Erik Sveiby assesses individual attitude as well as the support provided by colleagues, immediate managers and organizational leadership (Sveiby and Simons, 2002).

● Assess the level of collaboration through attitude surveys, extent of recognition for knowledge sharing, measures within the appraisal system, etc.

3. Communities of practice

A well-connected network of communities of practice can overcome problems caused by knowledge 'stickiness' and social barriers to knowledge flows. Communities of practice thrive when there is clear benefit to individuals from participating.

 In *Competence Area 3: Learning* we saw that building effective communities of practice involves sustaining the delivery of value for both individuals and the organization and aligning those sources of value so that they are complementary.

Effective communities of practice thrive on the enthusiasm and commitment of individuals. They should not require significant organizational intervention.

Efforts are needed to connect communities of practice to prevent knowledge 'sticking' within their boundaries.

The best measures of communities of practice are 'outcome measures', in other words their bottom line contribution to the business. Shell has adopted this approach in their oil exploration business (McDermott, 2002). By conservatively estimating the value of knowledge to specific activities, the contribution of community discussions to that knowledge and the certainty of their contribution, they could make financial calculations to estimate return on the investment in supporting the organizational communities. For example, it was felt that community discussions reduced the need to drill and test three potential well sites per year in oil-bearing sand beds, because the experts could draw on a wider base of comparative knowledge about other similar sites around the world. This produced cost savings of about $24 million annually, compared with costs of only $300–400 000 for running the community that contributed the knowledge.

Measurable elements in this category could include:

- Savings and/or improvements in quality and efficiency as a result of community activities (Hanley, 2001).

- The attrition rate of community members versus non-members, representing reduced recruitment costs and higher levels of experience being retained in the organization.

- The rate of knowledge transfer between communities; for example, assessed through Social Network Analysis.

4. Managing relationships

We have seen that collaborating effectively with external partners gives us access to a broader range of knowledge resources than our organizations can otherwise sustain. A corporate reputation as a good alliance partner also has the advantage of attracting other institutions as potential collaborators, thus giving our organizations greater flexibility and better chances to adapt. The opportunity to leverage the value of our relationships relies on our organizations developing the capability to manage and learn from each one (Dyer, Kale and Singh, 2001).

 Signpost In *Competence Area 5: Relating* we saw the importance of allocating responsibility for actively managing relationships with network partners.

Elements of a monitoring system to provide insight into the effectiveness with which relationships are being managed for knowledge value could include:

- Analyzing the results of satisfaction surveys of alliance partners that assess whether mutual expectations are being fulfilled.

- The number of collaborative activities between alliance partners that have achieved their objectives.

- The longevity of relationships amongst core partners. This is important because the longer they endure the more likely it is that valuable tacit knowledge will be shared (Reid, Bussiere and Greenaway, 2001).

5. Leadership

Everyone in the Knowledgeable Organization needs to demonstrate leadership behaviours so that, in a dynamic market environment, decisions can be made rapidly in response to customer needs. Relevant knowledge needs to be widely disseminated to allow decision-making to be distributed to individuals closest to customers. We need shared values to act as a framework to guide these decisions.

In *Competence Area 2: Deciding* we saw that people need to be encouraged to accept responsibility for their own performance and their impact on the performance of others. Required behaviours include attentiveness, flexibility, co-operation and learning.

Senior managers need to create the conditions for effective collaboration and shape and communicate the knowledge-based strategies of our organizations. In this category, elements of a Knowledgeability Monitor could include:

- The extent to which the knowledge-based strategy has been understood, assessed through consistency of actions, employee satisfaction surveys, ability to proceed with change initiatives smoothly, etc.
- The effectiveness of managers in exemplifying values and supporting collaboration, assessed through 360-degree appraisal systems.
- The levels of flexibility and empowerment evident in the behaviours of individuals, assessed through a reduced need for problem escalation combined with increased customer satisfaction measures.

Together these two categories of *the means by which we process intellectual capital* to create value and the *co-ordination mechanisms to link intellectual resources* gives us a comprehensive perspective on the domains of knowledge activity that give us 'stability'.

EDS, a US-based systems consulting firm, is an organization that has developed an 'Intellectual Capital Dashboard' to monitor many of the categories that we have looked at in this section (Wick, 2001). They launched an intellectual asset management programme that started by looking at what was already happening across the organization. They found that some areas of EDS were already tracking intellectual assets and looking at factors that inhibited their growth (such as the limits on productivity caused by a confusing information architecture on an intranet site). Their approach was to aggregate existing data and also map and source uncollected data that would allow managers to make more informed decisions.

They developed a Web-enabled, automated monitoring tool, the Intellectual Capital Dashboard, that gave access to 'useful links, news, comparison tools, intellectual capital classifications and key metrics with colour-coded arrow indicators'. This was in the same format as an existing widely-used management information system, so was readily accepted across the organization. Making the Dashboard widely available allowed better decision-making, plus the additional benefit that managers could benchmark local performance against other areas, decide where they needed to improve, and then easily identify top performing areas to seek assistance from. This enabled them to 'leverage collective expertise in managing intangible assets'.

Many of the Intellectual Capital Dashboard metrics fell into the two domains that we have been looking at; for example:

Means to process intellectual capital. Employee satisfaction, contractor usage, customer satisfaction, net present value of employees, employee development ability, number of alliance partners.

Co-ordinating mechanisms. Number and value of communities, value of alliances.

Additionally, they included some 'change'-oriented measures, including the number of innovations approved. This falls into one of the domains that we will be looking at in the next section: Strategic Appraisal. EDS felt that by leveraging existing approaches and supporting collaboration, they were able to accelerate their intellectual asset management programme and focus on areas that would yield the highest value to the organization.

We will now move on to look at the domains in a viable organization that emphasize 'change' and see how we can develop indicators of our capability to understand changes in the environment and adapt to them.

Paying attention to developing foresight and our capability to adapt to change

The 'change' domains of the Knowledgeability Monitor help us to evaluate the long-term survival prospects for our organizations. Clearly this is important to investors, employees, customers and suppliers.

One obvious starting point is to examine the strength of the measures that indicate stability in an organization. In rapidly changing markets 'core competencies become core rigidities' (Lewin and Volberda, 1999) or competence traps (Levinthal and March, 1993; Levitt and March, 1998; Teece, Pisano and Shuen, 1997). Consequently, the elements of the Knowledgeability Monitor indicating stability are effectively reverse indicators of adaptability. For example, if staff turnover and recruitment are low, existing employees may be more efficient and effective, but the introduction of diverse perspectives and creative thinking is also likely to be low. The result is likely to be a reduced capacity to recognize the need for significant change and design innovative responses to challenges from competitors.

In general, since our focus has now shifted to the future, quantitative measures are likely to be less meaningful. It may not be possible to directly extrapolate current trends. Instead, we need probing mechanisms to achieve real foresight; intuition and judgment also play a part. The aim is to track the performance of the activities in our organization that help us identify the forces threatening both our status and position and our ability to generate creative alternatives.

We will consider the two domains of *Alertness* and *Strategic Appraisal*. Alertness assesses the intelligence capabilities within our organizations, in particular, how well they give us knowledge about the actions and capabilities of other players in our industry. Strategic Appraisal considers the choices we make to adopt particular patterns of action, the mechanisms we employ to determine new knowledge domains to explore and the patterns of influential information channelled in and out of the organization. We will identify the categories of Knowledgeability Monitor to give us useful feedback in each of these domains.

Monitor alertness through collecting intelligence to signal the need for change

In the viable systems model outlined in Figure 6.1 and Table 6.2, the activities in this domain are aimed at sensing what is going on outside our organizations and providing suggestions for innovations and adaptations that will align internal activities with environmental changes (Achterbergh and Vriens, 2002). In measurement terms, we need to assess how effectively these outwardly facing activities collect and interpret relevant information about the outside world.

Those involved in intelligence gathering will need some knowledge about the goals and performance status of our organizations, but only as a background against which to evaluate opportunities and threats. They should not feel bound by ways we have collectively come to see the world and our place in it.

 Signpost   In *Competence Area 2: Deciding* we saw that dominant logic constrains what the members of an organization collectively recognize as important and worthy of attention.

The objective of the Alertness domain is to generate ideas and make proposals that challenge current strategy and objectives. Activities to explore widely and create links between opportunities are important. We can evaluate our organizational capability to access sources of intelligence and assess their potential impact by tracking knowledge flows against three important categories in a Knowledgeability Monitor: speed, diversity and connectivity.

1. Speed

Elements might include:

- Speed of accessing relevant information, assimilating it and translating it into explicit knowledge to influence research plans, product, market or process development.

- The rate of knowledge absorption in terms of the number of routes that information can flow along (in other words, the ranges of sources of intelligence that we are employing), and the potential absorptive capacity of the people involved. This could be assessed in terms of their levels of qualifications and relevant experience.

 Signpost In *Competence Area 4: Connecting* we saw that absorptive capacity explains why the more knowledge we have, the more we can have.

2. Diversity

There are a number of sources of diversity. Diverse knowledge-based relationships in our external network encourage a broad and robust scanning process that can generate early warning signals. In contrast, close ties with only a few partners can inhibit new knowledge acquisition from other sources (Yli-Renko, Autio and Sapienza, 2001). The diversity of our customers, the diversity of the markets that we operate within and the diversity of suppliers that we use are all connections that potentially feed in new perspectives and intelligence about opportunities that we can pursue, or the potentially damaging competitive activities of others.

 Signpost In *Competence Area 5: Relating* we saw that the type of external relationship affects the permeability of an organizational boundary to knowledge flows in both directions.

The diversity of the competencies of the individual employees is another source of value. By having people from different cultures, backgrounds and industries working in our organizations, we expand the range of perspectives that we have access to. The range of different projects an individual has worked on and the number of countries they have worked in will also broaden perspective. This richness helps individuals make connections between new knowledge and increases the potential of our organizations to use it for value. In this category, elements of a Knowledgability Monitor might include:

- The relative proportions of loosely-connected and closely-tied relationship within our organization's network of external relationships.
- The conversion of ideas from external partners such as customers, suppliers, consultants and alliance partners into product or market development plans.
- The diversity of background and experience represented within the individual people that our organizations employ.

We should also recognize that the degree of diversity an organization can sustain will differ greatly according to size, experience and the constraints upon communication. Great care is needed in the interpretation of simple numerical proportions. Too many relationships can distract attention from important issues. It may seem attractive to recruit lots of new expertise to bring new ideas into the business, but these ideas need to be adopted if the individuals are to be retained and motivated.

3. Connectivity

It is the pattern of repetition and information overlaps that usually alert us to the significance of what are often weak signals from outside. We notice these most when we are well-connected to the outside world and when we have the means to collect the signals in one place and relate them to each other. A competitor intelligence function can provide a useful point of connection for various incoming signals and so help to shed light on blind spots and new opportunities. Making connections between different pieces of knowledge is the basis of creativity. Collaboration supports that process; whether that is collaboration in internal communities of practice, or collaboration in close alliances such as joint ventures. Collaborative activity tends to present all sorts of challenges to the mindset and established operations of our organizations. The more we connect with different organizations, the more conflicts we may potentially have to deal with. Yet the more densely connected we are to other people within one collaborative relationship, the greater value it can deliver. The number of collaborative relationships in our network is an indicator of our openness to adapt, but the number of connections within a relationship is an indicator of the ability to turn that relationship into value.

In this category, elements of a Knowledgeability Monitor could include:

- Number of collaborative relationships initiated for innovation.
- Number and density of interactions between members in a collaborative venture (for example, assessed using Social Network Analysis).
- Usefulness of competitor intelligence, assessed, for example, by the financial impact on investment decisions.

Strategic Appraisal is the second 'change' domain in our model. It is the means by which we evaluate the range of new options identified through the Alertness domain, and set them in the broader context of our knowledge-based strategy.

Monitor strategic appraisal mechanisms

In the Strategic Appraisal domain, we evaluate whether we have the organizational potential to adopt the innovation ideas that intelligence gathering provokes and whether the ideas are appropriate given the external conditions. Strategic Appraisal ensures that change is feasible and purposeful. Monitoring performance in this domain requires:

- Mechanisms to assess opportunities in the light of knowledge about social, political and regulatory trends.
- Evaluation of how much attention is given to things that challenge the dominant logic and encourage new developments.

- Ways to measure the innovative capacity of the organization.
- Indicators of our ability to influence the external environment.

To this end, an effective Knowledgeability Monitor needs to contain categories that give feedback in three areas: our capability to *interpret the environmental context, shape strategic direction* and *influence the environmental context*.

1. Interpret the environmental context

We need knowledge of external activities in three different contexts if our organization is to develop an informed knowledge-based strategy: the market context, the sociopolitical context and the technological context (Cummings and Doh, 2000).

Market   Knowledge of stakeholder activity is essential for an informed strategy of innovation and adaptation. We can use stakeholder maps to describe the interactivity within our industry context. They give us a picture of the levels of activity and the strength of the relationships between other players. These are different from the value net approach that gives feedback on our own relationships (see Figure 6.2, p. 251). Stakeholder maps show how the activities of competitors and organizations producing complementary products or services are likely to impact our own organizations' access to and interaction with customers and suppliers. For example, two local hospital trusts in a big city might be able to co-operate with each other when they purchase drugs and medical supplies, while being competitors for the supply of local doctors and nurses, and complementors in the eyes of customers if they each specialize in different treatments but provide flexible general care beds to the local population. By mapping the different aspects of stakeholder activity in the marketplace, we get a picture of where strategic action could make a difference in terms of sharing or protecting knowledge.

Consideration of other players' perceptions also affects strategic decisions. For example, when Lucent Technologies was owned by AT&T, MCI and Sprint saw it as part of a competitor for long-distance services, despite the fact that in network equipment it was a common supplier to all (Cummings and Doh, 2000). When Lucent became an independent business, it was more successful because the long-distance providers now perceived it to be one of the premier suppliers of network equipment.

In this category, elements of a Knowledgeability Monitor could include:

- Dynamic maps of the external interactions of competitors and producers of complementary products and services with respect to customers and suppliers.

Socio-political   The actions of governments, regulators and special interest groups affect the ability of our organizations to realize the potential of knowledge-based innovation. We need feedback into the activities of influential parties. Public policy-makers create constraints and limits on our options, while special interest groups evaluate and either legitimize or constrain the activity of our organizations within the wider social context. The media has a critical role to play in the power of interest groups and the impact these have on our strategic options.

Elements of a Monitor could include:

● Maps of the activities of influential external parties.

● Assessments of external perceptions of our organizations through measuring positive and negative publicity.

Technological   In the technological context, we can use the intelligence gained from mapping stakeholder activities to plan where we might gain advantage, either by being first to market or otherwise shaping the pattern of customer adoption.

We saw in *Competence Area 4: Connecting* that strategies to generate value through knowledge need to consider the possibility of gaining increasing returns.

Usually, this requires defining a standard for an industry, which is hard to do alone. For example, Toshiba, Time Warner and Sony-Philips got together early in the development of DVD technology to define a standard across all modes of use. Other organizations adopt a 'Trojan horse' strategy, giving away basic knowledge to capture users and then getting large revenues from upgrades and complementary products. In either case, Strategic Appraisal needs some way to assess the risk and rewards of increasing returns from opening access to knowledge assets. Useful elements for the Knowledgeability Monitor might include:

● Models of product adoption and usage under various scenarios; for example, created using risk assessment tools.

2.   Shape strategic direction

To produce a knowledge-based strategy that has synergy between all the domains of activity supporting a viable organization, we need guidance on what strategic issues should inform our choices. The net effect of Strategic Appraisal-related mechanisms should be to give our organizations the means of ensuring that the dominant logic that underpins decision-making evolves and remains relevant. For this, our organizations need to be able to evaluate their capacity to discriminate between available strategic options and also to assess the appropriateness of the scale and scope of internal innovation activities.

If we start with the capacity to discriminate between strategic options, then a useful tool is scenario planning, which challenges the mental models of individuals and shapes the potential strategic directions that could be followed by our organizations. It also helps us discriminate between strategic options by making evident the innovations we might need to make in order to thrive in each scenario.

In *Competence Area 4: Connecting* we saw that scenario planning is a way of prospectively making sense of knowledge potential by exploring alternative futures in an orderly manner. Scenarios are plausible and internally consistent stories about possible futures.

Other approaches might include using internal experiments within parts of the business, or prototyping products and services so we can test them with customers. A broad network of external relationships is a valuable test bed.

Once we have identified a necessary change, we also need to assess whether we could respond to it effectively. We need to have some elements within the Knowledgeability Monitor that evaluate the existing innovative capacity of our organizations, particularly relative to the strength of the absorptive capacity that we can draw on as the basis for knowledge creation.

In *Competence Area 4: Connecting* we saw that absorptive capacity means that the more knowledge we have, the more we can have. It is the basis for recognizing the importance of external opportunities and creating new knowledge.

The ability to access tacit knowledge, which is also fundamental to our innovative capacity, is associated with the close relationships between people; either internally through well-developed communities of practice, or externally through our networks. In general, the more that partners can 'overlap' their technological resources, the greater the potential for innovation. The levels of cross-licensing and combinations of partners' patents has steadily increased within alliances in recent years (Mowery, Oxley and Silverman, 1996).

These ways of shaping strategic direction are interdependent, since the extent to which our organizations recognize triggers for change and the extent to which we can respond are mutually re-enforcing.

Elements of a Knowledgeability Monitor that assess the net effect of discriminatory capacity and innovative capability include:

- An assessment of the extent of change in the strategic direction of our organizations over a given period of time.

- The plans that have been prepared in anticipation of the outcomes suggested by a number of scenarios.

- The number of close ties in our relationship networks that produce new combinations of knowledge, measured through cross-licensing and patent sharing.

- The openness to experimentation measured, for example, by the number of experimental evaluation projects relative to the number of developmental projects, or the number of loose associations entered into with other organizations for strategic evaluation purposes.

- The proportion of potential absorptive capacity to realized absorptive capacity evidenced by the ratio of new ideas to useful processes, products or services emerging out of the innovation process.
- The track record of major innovations measured, for example, through the number of truly new products in the portfolio.

3. Influence in the environment

Activities within the Alertness domain may suggest that greater value can be derived from releasing knowledge assets to influence the shape of the industry knowledge landscape, rather than protecting them within the boundaries of our organizations.

 In *Competence Area 4: Connecting* we saw that releasing knowledge has the potential to generate increased value by enabling the development of complementary products, the establishment of dominant standards or the creation of a critical mass of users.

Assessing the capacity to make these strategic decisions falls within the Strategic Appraisal domain because the other elements of feedback in this part of the Monitor give us an overview of trends in the environment and possible choices of direction our organizations could take in the longer term.

Membership of industry associations can also act as a mechanism for influencing the external context. For example, the Chemical Manufacturers Association actively lobby for non-punitive environmental laws, whilst simultaneously leading a 'Responsible Care' initiative that demonstrates the concerns of the industry for environmental matters (Cummings and Doh, 2000).

The elements of a Knowledgeability Monitor could include:

- Numbers of licenses and franchises.
- Revenue generated from complementary products that support knowledge that has been made freely available to others.
- The revenue generated from collaborative innovation projects with alliance partners.
- Growth in market space: opportunities to extend revenue from existing products and services into new markets.
- Active participation in complementary public working groups and industry fora.

The combination of intelligence and strategic appraisal can show where new outlooks are able to change the shape of an industry. For example, several years ago the Canadian Imperial Bank of Commerce started to see the importance of intellectual capital as a hidden driver in Canadian industry. This led them to re-evaluate their own role in supporting knowledge-based activity in the economy. Having realized this needed dedicated expertise, they set up a new lending division to serve businesses that operated predominantly through intangibles and intellectual assets. They provided advice on how to manage innovation capabilities, organizational know-how, human resources, intellectual property and intangible assets. As a result, the Bank gained considerable strategic influence on the external conditions. Having recognized this opportunity, the Bank also saw the need for a new evaluation framework that would allow them to assess how well they were doing in this new area. They called this the Knowledge Framework. According to their President, it 'allowed us to develop a new set of practices, new business models that would help us understand the risk, and new value models that would provide a view on non traditional sources of value' (Dzinkowski, 1999).

Balancing stability and change is a source of tension

Having seen how we can monitor the pairs of domains that provide stability and encourage change in our organizations, we now need to consider how we monitor the consequences of too much emphasis on either one or the other. What do we need to do to find an appropriate balance between them?

The problem with paying too much attention to the current means to process intellectual capital and the existing co-ordination mechanisms is that our organization can become myopic and introverted. Too much stability can lead us to become unresponsive. Over time, our knowledge becomes highly-specialized and we tend to cling to our well-refined and distinctive areas of competence. Returning to the landscape metaphor, the knowledge landscapes of our organizations are then characterized by relatively few very high knowledge peaks. Our knowledge is continuously refined through adaptive learning as we respond to and cope with environmental demands with only incremental improvements (Senge, 1990).

 Signpost   In *Competence Area 1: Competing* we saw that continuous improvement initiatives and reflection on current activities are the basis for adaptive learning.

This has also been called 'single loop' learning (Argyris, 1977). This means that our organizations learn through small changes in behaviours and actions in response to a mismatch between actual conditions and what is believed to be a desirable state of affairs.

Unfortunately, such highly-refined knowledge can also become a liability. It becomes a source of inertia that discourages change. We are reluctant to write off past investments in developing knowledge and find it hard to let go of ways of working and responses that have proved valuable in the past (Lewin and Volberda, 1999). A strong cultural orientation that verges on 'group think' may also have developed based on knowledge becoming deeply embedded at a tacit level. Tacit knowledge is slow to change.

In *Competence Area 1: Competing* we saw unlearning is difficult because existing knowledge gets in the way of new knowledge.

Too much emphasis on refining current knowledge can reduce the capacity of our organizations to appreciate opportunities presented by new areas of knowledge. In contrast, if we pay too much attention to feedback from the domains associated with change, namely Alertness and Strategic Appraisal, we can damage the value we get from exploiting existing knowledge resources. Particularly when environmental turbulence is high, Alertness activities may be continually signalling new areas to explore on the industry knowledge landscape and Strategic Appraisal may drive an incessant process of organizational re-invention. Although there may be high levels of generative learning (Senge, 1990) from frequent creative experimentation and constant strategic re-organization, it is unsettling for the people involved and our organizations become inefficient and fragmented.

In *Competence Area 1: Competing* we saw that generative learning underpins the development of new knowledge.

The term 'double loop' learning describes the process of correcting the mismatch between an actual and desired state by re-evaluating our underlying assumptions, rather than simply modifying existing behaviours (Argyris, 1977). One of the major objectives of the Strategic Appraisal domain is to challenge the dominant logic (or commonly-shared assumptions) within our organizations. If Alertness provides too many ideas and Strategic Appraisal is immoderate in its discriminatory ability, constant double loop learning can drive our organization towards chaos (Stacey, 1993; 1996).

In the viable systems model that has guided our ideas in designing the Knowledgeability Monitor, we find indicators of how other complex systems offset the risk from either excessive stabilizing influences or excessively strong change domains. The most viable systems live on the edge of chaos (Kauffman, 2000; Lewin, Long and Carroll, 1999; Lewin and Volberda, 1999; Stacey, 1996). This is where the system is most productive. Here it is neither too stable nor too changeable, but exists in constructive tension between the two.

All viable systems have a control domain, which effectively provides the bridge between stability and control. For our organizations, this domain encompasses a set of mechanisms that offer feedback on how well we are simultaneously improving our performance in leveraging knowledge for current value *and* strengthening our capacity to reinvent ourselves. We will move on now to look at what mechanisms need to be included within the control domain of our organizations.

Reduce the tension by comprehensively monitoring organizational learning capacity

Monitoring the comparative performance of stability and change activities could be seen as an assessment of the learning capacity of our organizations: both single and double loop. These forms of learning are both contradictory and complementary and we need to become skilled at managing both simultaneously (Lewin and Volberda, 1999). Our ability to thrive depends on this capability to balance single and double loop learning (Volberda, 1996).

The categories for monitoring Control in our organizations should track and integrate the categories we pay attention to on either side of the Knowledgeability Monitor. This gives us the feedback to correct any imbalance. Although measurement is crucial to help us achieve this balance, we also need ways of interpreting the results to assess the impact of inter-relationships between the various different elements. Trends are likely to be more important that any specific numbers. Paying excessive attention to any individual element is likely to trigger an over-correction.

These overview measures fall into three categories: the *strength of the stabilizing mechanisms,* the *strength of the drivers for change* and the *moderating factors* that show the risk propensity of our organizations.

1. Strength of stabilizing mechanisms

Effective performance of these mechanisms within a knowledge-based strategy ought to be evident in 'stability'-related financial and operational measures: 'an improvement in organizational efficiency and measured by cost savings, profits, revenue growth, return on investment' (Dzinkowski, 2000).

Elements of The Knowledgeability Monitor could include elements such as:

- the proportion of projects completed on time and within budget,
- improvements in quality assurance standards,
- the number of product improvements achieved per year,
- increases in productivity,
- progress in meeting cost reduction targets,
- growth in revenue per employee,
- ratio of sales leads to sales closed: the efficiency of the sales process,
- duration of customer and supplier relationships,
- talent retention ratios,
- duplication ratios: how often the business model can be replicated in new areas (von Krogh and Cusumano, 2001).

2. Strength of drivers for change

Effective performance of these drivers within a knowledge-based strategy ought to be evident in 'change'-related financial and operational measures. Elements within The Knowledgeability Monitor could include elements such as:

- proportion of revenue from new customers and new projects (Bontis, 2001),
- proportion of revenue from collaborative ventures,
- proportion of investment in research versus development,

- Number of alliances that produce new revenue streams,
- Level of investment in education and training,
- Increases in employee diversity,
- Level of investment in new technology,
- 'Slack' in the system (which encourages care and innovation) (von Krogh, Ichijo and Nonaka, 2000).

3. Moderating influences

These show the tendency of our organizations to take risks – effectively the degree to which our culture and pattern of previous decisions inclines us towards stability or change, and therefore the level of effort we may need to exert in order to regain balance. The pattern of organizational response to risk may be driven by things like legacy investments in infrastructure, since the time periods over which investments are written off can constrain future choices. Past experiences of failed innovation, or leadership preferences can also influence willingness to take risks.

Other influences on the pattern of risk could be related to the strength and nature of the shared sense of identity within our organizations. Enduring shared values can create a strong sense of identity that leads to coherent patterns of action across the organization over time. Our shared sense of identity is evident in how we behave together and what we jointly believe matters.

 Signpost   In *Competence Area 2: Deciding* we saw that the shared perception of identity is an important component of the 'collective mind' of our organizations. This is the means by which we jointly make sense of the environment, integrate our knowledge and commit to action.

The sense of identity and nature of the shared values can predispose our organizations to either stability or risk. Worthwhile elements of a Knowledgeability Monitor would track significant behavioural shifts that suggest whether the previous propensity to risk (high or low) may have changed. If we reflect on the ideas in Box 6.1, pp. 241–42, we can see that a change in risk orientation should alter the operating balance between stability and change mechanisms. Whether this balance is appropriate to the turbulence in the external environment is another matter.

One organization that has clearly defined what it does not want to change whilst it evolves and grows is the Swiss-based food and consumer products company, Nestlé (Wetlaufer, 2001). The CEO, Peter Brabeck, consciously adopted an approach of adapting, improving and restructuring the business as a continuous process, rather than expecting to make periodic disruptive changes. His view was that in a consumer food business, the relationship of trust with customers would be undermined by continual re-invention. The value system and its focus on quality and safety were the basis of that trust.

At the point where he was appointed as CEO, Brabeck chose to widely distribute a document about what he saw as the 'untouchables' of the business. These included the fact that Nestlé is about people, products and brands first and foremost. Technology was simply an enabler for the business, rather than a driver. Decision-making related to consumer needs (branding, pricing, communication and product adaptation) should be decentralized as far as possible in the organization, in recognition of the fact that people have local tastes in food and beverages. Balancing this distributed activity was a centralized approach to production, logistics and supply chain management, which achieved economies from the scale of the business. The strategy also shaped the choices made in the organization, with the most important strategic objective being long-term optimization of shareholder value, rather than short-term profits. Brabeck spent considerable time explaining this strategy to investors and used it to justify substantial investments in research and development.

The final way in which Nestlé's commitment to deliberate, paced change was sustained was through the selection criteria applied to its managers. These were widely communicated and reinforced through training and compensation. The criteria included: 'a honed ability to communicate and motivate people, open-mindedness, credibility and a strong work ethic. Together with modesty, courage, solid nerves and composure, and the ability to handle stress'. One important consideration Brabeck used to assess promotion potential was 'the biggest mistake that person had made'. He argued that if the person had not had the courage to make a big mistake, then he or she had not had the courage to make big decisions, nor the chance to learn from them.

Together, the clear strategy of paced growth, the 'untouchables' and the management criteria provide a good indication of the 'moderating influences' at Nestlé. These shaped the pattern of decisions in the organization. Including elements related to them in a Monitor would indicate the strength of the factors driving sustainability. However, they could also indicate the inertia that might be encountered should more radical disruptive change become necessary.

When the levels of turbulence in the environment change, our immediate response is likely to be the one patterned into our organizations as a result of past experience. If the external environment has been stable for a significant period of time, our organizations have been successful and incremental adaptation has worked well, then it is likely that increased turbulence will initially stimulate faster incremental refinement of our practices, rather than the necessary shift in our fundamental assumptions about how to operate. Activities within the Control domain need to monitor the signals and assess whether further stimulus to more radical change is needed.

In general, the more successful an organization is at recognizing and responding to opportunities to change, the better it is likely to get at it (McKenzie and Reynolds, 1997). Practice embeds the capability until it becomes a core competence. Also, the very process of continued knowledge exploration enhances absorptive capacity and therefore the capacity to recognize the value of new knowledge. As a result, the more exploration an organization does, the less likely it is to be selected out of the economy (Lewin, Long and Carroll, 1999).

A study of investments in intangibles by MIT's Sloan Management School supports this assertion (Pearl, 2001). Of 3500 companies followed for 34 years, it was found that a 1 per cent rise in R&D spending produced a 4.3 per cent rise in market to book ratio. In other words, the market recognized the value of R&D and the firms gained better access to capital to sustain their businesses.

Elements of a Monitor could include:

- The balance of the portfolio of organizational investments in products and markets using standard financial risk assessments of each.
- The return on capital expected by the organization for new investments.
- Employee attitude surveys that show patterns of alignment with organizational values.
- Employee turnover rates, the average length of service of employees or the proportion of new employees to longer service ones. This may indicate the level of commitment to the organization's value that can be expected.
- The number of innovation projects that do and do not produce returns (unsuccessful projects suggest a higher willingness to experiment and take risks).
- The increase in market to book ratio produced by a rise in R&D investments.

We can now bring together all of the mechanisms that we have looked at in this chapter. We can combine the categories within the two domains that relate to stability, those within the two domains that relate to change, and those within the balancing domain into a single Knowledgeability Monitor (Table 6.3). The detail of how we assess each element in the monitor will change from one organization to another. We have made some suggestions that might form a useful starting point for discussions. We see that the Control domain integrates and interprets the domains above it to adjust the balance and avoid both stagnation and chaos. In other words, it ensures there is 'enough exploitation to ensure the organization's current viability and enough exploration to ensure its future viability' (Levinthal and March, 1993).

It is worth remembering that stability mechanisms (which encourage refinements of what we already know) are likely to be stronger than mechanisms that drive major change (Lewin, Long and Carroll, 1999). This is partly because, in general, investors prefer more certain and immediate returns to the potential of high returns at some time in the future, and therefore discourage risk. However, it is also because our organizations can find it difficult to absorb too many new routines and adapt to lots of new technology so incremental change is more comfortable (Nelson and Winter, 1982).

Working through the process of understanding how to maintain a dynamic balance between stability and change offers a number of rewards (Bontis, 2001; Postman, 1985). By immersing our organizations in a process of surfacing the effects of decisions upon knowledge stocks and flows and reflecting on the reasons for the results, we begin to understand more about how our organizations

Table 6.3 The main categories of the Knowledgeability Monitor

Insights into current performance (Measures of stability)	Foresight from feed-forward triggers (Indicators of capability to change)
Means to process intellectual capital • Individual and organizational competence • External relationships • Brand image • Patents copyright and trademarks	**Alertness** • Speed • Diversity • Connectivity

Co-ordination of intellectual resources
• Processes and infrastructure
• Culture
• Communities of practice
• Management of relationships
• Quality of leadership
	Strategic Appraisal
	• Environmental interpretation
	  – Market
	  – Sociopolitical
	  – Technological
	• Shaping strategic direction
	• Influence in the environment

Control
- Strength of stabilizing mechanisms
- Strength of drivers for change
- Moderating influences

learn. Then we can identify what we can do to influence this. This establishes a means by which we can exert even greater influence on our own future, despite the uncertainty and turbulence of the external market.

We have already looked at single and double loop learning and related the former to stability mechanisms and the latter to drivers for change. The ability to reflect on how to combine and work with both to redefine the future of the organization has been called triple loop learning (Snell and Chak, 1998). This challenges whether the purpose of the organization is appropriate and it is learning at the level of identity and being (see Figure 6.3).

Comprehensively monitoring how intellectual capital affects current performance and future sustainability may appear an onerous task. However, we would argue that the process delivers significant returns. Feedback on the performance of intellectual capital is a fundamental stimulus to learning at all levels and learning is the basis of sustainability. Knowing that an organization takes an interest in human capital development makes the company an attractive employer. The same applies to suppliers; they know what is expected of them and understand the basis for mutual value in the relationship. For customers, the metrics are concrete evidence (rather than perhaps what has become standard rhetoric) of the importance the company places on customer

Figure 6.3 Single, double and triple loop learning

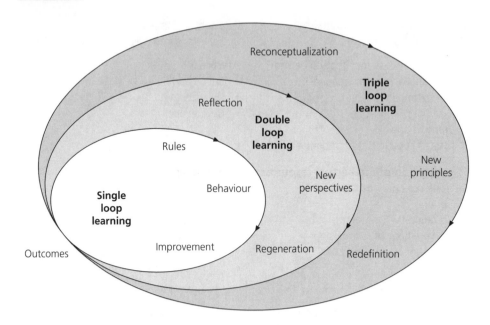

satisfaction. For investors, the very act of monitoring shows the importance our organizations place on the return on intellectual capital.

We may have concerns about publicizing intellectual capital reports, perhaps that they might produce a fall in share price if current performance is actually not very impressive. Those companies that have already published results are usually leaders in knowledge management and knowledge growth has been an integral part of their strategy for some time. Consequently, they have had time to invest to ensure that their performance is creditable. Yet, intellectual capital reporting is likely to become a requirement within most standards of accounting practice in the next decade. Even if it does not become mandatory, companies that ignore the issues we have been looking at are likely to be perceived as weak and a greater investment risk that those that do provide such information. Producing an intellectual capital report is a tangible output of efforts invested in all six areas of competence of the Knowledge Organization and provides a way to communicate the real value generated within the organization, as well as monitor performance to trigger future development. We propose that success today and sustainability into the future are the results that we should expect from these efforts.

Summary

In this chapter, we started with a series of questions:

How can we communicate the value of our intellectual capital to investors?

How can we evaluate the current performance of intellectual capital?

How do we know whether we have the capacity to adapt in the future?

How do we construct a comprehensive monitor to review the balance of our intellectual capital investments and make sense of the interdependencies?

How can we learn from the feedback a monitor gives us?

To answer these, we set out to understand how to develop *insight* into our ability to leverage our intellectual capital for current advantage. We also wanted to develop *foresight* about the way the knowledge landscape of our industry is changing and how well we can identify and respond to the changes. We looked at the characteristics of knowledge that make it difficult to measure, including subjectivity, complexity and comparability. We also saw that various techniques have been developed to measure the value of intangibles and intellectual capital.

We recognized that to be successful today and in the future, we need to track indicators of our tendency to both stability and change so that we can adjust the pattern of our actions appropriately. Starting from a model of the characteristics of viable systems, we developed a Knowledgeability Monitor based on five domains of activity in our organization, two associated with maintaining stability, two that stimulate change and one that controls the balance between the two.

Paying attention to developing insight into the current performance of intellectual capital involves monitoring the activities of our organizations within the two domains that support stability:

- The means to process intellectual capital in the form of:
  - individual and organizational competence,
  - external relationships,
  - brand image,
  - patents copyright and trademarks.

- Coordination mechanisms that link intellectual resources for value generation:
  - processes and infrastructure,
  - culture,
  - communities of practice,

▶

▶

- management of relationships,
- quality of leadership.

Paying attention to developing foresight and our capability to adapt to change involves monitoring the activities of our organizations within the two domains associated with change:

- Alertness measured in terms of:
  - speed,
  - diversity,
  - connectivity.

- Strategic Appraisal shown through capacity to:
  - interpret the environment (market, sociopolitical, technological),
  - shape strategic direction,
  - influence the external environment.

The two 'stability' domains are the basis for single loop learning within our organizations, through which we incrementally adjust our actions and refine our knowledge. An excessive emphasis on this approach can lead to highly-specialized, but potentially irrelevant knowledge. The two 'change' domains are the basis for double loop learning within our organizations through which we change by adjusting our fundamental assumptions about how we operate. An excessive emphasis on this approach can lead to continual reinvention and a failure to exploit the potential of innovative opportunities; in the extreme, chaos results.

The Control domain encompasses the activities within our organizations that balance the stability mechanisms and the drivers of change. It provides a 'lens' through which to interpret the stability and change domains of the Knowledgeability Monitor. Additional measures are needed to show the relative strength of the stabilizing mechanisms and drivers for change. Moderating influences that assess the risk propensity of our organizations show where we need to rethink our position. When combined, these form a feedback mechanism to show whether the stability–change balance is appropriate in context. Learning how to maintain the balance is the basis for triple loop learning, which is the process of redefining the identity and purpose of our organizations to meet the challenges of the future.

References

Achterbergh, J. and Vriens, D. (2002) 'Managing viable knowledge', *Systems Research and Behavioural Science* 19: 223–41.

Allee, V. (2000) 'Reconfiguring the value network', *Journal of Business Strategy* 21(4): 36–40.

Argyris, C. (1977) 'Double loop learning in organizations', *Harvard Business Review* Sept–Oct: 115–25.

Barchan, M. (1998) 'Capturing knowledge for business growth', *Knowledge Management Review* 1(4): 12–15.

Beer, S. (1979) *The Heart of the Enterprise*. Chichester: Wiley.

Beer, S. (1985) *Diagnosing the System*. Chichester: John Wiley.

Bontis, N. (2001) 'Assessing knowledge assets: a review of the models used to measure intellectual capital', *International Journal of Management Reviews* 3(1): 41–60.

Bontis, N. (2002) 'Managing organizational knowledge by diagnosing intellectual capital: framing and advancing the state of the field', in *The Strategic Management of Intellectual Capital and Organizational Knowledge* (ed. N. Bontis). Oxford: Oxford University Press.

Brooking, A. (1996) *Intellectual Capital: Core Assets for the Third Millenium*. London: Thomson Business Press.

Brown, S. L. and Eisenhardt, K. (1998) *Competing on the Edge: Strategy as Structured Chaos*. Boston, MA: Harvard Business School Press.

Cummings, J. and Doh, J. (2000) 'Identifying who matters: mapping key players in multiple environments', *California Management Review* 42(2): 83–104.

Dyer, J., Kale, P. and Singh, H. (2001) 'How to make strategic alliances work', *California Management Review* 42(4): 37–43.

Dzinkowski, R. (1999) 'Managing the brain trust: reporting intellectual capital', *CMA Management*, 73(8): 14–19.

Dzinkowski, R. (2000) 'The measurement and management of intellectual capital: an introduction', *Management Accounting*, 78(2): 32–6.

Edvinsson, L. (1997) 'Developing intellectual capital at Skandia', *Long Range Planning* 30(3): 366–73.

Edvinsson, L. (2002) *Corporate Longitude*. London: Prentice Hall.

Edvinsson, L. and Malone, M. S. (1997) *Intellectual Capital*. London: Judy Piatkus.

Hall, R. (1992) 'The strategic analysis of intangible resources', *Strategic Management Journal* 13: 135–44.

Hanley, S. (2001) 'Show me the money: a practical framework for KM metrics', APQC Annual Conference.

Kauffman, S. (2000) *Investigations*. Oxford: Oxford University Press.

Kish, P., Riskey, D. R. and Kerin, R. A. (2001) 'Measurement and tracking of brand equity in the global marketplace: the PepsiCo experience', *International Marketing Review*, 18(2): 91–7.

Levinthal, D. A. and March, J. G. (1993) 'The myopia of learning', *Strategic Management Journal* 15 (Special issue): 45–62.

Levitt, B. and March, J. G. (1998) 'Organizational learning', in *Annual Review of Sociology* (ed. W. R Scott). Palo Alto, CA: Annual Reviews Inc.

Lewin, A., Long, C. and Carroll, T. (1999) 'The co-evolution of new organizational forms', *Organizational Science* 10(5): 535–50.

Lewin, A. and Volberda, H. (1999) 'Prologomena on co-evolution: a framework for research on strategy and new organizational forms', *Organizational Science*, 10(5): 519–34.

McDermott, R. (2002) 'Measuring the impact of communities', *Knowledge Management Review* 5(2): 26–9.

McGaughey, S. L. (2002) 'Strategic intervention in intellectual asset flows', *Academy of Management Review* 27(2): 248–74.

McKenzie, J. and Reynolds, A. (1997) 'Innovation success in the food and drink industry: maximizing opportunities and minimizing risks', FT Retail and Consumer Publishing. London: Pearson Professional.

McMahon, F. and Moore, K. (1999) 'Knowledge exchange', in *Liberating Knowledge* (ed. IBM Lotus CBI). London: Caspian Publishing, 66–72.

Mowery, D. C., Oxley, J. E. and Silverman, B. S. (1996) 'Strategic alliances and interfirm knowledge transfer', *Strategic Management Journal* 17 (Winter special): 77–91.

Nelson, R. R. and Winter, S. G. (1982) *An Evolutionary Theory of Economic Change*. Cambridge, MA: Belknap.

Pearl, J. (2001) 'Intangible investments, tangible results', *Sloan Management Review* 43(1): 13–14.

Pike, S., Rylander, A. and Roos, G. (2002) 'Intellectual capital management and disclosure', in *The Strategic Management of Intellectual Capital and Organizational Knowledge* (ed. N. Bontis). Oxford: Oxford University Press.

Postman, N. (1985) *Amusing Ourselves to Death: Public Discourse in the Age of Show Business*. New York: Viking.

Reid, D., Bussiere, D. and Greenaway, K. (2001) 'Alliance formation issues for knowledge-based enterprises', *International Journal of Management Reviews* 3(1): 79–100.

Senge, P. (1990) *The Fifth Discipline*. London: Century Business.

Skyrme, D. and Amidon, D. (1997) 'Creating the knowledge-based business'. London: Business Intelligence.

Snell, R. and Chak, M.-K. (1998) 'The learning organization: learning and empowerment for whom?', *Management Learning* 29: 337–64.

Spender, J. C. (1996) 'Making knowledge the basis of a dynamic theory of the firm', *Strategic Management Journal* 17 (Special issue): 45–62.

Stacey, R. (1993) *Strategic Management and Organizational Dynamics*. London: Pitman Publishing.

Stacey, R. (1996) *Complexity and Creativity in Organizations*. San Francisco, CA: Berret Koehler.

Stewart, T. A. (1998) *Intellectual Capital: The New Wealth of Organizations*. London: Nicholas Brearley.

Strassman, P. (1999) 'The value of knowledge capital', www.strassman.com (accessed October 2002).

Sveiby, K.-E. (1997) *The New Organizational Wealth: Managing and Measuring Knowledge-based Assets*. San Francisco: Barrett-Kohler.

Sveiby, K.-E. (2001) 'A knowledge-based theory of the firm to guide strategy formulation', *Journal of Intellectual Capital* 2(4): 344–58.

Sveiby, K.-E. and Simons, R. (2002) 'Collaborative climate and effectiveness of knowledge work – an empirical study', www.sveiby.com (accessed 30 July 2002).

Teece, D. J., Pisano, G. and Shuen, A. (1997) 'Dynamic capabilities and strategic management', *Strategic Management Journal* 18(7): 509–33.

Volberda, H. (1996) 'Towards the flexible form: how to remain viral in hypercompetitive environments', *Organizational Science* 7(4): 359–74.

von Krogh, G. and Cusumano, M. A. (2001) 'Three strategies for managing fast growth', *Sloan Management Review* 42(2): 53–61.

von Krogh, G., Ichijo, K. and Nonaka, I. (2000) *Enabling Knowledge Creation: How to Unlock the Mystery of Tacit Knowledge and Release the Power of Innovation*. Oxford: Oxford University Press.

Wetlaufer, S. (2001) 'The business case against revolution: an interview with Nestle's Peter Brabeck', *Harvard Business Review* 79(2): 113–19.

Wick, C. (2001) 'Measuring intellectual capital at EDS', *Knowledge Management Review* 4(5):14–17.

Yli-Renko, H., Autio, E. and Sapienza, H. J. (2001) 'Social capital, knowledge acquisition and knowledge exploitation in young technology-based firms', *Strategic Management Journal*, 22: 587–613.

7 Taking an Overview
Integrating

Business Challenges

- What makes a Knowledgeable Organization?

- Why is a holistic approach important for nurturing knowledge competence?

- How do the areas of competence in this book complement one another?

- How do we keep them all in mind simultaneously?

- What happens when they do work together in a complementary way?

Introduction

In this book, we have chosen to look at six aspects of managing knowledge as a primary source of business value in the knowledge economy. In the chapters on Competing, Deciding and Learning, we examined how people, processes and some technology can be blended in context to integrate knowledge into our business operations. In co-ordinating these activities, we came up against sources of tension that occur largely because knowledge resources have unusual characteristics. Unmanaged, these tensions can dilute possible returns on investments in knowledge-based activities. Well balanced, they give an organization the internal knowledge-based capability to thrive. In the last three chapters, we changed our perspective and looked outwards to review our organizations in the context of external activities. In Connecting, Relating and Monitoring, we explored how the dynamics of knowledge exchange create new economic conditions and challenge us to pay attention to three further tensions. The speed, interdependence, and intangibility of everyone's knowledge activities (Davis and Meyer, 1998) impose new demands on our own knowledge capabilities. Unmanaged, these can leave us strategically disadvantaged: we are cut off from the dynamics that affect our performance on the knowledge landscape of our industry. Well balanced, the tensions give us the ability to use knowledge effectively and respond flexibly to a broad range of circumstances.

We believe that the Knowledgeable Organization is a paradoxical entity, shaped by the tensions inherent in constantly translating fluid and versatile knowledge resources into tangible value. Paradox is an inevitable consequence of organizational existence, driven by the need to adapt constantly to changing conditions, whilst still remaining in essence a co-ordinated and coherent vehicle for value generation. Getting premium value from knowledge is an art – the art of recognizing the paradoxes affecting performance and handling them in such a way that each side of the tensions becomes mutually supportive. However, it is not simply a question of handling them individually. The way we deal with each of the six sources of tension must also be complementary and self re-enforcing, or once more we run the risk of conflicting pulls undermining our good intentions. In this chapter we will see how the tensions in the six competence areas are closely connected. They can be fitted together into a holistic mental orientation, designed to address essential aspects of getting value from knowledge. We suggest that such a tautly integrated approach to organizing is an appropriate response to the charge (Child and Gunther McGrath, 2001) that knowledge requires us to:

- shift 'the goal of organizing from buffering against uncertainty to responding to it',

- adopt 'a strategic focus on structure and process design',

- re-emphasize 'the social and interpersonal',

- reconsider 'issues of legitimacy'.

Handling paradox

Throughout this book we have been considering tensions: apparent dichotomies between two equally desirable capabilities. These are paradoxes. A paradox or dilemma (we use the terms interchangeably) is not an unresolvable problem, but simply a pair of apparently conflicting pulls that exist in tension. Each side of a tension has its strengths and benefits, but if emphasized in the extreme it can become weakness. So, for example, if we concentrate on exploiting knowledge excessively, we run the risk of becoming narrow minded and possibly irrelevant in a changing world. Whereas, if we concentrate excessively on creating new knowledge, we risk failing to exploit and generate value from the opportunities we have created. Each side of a tension can also be mutually re-enforcing. For example, exploiting best practices can 'raise the bar' for knowledge creation with examples of excellent practices stimulating even greater heights of innovation. To harvest the benefits of each, we must choose to pay attention to both sides of a tension.

There are four main ways that we can handle these tensions (Scott Poole and Van de Ven, 1989) and these are summarized in Table 7.1.

Table 7.1 Ways to handle paradoxical tensions in our organizations

Ways to manage paradoxes	Implications
1. Opposition Accept the contradiction and live with it. An either/or response.	Proponents of each side of the tension become polarized. They resolve their differences through argument and weight of opinion. This produces violent swings between each aspect of the paradox, as weight of opinion sways action from one side to the other. Each side vies for attention, generating conflict and confusion for those involved. We can see evidence of this in the division over where knowledge management belongs in the organization. For example, should it sit with the IT department or the HR department or elsewhere?
2. Temporal separation Handle the conflicting pulls at different times. A pendulum approach.	We can address one aspect of the tension and then the other in sequence, as long as we keep both in view. So, for example, we might invest in individual training in one budgeting period and then concentrate on investing to create the organizational conditions for collective learning in the next. As long as we keep in mind both needs and explain the pendulum effect to those involved, we can deal with the tension effectively over time.
3. Spatial separation Assume one side of the dilemma operates at a different level to the other or use physical or social distance to isolate the conflicting pulls. An isolation approach.	We can create parts of the organization that focus on one side of a tension (such as knowledge exploration) and parts that focus on the other (such as knowledge exploitation). Some of the organisational forms we looked at in *Competence Area 5: Relating* are designed to do just that. By institutionalizing the tension at different structural levels of the organization we can simultaneously pay attention to both aspects.
4. Synthesis Introduce a new dimension that encapsulates both pulls and merges them into a concept that transcends the problem. An integrative approach.	We develop a new solution that allows us to act strongly on both sides of the tension simultaneously. For example, communities of practice encourage both individual and organizational learning simultaneously.

Reframe the problem to see the balance more clearly

To select the most suitable method from the ones described in Table 7.1, our starting point needs to be to make each paradox explicit. This allows us to acknowledge the desirable benefits of each aspect and recognize where they are complementary. If we reconsider each aspect through the 'lens' of the other (in other words, we look at the context of one side within the complementary context of the other – Hampden-Turner, 1990), we start to see a way forward. This is known as reframing. For example, in Figure 7.1 if we look at our capacity for exploiting current knowledge through the frame of our exploratory capability, we may notice where the two do not mesh effectively and see where the knowledge we currently exploit does not match the pattern of new ideas that we are tapping into. If we reverse the process to examine our exploratory capacity in the light of our capability to exploit knowledge, we might notice that we set out to explore without full understanding of what we know well. Both are equally limited strategies in isolation and we need to do both.

Where we find an imbalance between two equally important aspects of managing knowledge, there will be a performance problem. Our organizations will not be returning the best value from knowledge activities. Frequently, we try to resolve performance problems by doing something to reduce the bad effects. However, this is not tackling the underlying cause. For example, we generally find we cannot resolve poor technology usage by improving the technology, instead we have to address the people issues. With most tensions, it usually proves more effective to switch attention to the side that is being ignored. That way we can use the benefits of a complementary opposite to counteract the negative effects of polarized attention. We break a vicious circle and turn it into a virtuous spiral. This is a more powerful way to drive performance upwards to

Figure 7.1   Reframing each aspect of the tension in the light of its complementary
opposite (adapted frorn Hampden-Turner,1990)

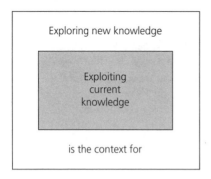
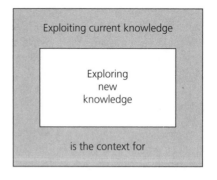

As we consider the current focus of activity at the centre of either picture, we need to
make sure we are reviewing it in the context of the activities that frame it.
Then reverse our perspective and assess the implications.
The process of reframing helps us keep our eyes on the bigger picture, whilst still being
able to address the detail.

the ideal point of balance, where we are paying equal attention to both sides of the dilemma.

Thinking in an either/or mode weighs the benefits of one dimension too strongly and ignores its downsides, as well as the potential upsides of the opposite perspective. This leads us to the polarized response. We can usefully frame the polarized response as a metaphor, possibly drawing upon an extreme figure of ridicule. This helps us to identify with the risks of excessive attention to either aspect. For example, many of us will sympathize with individuals overwhelmed by a flood of information they cannot use to survive, or the lonely specialist commanding peaks of expertise separated by rivers of information and no way to cross the flood. By extending the metaphor, we can see that in knowledge management terms, the ideal is to build the bridge between them that carries only the knowledge they need to act in an informed way. From that image we could envisage a balance of 'push' and 'pull' feeds using a combination of technology-enabled conversations in communities. We can capture the full metaphor in graphical form (Figure 7.2), showing the impact of either/or thinking (top left and bottom right), the process of temporal or special separation as a spiral between aspects of the tension (through the middle) and the resolution as a synthesis (top right). We will be using this format to show the implications of each of the paradoxes in the six competence areas.

Figure 7.2 Capturing the risks and rewards of paradoxical activity in one graphical image

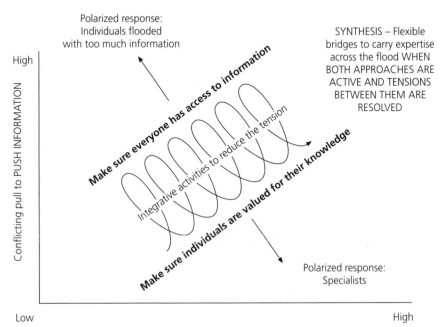

In the last six chapters we have looked at a range of alternatives that can be used to adjust each aspect of the tensions surrounding competing, deciding, learning, connecting, relating and monitoring. Our next step is to move our attention to a more integrative level and consider how we might pay attention to combinations of tensions. Let us start with the issues raised in the first three chapters to see how they can complement one another. They all focus on paying attention to internal priorities for knowledge activities.

Paying attention to reframing the internal priorities

The versatility of knowledge presents some conflicting pulls that stretch us in our efforts to fulfil three essential organizational capabilities (Table 7.2): competing, deciding and learning.

In the first three chapters, we identified various ways that our organizations can take action to improve each side of these tensions. To remind us of the issues involved, we have summarized the various complementary forces in Table 7.3.

First, let us see how the approaches to paradox we have looked at can make the aspects of each tension mutually re-enforcing, rather than destructive, to overcome the obstacles in Table 7.3.

Competing sustainably

We will start with *Competence Area 1: Competing*. The tension here is associated with the need to use knowledge to achieve competitive advantage now and in the future. In other words, how can knowledge help us compete *sustainably*? The route to achieve this is to create a mutually re-enforcing cycle in which the 'financial capital' produced from exploiting knowledge gives us the funds to explore new knowledge domains and regenerate our 'knowledge capital', so we can sustain future financial capital performance and so on, in a virtuous, self re-enforcing spiral (Figure 7.3).

The returns from each side of a tension may be realized over time and in different parts of the organization (Zack, 2002). Given the restrictions on financial resources and the staying power of embedded knowledge, it is hard to optimize both sides of this tension at the same time. So, inevitably, most organizations are handling the paradox by separating it in time and/or space. However, it is still important to aim for synthesis in order to avoid the risks inherent in the polarized response. Too much exploration leaves our organizations climbing up and down knowledge peaks, perpetually searching like a restless explorer, discovering lots of promise for the future, but finding it hard to deliver value now (top left of Figure 7.4).

On the other hand, if we pay too much attention to exploitation, our organizations become staid old workhorses that produce high value now, but without the nimbleness to move around a rugged knowledge landscape (bottom right of Figure 7.4). Our organizations can combine the benefits of both capabilities by spiralling back and forth, whilst keeping both sides of the tension in view

Table 7.2 Internal priorities to take advantage of the versatility of knowledge resources

Competence area	Versatile characteristics of knowledge which we can use to our advantage	Complementary aspects of knowledge activity	Stretch in order to BOTH
Competing	• 'Know what' multiplies with use. Knowledge is accessible to many simultaneously in slightly differing forms. • Knowledge only represents potential until we combine it with the appropriate 'know how'.	Promises future value. Delivers current value.	Explore new and uncertain knowledge domains (generative learning) *and* Exploit existing expertise and capability (adaptive learning).
Deciding	• Knowledge is socially constructed so it is constantly evolving. • Knowledge is infinitely usable in different contexts. • Knowledge is not consumed with use and is accessible to many simultaneously.	Diverse knowledge broadens perspectives. Fit between ideas brings depth and efficient usage.	Draw on knowledge diversity for better distributed decision-making *and* Align patterns of decisions to achieve coherent organizational performance.
Learning	• Knowledge resides in heads of individuals, but needs to be harnessed by organization. • No one person can know it all.	Expertise is individual. Business capability is communal.	Encourage individual learning *and* Foster organizational learning.

Table 7.3 How to pay attention to the various aspects of the three internal knowledge competence priorities

Competence area	To address each side of the tension...	... pay attention to the following	but there are obstacles to doing both well
Competing	Exploring new knowledge	Establish the conditions that nurture new knowledge development. Evaluate new potential against the organization's value drivers. Use rapid prototyping to provide tangible evidence of value potential. Encourage people to be creative and support risk-taking.	The organizational processes to support each aspect are generally incompatible.
	Exploiting existing knowledge	Build and maintain knowledge stocks through adaptive learning processes. Put in place the right forms of organizational memory. Help knowledge flow through standardizing interfaces, technology connections, cultural comfort and diffusing good practices.	Embedded knowledge is hard to change and gets in the way of new knowledge.

Deciding	Diversifying decision inputs	Extend relationships across the organizational boundaries. Actively adopt employment policies that encourage diversity.	Conflicting individual interests and political power increase with diversity making it harder to align decisions.
	Aligning patterns of decisions	Create a caring context that encourages individuals to think of communal interests. Cultivate background common knowledge. Rely on values and ethics as flexible boundaries for decision-making.	
Learning	Encouraging individual learning	Design meaningful training activities to help learners construct understanding in context. Support on-the-job learning. Create the conditions for tacit knowledge exchange.	The 'stickiness' of knowledge means it does not travel easily in some contexts.
	Creating the context for organizational learning	Use dialogue, narrative and metaphor to develop a shared language. Design *Ba** spaces to encourage communal knowledge interactions.	

*See *Third Competence Area: Learning*

Figure 7.3   Mutually re-enforcing competitive activities

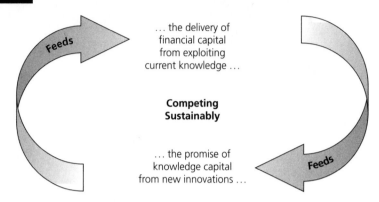

Figure 7.4   Avoiding the risks and integrating the requirements to compete sustainably

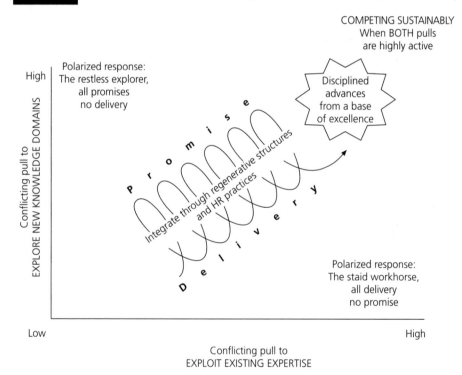

through sound structures, processes and HR practices that consistently and compatibly encourage regeneration. Building in the discipline that encourages the spread of knowledge and good practice alongside flexible attitudes provides an excellent base camp from which our restless explorer can make sorties on a nimble horse. This is the route to competing sustainably.

Deciding knowledgeably

Following this same process, let us review *Competence Area 2: Deciding*. For organizational decisions to be truly knowledgeable, we need to rely on the diversity of distributed expertise to decide locally, but within a context that helps keep the decisions well aligned. As we have seen, when a tension is well managed, the two aspects should be mutually re-enforcing. The problem is that each individual has a uniquely constructed perspective on the world, derived from experience and embedded in mental models. Inevitably, they feel strongly about their views and will defend positions that may not be compatible with those of others. Our organizations also have a dominant logic that can be hard to change. We develop a 'collective mind' that creates a predisposition to patterned behaviours. The value of diversity is to constantly challenge the blinkered disposition while the value of the 'collective mind' is to align distributed decisions, as shown in Figure 7.5.

Many decisions must be taken daily, all across our organizations. Ideally, we want individuals to apply their knowledge closest to the point of need, yet we want the sum of all decisions to coalesce into harmonious organizational activity. Individuals will also be involved in various projects and have many different personal and business commitments pulling on their time and energy. The mix of personal and organizational interests can create power struggles and conflicts between individuals, as well as between individuals and our organizations.

To handle this paradox, we need it to be synthesized within each individual. We can encourage everyone to develop the skills to reconcile their own interests with those of others. Organizationally, we can develop a framework of commonly-accepted values and ethics against which all decisions can be evaluated. We can also encourage dialogue and cultivate shared mental models that provide a suitable context for decision-making, but ultimately we have to depend on the emerging patterns of individual leadership actions to produce the best results.

Figure 7.5 Mutually re-enforcing aspects of decision-making

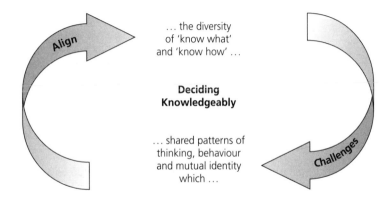

If we do not set the context appropriately, by developing a framework for leadership behaviour to be exhibited, senior management teams will be presiding over organizations of solo musicians, all performing their individual repertoire and generating a discordant cacophony of noise (top left, Figure 7.6). If we frame the context too rigidly, without room for interpretation, we devalue the diversity of knowledge by conducting a choir that never digresses from the predetermined song sheet (bottom right, Figure 7.6). But if we can trust caring and heedful individuals, who respect each others' contributions, to reconcile communal interests with their own and those of others, then like a jazz band in which everyone is a leader, we will find that the decisions of each individual merge to produce harmonious and coherent improvisation that benefits all (top right Figure 7.6). This has been called a 'culture of critical enquiry' by the construction services firm Ove Arup. Individuals are expected to both challenge the perceived wisdom of the organization and to collaborate with each other (Sheehan, 2003).

Figure 7.6   Avoiding the risks and integrating the requirements to decide knowledgeably

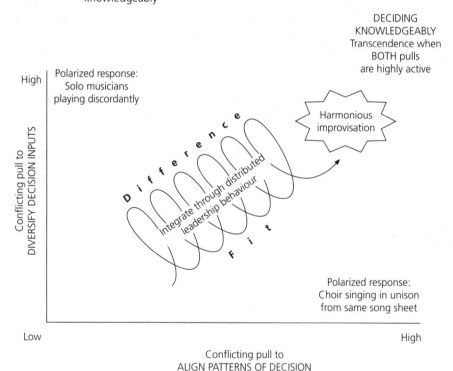

Learning dynamically

In the last of the internally-focused competence areas, we considered the tension created by the processes of individual and organizational learning. For our organizations to derive value from knowledge, we have to create the context for individual development, which is the 'seed corn' for organizational development. The individual and the organization *learn dynamically* together (Figure 7.7), integrating their expertise into a capability that has more influence over the knowledge landscape because it is a communal power.

Figure 7.7   Mutually re-enforcing aspects of learning

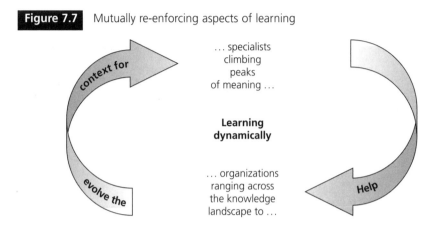

The mutually re-enforcing cycle revolves around 'languaging'. Language is the dynamic medium through which we communicate and explain the meaning that we draw from learning experiences. It can be both a unifying and a divisive force, depending on how well words and sentences resonate with other experiences and understanding in a context. The role of organizations is to absorb, comprehend and apply the refinements of meaning constructed by specialists as they climb peaks in their knowledge landscapes. As our organizations develop the capability to range across the landscape, they alter the context for that exploration and change the value of specialist expertise. To ensure that the two activities work in harmony, we need to pay attention to the languaging processes and the context that helps specialists share and co-ordinate their knowledge.

There are two things that prevent this virtuous spiral from progressing. Knowledge is 'sticky', because language is often inadequate to communicate the full range of experience that an individual has accumulated, and social pressures (together with the power and political forces we encountered in the area of deciding knowledgeably) create barriers to sharing.

If we do not pay attention to both sides of the tension, then we run the risk that language and refined perspectives isolate specialists on peaks of expertise, divided by rivers of specialized language. This restricts the chances of them working together to develop complex organizational capabilities that can make a difference in the knowledge landscape (top left Figure 7.8). If we focus solely on improving the conditions for organizational learning, without developing the individual appropriately, we risk ploughing the ground and fertilizing the soil but not having the necessary seeds of individual learning to grow any

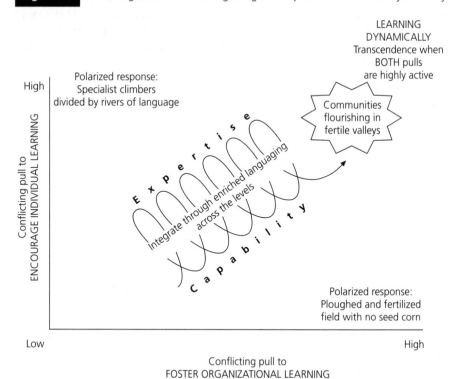

Figure 7.8 Avoiding the risks and integrating the requirements to learn dynamically

capability (bottom right Figure 7.8). We need to cultivate a context that helps bridge the divide between individuals by providing tools to enrich shared language and germinate the seeds of experience. Communities of practice provide a place where the specialists can meet in a fertile context and there is a joining of individual and organizational learning interests that enable both to grow together (top right Figure 7.8). The result is dynamic learning that stimulates both sides to higher and more valuable knowledge peaks.

Balancing both requirements gives us progressive knowledge capabilities

Clearly, these three tensions are closely related. Encouraging individuals to learn automatically extends the diversity of knowledge drawn on in decisions and also helps them to be more comfortable exploring new and uncertain knowledge domains. For organizations to exploit their capabilities they need to ensure that the pattern of distributed decisions is sufficiently aligned and that the organizational context encourages continuous improvement and learning from those decisions.

The complementary nature of these tensions suggests that we need to try to pay attention to both sides of all of them, so that knowledge investments and actions are mutually re-enforcing rather than counterproductive. We can start to keep this in mind by framing the combined text of one aspect of each tension in the context of its opposite aspects, as in Figure 7.9.

The suggested integrative activities within each spiral of Figures 7.4, 7.6 and 7.8 address the obstacles (identified in the last column of Table 7.3) that prevent the virtuous spirals in Figures 7.3, 7.5, and 7.7 from operating. The solutions are also internally consistent and mutually supportive. Disciplined exploration would rely on harmonious improvisation in decisions and be helped by communities of practice for learning. We could equally well argue that communities of practice integrate harmonious improvisations into disciplined advances. If the solutions were not mutually re-enforcing, we would be introducing incompatible forces into our organizations that would work against one another to devalue the various positive attributes of knowledge we are seeking. All of the recommendations we should be paying attention to are designed to stimulate individual autonomy and independent thinking within a coherent context. Then our organizations can fulfil their role of co-ordinating and integrating the value of individual contributions into capabilities that are more than the sum of their parts. If our organizations can develop the competence to decide knowledgeably and learn dynamically, they have all the basic ingredients to compete sustainably. To illustrate what happens when these tensions are not aligned, let us look at the case of Xerox in the 1970s and early 1980s. The case can be read in the right hand column: the linkages with the tensions we have been discussing are described on the left hand side.

Figure 7.9 Reframing three aspects of internal knowledge priorities in the light of their complementary opposites

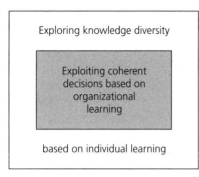 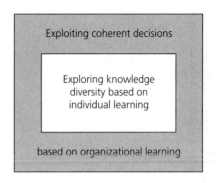

As we consider the current focus of activity at the centre of either picture, we need to make sure we are reviewing it in the context of the activities that frame it.
Then reverse our perspective and assess the implications.
The process of reframing helps us keep our eyes on the bigger picture, whilst still being able to address the detail.

Where Xerox went wrong

XEROX CASE – *PART 1*

Exploiting knowledge was easy.

The organization had learned to be arrogant.

Protection for their knowledge-based competitive position was receding.

Innovation was stifled by rigid processes.

Xerox tried to exploit more of their existing expertise.

Xerox, the multinational document company, was faced with several unbalanced situations with respect to Competing, Deciding and Learning during the mid-1970s. By 1975, the growth of consumer demand for copying was enormous, but Xerox's range of copiers was really the only choice on the market. Xerox's experience of competing to date was largely monopolistic. 'Operating in an expanding market with virtually no competition, the corporation learned that selling copiers was easy and that they were doing the customer a big favour by democratising information' (McKenzie, 1996). They were exploiting a proprietary technology, though not necessarily efficiently. Unfortunately Xerox's position was being challenged by anti-trust suits and their patents were expiring. Unaccustomed to the need for innovation and without the right structure in place to enable it to become innovative, the company quickly found its market shares being eroded by companies such as Canon and Ricoh, which were launching competitively-priced products with many new features. The limited experience with innovation was further aggravated by the fact that the Board of Directors brought in new management from the Ford Motor Company. This new top team focused heavily on process and structure, driving alignment through strong financially-based decision-making. Anyone proposing a new product was required to provide 3500 input assumptions for a model that would predict the impact on profits to 3 decimal places! 'The managers screwed down the clamps of process so tight that for a time they stifled a highly creative company' (Brown and Duguid, 2001).

Xerox made the mistake (Christiansen, Johnson and Rigby, 2002) that when their markets were threatened, rather than trying to innovate by developing low-end competitive products to compete against the threat from outside, they moved up into the high-end of the market. By 1982, they were so squeezed that their new CEO David Kearns believed that they would soon be out of business (Kearns and Adler, 1992).

Serious problems arose.

The problems were further compounded because the organizational processes were inadequate to allow effective learning. For example, customer service technicians were trained to resolve problems with broken machines. They were given directive documentation to guide their repair work. Unfortunately, the directive nature of the manuals was too rigid, explaining 'how' without explaining 'why'. Technicians were then completely unprepared to resolve unforeseen problems. 'Directive documentation wasn't designed for sense-making '(Brown and Duguid, 2000). Individual engineers accepted the poor quality of the repair manuals and then did what anyone in their position would do, they improvised. Until the anthropologist Julian Orr studied the real practice of the engineers, the systems and processes of Xerox made them 'blind to what lies outside the narrow tunnel of process . . . routines and processes encourage employees to hide their insights and improvisations. Valuing and analyzing the improvisations by contrast can be highly informative. Indeed it has been suggested that Xerox stumbled so badly in the 1970s in part because it failed to gather evidence of poor quality from its field representatives' (Brown and Duguid, 2000).

Directive alignment of decisions restricted sense-making at the point of need.

The value of diversity was stifled . . ..

. . . and prevented learning.

The result of unresolved tensions was serious.

As the then CEO David Kearns and the consultant David Adler explained 'we had lost touch with our customer, had the wrong costs-base and inadequate products' (Kearns and Adler, 1992).

What did Xerox do to correct this situation? The organization set out to re-invent itself. First, they decided to diversify into financial services and computers, although they finally had to close the financial services operation through lack of funds. The move into computers required them to explore several new knowledge domains to offset the problem of solely exploiting copier knowledge. To generate

By placing more
emphasis on
innovation . . .

the new knowledge they strengthened their investment in the Palo Alto Research Centre (PARC), concentrating innovative activity in a separate structure
within the organization. Separating the structure
that was to generate radical innovation from the
mainstream business that exploited the knowledge
was probably a wise move at the time, since the
dominant logic within the organization was that
'Xerox knows best' and the 'collective mind' considered Xerox to be a copier company. This would
undoubtedly have restricted the diversification
process into technology that was to prove to be so
crucial to Xerox's transformation into the Document
Company, and subsequently its wide recognition as
one of the world's leading knowledge companies.

. . . outside
the existing
'collective
mind' . . .

'As tightening ties of formal co-ordination inevitably
inhibits creativity, firms often loosen them to
encourage it. Loosening ties in this way is a well-
established business practice. Lockheed did it with
its "skunk works", Xerox did it with PARC.
Decoupling organizational links in this way does
more than provide room for new ways of thinking
outside the old prescriptions, it also keeps exploration safe from those organizational antibodies
that flock to protect the corporate body from in-
vasions of the new. Power struggles between old
ideas and new inevitably favour the old and established, which have a proven track record. So fledg-
ling ideas are easily pushed from the nest. The
defenders of the old copier business within Xerox
for example, had much more collateral (epitomized
by an established revenue stream) than the cham-
pions of the new digital technology when the
struggle developed for resources' (Brown and
Duguid, 2000).

. . . Xerox broke
the hold of the
old paradigm
over decisions
and increased
diversity.

This allowed
new values to
unite those
dedicated to
innovation...

Unfortunately, once separated, communication
failed with the rest of the organization. For example,
'when managers tried to extend the knowledge
created at PARC to the rest of the company, what
had been intuitive among the scientists working on
the Graphical User Interface (GUI) proved almost
unintelligible to the engineers who had to turn the

... but created an obstructive divide between those who exploited knowledge and those who explored the new knowledge domains ...

... and created a disconnect between individual and organizational learning.

ideas into marketable products ... The knowledge that flowed easily within PARC did not flow across its borders to the rest of the corporation' (Brown and Duguid, 2001). The result of this divide and lack of internal willingness to exploit the new knowledge was that it leaked out to Apple Computers, Adobe Systems and Microsoft: 'companies that had better processes in place turning such embryonic concepts into products'.

By isolating innovation from other internal processes, Xerox created a divide in terms of the mental alignments between the various people involved. 'The scientists dismissed the engineers as copier obsessed "toner-heads" and the engineers found the scientists arrogant and unrealistic'.

The end result was local learning in pockets that was not transferable across the organization and so could not be exploited effectively.

We will return to the Xerox story later and see how these three tensions linked with the second three areas of knowledge-based activity – connecting, relating and monitoring – to turn Xerox into one of the most admired knowledge-based organizations in the world.

Paying attention to reframing the external dynamics

When we look at the way knowledge characteristics affect conditions outside our organizations, we find that there are three further dilemmas that we need to pay attention to. As with the internal dilemmas, they are all mutually supporting and need to be viewed as elements of a bigger picture that should be tackled inclusively as part of a knowledge-based strategy.

To make it easier to keep all the tensions in mind we have summarized the complementary aspects of the remaining dilemmas in Table 7.4.

In Table 7.5, we start to highlight the most obvious vertical links between the internal priorities at the level of practice and the ways we address the external dynamics created by knowledge at the level of strategy.

Let us begin by looking at how each tension individually can produce complementary benefits; and in the process we will see that the links between the tensions become more evident.

Table 7.4 How to pay attention to the various aspects of managing external knowledge dynamics

Competence area	To address each side of the tension....	... pay attention to the following	but there are obstacles to doing both well
Connecting	'Outside-in' knowledge flows	Reducing blind spots by scanning the horizon, challenging current thinking and developing potential absorptive capacity. Exploring new knowledge domains with the tools that identify patterns in external activity – for example, data mining, scenario planning and collaborative projects.	Limited resources. The constant need to flex the boundary dynamically to adjust to external conditions.
	'Inside-out' knowledge flows	Knowledge that may create more value if it is given away. Protecting the knowledge that makes a real difference to competitive position.	
Relating	Associating loosely	Managing outsourcing relationships. Monitoring the performance of each relationship to see whether it might deliver more value if it was closer.	Maintaining a dynamic mix relevant to strategy, so the organization can adapt effectively, even though only some relationships are perceived as strategic and so many may not be actively managed.

	Relating closely	Progressively strengthening ties with customers, suppliers, competitors and complementors. Allocating specific responsibility for relationships. Managing problems as they arise.	A preference for the comfort of stability and accumulated tacit knowledge can block the will to see triggers for change.
Monitoring	Achieving foresight	Developing measures for the two change domains: *Alertness* concerning speed, diversity, connectivity. *Strategic Appraisal* which involves interpreting the environment (Market, Sociopolitical, Technological), shaping strategic direction and influencing the environment.	
	Achieving insight	Developing measures for the two stability domains: The *Means to Process Intellectual Capital* in the form of individual and organizational competence, external relationships, brand image, patents copyright and trademarks. *Co-ordination* mechanisms that link the intellectual capital resources for value generation: processes and infrastructure, culture, communities of practice, relationship management and quality of leadership.	

Table 7.5 Highlighting the links between internal priorities and external strategic choices

Conditions in the knowledge economy and their link to internal priorities	Complementary activities in competence areas 4, 5 and 6 and how they link to competence areas 1, 2 and 3	Issue to be tackled
Knowledge is a more fluid and versatile source of power than money. It can only contribute to competitive influence when the flow is managed strategically.	Absorb appropriate amounts of new knowledge to keep the organization abreast of the forces that are influencing activity in the external environment.	How permeable the organizational boundary should be to 'Outside-in' knowledge flows and 'Inside-out' knowledge flows.
This connects to *Competence Area 1: Competing* because the speed at which information flows between organizations in an industry affects the pace at which our organizations can exploit knowledge and the rate at which we need to explore new knowledge domains.	Exploit the value of existing knowledge by manipulating 'inside-out' flows to strategically influence the external landscape and shape the competitive context.	
Value is optimized when we make sure that the knowledge flows are channelled smoothly and efficiently. Different types of knowledge need different conditions to enable them to flow.	Associating loosely to absorb patterns of weak signals gives the organization the flexibility it needs to respond to environmental turbulence. Loose associations increase the diversity of inputs to decisions.	How to manage the relationships in our network to balance the value of loose associations *and* the value of close ties, to give our organizations the capability to respond intelligently to environmental turbulence.

Knowledge flows through language and social interaction, so enabling smooth connectivity means managing the various aspects of relating. This also links to *Competence Area 2: Deciding* because the external relationships increase the potential for richness and diversity in the organizational network, but challenge its coherence at a strategic level.

Close ties provide the context to absorb difficult tacit knowledge, explore risky areas and develop the depth of understanding needed to exploit new knowledge well. Allocating responsibility for managing close ties makes it easier to align the influence of external diversity on patterns of decisions in the organization.

How to strategically monitor our organizations' intangible value-generating capability by measuring how well intellectual capital investments allow us to create future potential *and* deliver value now.

Increasingly, organizations deliver value by the way they manage intangibles. To gain the necessary feedback as to whether the organization is getting value from its investments now and creating the knowledge potential for the future is difficult when there is less obvious connection between cause and effect to learn from.

This links to *Competence Area 3: Learning* because feedback on performance is vital to improve the contribution of investments in individual and organizational learning and to encourage the organization to redefine itself when required.

Develop the foresight to know what knowledge investments will be valuable in the future (feedback for generative learning).

Gain insights about existing performance in order to refine the way current knowledge is used to deliver value (feedback for adaptive learning).

Connecting influentially

Exploring new knowledge domains depends on knowledge flowing into our organizations to generate new ideas. Exploiting existing knowledge requires that we manage the flow of knowledge from inside our organizations to the outside, either by deliberately leaking it for greater returns, or by protecting it to create competitive advantage. When we do both well we absorb new influences from outside and gain the ability to influence competitive conditions for others. If we keep this larger picture in mind all our connections can be viewed as strategically influential (Figure 7.10).

To generate economic value by co-ordinating and integrating knowledge, our organizations need effective connections with external sources of knowledge. When there is upheaval in the external knowledge landscape, we need to absorb more knowledge into our organizations to help us make sense of the turbulence and influence our internal pattern of decisions. By channelling our own knowledge from inside to outside, we gain influence on the conditions in which we do business. The main obstacle to this process is the fact that strategy can only be an emergent process when there is little stability in external conditions.

If we do not try to manage both aspects of this tension we run two risks simultaneously. Either our organizations absorb so many ideas that we become confused, 'fat' and overwhelmed with the effort of constantly absorbing knowledge that we cannot process rapidly enough for real value (top left Figure 7.11). Or we exploit our knowledge resources inefficiently in the outside world and become weakened from lack of sustenance and reduced returns (bottom right Figure 7.11). There are two ways to fall into this trap – either by allowing knowledge resources to leak out unprotected, or by protecting them at great expense – in both cases without gaining worthwhile returns. Either way, we are wasting valuable resources.

Figure 7.10 Mutually re-enforcing aspects of connecting

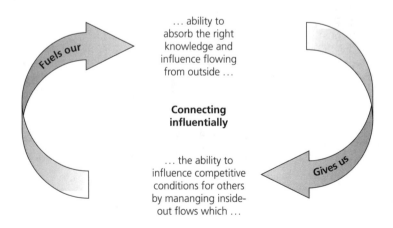

Fuels our

... ability to absorb the right knowledge and influence flowing from outside ...

Connecting influentially

... the ability to influence competitive conditions for others by mananging inside-out flows which ...

Gives us

Figure 7.11 Avoiding the risks and integrating the requirements to connect knowledge flows influentially

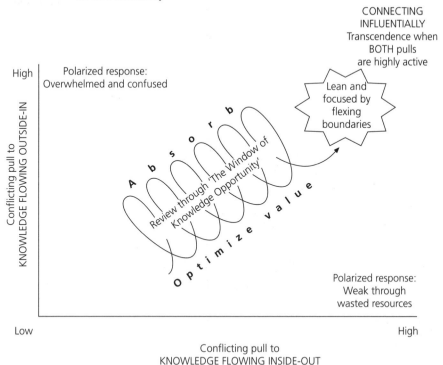

This process is strongly linked to *Competence Area 1: Competing*. The fluid and accessible nature of knowledge means that we cannot insulate our organizations from what is going on around us. So, to compete sustainably, we need to connect influentially with the economic activity beyond the perceived boundaries of our organizations. We can see how this fits together in Figure 7.12.

It is almost impossible to disassociate the activities of our organizations from the turbulence in the environment. The level of external activity determines how much new knowledge is required to stay ahead of the game. The level of internal activity determines the influence our organizations can have on conditions outside. The only answer is to constantly flex the boundary of our organizations to change the permeability to knowledge flows. One way to do this is to relate intelligently.

Relating intelligently

The picture starts to get even richer when we start to consider *Competence Area 5: Relating*. As we seek access to knowledge beyond traditional boundaries, our organizations become involved in networks of relationships. Some are loose associations and some are closer ties. An intelligent approach to relating is to invest time and effort in paying attention to managing these relationships

Figure 7.12 Connecting influentially to support competing sustainably

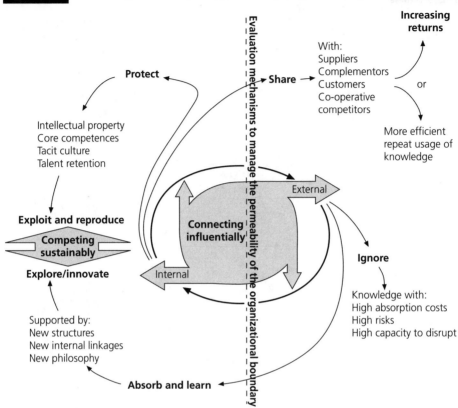

according to the potential returns to be gained from each (Figure 7.13). Once again, the two aspects of the tension are mutually supportive as loose associations become progressively closer and then act as a filter to evaluate the compatibility of future loose associations. In addition, the strategic aspects of relating are closely associated and mutually supportive of the practical aspects of deciding, which we looked at in Competence Area 2.

Although we can create connections with the outside world, the way we configure and support relationships has a significant influence on their contribution in both knowledge and monetary terms. In addressing this within any one relationship, we generally separate the tension in time and space: it is difficult for the relationship between two organizations to be simultaneously loose and tight. However, across the network itself, we can reconcile the value of both types of relationships to avoid the pitfalls of a polarized response. High-quality relationships based on trust, as well as ones based on more traditional economic co-ordination mechanisms like price and authority, can deliver far greater organizational returns in both exploitation and exploration than either form alone. As with all the tensions so far, there are risks in the polarized response as illustrated in Figure 7.14.

Figure 7.13 Mutually re-enforcing aspects of relating

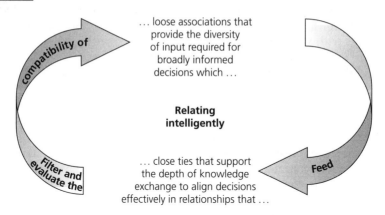

... loose associations that
provide the diversity
of input required for
broadly informed
decisions which ...

**Relating
intelligently**

... close ties that support
the depth of knowledge
exchange to align decisions
effectively in relationships that ...

compatibility of

Filter and
evaluate the

Feed

Figure 7.14 Avoiding the risks and integrating the requirements to relate intelligently

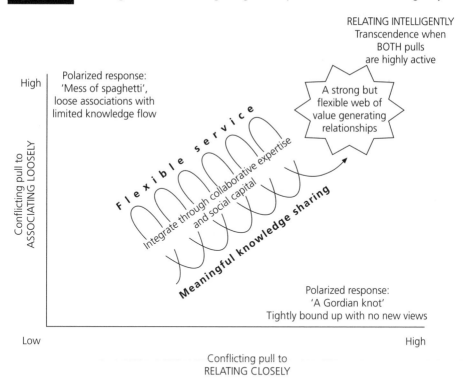

RELATING INTELLIGENTLY
Transcendence when
BOTH pulls
are highly active

High

Polarized response:
'Mess of spaghetti',
loose associations with
limited knowledge flow

A strong but
flexible web of
value generating
relationships

Flexible service

Integrate through collaborative expertise
and social capital

Meaningful knowledge sharing

Conflicting pull to
ASSOCIATING LOOSELY

Polarized response:
'A Gordian knot'
Tightly bound up with no new views

Low

High

Conflicting pull to
RELATING CLOSELY

If we try to manage too many loose associations in our network, we run the risk of becoming a hollow and tangled mess of spaghetti: too diverse and opportunistic to create any sustainable mass of valuable knowledge activity. This is a difficult proposition to co-ordinate strategically (top left Figure 7.14). On the other hand, too many close ties mean that we can get ourselves tied in a Gordian knot made up of an intricate set of conflicting agendas between the various organizations with which we have bonded (bottom right Figure 7.14). Our network needs to be a strong and flexible web (top right Figure 7.14). The web should contain an appropriate mix of close, meaningful knowledge-sharing ties with strategic partners and flexible knowledge-based interactions that stimulate diversity through a mass of loose associations in our network.

It is hard for everyone to know how to respond to these conflicting demands, so it becomes invaluable to give specific responsibility for co-ordinating relationships, prioritizing resources and reviewing the value of the relationships in the light of changing strategic priorities. This may be a specific function within larger organizations. Responsibility needs to be allocated for focusing on developing a strategic level of cross-boundary collaborative expertise to manage the network in the way indicated in Figure 7.15. In so doing, we enable our organizations to make best use of external diversity, whilst simultaneously aligning decisions with strategic priorities – the source of tension that we addressed in *Competence Area 2: Deciding.*

Figure 7.15 Using a network of relationships to make more informed decisions

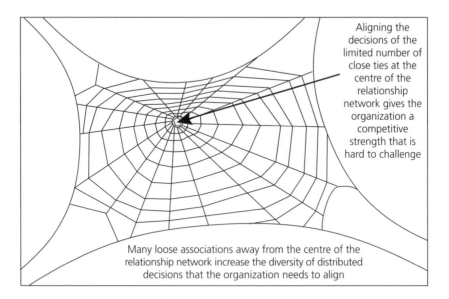

Aligning the decisions of the limited number of close ties at the centre of the relationship network gives the organization a competitive strength that is hard to challenge

Many loose associations away from the centre of the relationship network increase the diversity of distributed decisions that the organization needs to align

Monitoring perceptively

Finally, if we are going to learn from all our activities and investments in knowledge-based resources, then we need feedback mechanisms. However, an historic perspective is not always adequate. To monitor perceptively, we also need feed-forward mechanisms to give us the foresight to adapt to changes in the knowledge landscape (Figure 7.16).

This mutually re-enforcing loop gives us the depth and breadth of perspective we need if we are to learn how to improve, as well as how to advance strategically. In *Competence Area 6: Monitoring* we found that stability and change are two facets of any viable system. Indeed, in each of the competence areas in this book, we find that one aspect is driving stability and coherent activity and the other is driving change (see Table 7.6).

Focusing on only one aspect is not enough to give us the input we need to survive now and continue to thrive as the knowledge landscape changes. If we are to navigate through the upheavals constantly reshaping the knowledge landscape, we need to monitor the performance of all aspects of knowledge-based activity so that we have a strategic perspective on our capability to simultaneously maintain stability and respond to the need to change. We can then evaluate whether our organizations are properly positioned to respond to future

Figure 7.16 Mutually re-enforcing aspects of monitoring

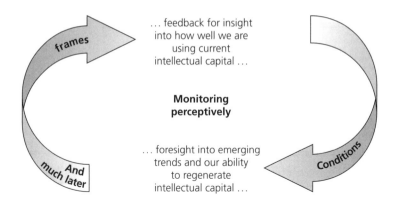

... feedback for insight into how well we are using current intellectual capital ...

Monitoring perceptively

... foresight into emerging trends and our ability to regenerate intellectual capital ...

frames

And much later

Conditions

Table 7.6 Monitoring all aspects of internally and externally-focused areas of competence

Stability	Change
Exploiting – now	Exploring – novelty in the future
Aligning – for coherence	Diversifying – for difference and richness
Organizational Learning – for improvement	Individual Learning – for diversity

'Inside-out' knowledge flow
    – for better exploiting
	'Outside-in' knowledge flows
	    – to absorb new influences

Close Ties – for stable relationships	Loose Ties – to give flexibility

Figure 7.17 Avoiding the risks and integrating the requirements to monitor perceptively

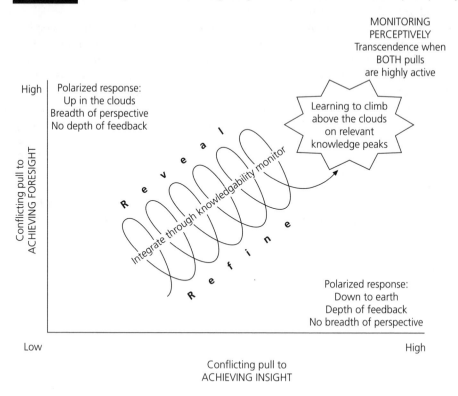

changes (generative learning), as well as whether we are learning from what we are doing now (adaptive learning) (Senge, 1990).

Although it is important to monitor activities on both sides of this tension simultaneously, the output from monitoring future potential will not shape insight until our organizations have travelled around the whole loop of exploiting knowledge through patterns of coherent decisions, diffused by organizational learning, that benefit from inward flows through close relationships. Once we have paid attention to all of these factors, the foresight about new knowledge ideas will have been translated from exploratory potential to realized capability. Then we need to monitor current performance to gain insight from the way we are managing our knowledge investments for present returns.

As always, there are risks in ignoring either side of this tension. It is important to have plenty of foresight, but the activities that monitor this broad perspective are subjective and ambiguous. We can easily lose our way in the clouds of future possibilities (top left Figure 7.17); whilst they might bring us many revelations about future patterns of knowledge activity, if we are not simultaneously paying attention to improving the performance of current knowledge activities we forget to improve what we are doing now. As a result, we may open unnecessary connections and build the wrong relationships, compete ineffectively, decide in ignorance and thwart learning without the opportunity to correct the error of our ways to ensure we produce value now. On the other hand, we can be too down to earth and focused on current activities (bottom right Figure 7.17). Feet of clay are slow to respond to the need for change.

The value of monitoring perceptively is to provide meaningful input to enhance the process of learning dynamically. If we use the Knowledgeability Monitor perceptively, we also have the opportunity to learn about how our organizations learn. We have seen that this is the basis of triple loop learning, which better positions us to foresee and respond to the radical changes that occur in industries from time to time (top right Figure 7.17). This capacity for higher learning allows our organizations to redefine the nature of their identity when environmental conditions demand such a change.

Balancing both requirements gives us progressive strategic capabilities

Having explored the way each tension is mutually supportive, let us again reframe them to see how they complement each other as a system of knowledge-based performance (Figure 7.18).

We argue that the solutions to each of these three paradoxes are once again internally consistent. Evaluating knowledge opportunities through 'The Window of Knowledge Opportunities' (which we developed in *Competence Area 4: Connecting*) helps guide our choices of collaborative activity and manage relationships for better value. Connecting and Relating are strategic necessities to adapt effectively in the knowledge economy. However, we do not know when

Figure 7.18 Reframing three aspects of external knowledge priorities in the light of their complementary opposites

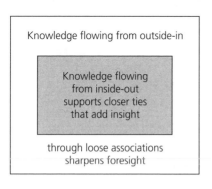
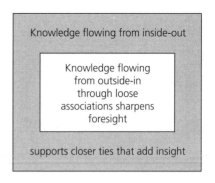

As we consider the current focus of activity at the centre of either picture, we need to make sure we are reviewing it in the context of the activities that frame it.
Then reverse our perspective and assess the implications.
The process of reframing helps us keep our eyes on the bigger picture, whilst still being able to address the detail.

to adapt without perceptive performance monitoring. The Knowledgeability Monitor provides the feedback on all choices, both internal and external. From it, we develop the depth and breadth of perspective needed to actively generate a higher-level strategic awareness of our ability to re-conceptualize the whole organizational purpose, if the external situation changes sufficiently to require it. If the solutions were not mutually re-enforcing, we would be introducing incompatible strategic activities into our organizations. All of the recommendations are designed to stimulate a comprehensive strategic perspective on the performance of our organizations in the knowledge economy. Then our organizations can fulfil their role of co-ordinating and integrating the value of knowledge resources into strategic capabilities that are more than the sum of their parts.

Let us return now to the Xerox story and find how they made this work in recent years. The case study does not exhibit all the aspects of all six tensions, but it does show how many of them work together in a mutually supportive fashion.

How Xerox worked effectively with internal and external tensions

XEROX CASE – *PART 2*

Innovation driven by values-based decision-making aligned the diverse work orientations of individuals. This linked exploration and exploitation activities and encouraged organizational learning.

Here we compare the early years of Xerox's efforts to increase innovation with later more successful attempts. We will see that useful learning required connections internally as well as externally. In addition, uniting people with common values allowed innovation to be more readily exploited. Four aspects of Xerox's approach form the basis of the comparison.

1) New product development

The first illustration is the example of the Xerox 'Lakes' team that developed the 'Document Center 265' copier (Senge and Carstedt, 2001). This was Xerox's first fully digitized copier and 90% of its parts were re-manufacturable, with 97% recyclable. There were only half the number of parts in the machine compared with its predecessors, so it was simpler and easier to maintain. The re-manufacturing and waste reduction initiatives were estimated to have saved Xerox $250 million in 1998 alone. The Lakes project produced more than 500 patents and the innovation team's vision of 'zero-waste' was wholeheartedly taken up in the manufacturing process and eventually was also adopted by many suppliers. The innovative design used leading edge technology, but this was still adopted easily in production. A significant reason for this success was that the values on which the project was based were attractive to everyone. The Lakes project motto was 'Zero for the landfill for the sake of our children'. Everyone could buy into that and feel good. It was a constraint, but because it was an uplifting one, people found it worth pursuing.

Relating to other companies through loose external ties improved the performance of the close internal team, provided greater returns and enhanced learning throughout the network, so making it more difficult for other competitors to attack Xerox's market.

Given the radical nature of the Document Center 265, the team took care to make sure that the supplier network was involved with the new developments. They hosted symposiums to educate suppliers about the meaning of re-manufacture and shared their knowledge about the techniques required to achieve it. They also worked on the basis of mutual co-operation where suppliers would share in the cost saving, since used parts would go back to the suppliers for re-manufacture. The Lakes Chief Engineer John Elter commented, 'the key is that suppliers participate in the economic benefits of re-manufacturing, because they don't have to make everything new. This is a big deal. Plus, they are developing new expertise they can apply with other customers' (Senge and Carstedt, 2001).

2) Culture change and a new vision

By changing the values that aligned decision-making . . .

At the same time as investing in the Palo Alto Research Centre, Xerox began to focus on quality as a means to change the corporate culture. In 1983, they launched a Leadership Through Quality (LTQ) programme. This focused on process improvement, and in so doing started to encourage the capture of individual (adaptive) learning that had been missing in the workplace up until then. The programme was to gradually alter the influences on decision-making, aligning people behind more customer-oriented values and moving the company away from the historic arrogance of the past.

. . . and connecting with other organizations to draw in knowledge from outside . . .

Realising that Japanese competitor production costs were 40–50% of those of Xerox, a major benchmarking exercise was instituted under the banner of the LTQ programme. 'This initiative played a major role in pulling Xerox out of trouble in the years to come' (Radhika and Mukund, 2002).

. . . whilst monitoring performance throughout the initiative . . .

. . . Xerox was able to identify knowledge blind spots and feed back ideas to improve both efficient exploitation of existing knowledge . . .

Xerox started with competitive benchmarking, but found that did not always identify all the best practices in processes and operations. They subsequently moved to benchmarking by function, looking to companies who were complementary, such as LL Bean for warehousing and inventory management, American Express for billing and collection, Florida Power and Light for quality improvement and Honda for supplier development. The success of the programme was evident in that overall customer satisfaction improved by 40% and complaints to the President declined by 60%. The number of defects per machine, service response time, inventory costs, defects in incoming products and inspection time and errors in billing all fell by significant proportions. Productivity, distribution, product reliability and sales also all improved markedly. Xerox went on to win several quality awards, but the real value of these benchmarking exercises was the knowledge that was coming into the organization from the outside.

The realization of value from the quality initiative led Xerox to expand their vision of the value of knowledge both inside and outside their business. Dan Holthouse, the Director of Corporate Strategy and Knowledge Initiatives said, 'knowledge management initiatives require cultural changes, and the lessons learned from the Xerox quality experience will be key for implementing cultural change again. We see knowledge management as a build onto quality not a replacement' (Biren and Dutta, 2000).

. . . and identify real innovation potential.

In Xerox's annual report in 1998, Paul Allaire, CEO then Chairman of Xerox said, 'Managing for knowledge means turning working environments into learning environments, where generating ideas and sharing knowledge creates new business value. It means recognizing that knowledge is not only in people's minds, but also in the digital and paper documents they use'.

By absorbing the relevance of external knowledge developments . . .

Rick Thoman, the President and CEO of Xerox in 1999 explained how knowledge as both an internal imperative and an external market space became a compelling logic for Xerox's strategy, 'If X(erox) equals D(ocuments) and D equals K(nowledge) then X also equals K' (Biren and Dutta, 2000).

. . . into the organizational strategy, the values that aligned internal decision-making . . .

In 1996, knowledge became an integral part of the Xerox long-term plan, called X2005, from there it became part of the marketing identity of the company, as well as part of the internal values that aligned decisions and provided something for people to identify with.

. . . were seamlessly associated with the external customer requirements.

'At Xerox, the sharing of knowledge translates into accelerated learning and innovation. Eventually, that is where its competitive advantage lies. Indeed, it was the internal reflection on KM that led Xerox away from the analog copier business to digital copiers in the mid-90s and to digital document networking today. Xerox's overarching KM strategy is to create added value by capturing and leveraging knowledge. This strategy is rooted in the lessons learned from Xerox's near collapse in the 1970s. It also had failed to exploit numerous advanced technologies it had developed, such as the mouse and pull-down menus that were later commercialized by Apple. These lost opportunities led to the thinking behind the Year 2005 plan' (Hickins, 1999).

From this turning point the company went from strength to strength.

3) Generating value from knowledge flowing across the organization's boundaries

Research initiatives focused on developing knowledge-based products that the organization could sell, avoiding the mistakes of the early days of PARC.

Knowledge
generated
by internal
learning . . .

DocuShare was one such product. First developed in 1996 to help the employees at the Rochester research laboratory to share information, it quickly became a company-wide tool to help teams create a virtual office space on the corporate intranet. Using visual technology, teams could set up a three dimensional 'room' with 'filing cabinets' full of electronic documents. This significantly reduced product development costs, encouraged knowledge re-use and also 'stimulated new applications for the same knowledge' (Hickins 1999).

. . . was
packaged into
products and
services, that
flowed from
inside to the
outside to create
new markets . . .

The tool worked well because it replicated human behaviour. A team of anthropologists had studied how scientists exchanged knowledge and an environment was re-created in which they could do the same things with no training and no bureaucracy. Each user could set his or her own priorities on what knowledge to protect and what to release. The tool was launched as a commercial product and in 1999 Docushare 2.0 became KM World's product of the year.

. . . and the
potential for
increasing
returns.

Another way that Xerox allowed knowledge to flow across its boundaries was through establishing a consulting business. Once the company had gained a good reputation as an expert company in managing knowledge, consultancy was a natural extension of the core business. 'Xerox Professional Services (XPS), is expected to generate at least 50 percent of the company's revenues within 10 years' (Hickins 1999).

The initial model
for knowledge
flows from the
inside of the
company to the
outside was not
ideal because it
did not fit the
culture.

In addition, Xerox developed other ways to exploit innovative ideas. In 1989, the company had recognized the need to bring to market some of its technological developments that were not strategically central to its business (Altman, 2002). It set up Xerox Technology Ventures (XTV), a venture capital organization with rights to commercialize the knowledge from PARC and other research centres. This proved to be an unsuccessful model for gaining external value from internally created knowledge, largely because of the ill feeling that it generated.

For example, XTV was unofficially banned from entry to PARC.

When the model was changed to integrate innovation and exploitation into one corporate entity partly owned by Xerox, but outside the parent culture . . .

Xerox New Enterprises (XNE) was set up in 1996 as a division of Xerox Corporation to overcome the problems of XTV (Altman, 2002). It was set up to protect the returns from future inventions being harvested by competitors. Xerox Corporation would vet opportunities emerging from the research centres and if they did not fit with their core strategy or were not viable within the large organizational structure, XNE would be given the opportunity to evaluate their viability. Commercialization was based on a model of divisions that operated independently in a sort of family environment, but were open to external investors as minority shareholders. Employees were offered stock options in their own spin-out business and calculated risks were encouraged.

. . . it became possible to diversify and simultaneously align decisions around appropriate values . . .
. . . as well as gaining greater returns from centralized resources.

XNE was the link with Xerox, which supplied funds and central resources such as best practice advice and proprietary internal information, in return for a percentage of revenues as a royalty fee. With these advantages, but none of the corporate decision-making limitations, the individual spin-outs could reap the benefits of local employee commitment, flexibility of response and their own culture. They developed innovative products that were not core to the Xerox strategy, turning them into viable and coherent businesses that could ultimately be either sold off, or reabsorbed back into Xerox.

Individual learning could be absorbed back into the organization through reintegrating successful spin-out operations.

At XNE the focus was on the individual as the source for good ideas, and this generated an entrepreneurial spirit. Xerox changed some of its established reward plans for XNE employees to encourage an entrepreneurial culture. They also adapted their recruitment and selection processes to select the sort of energetic risktakers who could help new enterprises to succeed.

4) A balanced approach to managing knowledge

The internal Knowledge Work Initiative (KWI) focused attention on 10 key knowledge domains. These can be mapped onto the tensions in the areas of competence described in this book as follows

Internal initiatives balanced attention to knowledge exploitation and exploration . . .

Exploiting
1 Capture and re-use of past experience bases
2 Embedding knowledge in products and services
3 Producing knowledge as a product

Exploring
4 Mapping knowledge of experts
5 Driving knowledge for innovation
6 Building and mining customer knowledge

. . . encouraged individual and organizational learning . . .

Individual Learning
7 Instilling responsibility for knowledge-sharing

Organizational Learning
8 Facilitating knowledge sharing
9 Leveraging intellectual assets

. . . and made feedback a priority.

Monitoring
10 Understanding and measuring the value of knowledge

Knowledge-based initiatives were developed in four key areas:

- Knowledge repositories.
- Communities.
- Navigation and access.
- Knowledge flows.

We will look at two of these in particular, the knowledge repositories and communities.

The knowledge repository was based on the Eureka database.

A standardized method of communication allowed the organization to

Signpost In *Competence Area 1: Competing* we saw that Xerox's Eureka database enabled the learning by engineers in the field to be captured, validated and shared more widely with colleagues. Manufacturing

harness individual learning and enhance innovation.

and logistics also used the inputs to the system to improve future product design.

The use of Eureka was tracked and in 1999 led to 5 per cent cost savings in parts and engineers' time and 5 per cent reduction in repair time and increased customer satisfaction.

Communities were a solution to the paradox of linking individual and organizational learning.

One particular community that worked very effectively was the 'Transition Alliance', a community of senior information systems managers from many of Xerox's business units, who worked together to manage the transition from a legacy IT infrastructure to one that could support a range of strategic initiatives. The objective was to establish an industry standard office environment that would allow knowledge to flow seamlessly to where it was needed (Storck and Hill, 2000).

Communities involving many people willing to exhibit leadership behaviours worked outside the formal structure to draw on diverse perspectives and produce more innovative solutions that were more acceptable and easier to diffuse even in a stable culture.

Xerox encouraged the Alliance, but corporate intervention was very limited, giving the community the freedom to develop new ideas and achieve goals without the constraints of the formal management processes such as the Information Management Council, or the Technology Strategy and Infrastructure Group. The lines of communication between the Alliance and these standing committees were ad hoc, though the group gained feedback from them through some common membership. The notion of a strategic community made up of fairly senior organizational members who engaged because they wanted to, used informal communication patterns and largely determined their own directions, tasks and activities, was a new knowledge management capability for Xerox. It was found to have several benefits

- Higher quality knowledge creation.
- Fewer revisions to plans.
- High knowledge sharing amongst business units.
- Improved likelihood of implementation.

The conditions for both individual and organizational learning were fostered.

Members were surprised at how much they learned at Alliance meetings. The Alliance developed a culture and language of its own, but members returning to their business units were able to transfer the learning effectively.

Integrating twelve conflicting forces is another source of tension

As we have been careful to point out, none of the tensions inherent in each area of competence can be viewed in isolation. The paradoxes that affect how we respond to external knowledge dynamics are closely associated with the internal priorities that we need to address in order to compete sustainably, decide knowledgeably and learn dynamically. They are an integrated system that shapes the performance of our organizations' use of knowledge.

F. Scott Fitzgerald once said that 'The test of a first-rate intelligence is the ability to hold two opposed ideas in the mind at the same time and still retain the ability to function'. He was essentially referring to the ability to take a paradoxical perspective on life. In Western thinking, we tend to be trained to be much less inclusive in our thinking, much more individualistic, competitive, unique, and distinctive, and much less communal, co-operative, inclusive and integrative. The problem lies in the fact that we tend to turn categories of values, beliefs, ideals and even systems such as ideologies into things (reification), giving them the characteristics of immutable objects and assuming everyone perceives them in the same way. A paradox or dilemma is nothing more than two points of view, which have taken on a reified form in a particular context. Abstract language exacerbates the problem by giving the ideal, concept or theory, a single label. We tend to assume that the label is interpreted commonly by everyone, whereas in reality it tends to be interpreted through the 'lens' of each individual's unique and complex system of meaning that has developed as a result of their experiences.

Figure 7.19 Reframing three internal priorities in the light of three strategic responses to external dynamics

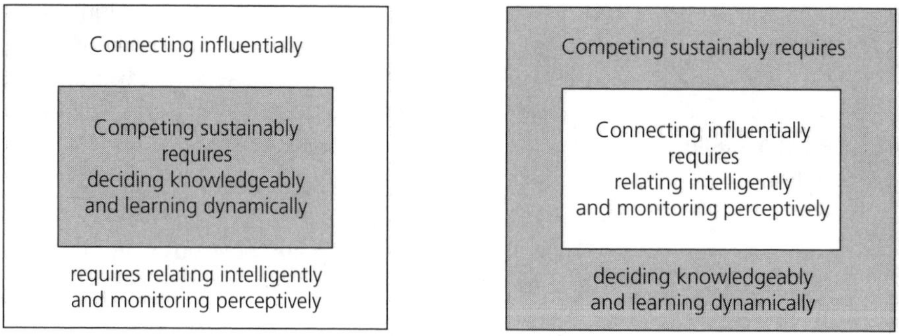

Connecting influentially

Competing sustainably
requires
deciding knowledgeably
and learning dynamically

requires relating intelligently
and monitoring perceptively

Competing sustainably requires

Connecting influentially
requires
relating intelligently
and monitoring perceptively

deciding knowledgeably
and learning dynamically

As we consider the current focus of activity at the centre of either picture, we need to
make sure we are reviewing it in the context of the activities that frame it.
Then reverse our perspective and assess the implications.
The process of reframing helps us keep our eyes on the bigger picture, whilst still being
able to address the detail.

Yet, there is evidence that people can learn to manage systems of tensions. Socrates taught people to do this by forcing them to face up to the apparent contradictions in their systems of thinking. His approach was to make the tensions explicit at a level that was meaningful and relevant to an individual and then encourage that person to mentally rise above the conflict and find a way to reconcile the tension.

We recognize that it is hard to keep in mind twelve different opposing forces unless they can be encapsulated into a single framework. The starting point for creating such a framework is to reframe the three internally-focused areas of competence through the lens of the three externally-focused areas of competence and *vice versa* (Figure 7.19).

We will continue to explore this framework in the next section. However, to hold all of the twelve aspects in tension and be able to work with them effectively requires that we have people within our organizations that have a well-developed level of intellectual complexity. We need to start by looking at what this means first, since this is the way in which all the tensions can be integrated and resolved.

Resolve the tension through developing intellectual complexity

Intellectual complexity is an important element of a managers' ability to process complicated, novel, ambiguous or dynamic strategic information in turbulent environments (Wang and Chan, 1995). The more intellectually-complex an individual's mental processes are, the better they will handle complex job problems, because they can flexibly handle many different situations (Wofford, 1994).

Intellectual complexity can be described (Kegan, 1994) as the extent to which a person can mentally:

> *Differentiate* – the number of dimensions they use to perceive environmental stimuli. (The word dimensions could be interpreted as nuances, subtleties, senses, implications, or interpretations.)
> and
> *Integrate* – the complex system of rules they use to organize the differentiated dimensions.

Essentially, it affects the richness that we perceive in the world and the comprehensiveness of our response to that richness. Intellectually simple people only perceive a few dimensions in a situation and use a fixed rule set to interpret them. In contrast, intellectually complex people:

- Perceive many dimensions and interpret the phenomena using more complex and adaptable reasoning (Calori, Johnson and Sarnin, 1994; Goodwin, 1991).

- Search for more information (Tuckman, 1964).
- Take notice of broader ranges of information (Streufert, Garber and Schroder, 1964).
- Spend longer interpreting information (Dollinger, 1984).
- Have a more accurate perception of the complexity of the environment at intermediate information loads (Streufert and Driver, 1965).
- Try more approaches to solving a problem (Streufert and Nogami, 1989).
- Possess more functional constructs in memory (Lundy and Berkowitz, 1957).

It seems that intellectual complexity develops through various stages (Kegan, 1994). At each level an individual relies on different mental structures to organize three aspects of thinking:

1 knowledge (cognitive),
2 interpersonal relationships,
3 intrapersonal understanding.

Five stages of development have been identified. The first three stages are age-related and happen naturally.

Stage one. When we are born we have no ability to differentiate. We cannot even distinguish ourselves from our mother. All is Unity. Gradually from birth to about the age of six, we learn to:

1 recognize objects exist independent of our senses (knowledge),
2 recognize people exist independent of oneself (relationships),
3 distinguish between inner sensation and outside stimulation (intra-personal understanding).

Figure 7.20 Stage one intellectual complexity

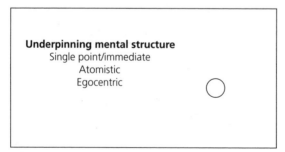

Underpinning mental structure
Single point/immediate
Atomistic
Egocentric

Stage two: Between the ages of six and our teens, our mental development produces durable categories of experience, which enable:

1 Knowing to become more concrete and logical, as we perceive that objects have properties irrespective of our own perceptions. New perceptions can be classified against previous categories.

2 Social relating to allow for others to have a point of view, distinct from our own and fully manipulable.

3 Intra-personal responses to be driven by enduring needs and beliefs rather than impulses. Impulses are regulated and organized into categories that produce results. We can delay gratification.

Figure 7.21 Stage two intellectual complexity

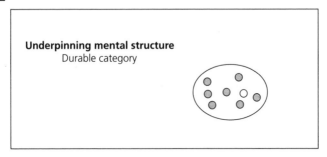

Stage three: From teens to adulthood we learn to make meaning by connecting categories. To make sense of the world, we have to learn to subordinate categories and consider the impact of the interaction between them. In other words, we learn to recognize tensions, but not always to handle them integratively. This is the beginning of an either/or response to any situation. The ability to relate categories of knowledge allows us to:

1 Reason abstractly, think hypothetically and deductively, distinguish what is from what is not and see relations as simultaneously reciprocal.

2 Be aware of shared feelings, agreements and expectations that override individual interests.

3 Internalize others' points of view, empathize, recognize emotions as internally subjective states rather than social transactions.

Figure 7.22 Stage three intellectual complexity

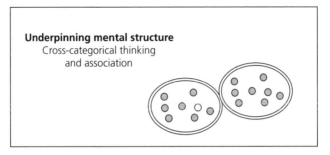

Not all adults go beyond level 3. To move to a higher level of intellectual complexity needs continuous exposure to experience and training, with reflective opportunities to help the individual integrate new thinking. Progress can be limited to some extent by innate potential, though there is evidence that we can develop the necessary skills. Several studies suggest that education can raise the level of intellectual complexity at least one level. Longitudinal studies of students in graduate programmes show that around 70 per cent of men and women between 20–50 years old entering graduate programmes were at the third stage of intellectual complexity. By the end of the programme, 70 per cent of the population studies were either almost at level 4 or well into level 4 thinking (Kegan, 1994). Although no comparative studies were made of similar groups of adults not following graduate programmes, there are many studies of adults at various ages and the percentage of fourth stage intellectually complex individuals in the population is always lower. Other studies suggest that the introduction of formal processes to encourage dissent or disagreement into group discussions can help increase intellectual complexity (Stone, Sivitanides and Magro, 1994).

Stage four: When we reach this fourth stage we learn to recognize and integrate multiple perspectives into a system, which allows us to:

1 Develop ideologies that relate abstract concepts into generalizable theories, be innovative, generate one's own vision and develop expertise in an area.

2 Evolve regulating institutions that can encompass multiple roles and relationships, conceive of the organization from outside in and recognize our relationship to the whole.

3 Acknowledge our own self-authorship, identity and autonomy, and not be threatened by difference in others. Take the initiative and take responsibility for what happens to us at work, rather than seeing others as the cause of now and the future.

Figure 7.23 Stage four intellectual complexity

Underpinning mental structure
Complex system

Clearly, these are important capabilities for dealing with the issues we discussed in *Competence Area 1: Competing* and *Competence Area 2: Deciding*, where we saw that we need individuals to work flexibly and adopt what we described as leadership behaviours to resolve the tensions in their local context. However, we do need go one stage further to cover all the tensions in a holistic approach to the six Areas of Competence.

Stage five: At this level we can use advanced thinking. We can accept and learn from difference by understanding how to resolve tensions in three different domains:

1 Using oppositeness and contradiction as a stimulus to more integrated perspectives. Synthesis of complex theories and critical reflection on a discipline from outside the 'ideology'.
2 Building relationships across value systems for the benefits of both parties.
3 Purposeful re-evaluation of one's own identity in the light of the identity of others.

Figure 7.24 Stage five intellectual complexity

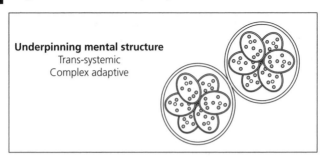

The focus of our attention at this level tends to be on the paradoxes presented in abstract systems of thinking, institutional relationships and self-regulatory values and beliefs. Clearly, these are critical aspects of our capacity to address the tensions in this book.

Working at the fifth stage of intellectual complexity is undoubtedly a stretch, because we need to be constantly aware of whole interacting systems of conflicting tensions, evaluating them to find integrative solutions that extract the communal benefits of co-operative value systems. Yet we would argue this is what is required to manage knowledge effectively. To reach this stage we have to:

- Recognize that interacting systems of opposing categories are part of the way we view our world.
- Objectively identify the risks and downsides of conflicting views.
- Acknowledge the upsides and potential benefits of the opposite perspectives.
- Take action in the less well-emphasized areas to compensate for previous over-emphasis in one domain.
- Focus on finding ways that the upsides and benefits of the opposite view can alleviate the risks and downsides of our favoured perspective.

This must be the aim of the managers of the Knowledgeable Organization if they are going to get full value from knowledge resources.

Synthesis: integrating cycles of knowledge capabilities

Building on this idea of intellectual complexity, let us envisage the issue of paying attention to internal priorities at the same time as paying attention to external dynamics. In Figures 7.25 and 7.26 we illustrate the systems of opposing categories that are fundamental to the way we manage knowledge. In earlier chapters we have explored the risks and downsides of these views, together with the upsides and benefits of the opposite perspective. We have also suggested ways to take action to address the less well-emphasized areas, and made recommendations for integrating the two kinds of activities.

Finally, in Table 7.7 we come back to our response to the questions posed at the start of this chapter.

At stage 5 of intellectual complexity we can see how the internal and external perspectives can be complementary activities that work together to deliver best value from knowledge resources. When those in our organizations are con-

Figure 7.25 Paying attention to internal capabilities of Competing, Deciding and Learning

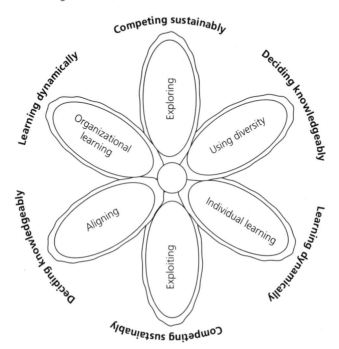

Figure 7.26 Paying attention to external interactions by Connecting, Relating and Monitoring

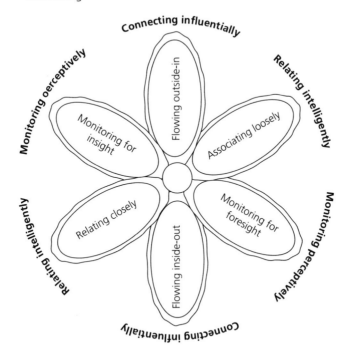

sciously aware of the tensions involved in handling knowledge as a resource and consistently and consciously aiming to achieve a balanced approach to all twelve categories in Figure 7.27, we believe that they will be well placed to achieve the elusive but very real returns from good knowledge management.

Table 7.7 A perspective on Knowledge Management

Question	Our response
What makes a Knowledgeable Organization?	The ability to handle systems of knowledge-related tensions in a balanced manner.
Why is a holistic approach important?	To make sure all knowledge-oriented activities are mutually supportive.
How are knowledge competencies complementary?	Together they provide a system of dynamic capabilities carefully tailored to manage the versatility and fluidity of knowledge as a resource.
How do we keep them all in view simultaneously?	By encouraging people within our organizations to develop both stage 4 and stage 5 intellectual complexity.

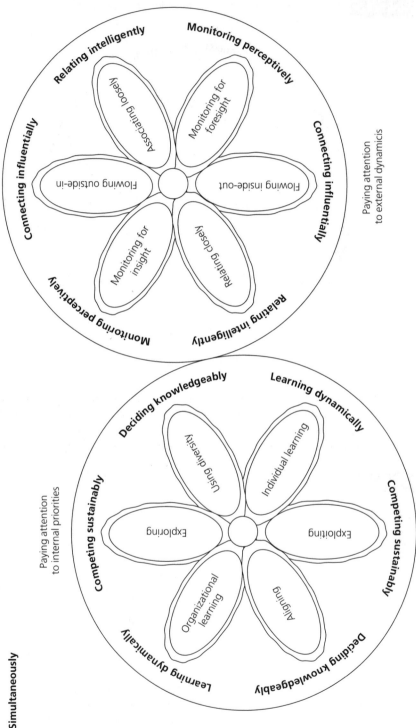

Figure 7.27 A complex adaptive system for using the characteristics of knowledge to best economic advantage

References

Altman, J. W. (2002) 'Xerox new enterprises', 802-071-1 European Case Clearing House, Babson College.

Biren, B. and Dutta, S. (2000) 'Xerox: building a corporate focus on knowledge', 600-015-1 European Case Clearing House, Insead, Fontainbleau, France.

Brown, J. S. and Duguid, P. (2000) *The Social Life of Information*. Boston, MA: Harvard Business School Press.

Brown, J. S. and Duguid, P. (2001) 'Creativity versus structure: a useful tension', *Sloan Management Review* 42(4): 93–4.

Calori, R., Johnson, G. and Sarnin, P. (1994) 'CEO's cognitive maps and the scope of the organization', *Strategic Management Journal* 15(6): 437–58.

Child, J. and Gunther McGrath, R. (2001) 'Organizations unfettered: organizational form in an information-intensive economy', *Academy of Management Review* 44(6): 1135–48.

Christiansen, C. M., Johnson, M. W. and Rigby, D. K. (2002) 'Foundations for growth: how to identify and build disruptive new businesses', *Sloan Management Review* 43(3): 22–31.

Davis, S. and Meyer, C. (1998) *Blur: The Speed of Change in the Connected Economy*. Oxford: Capstone.

Dollinger, M. J. (1984) 'Environmental boundary spanning and information processing effects on organizational performance', *Academy of Management Journal* 27(2): 351–68.

Goodwin, V. L. (1991) 'Antecedents, consequences and covariates in the study of organizational cognitive complexity', University of Texas, Arlington.

Hampden-Turner, C. (1990) *Charting the Corporate Mind*. Oxford: Blackwell.

Hickins, M. (1999) 'Xerox shares its knowledge', *Management Review* 88(8): 40–6.

Kearns, D. T. and Adler, D. A. (1992) *Prophets in the Dark*. New York: Harper Collins.

Kegan, R. (1994) *In Over Our Heads: The Mental Demands of Modern Life*. Boston, MA: Harvard Business School Press.

Lundy, R. M. and Berkowitz, B. (1957) 'Cognitive complexity and assimilative projection in attitude change', *Journal of Abnormal Social Psychology* 55: 34–7.

McKenzie, J. (1996) *Paradox the Next Strategic Dimension: Using Conflict to Re-energize your Business*. Maidenhead: McGraw Hill.

Radhika, A. N. and Mukund, A. (2002) 'Xerox: the benchmarking story', 602-051-1 European Case Clearing House, ICFAI Center for Management Research, Hyderabad, India.

Scott Poole, M. and Van de Ven, A. H. (1989) 'Using paradox to build management and organization theories', *Academy of Management Review* 14(4): 562–78.

Senge, P. (1990) *The Fifth Discipline*. London: Century Business.

Senge, P. and Carstedt, G. (2001) 'Innovating our way to the next Industrial Revolution', *Sloan Management Review* 42(2): 24–38.

Sheehan, T. (2003) 'KM and project management in the construction industry', 11th Henley Knowledge Management Forum Meeting, Henley Management College.

Stone, D. N., Sivitanides, M. P. and Magro, A. P. (1994) 'Formalized dissent and cognitive complexity in group process', *Decision Sciences* 25(2): 243–62.

Storck, J. and Hill, P. A. (2000) 'Knowledge diffusion through strategic communities', *Sloan Management Review* 41(2): 63–74.

Streufert, S. and Driver, M. J. (1965) 'Conceptual structure, information load and perceptual complexity', *Psychological Science* 3(5): 249–50.

Streufert, S., Garber, J. and Schroder, H. M. (1964) *Performance and Perceptual Complexity in Tactical Decision Making*, Princeton, NJ: Princeton University Press.

Streufert, S. and Nogami, G. Y. (1989) 'Cognitive style and complexity: Implications for I/O psychology', in *International Review of Industrial and Organizational Psychology* (eds C. L. Cooper and J. Robertson). New York: John Wiley.

Tuckman, B. (1964) 'Personality structure, group composition and group functioning', *Sociometry* 27: 469–87.

Wang, P. and Chan, P. S. (1995) 'Top management perception of strategic information processing in a turbulent environment', *Leadership and Organization Development Journal* 16(7): 33–49.

Wofford, J. C. (1994) 'An examination of the cognitive processes used to handle employee job problems', *Academy of Management Journal* 37(1): 180.

Zack, M. (2002) 'Developing a knowledge strategy', in *The Strategic Management of Intellectual Capital and Organizational Knowledge* (eds C. W. Choo and N. Bontis). New York: Oxford University Press, 255–76.

Index

Page numbers in *italics* refer to illustrations and tables; page numbers in **bold** refer to main discussion.